The Secret
Dossier

of a Knight Templar

of the Sangreal

by

Gretchen Cornwall

thesecretdossier.co.uk

October 13, 2016

Contents

Acknowledgements

To John - for paving the way in love –
and for the gift of the most valuable commodity of all – time.

I owe much to my family, friends and inspirational acquaintances I've met along the way - without their valiant encouragement I would not have had the resilience to cross the threshold of a first book.

Thank you Mother Divine, Marcia Winter, for instilling within the love of books and a good cup of coffee at a young age. I'll always treasure our trips to the library together and seeing you read in your chair late into the night searching for the answer to inner mysteries.

For my father volunteer fireman, Captain Lee Schroeder, who cared enough to save lives. You taught me about faith and the determination to get back on that pony when she unceremoniously dumped me on the ground.

To my siblings who are also my best friends – Shirley, Raymond, Judith, Ruth and Tracy. They are remarkable people who fight the good fight to make their dreams come true. They serve their communities and are mirrors of life which I respect and hold dear.

To Sarah Vickery for her continued positivity, advice and open door and Colin for those fabulous buckets of strong coffee.

With gratitude to friend Sue Cowling who has believed in me whatever mad venture I've embarked upon over the years.

Tim Stouse, I appreciate that your knowledge of punctuation is far less creative than my own. You have a sharp eye for a carelessly spelled word. Thank you for the generosity of your precious time.

Without the friendship of Grail composer Adrian Wagner and Helen Wagner, I would not be living in England. To author Laurence Gardner who lit the fuse to my journey.

Thank you to all those authors who have dug deeper than the veneer of shallow authority and had the courage to plunge down the rabbit hole with Alice.

To those who have stood on the shoulders of giants in centuries past so that we have a continued thread to follow through the maze of history and clues as to what it means to be truly human.

To the modern Knights Templar Order who have never left the field

This book would not have come to life without the golden gift of information from the Comte de Mattinata de Medici

Introduction

"I'm going to build my secrets into the geometry of these buildings because I know that books can burned but buildings not so easily."
Thomas Jefferson

The Knights Templar survived the arrests of 1307 - period. It is not pseudo history, it is a fact...

The evidence for their survival and resurgence in Europe and the Americas is stunning, leaving an observable trail into the present that would make a detective blush.

It was absolute common knowledge in the 14th century that they had survived, often in their own host country such as Spain, Portugal, Scotland, Switzerland, England and Germany – those still in France kept their heads down.

Localized preceptories changed their names, often without any attempt to disguise their identity, forcing the Vatican to negotiate with them as if they were a hostile nation capable of defending themselves which they were. The Vatican at this time had been relocated to France by the French King who used the Pope as a weapon against the Templars.

Legends that the first Templars found sacred treasures and texts in the Holy Land have increased their glamour and mystique. They were the rock stars of their day when religion was the only game in town.

The origins of the Order lay within the hands of one man, Bernard de Clairvaux. The saint was the focus of controversy when he put swords in the hands of the first fighting monks, his very own Cistercian brothers - a small and failing order which he turned into an international success.

Often the Cistercians and St. Bernard are given very little space when discussing the Templars – in order to understand the fighting monks it only made sense to explore the life of the man himself.

I hope that I've managed to bridge the gap of time in sympathy to his genius, compassion and tireless energy. He lived his life with unabashed mysticism and unapologetically worshiped the Queen of Heaven and the King of Kings. He changed the culture of Europe and improved life for women.

Bernard was intriguing as a person and I wanted to explore the possibility that his ideals, organizational skills and leadership abilities might have sprung from ancient gnostic family traditions.

During the search for his family's past and that of the Cistercians, I found myself researching Templar locations in Britain that still bore the footprint of the Celtic Christians.

The subversive teachings of a radical man named Jesus had become legalized in 325AD by Rome but the Celtic Christians in Britain came without swords into a dangerous landscape and left indelible foundations on which flourished high art and a beautiful culture distinct from Europe and Rome itself.

The Romano Britains believed their line of transmission from the radical teacher was of an earlier form and purer intent. Had their message been infused into Templar traditions?

Jesus's life as recorded in the Bible is missing 18 formative years. Legends place Christ with his uncle Joseph of Arimathea as having travelled by sea to Cornwall in

The Secret Dossier of a
Knight Templar of the Sangreal

Britain as metal merchants and engaging with the Druids.

One route for tin and metal trade was through the port of Marseilles and north, *over land*, to the English Channel. Northern inland France was famous for its gold mines originally held by the Gauls who wove it into mesmerizing ornaments fit for kings.

Jesus would have had the opportunity to be in direct converse with the peoples and cultures of interior France north to south with his further choice of locations in Britain to choose from, depending on the needs of his Uncle Joseph's business.

Joseph is said to have had ships which went from the Mediterranean sea around to Cornwall. Is it possible that the gold of interior France lured as well and that a sea journey commenced from northern France to other ports in England?

Author Laurence Gardner of Bloodline of the Holy Grail suggests that there was a Jewish enclave in Marseilles already which is why the family of Jesus and Mary Magdalene fled to France in the first place. His grandparents were said to have migrated to Gaul from Marseilles after the crucifixion with Veronica's Veil.

Christ's possible links to northern England can be surmised by the Roman connection as they were mining precious metals in the Cumbrian landscape, its wealth flowing into the broader Empire.

Cumbria is rich with as many as twenty desirable and useful minerals. The mining tradition of the North West existed up through the centuries and had been a guarded secret of the Templars.

Why would Joseph of Arimathea, who was known to be very wealthy, restrict his trade simply to the tin of Cornwall when the Island of Albion was rich in so much more and had already been leveraged by the Romans and the earlier indigenous culture?

The missing eighteen years of the life of the historic Jesus can now be put into a different framework, though perhaps fanciful, new speculation can lead to new knowledge.

The Cathars have long associations with the French Templars, but it seems as if another stream had been introduced via the early Celtic Church.

The Vikings have also become part of the pre Templar historic enigma. Those brave explorers who settled in Ireland, Britain and Western Europe were eventually lured into the Celtic Christian story, weaving their artistry into a body of work that opposed Rome for many centuries. Their mastery of the seas was inherited by the historic Templars along with their technology.

The Celtic Christians took great care to erect stone crosses in the landscape capturing ley lines and sacred sites of worth. The tall stones were filled with twisting serpents, runes and topped with the famous encircled and equal cross.

Did the Dark Age Christian Celts have a secret navigation device which was translated into these monuments? Author Crichton E. M. Miller believes he has reverse engineered the Celtic Cross to find a complex navigation system encoded in religious symbolism which allowed the Templars to discover the New World.

Based on his stunning find, I followed an ancient technology trail up through the historic Templars and Renaissance painters to Chaucer's Astrolabe. What made the Templars the masters of the seas and had they learned their craft from the Vikings who were amongst their genetic predecessors?

Introduction

*

The Isle of Thanet on the S.E. coast of England is a small community. Word seeped out that I had plans to write a book which included the Knights Templar. As a result I had the good fortune to be contacted by a modern day descendant. For the sake of his privacy I initially chose to call him John Temple.

But as I was writing the last chapter of this book, I found out a great deal more about his true identity. I took the decision to reveal this information in chapter one. With the Knight's permission I used his anglicized family name, my chosen alias for him and also his title throughout the book. His actual first name will not appear in this volume.

John Temple contributed historical, sacred-geometric and mystical content that he asked to have included in this book. I approached the meeting with hope but also a touch of reservation as I had met others in the past who claimed to be Templars.

I was greatly surprised during the meeting when he shared a map with 'magnetic lines' crossing over the United Kingdom and the world. I was intrigued as the lines intersected with specific Ordnance Survey grid reference points across England and Scotland which were related to historic and modern Templar locations. What are the odds of a correlation between 'ley lines' and a rigid navigation grid of specific historic sites, surely it must be impossible? I was told that there '...was no such thing as coincidence'.

John Temple also pointed out an odd geometric 'kite' which was described as the Keystone of the energetic map. The Heronian Tetrahedron rests upon the altar of Saint Kentigerns in Caldbeck Cumbria. The 'tail' stretched east across the Pennines, a tiny church dedicated to Saint John - the patron of the Order - and finally to Bornholm Island famous for its round Templar churches.

I suddenly found myself in the deep waters of Quantum Mechanics as I searched for the connections between sacred geometry, sacred numbers, while pondering the nature of the soul and our relationship to the Universe and the Ark upon which we live, earth. And all were connected to the history of Templarism.

It was my privilege to include the Templar Matrix Map and in the years that have followed the initial meeting; they have not given me reason to doubt their story or the information that I was given. In fact quite the opposite, I became more convinced as I explored the content I was given.

I would be lying if I said that it was smooth sailing as more questions were generated by the information but full explanations were not forthcoming. I have read other accounts of Sub-Rosa contactees having similar experiences where esoteric information is given but not fully explained.

I did not view this with suspicion but decided to play the game by donning my Indiana Jones hat. As a result and by my own hand - I learned. Having the opportunity to engage in a real life quest which challenges the inner domain with outer measurable discoveries is more rewarding than a video game or film could ever be.

I have endeavored to research every possible angle as a result and hope that I have grasped the metal of esoteric Templarism and have conveyed its overall intention in the following pages amongst my own work.

The Secret Dossier of a
Knight Templar of the Sangreal

*

In recent years there has been much debate regarding Mary Magdalene and the now famous Da Vinci Code. I was told that she had been the wife of Jesus and that their children merged with the Merovingians of France.

John Temple stated unequivocally that Jesus had not died on the cross, was resurrected and did not experience death. In other words the Son of Man had a human experience, a Divine experience and we are His inheritors.

The Divine is not inaccessible to humanity and we can have direct experience without the need of an intercessor such as a politically driven or economically driven church sate.

Matthew 6:6 But thou, when thou prayest, enter into thy closet, and when thou hast shut thy door, pray to thy Father which is in secret; and thy Father which seeth in secret shall reward thee openly. - *King James Bible "Authorized Version", Cambridge Edition*

The Templars have been accused of withholding their secrets from the world but I would like to state that what one chooses to think in the privacy of one's sovereign domain – the mind – is and should be off limits to all and sundry. Our own personal space, the mind and soul, is just that, deeply personal and therefore private.

Fortunately in today's western democracies we have the assurance of freedom of religion without the threat to life. Hopefully our world will maintain this freedom in the west and that the events of 1307 will never occur again nor any more deaths be attributed to an Inquisition of any nature by any religion.

We do not have consensus however as to the nature of the soul and to speak of these matters without hesitation or context can bring about social derision, the potential loss of income through job loss or worse.

It is much easier to speak with people of like mind than to beat one's head against an unrewarding door which has been closed with accusations of lunacy, fear or ignorant materialism.

There are innumerable mystic scholars down through the centuries which one may read, often free online, that will fill in any information gaps for the serious student. I have done my best to search these references out and hope you will avail yourself of them via the bibliography.

*

Having followed Magdalene art through history I discovered a few years ago that her secret was hidden in the stars of a constellation which revolves in the northern hemisphere to alternately appear to be an exaggerated 'M' or 'W' respectively. It is a throne attributed to Cassiopeia by the Greeks but in the 12th century if not earlier became secretly associated with the Magdalene.

This constellation is remembered in the gesture of an obscure hand sign. The 'M' hand sign was recently found by author and TV host, Scott Wolter, on the Statue of Liberty which I have traced back as early as the 12th century up through Renaissance masters and the Tudor era alchemists. I believe that the 'M' hand sign is related to the constellation of Cassiopeia which was secretly attributed to the Bloodline of Christ.

I believe there is much more to learn and that Templarism has much to offer the modern seeker, including the confirmation that the sovereign freedom of the individual has automatic & natural right to have personal and direct experience of the Great Divine. I found the quest for knowledge to be a joyful experience which has led to broader vistas than I could have expected.

The interconnectivity and beautiful synchronistic overlays of historic places, people, art and architecture has been a breathtaking journey for this American writer from Seattle.

I have the good fortune to call 'this Sceptred Isle' of Great Britain my home where I believe I have found those who are the inheritors of the historic Templars and Christ. It was a privilege to represent the Templar ambassador's Secret Dossier on his family and Order containing information thought lost in centuries past.

One

The Royal Priests of Cumbria

All roads lead to Cumbria – and to one family in particular. The Mattinsons have been guardians of the secrets of the Sangreal and the Knights Templar for centuries from the anonymity of shadows.

There is a grave that was placed at the western entrance of Saint Kentigerns, Caldbeck, as a guardian to the sacred space of the churchyard. Francis Mattinson died 20th September, 1823 and is just one of many his kin interred at the Keystone church.

My Templar contact is a Mattinson and the son of the 7th son, of the 7th son, which raises interesting folklore overtones.

During the course of almost nine years of writing this book and research, I would occasionally be given leads as to the identity of my contact. The leads bore amazing fruit and when pressed for further information I was given an explanation straight out of a novel. Alexander Dumas to be exact.

The leverage came from a glaring anomaly in the Mattinson family history. Reverend Morris's book titled the Records of Patterdale is just that, a record of the peoples of his parish and its history written in 1905 directly from the decaying parish records in an effort to preserve them.

Under chapter IV titled the Clergy of Patterdale, there was much discussion about a John Mattinson who was born in 1669 and passed away many decades later on 19 December 1765. An unusual feat in that era as life expectancy for most was a great deal shorter, in fact, by half.

John Mattinson was buried at the ancient yew tree of Saint Patrick's – the name of the village of Patterdale is derived from Patrick's Dale. The famous tree stood on a mound and had a circumference of about ten feet at its base but was felled by a horrendous storm in 1883. The site had been a meeting place for many centuries and it seems a fitting location for a remarkable man to be laid to rest.

John Mattinson became the Curate and Schoolmaster of Patterdale in 1706 and was ordained a priest of the Anglican Church in 1707 by Bishop William Nicolson of Carlisle. A curate has the charge of care or *cure* of the souls of his parishioners and is considered a parish priest in this sense.

According to the Clergy of the Church of England Database, Mattinson, now aged approximately forty-four to forty-five, became Curate of Matterdale as well and was listed as Johannes Mattinson between the years of 1713 and 1723. Why was he given a Latin name in the *Anglican* Church as an adult and then in 1736 to 1754 he was then listed as John Mattinson as he had earlier in his career?1. Aside from the Latin use of the name John, as a function of church records, its spelling sits much more comfortably in European circles and the Catholic Church not England. It is almost as if there is an attempt to recall - in the formal setting of church records - a tie to Europe with the cooperation and knowledge of his Anglican upline. In other words, Bishop Nicolson (and future officiants) during the years of the use of the name of Johannes, had to have known of the priest Mattinson's actual identity.

I came across a reference via Lodge St. Andrew #518 regarding *A. C. Mackey's Encyclopedia of Freemasonry and its Kindred Sciences 1909* – in a discussion regarding the importance of abbreviations in Freemasonry, the initials H. J. stood out immediately. According to Mackey, H.J. equates to Heilige Johannes. *"German, meaning Holy Saint John."* 2.

According to Morris, he lived comfortably on approximately £18.00 per annum with his wife Elizabeth and four children and remained a Curate for sixty years. Elizabeth was a skillful midwife from which she earned a stipend and presided over the christening dinner for which she was also paid a small amount. John was known to help her spin the 'tithe wool'. It seems as if the Curate did not mind helping his wife with 'women's work'.

"On the day of her marriage her father boasted that his two daughters were married to the two best men in Patterdale—the priest and the bagpiper." 3.

The Curate performed the christening and marriages of all four of his children and presided over the funeral of his parents. His father had married twice and John performed that wedding as well. John educated his son who was then able to enter college and another young man who succeeded him as schoolmaster.

John lived to the age of 96 and was 'possessed' of £1000.00 at the time of his death. 4.

It was considered so strange that the account of his life and death (and more to the point the amount of money he had) was written about in a book titled "The Recreative Review: Or Eccentricities of Literature and Life Vol II" – please note the term 'eccentric' in the title of the book which was filled with astonishing oddities of the day.

"Surely, the good old parson resembled the soldier in the song, which begins –
"How happy's the soldier that lives on his pay, And spends
half-a-crown out of sixpence a day!" 5.

So, how much is £1000.00 worth today and why was it so incredible as to be remarked upon? Due to inflation, £1000.00 is the near equivalent of £10,000,000.00 today.

What in the world was a man in a rural backwater of Cumbria, living the life of a simple parish priest, doing with near to ten million British Pounds Sterling at the time of his death?

He could not have saved this amount while supporting a wife and children and there was no way he could accrue it without having been a known captain of industry. If John had inherited his money, why didn't he live ostentatiously, perhaps building a large house that would stand the test of time? Why didn't his father 'live large' as most would with such deep pockets? According to my Templar contact, embracing poverty was just as important to his ancestral family line of priests as it was to those who joined the chivalrous order in the Middle Ages.

John Mattinson was wedded to the land in service and not to the acquisition of expensive personal belongings. Once the source of these funds had been revealed to me I was told that there had been careful investments made in land through the generations. As an example King George III bought Buckingham House (now Palace) for Queen Charlotte in 1761 at a cost of £24,000.00 which is now estimated to be worth one billion though admittedly by experts to be priceless. I was told the Mattinson family provided the financing for the transaction but of course

The Man in the Leather Mask

John was born in Patterdale, Cumbria, to a Henry Mattinson. Alexander Dumas knew the history behind Henry and was inspired to write his heroic tale, The Man in the Iron Mask from the account of his life.

Henry IV (1553-1610) King of France was remembered as 'Good King Henry' for his religious tolerance and had been Protestant before inheriting the crown from his cousin. He was forced to convert to Catholicism in order to reign after four years of failed negotiation with the church.

He ended the Wars of Religion and after having survived twelve assassination attempts was murdered by a fanatical Catholic. The poor man did not have a chance as the Catholics did not trust him due to having been a Protestant and the Protestants thought he'd turned traitor.

Into this unsettled scenario of religious war and social upheaval, two sons were born 27 September 1601 at the secluded Château de Fontainebleau far from Paris and prying eyes.

Maria de Medici became regent upon Henry IV's death as her sons were only nine years old.

Louis XIII ascended the throne of France under his mother's eye, while his twin brother Henri was hidden. The political situation remained turbulent and dangerous.

The queen insisted that 'only one son should take the throne'. Identical sons could be used by ambitious courtiers in a game of chess for power over France; such deadly games were already in full swing. It was best to hide one and remove temptation altogether, but what to do with the other prince?

John Templar stated that the young prince was kept locked away in order to *'de-royalise him'* and as he grew he wore a leather mask. *'He remained unidentified until a plan could be worked out.'*

Prince Henri was sent into exile to the small town of Mattinata Italy on the Adriatic Sea, which is towards the south and far from his mother's place of birth in Florence. Mattinata is on a peninsula and therefore on the way to nowhere making it unlikely he would be recognized by local people nor stumbled upon by unauthorized nobility. According to my source *'He was well received as Henri de Mattinata de Medici'*.

I found the coat of arms for Mattinata to be rather odd considering the topic of hidden identities and the Templars. Its motto reads as 'Lux Vera Illuminet – 'The True Light Illuminates' and is emblazoned with Venus the Morning Star. 6.

Prince Henri was blessed to have a younger sister who at the young age of sixteen caught the eye of the King of England. Henrietta Maria of France (1609-1669) became the queen consort of King Charles I of England in 1625 but never had a coronation due to her strong Catholic faith which made her unpopular with Protestants in England.

At Henrietta's suggestion, Henri was sent to safe, distant, Patterdale in Cumbria with a sizeable amount of money to help him live as his birth right demanded. I wonder if the two siblings were close and perhaps the young queen felt familial sympathy for the man in the leather mask. Perhaps just knowing her brother was in England gave her a measure of emotional support while dealing with the difficulties of being unpopular at her own court.

Upon arrival his name was changed to Henry Mattinson having dropped the last three letters of ATA from Mattinata and replacing them with SON – in other words the 'son from Mattinata'. In this way future generations in Cumbria would be identified with Prince Henri and as a De Medici.

At the very minimum this suggests that Prince Henri had matured to at least twenty four years of age and more likely older when he lived in Mattinata considering that Queen Henrietta would have needed time herself to move and settle into court life in England.

The Mask

Henri would then be old enough to be easily recognized with his twin, thus allowing perhaps for rumors to have circulated amongst all the nonessential members of his household and locals as to his identity. Obviously someone close to him knew who he was in order for his mother and sister to 'keep tabs' on him. Had disguised royal visitors to Mattinata caused raised eyebrows over the years? If he'd been *'well received'* then certainly he was popular with the social elite of the area as well. It seems as if some concern was leveled at Henri if he were given such a large amount of money and more than likely, loyal household retainers went with him to Mattinata and Patterdale as his security detail.

In the Alexander Dumas novel, the Man in the Iron Mask, the prince was held in a dungeon and forced to wear an iron mask around the clock. There are multiple accounts of prisoners forced to wear masks to hide their identities in France, thus the confusion as to the original sufferer's identity. It does not appear to be a single incident as is commonly thought but a favored form of torture to hide a prisoner. Some prisoners were treated very harshly indeed.

I can't imagine having to wear a mask of this nature for very long, the damage it would due to one's skin and the psychological pressures can't be understated. Therefore in Henry's situation it seems to have been a temporary measure, removable and a kinder option as leather would suggest.

The wearing of masks to hide facial disfigurement from plague, accident, birth defects and any other misfortune was not uncommon. One would assume during this time period that if a man were seen wearing a mask it must be due to a horrible malady and the prudent measure would be to cross the street to avoid said person in fear of contagion or spiritual curse such was the mindset of the day. We are blessed today in this age with access to medical care that was just not possible in 17th century Europe. WWI saw the first attempts at facial reconstruction as so many young men were coming back from the war disfigured.

Wealthier people could afford to buy artful masks or even patches to cover pock marks and in Venice the Carnival had been in full swing since the 13th century where the mask was the norm. As a method of disguise, beautification and flirtation the mask was a truly useful device. Today, wearing a mask as a matter of daily life to disguise oneself would draw unwelcome attention and suspicion as it is no longer a cultural norm or harsh necessity.

Corroboration

In 1771 the philosopher Voltaire wrote that an older brother of Louis XIV was the man in the iron mask. Writer Alexandre Dumas made the story famous in circa 1840 and included it amongst the serialized adventures of the Three Musketeers.

A clue as to Dumas knowledge of Henry Mattinson lies in his parentage. He was able to gain access to French aristocracy through his father's noble connections. One of his employers was the King of the French, Louis Philippe I (1773-1850) who had supported the Revolution. Dumas could not have been closer to intellectual circles, the nobility and therefore information.

The difference within the Dumas story is that the prisoner was an identical twin of Louis XIV (1638-1715) and interestingly enough he added the figure of Cardinal Richelieu (1585-1642) to the same timeline but Richelieu had been the chief minister of Louis XIII decades earlier.

Louis XIII relied upon Richelieu to an exclusivity that brought about malcontent with his other courtiers and bordered on paranoia which no doubt the Cardinal preyed upon as it brought him great political powers.

Author Kathleen McGowan asserts that according to her sources, the Three Musketeers were inspired by actual Templars. It certainly makes sense that Dumas had woven Henri de Medici's story amongst the Templars. Had Musketeer/Templars gone to Cumbria with Henri to protect him in his new life? Had he been initiated and joined their brotherhood?

I'm certain Henri had other options in Europe but the island fortress of England with his sister as queen could not have been better. He could lead a real life undisturbed by potential enemies in France including his adult brother. He had the option to fall in love rather than have an arranged political marriage. Henri had priestly tendencies and could foster his inner life in the mountains of the Lake District with a freedom that would have been difficult in France.

Notable Visitors

I have not at this juncture been told how Voltaire and Dumas knew of the incident. Both stories are very close with changes as to which French king had been involved and there is the matter of the inclusion of the Cardinal in the Dumas version which is very close to the truth.

In the book, 'The Records of Patterdale' the Reverend Morris includes an entire chapter titled, Notable Visitors, with dates of visitations starting in the 17th through to the late 19th century.

During the 1870s, the Archbishop of Canterbury, Dr. Temple, stayed for several weeks in Patterdale. Lord Tennyson and William Wordsworth also had protracted visits.

"Patterdale has been visited by members of the royal family, dukes and duchesses, marquesses and marchionesses, earls and countesses, lords and ladies, viscount and viscountesses, barons and baronesses, archbishops, bishops, sirs and ladies." 7.

The visitors were from Britain but also from across Europe including France and Italy, such as the King of Naples. Due to the distance, the European nobles are of greater interest to this inquiry and certainly odd as there are picturesque idylls everywhere on the continent. They did not need to traverse the channel to see Patterdale.

Between those with potential sources who knew of the royal twins born in 1610 and the 'notable visitors' of Patterdale travelling back and forth, Dumas became privy to the riveting heritage of Henry Mattinson.

Why had so many cousins of Prince Henri visit Patterdale and his descendants over the centuries? They came to consult the royal Templar Priests who were from two of the most powerful families of early 17th century Europe.

The visitors had weighty problems on their minds from the very human personal questions to matters of state. Today the Dalai Lama, as a key holy man of this century, is sought out by world leaders and those of influence; who amongst the modern notables has not shaken the hand of the Tibetan priest or had his photo taken with him? So it was with the Princes of Patterdale.

The Secret Dossier of a
Knight Templar of the Sangreal

Genetic Heritage

The claims by my contact regarding his identity are incredible and fantasy royalty has always been a part of European history. With that said, there *is* a proportion of claimants who actually *are* who they know themselves to be and in the case of John Temple of the Cumbrian Mattinsons, I do not doubt him and am privileged to share his family history with the public for the first time in 405 years.

My Templar contact's actual title is -
the Comte de Mattinata de Medici.

It is a given that there were other Mattinsons across England as the name derives from the biblical Son of Matthew. However it is not an unduly common name and the children of Henri Mattinata de Medici were fruitful and multiplied in Cumbria. The Curate John Mattinson himself had seventeen grandchildren alone.

There are millions of known descendants of Jesus in the world today but few are able to actually trace their line back as the massive family branch has multiplied outside of direct documentation and direct descent knowledge. One must be able to trace a line back to a known Grail family.

The Comte de Mattinata de Medici is able to trace his ancestry back through family lore and Templar heritage which has stood the test of time and has been recently corroborated in a DNA test. The test was done between a direct line Mattinson and a known De Medici descendant resulting in a perfect familial match.

The family of the Comte de Mattinata de Medici would not have thought of a DNA test without actual knowledge of family history. Nor would a de Medici be willing to provide a DNA sample without some assurance that they were not wasting their time with charlatans. It is one thing to make a fantastical claim; it is another to back up a claim with historical references and modern science.

1. Clayton, Mary, Mrs. "CCED: Persons Index." CCED: Persons Index. Accessed August 05, 2015. http://db.theclergydatabase.org.uk/jsp/persons/CreatePersonFrames.jsp?PersonID=156311.
2. Russell, Duncan, Bro. "Lodge St. Andrew #518 Province of Aberdeenshire East Grand Lodge of Scotland." Lodge St. Andrew 518,freemason,masonic. April 25, 2004. Accessed August 05, 2015. http://www.standrew518.co.uk/encyclopedia/Abb.php - http://www.standrew518.co.uk/.
3. Morris, The Records of Patterdale, Historical and Descriptive With Illustrations, 29.
4. Ibid., 30.
5. Douce, Francis. The Recreative Review, or Eccentricities of Literature and Life. London: Wallis and, 1821. pg 106
6. Sri, Magilia. "Municipality of Mattinata." Mattinata.it/. http%3A%2F%2Fwww.mattinata.it%2Fnews%2F19260%2Fha-sessant-anni-e-li-dimostra-tanta-storia-tradizioni-e-cultura.
7. Morris, The Records of Patterdale, Historical and Descriptive With Illustrations, 102.

Two

The de Medicis

What can be gleaned from the Medicis in order to understand Henry Mattinson?

It seems as if Queen Maria de Medici chose to give Henri her own last name rather than identify him with the House of Bourbon so as not to destabilize Louis; however 'Comte' itself is derived from French and Occitan rather than Italian. So it would seem that both worlds are being honoured along with the tie to the Cathar language.

The equivalent in Britain would be that of an Earl.

Familial pride seems to be at play as she dangerously gifted her hidden son with a name which amounts to an instantly recognizable aristocratic title. But who are the de Medicis?

According to the mists of time and legend, the great Florentine family, de Medici, rose from an illegitimate son of Charlemagne named Averado who became a successful commander in his army.

The reference to this is from a 17th century book (*Origin and descendants of the house of the Medici of Florence*) written by family member, Cosimo Baroncelli (1569-1626). What sources he drew on are not known and of course due to the passage of time may not exist any longer.

Medici literally means 'doctor' – Averado was known to possess the 'king's evil hands' and could heal people by the laying on of hands. As a descendant of Jesus this tradition makes sense and it was employed as a genealogical test to prove that Charlemagne was Averado's father.

The Stuarts were also known to have employed this method of healing – the tradition lasted many centuries. The physician André du Laurens (1558–1609) claimed that the Merovingian King Clovis I (481–511) was the first king who used the healing touch regardless of the rank of his people.

There is a passage in the Bible which discusses this very act and certainly would have been an inspiration to the Merovingian's: Mark 16:18 KJV "They shall take up serpents; and if they drink any deadly thing, it shall not hurt them; they shall lay hands on the sick, and they shall recover."

Photo © Gretchen Cornwall at Canterbury Cathedral

The De Medici Coat of Arms

Sir Averado de Medici faced a giant of a man named Mugello in battle in order to free Tuscany from the invading Lombards.

Mugello struck at the knight with a mace, which is a rather nasty pole with a rounded head made of either stone, copper, iron or steel. They were far less expensive than a sword, required less skill and had an advantage in the hands of a large man. Maces did not penetrate armor but could shatter bone and crush organs. According to legend the blows left round indentations on the shield of the knight who valiantly won the day. 1.

It is a legendary possibility for the explanation of the de Medici family coat of arms.

The device is simple in its visual context: six red round balls on a gold shield or *six balls in orle gules*. At varying times there have been as many as twelve red balls, however six became the accepted standard and when in 1465 the Medicis became allies to the French Crown they were awarded the use of the Fleur de Lis which took the place of the top red ball and was of a larger dimension.

The 17th century chronicle goes on to state that Averado's family grew in wealth by land investment. By the early 11th century the family owned castles at Castagnolo and Potrone now in modern day Scarperia Italy.

At this time the Medicis were members of the textile guild Arte della Lana or the wool guild of Florence which of course was the bridge to the banking guild, the Arte del Cambio (Art Exchange), that would become synonymous with the family name.

There is debate as to the meaning of the 'red balls' of the Medici shield - that they represent the round tablets or pills of the physicians' trade. There were physicians in the Medici family but just as surely that Prince Henry the Navigator was a gifted cartographer did not mean that he automatically lost his genealogy due to his 'trade'.

The French court in the 16th century started the rumour that the Medici coat of arms was merely that of a doctor in order to discredit the background of Queen Catherine de Medici (1519-1589). She had married the French King Henry II and upon his death ruled as regent and as an 'outsider' gained French political enemies along the way.

Giovanni Medici leveraged his power in the banking/exchange guild and opened the Medici Bank which became the most powerful in Europe during the 15th century.

The Seven Major Guilds of the corporations of arts and crafts in Florence each had their own heraldic device. The currency exchange which dealt in metals, stones, loans, credit and deposits had a red background as its shield with gold bezants which is synonymous with roundels and balls. A bezant is a term meaning a Byzantine gold coin. 2.

I do not think that the Medici shield is in any way related to doctors or apothecaries. The medical profession is amongst the seven major guilds and its shield denotes that of the Madonna and Child whose provenance is easily ascertained. There is no connection between the Medicis and pharmacists, the round balls are coins due to their association with the banking guild which they belonged to for generations.

I am rather fond of Sir Averado's battle-dented shield as an earlier source and hope that in the future evidence may be found, for the time being the banking connection is the stronger link. Or may I state that perhaps due to the etheric guiding hand behind the world, perhaps both origins behind the coat of arms are correct?

Upon further research of the De Medici coat of arms I came across a frontispiece of an illuminated book dedicated to Piero de Medici (1416-1469) by his grandson Pope Clement VII (1478-1534).

The central image of the illumination is that of a gold medal or coin representing Piero de Medici. I found this to be fitting considering the bezants on their shield.

The Piero de Medici Medal

Rosselli, Francessco. *Aristotle's Physics*. Pope Clement VII. 1445 – before 1513 3.

The shield of the Medicis can be seen in the upper left in the above illustration. The six red coins surround a seventh which appears to be black. I edited the image by including two pentacles over the medallion of Piero Medici.

The medallion is surrounded by five vessels containing fiery foliage and is the basis for the inverted pentacle drawn in white. I cover the pentacle or pentagram in greater detail in following chapters due to its importance to esoteric Templarism. Likewise there are five Melusine figures which support the upright blue pentacle.

Melusine is an early medieval elf maiden of fountains and springs with the ability to transform into a dragon. She is the inspiration for the Lady of the Lake of Arthurian tales. Varying noble houses of Scotland and Western Europe counted her as their ancestor. I believe her to be an allusion to Mary Magdalene.

Each shield on the frontispiece is supported by a feminine dragon or Chimera. Their tails are woven round each other as infinity knots reminiscent of the Ouroboros. I found the hair colour to be of interest and wondered if the model might have been an attractive young lady of the family or perhaps copied from a prior painting?

Piero de Medici had engaged Sandro Botticelli to paint the Madonna del Magnificat in 1481. Those included in the painting are his family members and I think it likely that the Madonna may be copied into the cameo of the above dragon visage.

Madonna of the Magnificant Sandro Botticelli 1483 Photo by Livioandronico2013

The dragons in the frontispiece are a nod to the Order of the Dragon, founded in 1408 and based on the chivalric orders of the Crusades, created by Sigmund of Luxembourg (1368-1437), King of the Holy Roman Empire and of Italy and Germany.

The purpose of the order was to safeguard Europe against the aggressions of the Turks. The Order of the Dragon was based on the older Hungarian Order of Saint George (*Societas Militae Sancti Georgii*), which had been established in 1326 by King Charles I of Anjou.

It was the first secular order of knights to have been established outside the church which could have been a positive reaction by King Charles I upon the Templars having disbanded only 12 years prior. I have no doubts that the new order included actual forcibly retired Templars who could still swing a sword!

Saint George was the patron of the Order of the Dragon whose emblem was an Ouroboros with the Cross of St. George on its back.

King Rene d'Anjou of Naples (1408-1480) was born in the same year that the

Order of the Dragon was formed and 82 years after his ancestor had inspired its predecessor.

If there was an initiate guiding the rise of the Italian Renaissance it was Rene d'Anjou. He employed Christopher Columbus and Jewish astrologer and Kabbalist, Jean de Saint-Remy, who was reputed to be the grandfather of Nostradamus. The king wrote poetry, treatises on tournaments and also illustrated his own works. Arthurian and Grail romances were also a part of his field of interests. 4.

Rene befriended the Medici family and prompted Cosimo and his son Lorenzo de Medici to take up the beautification of Florence through architectural wonders and artistic endeavours.

During the years 1439 to 1444, Cosimo scoured Europe for manuscripts across multiple disciplines from Hermetic, Gnostic and Greek classics. He founded Europe's first public library of San Marco which was a step towards challenging the established church. 5.

Birth of Venus 1486 by Sandro Botticelli

1. Tarassi, Massimo0. The Buyer: The Medici Family from Its Origins to the Fifteenth Century. in G. Cherubini and G. Fanelli (curr.) op. cit, 2.

2. Roover, Ryamond De. The Three Balls of the Pawnbrokers. Vol. XX. Business Historical Society. Business Historical Society, 1946. 24

3. Rosselli, Francessco. Aristotle's Physics. Pope Clement VII. 1445 – before 1513

4. Baigent, Michael, Richard Leigh, and Henry Lincoln. The Holy Blood and the Holy Grail. London: Century, 2005. 158.

5. ibid p. 159

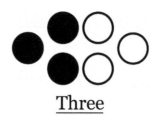

Three

The de Medici Code

Two Shields Converge in Cumbria

The similarity of the Medici coat of arms and that of the Earls of Lonsdale of the family name of Lowther in Cumbria is odd indeed - six annulets against a gold shield. An annulet may be described as a roundel or coin that has been voided by having the centre punched out.

The Lowthers raised their fortunes in service to King Edward I while helping to protect the boarder against the Scots. As they became of greater value to the crown their rewards also grew, from a manor house and castle to vast estates.

I wondered if there might have at some point been a connection to the Averado de Medici's of the 12th century and perhaps the Lowthers of Medieval England as philosophical cousins or literal and or both. It bears greater scrutiny.

Sir John Lowther (1642-1706), 2nd Baronet of Whitehaven Cumbria, kept meticulous records of his estate and also notations of those who were pertinent to helping run the community.

In his General Memoranda Book he notes that John Mattinson was nominated to the parish of Patterdale in 1705 as the schoolmaster. For the Baronet to have made this notation it had to have had personal relevance and implies acquaintance at the very least. 1.

I asked the Comte if there was a shared heritage with the Lowthers as the coat of arms is too close to be insignificant.

Prince Henri had indeed married a Lowther. As a rich man of the royal house of Bourbon and Medici, he would have been circulating with those of his own socioeconomic background and his new in-laws were the most powerful family in the area.

Wordsworth and the Cumbrian Templars

There entered Two by Two
Two only ever knew
As they grew
Two by Two
One only took the pew
Wordsworth unpublished –

The poet William Wordsworth (1770-1850) was sponsored by the Lowthers and actually lived at Lowther Castle for a time. He was part of a movement known as Romanticism which sought to reinvigorate ideals such as the power of emotion and love in an age of hard industrial revolution which was fast divorcing itself from spirit. Romanticism went hand in hand with the famous painters of the Pre-Raphaelite movement which pined after the beauty in nature and Arthurian legends.

In light of the identity of Henry Mattinson the above poem by Wordsworth is incriminating and places the poet with direct knowledge of the hidden prince.

During a final meeting for this chapter with the Comte de Mattinata de Medici, I was told that Wordsworth was given 'Kendal Black' by the Templars as a path towards altering awareness. He then wrote some of his most passionate works. Kendal Black was an opiate derivative developed in Cumbria.

"And labourers going forth to till the fields, Ah! need I say, dear Friend! that to the brim My heart was full; I made no vows, but vows Were then made for me; bond unknown to me Was given, that I should be, else sinning greatly, A dedicated Spirit. On I walked In thankful blessedness, which yet survives" Wordsworth 2.

Nostradamus

Deciphering the works of Michel de Nostradamus (1503-1566) has always been a challenge. His prediction that Catherine de Medici's husband, King Henry II of France, would die violently came true, thus cementing his reputation within her court.

His predictions of a terrifying war involving a man named 'Hister' seemed to echo that of WWII and Hitler. His financial fate was bound to the De Medicis and it must be probable that his predictions included the family's future.

The Quatrain, Century Eight, Sixty Six, by Nostradamus is fascinating:

"When the Inscription D.M. is found,
in the ancient cave, revealed by a lamp.
Law, the King and Prince Ulpian tried,
the Queen and Duke in the pavilion under cover."

What to make of this prediction? Is it possible that the initials D.M. may stand for de Medici? What hidden cave is being spoken of and what is within the cave?

There are many caves in Cumbria but also in France. Is there a relationship here to the mysterious tomb as painted by Poussin in the next century - the Shepherds of Arcadia? The tomb was supposed to have been of great antiquity and would have been in existence during Nostradamus' lifetime.

I immediately thought of the Shugborough Monument in England, which includes in its coded inscription, offset letters D and M opposite one another, leading me to think of Arcadian themes.

The Secret Dossier of a
Knight Templar of the Sangreal

The reversed monument of the tomb from the Poussin painting is under an archway and is carved to resemble the opening of a cave. Please see chapter 27 - The Erasmus Obelisk and the New World for photos and details.

Nostradamus does not give us a name for the other persons in this quatrain and the prior and further quatrains discus power struggles centred in France. Is it possible to glean more by finding out the identity of Prince Ulpian the only name in the Quatrain?

There may have been two 'prince' Ulpians – a father and a son - but dating them or separating the two from one another is a debate I will not embark upon. I will treat their legacy as the same individual as it is difficult to know which character Nostradamus was intending to identify from the Classical world as there are actually three total possibilities.

Ulpian was a 2nd to 3rd century Roman lawyer and scholar who served on the council to the Emperor Severus but through disagreement found himself in exile. Ulpian was called back to Rome in order to serve the next Emperor as his chief advisor. His is a tale of triumph over injustice.

Fast forward to the early 3rd century and Ulpian becomes a fictional character in the *Deipnosophistai*, which translates roughly into The Dinner Philosophers by Athenaeus, a Greek scholar who lived in Egypt.

Ulpian is a guest at a dinner party which lasts several days where he is expected to debate in the rigorous manner of Plato with other experts in various fields across the Seven Liberal Arts. It is a cerebral Table of the Grail being enacted where the debate creates human drama.

Ulpian is quoted as saying -

'To live honourably, to harm no one, to give to each his own.' 3.

Ulpian's quote rings loudly of what is considered to be the Neo-Pagan or Wiccan Rede, *'Do as thou wilt and harm none'* but is centuries older and of alchemical origin than the modern day Wiccan Rede.

The history of the Rede can be found in a work of fiction by a remarkable Benedictine monk, Greek scholar, savant and medical doctor, François Rabelais (circa 1483-1553) who was of course a contemporary of Nostradamus.

He was born in Chinon, attended university at Montpellier in the Languedoc region and had travelled the breadth and depth of France. His patron had been Francis I King of France and the father of Henry II whose early death Nostradamus had predicted. It is impossible that Nostradamus had *not* met Rabelais or read his books.

Rabelais has gone down in history as a literary genius for his satirical and humanist views in a series of tales about a giant named Gargantua and his son, Pantagruel. The good hearted giant Gargantua builds an Abbey called Thélème. Over the door of the abbey is an inscription:

Grace, honour, praise, delight,
Here sojourn day and night.
Sound bodies lined

The de Medici Code

> With a good mind,
> Do here pursue with might
> Grace, honour, praise, delight.

Within the walls of the abbey a world opened up which had more to do with going on holiday or vacation than slavish round the clock monastic work. Maid service was available, one could rise at any time of day and the residents did exactly as they pleased in all ways. Rabelais wrote, *'Do What Thou Wilt'*... a derivative of Ulpian's quote.

> "...because men that are free, well-born, well-bred, and conversant in honest companies, have naturally an instinct and spur that prompteth them unto virtuous actions, and withdraws them from vice, which is called honour."

In this case 'honour' equates with blind dogmatic pride that was being relentlessly pushed on society by the Roman church regardless of human need or suffering. According to Rabelais it is important to know how and when to break the rules out of forgiveness and compassion, if indeed the rules were of true human significance in the first place.

He caused a great deal of controversy within the church when his tales of Gargantua were published to great popularity. He was forced to go into hiding and his books were banned. He ended his life quietly outside of Paris as a Curate, an oddly similar theme to John Mattinson.

Rabelais as a Greek scholar was conversant in Ulpian's work and also in his fictional form at the pen of Athenaeus. He transmitted the body of philosophy that swirled around the character to Nostradamus. Therefore Prince Ulpian within the context of the Nostradamus Quatrains actually contains an entire alchemical and humanist point of view in just the name of the man himself.

> Law, the King and Prince Ulpian tried,

Is it possible that the line of this Quatrain might refer to the 'Law' as representing the heretical compassion of Christ, Henri de Medici is the King and Prince Ulpian, a lawyer, serves as a code for the philosophy of the Underground Stream which is 'tried' or persecuted by Inquisitional and or political forces.

If this quatrain is in reference to Henri de Medici - perhaps the next line may make some sense:

> the Queen and Duke in the pavilion under cover

The Queen in reference may be his mother, Maria de Medici. The Duke could have been his twin brother, as a duke is very close in rank to a prince; or any of the many courtiers around Maria who were in collusion with her during the imprisonment of Henri and as such they were 'under cover'. Is it possible that Henri de Medici was the better man and would have been the preferable king of France?

I am certainly speculating but one point is clear that Nostradamus was familiar with the heretical scholar Rabelais and chose to include his alchemical philosophy in his Quatrain VIII Century, Sixty Six under the guise of Prince Ulpian. The Medicis were his patrons and therefore his predictions centered on them and their future sons.

Triple Portrait of Cardinal de Richelieu 1642, Philippe de Champaigne

1. "Database." Cumbria Archive Service Catalogue. http%3A%2F %2Fwww.archiveweb.cumbria.gov.uk%2FCalmView%2Fdefault.aspx. Cumbria Archive Service Catalogue, Carlisle, DCC/2/27, General Memoranda Book of Sir John Lowther
2. Rawnsley, H. D. Literary Associations of the English Lakes. Vol. 2. Glasgow: J. MacLehose and Sons, 1901. pp.176-7
3. "Ulpian." Wikipedia. https://en.wikipedia.org/wiki/Ulpian#cite_note-3. Digesta 1.1.10 - The Digest or Roman law, a body of work adapted from ancient Greek in the 6th century.

Four

The Ancient Kingdom of Rheged Will Rise

A Lost Language

Wales, Ireland and Scotland have taken great pains to preserve their languages from being lost. Their cousin, the local dialect of Cumbria, is under greater threat as it is perceived to simply be a regional accent.

Celtic Christians lived between the 4th and 11th centuries - "They were Celts in that their first language was Celtic – British, and later its daughter-tongues Cumbric, Welsh and Cornish – and Christian in that nearly all the people named here were baptised, raised, schooled and laid to rest as members of an orthodox British Christian church." 1.

The Brythonic-Cumbric culture of this time period was distinct and separate from Rome. It had direct ties to Ireland and was partners to centres such as Iona and played no small part in keeping alive the earliest form of Christianity while Rome crumbled and lost its inner core.

It was a difficult period with influxes from Germanic tribes but over the centuries the newcomers wanted to fit in and so converted even if they had the upper hand and had taken political control over large swathes of England. Out of this melting pot the language of Brythonic merged with that of Norse into Old English.

Cumbric as an early medieval language is considered to have died but I wonder just how much of it actually survived? The dialect has much in common with Scotland due to proximity and therefore Gaelic.

Anna Garnett is trying to preserve the Cumbrian dialect on her blog and discusses local influences:

"The Cumbrian dialect contains Norse and Celtic influences, and there are distinct variations in the dialect between the county regions; for example the North/West Cumbrian accent was greatly influenced by the Scottish and Geordie dialects, in contrast to the South which preserves aspects of both the Lancashire and Yorkshire dialects."

You can visit her blog for further information:

http://annagarnett.blogspot.co.uk/2010/10/hoos-ta-gaan-on-traditional-dialect-of.html

Lancelot Salkeld Porter (1911-1998) Poet of the Cumbrian dialect and founder of the Lakeland Dialect Society described his group and plea for the public to join:

The Secret Dossier of a
Knight Templar of the Sangreal

THE LAKELAND DIALECT SOCIETY
[What is it?.. .. I'll tell the'.]
We're nut stuck up er prood i't mooth
Fer t'main on us was bred in't fells,
We're nobbut wiet, yammly, fwoak
Off t'seeam switch as yersels.
An' like yersels, we clag tight tull
o't bits o'country ways an' looar;
We like ta hod a crack aboot
T'auld dale-fwoak' at hev gone afooar.
Mi fadder, (an' nea doot he's reet),
Sez t's main o't' fell fwoak er o't seame
They "Hawk tagidder" on a drag,
Till Foxy's brush is hung on t'beame.
He sez 'at t' interest (like t' auld Fox)
Is rousan 'noo fer thee an' me,
Soo join, yersels, an git yer kin
Ta join oor own Society.

From The Works of Lance Porter - Lakeland Treasury
Compiled and edited by Ted Relph and Published by the Society
http://www.lakelanddialectsociety.org/

During the latest meeting I had with the Comte, he said that the well-known phrase of 'Merry Neet' in Cumbric was not slang for 'Merry Meet' but meant the 'Merry Knight'. In other words the 'Merry Templar Knight'. The term 'Templar' also became shifted into Temper/Tempre.

I thought I would rely upon the fame of Robbie Burns and include an excerpt from his epic poem, Tam o Shanter both in its original Scots dialect and also English translation as an example of the northern cousin dialects.

Original
Nae man can tether time or tide;
The hour approaches Tam maun ride;
That hour, o' night's black arch the key-stane,
That dreary hour he mounts his beast in;
And sic a night he taks the road in
As ne'er poor sinner was abroad in.

The Ancient Kingdom of Rheged Will Rise

Translated:
No man can tether time or tide,
The hour approaches Tom must ride:
That hour, of night's black arch - the key-stone,
That dreary hour he mounts his beast in
And such a night he takes to the road in
As never a poor sinner had been out in.

http://www.robertburns.org.uk/Assets/Poems_Songs/tamoshanter.htm

The importance of the Cumbric language is easy to put into context: it was spoken by the legendary King Arthur Pendragon of the 6th century. In other words, the kings English. The Comte places the lost seat of King Arthur in a hidden forest location in Cumbria.

King Arthur's Seat in Cumbria

Many countries claim King Arthur from Wales, Italy, France, Scotland, Germany and England such was the popularity of his equitable society. I believe this widespread knowledge of Camelot to be an indication of a hidden alchemical tradition which moved through Western Europe.

The name Arthur finds its roots in Brythonic and means 'bear-king' and Pendragon may be translated as 'head-dragon' which implies there were other dragons! We need only look to the Welsh flag for confirmation of what I believe to be an actual magical tradition.

According to Welsh legend two dragons fought for supremacy over the land - they were red and white in colour. The red dragon won and is shown as the victor on a white background on the flag of Wales which has been in use for centuries on an intermittent basis.

Several British dynasties from 12th century Scotland through to the Tudors have used the dragon as their banner in battle.

Why a dragon? The dragon is representative of the awakened human energy tree which indicates that the combatants behind the story of the Welsh flag were actually Magi or Priest-Kings. Many of the stories written about Arthur show him battling supernatural forces, visiting other realms and surrounded by courtiers with etheric abilities.

The Mabinogion are the oldest Welsh tales which name a King Arthur. It is automatically assumed that the historical Arthur was therefore from Wales however there is the shared language between Cumbric and Welsh.

Could this indicate that tales of an historical Arthur flowed *to* Wales and were then written down? Early Celtic Christian priests were known to travel widely; I don't think this is terribly far off the mark as a concept.

It is always assumed that the Arthurian tales also flowed from Bretton in France to Wales then to England but it is more likely that a Dark Age Chivalric Order, which came out of a supposedly heretical Celtic Christian tradition in Cumbria, actually flowed east to inspire the Dragon Courts of Europe. Had the Cumbric Court of Arthur who counted Melusine as part of his family tree inspired his continental cousins?

Michael Wood states boldly that the Arthurian court can be easily placed with *the Men of the North*:

"Whoever fought these battles, their names and the other early poetic references to Arthur (c 900) surprisingly do not take us to the southwest or to Wales, but to Cumbria, southern Scotland, and the ancient kingdom of Rheged around the Solway." 2.

Wood goes on to say that according to Dark Age sources one family line stands out from others including that of Arthur - King Urien of Rheged. Poems as a means of historical memory were sung by Taliesin the Bard who bestowed epithets upon Urien such as the Eagle of the Land and also the symbol of the Lion. 3.

Sir Wolfram von Eschenbach (1170-1220) claimed he had an earlier source for Arthur than Chrétien de Troyes of the 12th century. Citing Kyot from Provence, whose work no longer exists: Wolfram writes lyrically about Perceval who must perform Herculean deeds in his quest to find the Grail and be illuminated.

But the obsessive details of the poem are less to do with the Grail itself but with the lineage of Perceval and the Grail family. It goes far deeper than family as Perceval must be worthy of his blood and perform tasks successfully in order to inherit the Grail, the castle and to earn the right to marry. 4.

Physicist and Anthroposophy adherent, Walter Johannes Stein (1891-1957) dealt with the historical discrepancies of Arthur as though the earth plane of Western Europe was in symbiotic contact with a higher-realm intent upon imparting Christ consciousness through heroic archetypes that could impress upon individuals open to the shared ideals.

His theory is reminiscent of the emanations of the Kaballah which flow down to Malkhuth the earth plane. At varying points in history the Grail stories had to be ethereally revitalized when humanity was in need.

"Rudolph Steiner has said that the Grail narrative was made exoteric about the year 1180. The different Grail stories did, as a matter of fact, first become generally known at this period; but they had already been present in the souls of men since the eighth or ninth century in forms which finally took the shape given to them by Chrétien de Troyes or Wolfram von Eschenbach. For the present, a few indications will be given here from which it will be evident that the narrators of the Grail story knew that the Grail experiences actually dated from the eighth or ninth century." 5.

I appreciate that Stein places the Arthurian tales to the 8th and 9th centuries. The truth is they existed from AD 33 when the children of the Wise Serpent, Jesus, thrived in France and married into the thrones of Europe. The tales of the actual and historic Arthur were however generated from events which took place in the 6th century in Cumbria.

The Ancient Kingdom of Rheged Will Rise

King Urien of Rheged (now Cumbria and southern Scotland) was of the late 6th century whose deeds are recorded in the Book of Taliesin. His coat of arms was that of a raven on a white background. He married King Arthur's sister Morgan le Fay and had four sons. Owain mab Urien inherited his father Urien's throne and fought to repel the Angles of Bernicia.

King Owain became the knight Yvain in Chrétien de Troyes' narrative The Knight of the Lion. Yvain and his companion lion fought and vanquished a dragon amongst other deeds. Befriending a lion is an astonishing feat and this incident may be a precursor of the Strength card of the tarot.

Chretien de Troyes writes of Yvain, son of King Uryen, as going on a secret mission to defeat a black knight who had unjustly wounded a comrade. King Arthur, though outraged by the events and promising to avenge his wounded knight, literally decides to take a nap thus losing the opportunity to gain and save face by embarking immediately on the expedition of honour. While Arthur sleeps, Urien/Yvain sneaks out of the castle and goes alone.

Yvain is given a ring of invisibility by a fairy held in servitude to the Black Knight. Once the villain is defeated Yvain woos and marries his widow with the help of the fairy and becomes the guardian of the magical fountain in his new wife's lands. 6.

It is easy to see where Tolkien found his inspiration for the Lord of the Rings and the heroic Rangers of the north, one of whom is the fated king uniting all the lands and peoples.

Owain mab Urien also had a famous son by the princess Teneu. Saint Kentigern became a pivotal figure of the Insular or Celtic Christian church. The prophet Merlin is connected with Saint Kentigern who came from the same area in Cumbria. 7.

Like the fall of Camelot, it is not a happy ending for King Owain as he loses his battle against the Angles along with his life but according to the Comte the family line survives through the Lowthers and the marriage to Prince Henri.

The Kingdom of Rheged is tragically lost and the Men of the North gather once a year and are told to wait before melting back into the mountains, 'not yet, not yet' - they are told, but, 'rise we will'.

We are distanced by these events by almost 1400 years and during that time much was destroyed through natural decay, war and the sacking of monasteries and households in the Cumbrian-Rheged landscape. The 11th and 12th century chroniclers were using sources which were fading and now gone but the chroniclers left a firm footprint for us to follow.

Prince Henri and the Holy Grail

The Cumbric dialect had to have been adopted by Prince Henri de Medici in order to understand the culture of his new home. His son John was born into the landscape and language.

I've pondered what it must have been like for Henri to have a sense of true freedom in Patterdale after his incarceration. No matter how polite it might have been in Mattinata, he was still a prisoner. He had a life forced upon him by accident of birth which may have made him prone to philosophical interests and to ask the deeper questions of life.

If he became a Templar priest as the Comte asserts what was his spiritual inspiration? French Templar descendants? Had he brought books from Italy and France? Both were hotbeds of occult and alchemical practices. Regardless the Templars of Cumbria embraced him as a brother indicating there was already commonality.

The Melusine figure and dragon of the frontispiece commissioned for Piero de Medici is synchronistic of Arthur Pendragon. In other words the Dragon returns to his spiritual & physical home through Henry Mattinson.

The Nostradamus quatrain Century Eight, Sixty-Six might be considered in another light. Could Prince Ulpian be a deliberate code and misdirection? Ulpian was never an actual prince but a well-educated upper middle class father/son/ fictional person whose life was used in the context of early alchemical Grail Mysteries by two brilliant writers.

Is it possible that Nostradamus gave Ulpian his princely title as a way of letting us know that the identity of the man was not of the 2nd to 3rd century Rome, but that his name was Urien? A prince of the 6th century, who would one day rise again as a Medici to protect the ancient kingdom of Rheged? Nostradamus as a scholar was acquainted with the earlier Arthurian tales.

According to legend King Arthur sleeps under a mountain in a cave and will come to the aid of Britain when the time is right. It is interesting that Arthur's family blood of course flowed through his sister as well. Morgan le Fay was of the Fae Realm, a Fairy Queen, who had married into the line of the Rheged royal family.

Is it then possible that Nostradamus' prediction was for our own time period when the Arthurian-Urien, de Medici and Bourbon family lines came together in the house of Mattinson of the ancient kingdom now called Cumbria?

The quatrain 'Law, King and Prince Ulpian Tried' could be interpreted to mean that the reincarnated, physical heir and king will 'try' or 'put on trial' the follies of modern life in Britain?

Has the Medici Code been discovered and will there be a rejuvenation of the land and its peoples? Has the Once and Future King recovered the Grail Hallows remembered in the tarot? Is there a path open to the practical magician and Priest-King of the Merovingians?

Let us revisit the hidden history of the King of Israel and Mary Magdalene up through Bernard de Clairvaux, the Knights Templar and our modern day connection with these enigmatic people as a stepping stone to understanding the Comte de Mattinata de Medici.

As of yet I have not revealed the first name of the Comte and have continued to use the name John Temple and his title throughout the book. I have not been given permission to use a photo at this stage but I can say that the Comte bears a striking resemblance to my favourite monarch King Charles II the son of Queen Henrietta de Medici.

I'll leave you to ponder a quote regarding the Dark Age ancestor of the Comte whose emblem was the crow - englishmonarchs.co.uk -

The Ancient Kingdom of Rheged Will Rise

"Urien was assassinated at Aber Lleu (Ross Low) on the behest of Morgant Bwlch, who was jealous of the power he wielded in the north and his reputation as a great warrior. His assassin, a foreigner by the name of Llofan Llaf Difo, cut-off Urien's head. He was said to have been buried beneath a cairn, under a blue stone cover. Nennius recorded:-

'Four kings fought against them, Urien and Rhydderch Hen and Gwallawg and Morcant.

Theodoric fought vigorously against Urien and his sons. During that time, sometimes the enemy, sometimes the Cymry were victorious and Urien blockaded them for three days and three nights in the island of Metcaud (Lindisfarne). But during this campaign Urien was assassinated by the instigation of Morcant, from jealousy, because his military skill and generalship surpassed that of all other kings."

The Departure of the Knights, Edward Burne-Jones 1894

1. Thomas, Charles. Christian Celts. Stroud: Tempus, 2003. p.6

2. Wood, Michael. In Search of the Dark Ages. New York, NY: Facts on File, 1987. p. 45

3. Taylor, Rupert. The Political Prophecy in England. New York: Columbia University Press, 1911. p. 45

4. Baigent, Michael, Richard Leigh, and Henry Lincoln. The Holy Blood and the Holy Grail. London: Century, 2005. P. 334

5. Stein, Walter Johannes, Irene Groves, and John M. Wood. The Ninth Century and the Holy Grail. London: Temple Lodge, 1988. p. 9

6. Markale, Jean. King of the Celts: Arthurian Legends and the Celtic Tradition. Rochester, VT: Inner Traditions, 1994. p. 25

7. Ibid p 98

Five

Bernard de Clairvaux
Knight of the Morning Star

"In danger, in anguish, in uncertainty, think of Mary, call upon Mary. Let not her name depart from your lips, never suffer it to leave your heart. And that you may more surely obtain the assistance of her prayer, neglect not to walk in her footsteps. With her as guide, you shall never go astray; while invoking her, you shall never lose heart; So long as she is in your mind, you are safe from deception; while she holds your hand, you cannot fall; under her protection you have nothing to fear; if she walks before you, you shall not grow weary; if she shows you favor, you shall reach the goal." *Bernard de Clairvaux* Homilies on the Gospel 1120. 1.

Bernard de Clairvaux brought about unprecedented changes in the 12th century, which affected Europe and the Middle East, and reverberated down the centuries.

The charismatic force of this man has not been entirely appreciated by researchers of the historical genre of the Knights Templar. It is easy to give him no more than a cursory nod in favour of the perceived glamour of the knightly Order, which without his hand, would not have gained its influential foothold.

Bernard de Fontaine was born in 1091 AD, near Dijon, France into a Burgundian noble house. He is descended from the Merovingian dynasty made famous by Baigent, Leigh and Lincoln.

Tescelin Sorrel, also known as Sorus, lord of Fontaines and crusader knight, was his father and Lady Aleth (Elizabeth) de Montbard, his mother.

Though yet unborn a wise man had foretold that this child was destined for greatness. Born the third of seven children, it is thought that all were well educated, but it was decided that particular care must be given to Bernard's studies if he were to follow his star and fulfil his potential.

The highly intelligent nine year old was sent to a renowned school in Chatillon-sur-Seine, run by the secular canons of Eglise Saint-Vorles where he was known to have relatives. He was given a broad education, preparing the way for his literary skills, strength in debate and critical thinking.

Ambitious at an early age, he excelled in literature and poetry to better expand his studies of scripture in the future. He had won the full admiration of his tutors, showing, 'masterful cognition', launching himself with zeal into his studies.

Bernard suffered a great personal loss at the age of 16 with the death of his mother and there can be no doubt that she influenced his decision to follow a religious life. However, we cannot know if she was the main factor in his choice to join the Cistercian Order.

I am convinced that he was following a wisdom tradition held within his family, in what seems likely, over centuries. The very fact that he had relatives nearby during his years in school is a clue that there may have been other guiding lights which helped to direct his esoteric nature.

Bernard de Clairvaux
Knight of the Morning Star

There are echoes of evidence indicating that the family and their companions were familiar with operating in an organised manner, case in point, their takeover of the Cistercian Order en masse. The Abbot Bernard would reluctantly become the very public face of the tradition that he served so well.

His Parents' Influence

This was obviously a close-knit family, with a special bond that many do not share with their relations. It engendered in de Clairvaux a deep respect of compassion, loyalty and integrity. The family lived by a high moral code tempered with fairness and Aleth was as inspiring to her son as Monica was to Augustine of Hippo, the 5th-century saint.

What is this mysterious bond and purpose that held this familial group together? It has long been noted that the Knights Templar were the guardians of great secrets, sacred relics and writings, bloodlines, and ancient documents. Clues lie in the family ties of the Languedoc and that of the Cistercian Order about to make its debut on the world stage.

It is thought by some historians that de Clairvaux's father, Sorrel, may have died during the First Crusade (1096-1099) but it is also possible that he experienced a conversion and followed Bernard into monastic life. Indeed, this family appears to experience an unusual motivation to take up monastic life, more than can be explained by the pervading religious culture of the day. Only his sister, Humbeline, remained in secular life and then for just two years before leaving behind her husband and children, with his consent, for a Benedictine convent.

Authors Lionel and Patricia Fanthorp suggest that Tescelin survived the First Crusade and may have become privy to knowledge, or actual physical evidence, calling for further investigation by what they term as the Guardians of the Holy Grail Tradition.

They theorise that he transmitted this secret to his son Bernard, creating the impetus for an incredible shift in the lives of the entire family. The Fanthorps go on to speculate that Bernard may have been prompted by his father's witnessing of events surrounding the discovery of the Spear of Destiny, upon the crusaders' capture of Antioch from October 1097 to June 1098. I also think it highly likely that family memory and strong oral traditions meant that the guardians knew of lost information and artefacts buried in these sacred locations.

Nothing certain may be said about Sir Tescelin's genealogy as his recorded history is vague. However, he would have had to have been an individual of some calibre to be considered marriage material for the Lady Aleth whose mother, also of the same name, was married to William III, Count of Toulouse.

The Counts of Toulouse were known to have connections to the Albigensians, otherwise known as the Cathars. This is certainly a long-established family affair and keeping the archival knowledge in house was important. It seems probable that Tescelin was part of the Grail lineage as was his wife.

An incident that reveals Tescelin's temperament is that of a duel, one where he was clearly the stronger of the two combatants. Knowing that combat would end in the death or severe injury of the challenger, Tescelin adopted a conciliatory approach, saving face for both parties and appeasing his own spiritual convictions of peace and chivalrous conduct.

Aleth was known to have visions - as did other family members. While pregnant, Aleth had a dream that Bernard had taken the form of a barking dog with white fur and a tawny back. Alarmed, she consulted a holy man who prophetically told her that this was a good sign, that the child would be a guardian to the Lord's house, a marvelous preacher and healer.

The holy man went on to say that as dogs licked wounds to facilitate healing and offered protection, so too would the child's oration offer salve to the souls of his flock.

Saint Bernard is often seen with a small white dog in religious art; I would take this a step further and make the connection to Sirius the dog/god star that often makes its presence known in modern Grail mysteries. We have an echo here of ancient Egyptian priestly thought likening Saint Bernard as a reincarnated Pharaoh. Thus his life is intimately linked with the Black Madonna, also of Egyptian origin, which we will soon explore further.

Aleth knew she had been blessed in life, born into privileged nobility, married to a chivalrous knight and with seven remarkable children. She was known to seek out the poor of her community, attending to the sick and helping in their homes. It was said she even did their dishes! Later in life she dressed simply, striving for a monastic existence even within the confines of her familial duties. As a mother of seven children, mostly boys, this could not have been easy and her ascetic practices affected Bernard deeply. During times of Tescelin's absence, when he was away on campaigns, Aleth took centre stage in her household.

Aleth must have been a rather formidable individual too, as one legend states she would hold an annual feast for Saint Ambrose, whose day is marked on the 7th of December. She invited clergy to dine in their home and clearly participated in their discussions.

Interestingly, Saint Ambrose's emblem is that of a bee, a Merovingian device, but this cannot be a surprise considering the lady in question was of Merovingian descent. The bee denotes sacred geometry but the hive mind centres on a single queen. Saint Ambrose was also an avid Marionist, a path which the young Bernard would follow his whole life.

Aleth had a visitation and was told she would die on the feast day of Saint Ambrose, which indeed transpired. Upon hearing of her death the abbot of a convent near Dijon begged of the family that she be buried at his cloister, a request which was granted. This is rather remarkable and a sign of the influential life she must have led and the respect she engendered in the men of her day.

Throughout their lives her children would say she appeared to them to offer solace. Bernard stated that she would implore him to continue his work started as a monk. His "long path to complete conversion" had begun with her death in 1107 and Lady Aleth was an example to her young son of solitude and worldly renunciation. However, he would be continually drawn back into the world by those who relied on his leadership – people who came from all walks of life.

Bernard de Clairvaux
Knight of the Morning Star

The Queen of Heaven

"We approach the altar of God and pray, and, if we persevere, despite our own dryness and tepidity, grace will overpower us, our bosom will swell, love will fill our hearts...and the milk of sweetness will overflow everywhere in a torrent." 2.
Saint Bernard

As we have seen, Bernard de Clairvaux's character was formed at an early age by his mystical family traditions and arguably by Fontaines itself, a centre for the misunderstood cult of the Black Madonna. He was absolutely driven by the passion he held for The Queen of Heaven and her importance to the public chivalric orders he would help create. Not only is she representative of a deep spiritual tradition and transmission but also that of ancestral appreciation, not unlike that of Shinto.

St Bernard maintained through his life that as a child he received three drops of milk, whilst in meditative prayer, from the breast of the Black Virgin of Saint Vorles, Chatillon sur Seine.

As a boy he became ill with a dangerous infection. He recited 'Hail Star of the Sea, show yourself a mother!". The Madonna came to life and showered him with three drops from her breast instantly healing him. The boy's heart filled with a flame of love that would never dwindle during his life.

This is an indication of initiation practices long established in Fontaines. Indeed it is one harkening back to ancient Egypt of Isis and her son Horus. The act established the young Bernard as Horus.

Later in life the prominent Bernard de Clairvaux would be dubbed the Second Pope and the Doctor of the Church; though this was through accepted channels, it is nonetheless a reflection of his unique spiritual and political status as a High Priest within the tradition. This said he constantly refused offers of advancement on the public stage. He had ample opportunity to become a bishop and perhaps even Pope. He considered these worldly accolades an impediment to his mission.

There are several versions of the 'Maria Lactans' miracle. Later he would experience this grace again in 1146 at the Cathedral in Speyer, Germany, which of course is dedicated to Saint Mary. In the 13th century, a church to Mary Magdalene was installed within the Cathedral grounds of Speyer. The Magdalene is never a co-incidence in these matters.

The Lactation of St Bernard is indicative of the Saint receiving clear spiritual sight from the Madonna or opening the third eye as we would express in today's terms. In other legends the healing salve falls onto his lips gifting him with prophecy, wisdom in speech and curing his ills. All of these gifts can be associated with an awakening or initiatory process.

Is it any wonder that the earliest and most necessary protection and nourishment of a mother to her child should result in spiritual fervor and devotion? It is primal and of our earliest hidden memories both personally and as a race memory.

A baby's very survival hinges on the all-important first milk holding the key to inoculation against disease. The most dependent of offspring on earth is the human being who would die without a mother's love. Since pre-history human beings have been seeking grace from a wise, forgiving mother whose breasts pour out solace to her children.

In today's terms we do have a different way of expressing the initiatic experience than that of medieval parlance. Medieval Christians did not shrink from Saint Bernard's visions of receiving the breast milk of the Black Virgin.

European Christians started dreaming and also having their own experience of the Magna Mater upon hearing of the Saints miraculous encounters with Her. A breast feeding adult seems an odd notion today and very disquieting to our modern view of human sexuality due to the exclusion in the west of physical experience along-side the spiritual. Of course he was not speaking of a mere physical act with no basis in spiritual energy.

The mother goddess was alive and well in the persona of mother Mary which did not exclude, to the medieval worshiper, a physical experience which is echoed in all its totality in Saint Theresa of Avila's life.

Abbot Bernard transmitted these initiatic practices to the Templar Knights. "One of the most remarkable examples of religious convergence occurred at the Convent of Our Lady at Saidnaya about fifteen miles north of Damascus. This Greek Orthodox religious house, deep in Muslim territory, possessed a 'miraculous' icon of the Virgin Mary which had been transmuted from paint into flesh. Oil supposedly flowed from the icon's breasts and this liquid was treasured for its incredible healing properties." 3. Thomas Asbridge goes on to say that it was a particularly valued pilgrimage site amongst the Templars who also took vials of the miracle oil with them back to Europe.

Since the Queen of Heaven gave birth to the Son they were to Medieval thought, inseparable. Her blood mingled with his and supported his life while in the womb and afterward her milk gave him life. They were the same being. If the Christ shed his blood on the cross for humanity; then it would follow suit that she would pour forth sustaining milk also for humanity.

The Origins of the Holy Trinity –
Microcosm and Macrocosm

The Black Virgin, the Father and Christ together are the resultant model of the Rosicrucian Chemical Wedding. In the east it is expressed as the Kundalini awakening.

Those who have had brushes with sacred Dragon energies have described it as an all-encompassing ecstatic physical and spiritual experience.

It is the point of coming face to face with one's own soul as if being loved by another with no limits and total understanding and forgiveness of all past errors. A state where true humility exists and acceptance of others in compassion remains along with a heightened sense of utter joy, energy and confidence.

The experience described brings to mind the question, what happens when god beholds himself? The resultant alchemical experience within the individual brings forth a rebirth of the Universal Child. Hence each human being on the face of the earth has this innate ability to become the Holy Trinity. This deeply personal process can only be described as sexual on the soul level and reverberates physically. There is only one way to express this in art or prose and that is in the symbolic form of sexual imagery.

It is so often misunderstood in the modern west where centuries of un-natural repression has brought about a confused state deep within the cultural psyche, causing an ignorant recoil at sensual imagery or at the other end of the spectrum a salacious over response. We seem to be much more comfortable with violence than love in the West. In Hindu art divine union is expressed freely and without pause.

We are not without such artistic examples in the west. Our symbolic art has been of a more subtle coded nature due to the guilt sprung upon us by the weight of religion.

A fine example of Enlightened Art in Europe would be that of the brilliant sculptor and architect, Giovanni Bernini, who transformed Rome in the 17th century, infusing the city with bold Egyptian and Greek symbolism.

The closest we may come to seeing the blatant sexuality of Hinduism in art is through Bernini's masterpiece The Ecstasy of Saint Theresa. The marble statue is fluid and alive. Saint Theresa is in a swoon of passion with a handsome young angel known as a Seraph who represents the element of fire. He stands above her suggestively and metaphorically about to pierce her with his golden arrow.

To view a photo of the statue of Saint Theresa of Avila by Bernini – please visit:
http://en.wikipedia.org/wiki/File:Teresabernini.JPG

Author Mark Booth, AKA, Jonathan Black, suggests that beings from other dimensions interact with humanity to facilitate altered states where gifts are bestowed. Black describes the story of two friends living in Budapest in 1943 who realized they could speak to angels. One was told that every cell of the body can join in the 'process of prayer'.

"A theology emerged from these angelic messages that seemed to look back to Mani and Christian Rosencreutz. The women were told that ecstasy was a presentiment of the weightlessness that would come when our bodily matter was transformed. As in the Chymical Wedding, they were told to look forward to the sacred wedding of heaven and Earth. When that happened, the angels told them death itself would die." 4.

Ecstatic art is a description of union with a higher inner being at a cellular level and one which Saint Bernard experienced, spending his life trying to describe to those who would listen and follow.

Karen Ralls, Ph.D. states, 'In the traditions of many ancient cultures, a young initiate would often receive three drops of a special liquid, generally symbolic of wisdom and initiation, and often from a female figure.' 5.

Three itself is a sacred number and an echo of trinity worship that preceded that of patriarchal Rome, as it must have, simply due to the divinity inherent in the human being.

The dying and resurrected god Osiris, his sister/wife, Isis and their son Horus being the inspiration for the triune was infused into the Judaic culture via Moses.

Instead of an all-male trinity a more natural view would be that of Father, Mother and Child; the offspring being male *or* female. As Above so Below, on Earth as it is in Heaven. Father, Son, Holy Ghost is an obvious borrow from the older Trinity where the Holy Ghost rather than being male, is unmistakably feminine. The Mother was obscured simply and diabolically by making her invisible.

It is well established that no religion is simply born out of the ground fully formed, but borrows heavily on prior traditions and is often changed as is human nature to suit the prevailing cultural understanding of the day. Political expediency and economic control are often the main inspirations for a change in exoteric doctrine.

The earliest Judaic peoples worshiped the consort of Jehovah, the Shekinah, adopting a matrilineal line of descent prior to the final eradication of the Mother in later times; however stubborn vestiges of her existence remain within Judaism today as in Christianity and Islam.

According to Laurence Gardner, "The Universal Mother Isis is known as the mistress of all the elements, primordial child of time, sovereign of all things, and the single manifestation of all." 6.

It has long been established that Madonna statues, regardless of coloration, have their origins in the Isis/Horus image, though the noir Lady represents an Underground Stream of knowledge and what we would call today political ideals. Her religion spread far and wide including that of the British Isles.

The Black Madonna holds her child close in maternal protection and nourishment. Her guises stretch back 30 millennia as the first source and included incarnations as Cybele, Diana, Demeter and Juno. Names such as Astarte, Ashtoreth and Ishtar resound with the same themes. Of equal importance is the goddess Athena/Minerva who is synonymous with Isis. Southern France abounds with the name Minerva whose emblems are the wise owl, the helmet of invisibility and a sacred lance.

> Oettingen for Bavaria,
> Hall for the Belgians,
> Montserrat for Spain,
> Alba for the Magyars.
> For Italy Loreto,
> But in France, Liesse
> Is their joy and ever shall be.
> Poem as quoted by Ean Begg 7.

The Black Virgin holds many meanings to her followers around the world. Her shrines appear at earth energy centers which are highlighted by large scale sacred architecture of megalithic, Templar and modern construction. Claims of inner transformation, physical healing and divine inspiration are as multiple as her believers.

Bernard de Clairvaux, serving as knight to the Morning Star, ensured her esoteric memory and served as an important link for women in the long march towards personal sovereignty.

Bernard de Clairvaux
Knight of the Morning Star

Apparition of the Virgin to St Bernard by Filippino Lippi 1480

1. Asbridge, The Crusades: The Authoritative History of the War for the Holy Land Publisher: Ecco; Reprint edition (March 8, 2011) ISBN-10: 0060787295 ISBN-13: 978-0060787295

2. Warner, Marina. Alone of All Her Sex: The Myth and the Cult of the Virgin Mary. 2nd ed. OUP Oxford, 2013. p. 200

3. Asbridge, Thomas S. The Crusades: The Authoritative History of the War for the Holy Land. Reprint ed. New York: Ecco Press, 2011. p. 187

4. Black, Jonathan. The Sacred History: How Angels, Mystics and Higher Intelligence Made Our World. Quercus, 2013. p. 411

5. Ralls, Karen. Knights Templar Encyclopedia: The Essential Guide to the People, Places, Events, and Symbols of the Order of the Temple. Franklin Lakes, NJ: Career Press, 2007.p. 39

6. Gardner, Laurence. Bloodline of the Holy Grail: The Hidden Lineage of Jesus Revealed. Shaftesbury, Dorset: Element, 1996. p. 121

7. Begg, Ean C. M. The Cult of the Black Virgin. 2nd ed. London: Arkana, 1996. p. 1

Further Reading:

C.R. Evans, Bernard of Clairvaux Oxford University Press ISBN 0-19-512525-8

Joseph L. Baird, The Personal Correspondence of Hildegard of Bingen ISBN-10: 0195308239

Heinrich Schipperges The World of Hildegard of Bingen 0-86012-284-0

Thomas Bulfinch (1796-1867). Age of Fable: Vols. I & II: Stories of Gods and Heroes. 1913.

Kathleen Nolan Editor: Capetian Women. 2003 Palgrave Macmillan ISBN 0-312-29448-4

Gildas, M. (1907). St. Bernard of Clairvaux. In The Catholic Encyclopedia. New York: Robert Appleton Company

Six

The Black Madonna and the Bloodline

In AD 633 a boat with neither sail nor oars glided into the harbor of Boulogne-sur-Mer, with nothing on board save a three foot statue of a Black Madonna and a copy of the gospels in Syriac. Witnesses said the boat had been sailed by angels.

Just as remarkable were those present at the time according to legend. The Merovingian King of France, Dagobert I, was celebrating Sunday Mass when the little boat sailed into the harbor. The statue of the Black Virgin of Boulogne-Sur-Mer survived until the French Revolution when it was destroyed.

The scene was a reenactment of the famous landing of his ancestor Mary the Magdalene to her new home in France, with extended family, retainers and of course Guardians.

The legend links the Merovingian royal line directly to their ancestor queen who was the earthly personification of Isis and according to legend was thought to know the All - the secret name of god. Magdalene means literally tower. She was not Mary *of* Magdala but Mary *the* Magdalene, Watch Tower of the Flock and the right hand of Jesus' Priesthood.

Young Sara, who fled Israel with Mary Magdalene, is remembered as the Black Egyptian, she spurred on the emergence of the Luminous Lady in Southern France. As a priestess and political leader this would have been expected of the daughter of an important spiritual and kingly line. Sara translates literally as Princess in Hebrew, a title, and was the daughter of the Magdalene and her father Jesus of Israel.

Sara's children eventually founded the royal houses of France and later married into European noble houses. The dynasty became known as the Merovingian Long Haired Sorcerer Kings. Long hair is considered a statement of sacred power. The longer one's hair, the more mystical power flows through the individual.

The Magdalene line of kings called the Merovingians, springs from the French King, Merovee 374 AD to 425 AD, whose dual fathers were King Clodio and also a magical aquatic beast reminiscent of Neptune. The unfortunate lady in question was assaulted in true Zeus fashion while swimming and was left with the embarrassing task of admitting to her husband that their child would be a bit different.

The incident is resonant of the old religion in Europe of taking on the attributes of a god thought to be able to guide one through life. Today we would term this practice as recognizing the archetypal god/goddess, force of nature or animal totem within and endeavoring to embody their behaviors in our own lives. It is also indicative of shamanic practices where again one takes on the characteristics of a force of nature, light being or particular helpful beast which also becomes one's spirit guide through life. However these choices are usually made by a consenting adult and not a fetus. What might have actually happened here beyond the philosophical? What might we deduce from this wild legend in the murky past? Much.

The conception is certainly different than that recorded in the bible of the Virgin's supposed gentle insemination. Rape by a sea-beast is a very different matter than an announcement by Archangel Gabriel which certainly appears to have been much more civilized. Is there a connection between the biblical annunciation and the mysterious parentage of King Merovee?

Is this legend a code explained to the public in terms of a sea-beast rather than the hot potato of a male Holy Ghost? After all, that could only happen once. Right?

According to church doctrine there will be a second coming to save the whole world which has supposedly yet to occur, so our King Merovee may surely be discounted. However, why go through possible humiliation by announcing to the world that your child is half Neptune's son? What ego-boost could there have been to the proud father that he might bravely suffer public humiliation? It is simple; he wanted to have the incident remembered. That King Clodio's son, Merovee was 'touched' by a powerful hand and was therefore different and the son of an otherworldly god.

If we tear the legend apart and examine the symbology we will find the actual motivations behind Clodio's purpose. Water is a symbol for flowing intuitive energy which poured straight from the Holy Land and in the veins of a bloodline that was fast becoming inconvenient to Rome, that of the Fisher Kings.

Christianity's very emblem is that of a fish and fish swim in the astral waters. Clodio wanted history to recall who his family was at least in hidden form. Who actually spun the legend is difficult to know. Obviously Clodio's queen told him of the event which would alter their son. Was she herself Clodio's magical partner and engaging in a rite passed down through Solomon which would enhance the abilities of their son while still in the womb? Does this mean that King Merovee was in fact born a Christ? But instead of being called a 'miracle worker' as his ancestor Jesus, he was dubbed a 'long haired sorcerer king' – akin to Solomon who was known to have practiced magic. But this was not considered evil since they were obviously men of god and practicing natural magic was not a sin as god had created all that involved the natural world. Christianity at this time was a very different kettle of fish and may indeed have been much more tolerant than later extremists.

No one seemed to have any problem with this dynasty as practicing sorcerers as they were openly and sincerely Christian and all in the name of god. I hope further research may bring possibilities to the table; but we may never know the full mystery behind King Merovee's conception. For now this question is shrouded in darkness like the enigmatic Black Madonna whom Bernard de Clairvaux loved.

For Love of the Black Madonna

"In thee the angels find their joy, the righteous find grace, and sinners eternal pardon. Deservedly the eyes of every creature look to thee, for in thee, and through thee, and by thee, the kind hand of the Omnipotent has renewed whatever he has created" Bernard de Clairvaux 1.

The Black Virgin is utterly black, as is her child, with a golden halo of stars and sceptre in hand. She is the embodiment of Sophia which in Greek literally translates as wisdom. The phrase, 'the Sophia of Christ' may be more appropriately termed 'the feminine wisdom of Christ'. Our Lady represents the noble strength and equality of womanhood. She is a defender of her children, educator and endless source of sustenance and compassion.

Gnostic groups such as the Cathars linked the biblical author, John of Patmos' work, Revelation, to their Lady Sophia. 'A woman clothed with the sun and the moon under her feet, and upon her head a crown of twelve stars' Revelation 12.1.

The impenetrable colouration represents a primordial time of chaos from whence the Sun/Son sprang. It is our earliest Western creation story.

She is indicative of our unconscious mind and its unknowable vast resources. The Black Virgin is Isis and Notre-Dame de Lumiere. It has been said that the blackness protects her children from light which is her underlying nature and too strong to behold.

St Bernard's most influential work, Sermons in canticum canticorum (Sermons on the Song of Songs, c. 1136), comprising some 120 sermons illustrates spiritual desire through the erotic imagery of the bride and bridegroom. The famous line spoken by the female lover, 'I am black but comely' refers directly to Our Lady, her lineage and spiritual sovereignty.

On a physical level she represents the Queen of Sheba who, according to traditions in Ethiopia, bore Solomon's son. We must also count further incarnations such as St. Mary the Egyptian, St. Anne and The Libyan Sibyl. Sara the Egyptian and St. Catherine of Alexandria feature prominently, these later two were especially important to the Templars. Passionate themes of human love are also explored in De diligendo Deo (On Loving God, c. 1126-41)

By the 16th century nearly 200 Black Madonnas had been discovered in France and a total of 500 now exist globally, some of them modern and in the United Kingdom.

Her attributes of blessings supporting the local area around her shrine, are as wide ranging as those of Isis/Minerva-Athena. Her countenance is that of a Caucasian but oddly her body, hands and face are black. It cannot therefore be said she represents a racial group. Instead her visage is that of an ideal. When church officials have been asked why is she black? The reply is often vague, 'She is black because she is black'. This may indeed be out of innocent ignorance on the part of the individual being questioned or perhaps as Ean Begg suggests "charming-holy simplicity". 2.

However with the Church of Rome's record for brutal suppression and lack of tolerance, the fear of threat that She represents to the strictly male Church of Peter cannot be overlooked. Church officials have given rather feeble excuses for her appearance by stating that years of candle soot have caused discoloration. She is certainly one of many embarrassing aspects that the Roman Church cannot explain away. Some statues have been given a pale complexion in order to end a debate that does not, however, disappear with a coat of paint.

Art historians and other specialists think that the Romans carved some of the earliest statues of Cybele from fallen meteors and dubbed her the goddess Magna Mater or Great Mother. They were brought from Phrygia in 204 BC to what is now Vatican Hill Rome.

Meteorites have long been held as divine gifts from the gods and were used to imbue objects such as swords in the Celtic world with special powers. These legends eventually lead to Excalibur, King Arthur's magical sword. Meteoric statues have since become Christianized and are identified secretly with the Magdalene by those following the older tradition. Other materials have included jet and ebony making her coloration intentionally black.

Some statues have been removed from the public altogether and it has been noted that upon painting or removing the image, congregation numbers drop. Author Ean Begg, whose seminal work for English speaking countries, The Cult of the Black Virgin, states alarmingly, "The Black Virgins of France that survived the fury of the Huguenots and the Revolutionaries are now being subjected to a three-fold process of attrition from thefts of uncertain motivation, the indifference and neglect of a skeptical age, and embarrassed suppression by the Church, often disguised as protectiveness." 3.

Since Ean Begg's book was printed in 1985 there has been a ground swell of research across a wide range of expertise and supportive documentaries as well as books. The internet is also a new fertile domain for Our Lady, offering information as well as tours, revitalizing the old pilgrimages. Hopefully Ean Begg's outcry has influenced these activities and will cause the growth of shrines and protect those already in existence.

Ean Begg notes that the energetic St Bernard was well travelled, visiting many locations of the Black Virgin at Aachen, Clermont-Ferrand, Dijon, Hasseltm, Longpont, Paris, Rocadamour, Rome, Toulouse, Tournai and Valenciennes. Begg also offers the suggestion that the modern Black Virgin of the Abbey of Orval (which St. Bernard founded) may be a continuation of an older promise.

The Saint has a direct experience with the Luminous Lady at the Benedictine Abbey at Affligem. Upon his utterance of 'Ave Maria' he has a vision of Our Lady who replies 'Salve, Bernarde' encouraging him to focus on his writing, relieving him of the stumbling block he was experiencing.

Overcome, he gave his staff and chalice to the abbey where they remain to this day at Dendermonde, Belgium. The gift of the chalice is an intriguing gesture and linked with Mary Magdalene as she is the physical Holy Grail containing Christ's bloodline within her womb. As the Magdalene was the Watch Tower of the Flock, the handing over of his staff is also symbolic of his acknowledgement of her position as Shepherdess of his ancient priestly Order and the Christ's early Church.

1.   Goldberg, B. Z. "The Sacred Fire: Book Three. In the House of the Lord: Chapter II. Romance in the Church." The Sacred Fire: Book Three. In the House of the Lord: Chapter II. Romance in the Church. Accessed August 05, 2015. http://www.sacred-texts.com/sex/tsf/tsf15.htm.

2.   Begg, Ean C. M. The Cult of the Black Virgin. 2nd ed. London: Arkana, 1996. p. 11

3.   Ibid

Seven

The Virgin and the Magdalene

It is clear from the writings of Saint Bernard that he was well educated with a quick mind. His intellect did not however get in the way of his sublime love of the Queen of Heaven and Jesus. He often accused those in power in Rome that their own intellectual dogma were clouding love of the divine, impeding their own spiritual progress and that of their flock.

This is reminiscent of the tantric teachings of India, recognizing the complete surrender of the rational to the ecstasy of the soul creating an environment where inner transformation is possible.

His writings reveal an emotional intense individual. He introduces a creed of personal union with god through mystic contemplation and meditation. Contrary to the official thought of the day he believed in a personal relationship with both the male and female aspects of god versus an externalized form of worship.

His writings on the Black Madonna and her son are a clear indication of his unique beliefs. Understanding him through our secularized and modern world view is not always easy. He was a man of his day and we are distanced from him by nearly 900 years of social change.

Our society has completely altered since the Victorian era, a comparatively short time span in relation to St. Bernard's 12th century. I wonder how we will be perceived in three generations let alone 900 years. We must view his world through our own inadequate reference points within the context of the history and spiritual teachings of his Order and our understanding of them today through exhaustive research.

Saint Bernard envisaged his relationship to the father and the mother as a love union with himself as their child:

"Love, is sufficient by itself, it pleases by itself, and for its own sake. It is itself a merit, and itself its own recompense. Love seeks neither cause nor fruit beyond itself. Its fruit is its use. I love because I love; I love that I may love. Love, then, is a great reality. It is the only one of all the movements, feelings and affections of the soul in which the creature is able to respond to its Creator, though not upon equal terms, and to repay like with like." Saint Bernard 1.

In his visions the Mother would embrace him with such strength that he seemed to take flight from his body to join her in heavenly love. During her feasts he would celebrate enraptured. *"My Love! My Love! Let me ever love thee from the depths of my heart!"*

The Virgin and the Magdalene

Writer Evelyn Underhill eloquently states the following from her 1911 work, titled Mysticism:

"Saint Bernard was not only in love with the Virgin but also with her divine son. In this love relationship, the saint considered himself as the bride of Christ, assuming the feminine rôle. For to him, like too many other mystics, the soul was an entity entirely distinct from the physical organism. It dwelt in the body but was not of the body. It constituted a complete personality like the Word of the Gospel or the pneuma of the Stoics. One could, therefore, commune with his own soul as he might with another person. Once a separate being, the soul could be of the opposite sex. And since it was the object of the love of Jesus, the lover of souls, it came to be considered as feminine. The soul was the bride and Jesus the spouse. Love was the union of the soul with god. Hence, in speaking of his soul and his intimate attitude toward Jesus, Saint Bernard refers to himself as female. And he describes the spiritual love relationship in highly sensuous language:

Suddenly the Bridegroom is present and gives assent to her petition; He gives her the kiss asked, of which the fullness of breasts is witness. For so great is the efficacy of this holy kiss, that the Bride on receiving it conceives, the swelling breasts rich with milk being the evidence. . . . And the Bridegroom will say: Thou hast, O my Spouse that which thou prayedst for; and this is the sign: Thy breasts have become better than wine. By this may you know that you have received the kiss, in that you have conceived and your breasts are full of milk." Bernard de Clairvaux as quoted by Underhill 2.

Saint Bernard's new platform of a personal relationship with god was unusual during a period where one could gain access to heaven only through a priest or if one is a woman, your husband; indeed exoteric Christianity still demands this of its followers.

Services were spoken in Latin which the bulk of the population did not understand. Bernard was unusual in that he actually engaged the public and spoke directly to them. Whether they agreed was another matter. But the point was he tried to meet them honestly without hiding behind a language which they would never know.

Incredibly he states that the way to god is through Mary the Great Mother: "*per Mariam ad Iesum,*" through Mary we are led to Jesus.

He also states that:

"Believe me, for I know, you will find something far greater in the woods than in books. Stones and trees will teach you that which you cannot learn from the masters." 3.

Bernard's world was alive and teeming with inter-dimensional Life which spoke to him and transformed him as a person.

Though he practiced ascetic self-denial, the Saint had a high respect and love for life. He embraced the ideal that the kingdom of heaven is within - with the archetypal Mother/Father and Son as guide. One could commune with the creator anywhere within creation itself and be in the presence of the divine, under any circumstances. The worship of the divine within nature amongst the Christian community is actually known as the Celtic Church.

The mental domain of the individual is sacrosanct and not under the rule of another human being. Bernard's concern for the sovereignty of the individual brings up many interesting questions of manipulation which resonate in our modern world; such as in media, economics and politics.

We may have access to more information today with new freedoms our medieval ancestors did not enjoy, but are we as people of the West under less pressure from these forces of manipulation than in the past? What we do need today is accountability, transparency and economic equality from our religious representatives, governments, large businesses and banking institutions.

However, I am not disputing the positive nature of our ability to communicate with each other over borders through the new technologies of today. Just as the Abbot did, we must today seek out the truth of a situation, think for ourselves and fight for justice.

Bernard was also a very practical man as this last quote regarding nature also indicates. We are not separate from our environment and its rules of behavior.

Through history the tradition has displayed this attitude that everything that is undertaken is done so with a practical perspective and a spiritual purpose.

What further evidence is there for this mystery cult that St. Bernard gave new life, causing a firestorm of fervent admiration across Europe?

Bernard did not support the idea of the Immaculate Conception and spoke openly against it. He wrote to the canons of Lyons persuading them to drop their insistence on a new festival for the Virgin stating that it actually dishonored her memory. Was there an underlying reason for this besides the well-known public arguments? If he suspected that Jesus was his ancestor then, yes, he would have argued against the idea that the Virgin was conceived by the Holy Ghost, effectively cutting off her own physical royal lineage, indeed her human lineage, from the house of Judah and King David.

The Semitic term virgin translates as almah or simply a young woman. The physical state of virgin in Hebrew is actually bethulah and in Latin virgin simply means young woman. The term virgin today as we know it, is a modern interpretation and in Latin has had to be addressed by the adjective 'intact' therefore – virgo intacta. The result? A direct, politically motivated and purposeful mistranslation of the gospels. 4.

This was Mary's first child with Joseph. They went on to have possibly six to seven more children with Jesus being the elder and heir to the throne. The Christ fathered three children himself that we know of with his wife the Magdalene. To state that his own mother Mary was of virgin birth effectively cuts out the all-important Davidic line which also ran through his mother - the line that carried esoteric wisdom from Egypt.

It is known that the Virgin Mary's parents were named Saints Anna and Joachim, also related to the house of David. The case for her own virgin birth is positively ludicrous and outside the realm of any real historical fact. Diminishing the lineage of Christ by inserting a sole male Holy Ghost as father gives political power to the Popes of Rome whose descent is handed down from Peter outside of the line of Davidic Priest Kings. Certainly nothing could be wrong with celebrating her life but to form a feast day around an event which never occurred is a lie.

Bernard protected the memory of his ancestor's history from slow erosion and in some cases purposeful destruction and the esoteric wisdom they carried. He was not the only one of his day to be dumbfounded by this new step away from the human experience that was Mary's conception.

The general population was not in favor of this festival either. Unfortunately in 1488 the Feast Day of the Immaculate Conception went forward and is today accepted as fact within much of the Christian Community regardless of the Virgin's physical parentage which is marginalized and not taught.

The contemplative mystic, Bernard, kindled a new knowledge of the divine founded upon a personal ecstatic relationship with his spiritual lover the Mother of God. Through Her the Son became accessible in a way not expressed before in Catholic Europe converting thousands with new found imagination through the approachable Madonna.

She was known as the Mediatrix and Star of the Sea, the intimate encounter between earth and heaven. It is hard to know at times which individual he places higher than the other through his impassioned sermons though he does state; "*only Jesus is honey to the mouth, song to the ear, joy to the heart.*" It is from this quote that he was given the title of Doctor Mellifluus the 'honey tongued teacher'.

The Saint however, goes on to say, 'Let us not imagine that we obscure the glory of the Son by the great praise we lavish on the Mother; for the more she is honored, the greater is the glory of her Son.' 'There can be no doubt,' says the Saint, 'that whatever we say in praise of the Mother is equally in praise of the Son'. 5.

Because of the patriarchal slant of the Church he would in no way been able to raise her above Jesus but certainly stressed the subject of her as Mother God as much as he possibly could.

Bernard lived an extreme ascetic lifestyle that may have left him with gastro-intestinal problems for his whole life. Of course we do not know that his extreme life style was the cause of his ill health, but it could not have helped him. This type of life style is practiced across many religions today by their most ardent followers and is considered an act of faith and devotion. Fasting before meditation is known to help heighten senses, but taken too far can actually be harmful and today is known as anorexia. Perhaps the denial of physical comforts and acquisition is safer than extreme dietary denial? I wish he had not been so hard on himself as he did suffer ill health much of his life which makes his seemingly tireless contributions the more incredible.

He ate very little and slept in a cell under a stair with barely room to stand up without hitting his head. During one bout of ill health in 1124 which required time to convalesce, he wrote De in laudibus matris virginis (Sermons in Praise of the Virgin

Mother). In this treatise, Bernard takes the role of a knight who gallantly serves Mary as an expressive troubadour in service to his ideal lady. The love-struck Abbot played his part in the spread of Courtly Love. This may be the only time that he wrote without the promptings of political need or that of clarification of theology. 6.

The Madonna and her heiress by marriage, Mary Magdalene, was the new Eve in whom the Saint played a large part in spreading a transformed view of women in Europe during his ceaseless travels. The veneration of Mary, as woman and literal archetype of the physical church, was greatly responsible for transforming the Code of Chivalry. This new representation of women flowered in the Courtly Love poetry of Medieval and later Renaissance France. Women, ever blamed for Eve's transgression, came to be looked upon, instead, as objects of veneration and inspiration, whose hearts were to be won through gallantry and protected from the violence of the world.

Within the ranks of the Cathari there were those who advocated a married Jesus and those who did not – this has not changed today where many Christians around the world are comfortable with a married god and those who are not. Amongst the esoteric writers there is also a split - either way there is interesting evidence which is slowly emerging pointing towards a marriage or at the very least that people in the 1st, 2nd and 3rd centuries and heretical sects of the Middle Ages thought that there had been. Did Saint Bernard believe it? I cannot unequivocally say 'yes' but it may very well be that he viewed Mary Magdalene as the heir to the Virgin's role.

The Return of the Divine Feminine

..."Jesus said to them, 'my wife'....

From The Gospel of Jesus' Wife translated by Karen L. King, Harvard Divinity School Professor. Coptic 4th century papyrus fragment. 7.

Men in the Judaic tradition were to "Be fruitful and multiply" (KJV Genesis 9:7) simply put celibacy was viewed negatively and would have been considered outlandish behaviour worthy of social derision. In fact it was expected as a Rabbi that one must marry in order to be even considered as a potential Rabbi. Jesus was called Rabbi often and as the male heir to the throne of David; he would have been expected to take a wife to perpetuate the line.

The Gospel of Jesus' Wife appears to be a business card sized fragment from a codex only revealed to the public in 2012, an important year to those who focused so much hope on the new energy heralded by the Mayan calendar date of December 21st, 2012.

It is hoped that this particular winter solstice will bring a new understanding and a new age of enlightenment for earth. Much has been made of the Divine Feminine during 2012 and rightfully so, and it is interesting that this fragment surfaced at this time. This small fragment is only one of many however that have surfaced over the

The Virgin and the Magdalene

decades indicating that Jesus had taken Mary Magdalene as his wife but that he also had children.

"Peter said to Mary, Sister we know that the Saviour loved you more than the rest of women. Tell us the words of the Saviour which you remember which you know, but we do not, nor have we heard them." 8.

The Gospel of Mary is a 5th century AD papyrus discovered in Egypt in the 19th century indicating a special relationship of knowledge between Jesus and the Magdalene.

And

"There were three who always walked with the Lord: Mary, his mother, and her sister, and Magdalene, the one who was called his companion."

The Gospel of Philip, was discovered in 1945 and part of the library now called the Nag Hammadi Library or the Gnostic Gospels. 9.

And again,

....the companion of the [Savior is] Mary Magdalene. {But Christ loved} her more than {all} the disciples and used to kiss her [often] on her [mouth]. The rest of [the disciples were offended by it...]. They said to him, 'Why do you love her more than all of us?' The Savior answered and said to them, 'why do I not love you as [I love] her?' 10. The Gospel of Philip - Nag Hammadi Library or the Gnostic Gospels.

Saint Bernard's love of the Black Madonna formed the very basis of the Cistercian Order and that of the Knights Templar. The Saint, the Queen of Heaven and the Templars are experiencing a Renaissance in the public eye that shows no sign of abating. Bernard de Clairvaux, troubadour and protector of the Black Madonna, made certain that the Divine Feminine was worshiped once more in Europe.

It is ripe for the immortal themes represented by Clairvaux of the Divine Feminine to be recognized as powerful archetypal guides accessible to all.

The Devine Feminine shines light through the morass of uncertainty and in the face of personal and global crisis such as climate change, economic deprivation and war. In life it is natural that one wants to speak to our father and for other reasons our mother, why would there not be an interdimensional and sacred relationship?

42

The Secret Dossier of a
Knight Templar of the Sangreal

Taking the reverence of the mother and the father's relationship to us, humanity has a virtual family of planetary and interdimensional beings we are intimately related to by soul with physical resonance. Alchemical Marriage can only be the ultimate description of this path.

The desire to merge with one's equal opposite is hardwired into humanity so that we may overcome our fears, death and transform our lives. To merge and become the wife of our husband or the husband of the feminine, to behold the face of God the Great Devine and see ourselves looking back at us – is the great heresy of all time amongst flat-earthers and the answer to what humanity seeks.

Author Jonathan Black, sub-rosa contactee, puts forth the rationale that our body has seven energy centres and each one is ruled by a planet in the solar system. Our mother is earth with her own soul and the sun is our father whose light shines down on us day and night reflected from the moon. Ascension, according to Black, is no less than meeting and moving through these planetary spheres and their personalities within us - hence the phrase 7th heaven. Please see his work titled The Sacred History.

1. Butler, Cuthbert. Western Mysticism: The Teaching of SS. Augustine, Gregory, and Bernard on Contemplation and the Contemplative Life. London: Kegan Paul International, 2000. p. 112

2. Underhill, Evely. "Mysticism: Part One: The Mystic Fact: VI. Mysticism and Symbolism." Mysticism: Part One: The Mystic Fact: VI. Mysticism and Symbolism. http://www.sacred-texts.com/myst/myst/myst09.htm. p. 259

3. Duignan, Brian, ed. Medieval Philosophy: From 500 to 1500 CE. 1st ed. New York, NY: Britannica Educational Pub. in Association with Rosen Educational Services, 2010. p. 64

4. Gardner, Laurence. Bloodline of the Holy Grail: The Hidden Lineage of Jesus Revealed. Shaftesbury, Dorset: Element, 1996. p. 28

5. Coffin, Robert A. London Burns & Oates, 1868. p. 128

6. Krstovic, Jelena, and Gale Cengage. "Bernard of Clairvaux Essay - Critical Essays - ENotes.com." Enotes.com. February 01, 2010. Accessed August 05, 2015. http://www.enotes.com/topics/bernard-clairvaux#critical-essays-bernard-clairvaux. Vol. 71

7. Kaleem, Jaweed. "'The Gospel Of Jesus' Wife,' New Early Christian Text, Indicates Jesus May Have Been Married." The Huffington Post. September 19, 2012. Accessed August 05, 2015. http://www.huffingtonpost.com/2012/09/18/the-gospel-of-jesus-wife-n_1891325.html?utm_hp_ref=mostpopular.

8. Griffith-Jones, Robin. Mary Magdalene: The Woman Whom Jesus Loved. Norwich: Canterbury Press, 2008. As quoted in the Preface

9. Philip, Jean-Yves Leloup, and Joseph Rowe. The Gospel of Philip: Jesus, Mary Magdalene, and the Gnosis of Sacred Union. Rochester, VT: Inner Traditions, 2004. p. 64

10. Swidler, Leonard J. Jesus Was a Feminist: What the Gospels Reveal about His Revolutionary Perspective. Lanham, MD: Sheed & Ward, 2007. p. 93

Eight

The Rise of Abbot Bernard

Recruitment en mass to the Abbey of Citeaux

"If you desire to enter here, leave at the threshold the body you have brought with you from the world; here there is room only for your soul." St. Bernard de Clairvaux

In 1113 Bernard de Fontaines entered Citeaux Abbey with 30 male relatives and friends consisting of the local nobility, but not before spending six months in training together under the young man's watchful eye. Interestingly he waited until Easter Sunday to enter the abbey with his men on the day of the risen son.

Practical and esoteric plans for the immediate future of Citeaux had been drawn. When the time came to approach Abbot Stephen Harding of Citeaux for admission, the group had been working in concert with knowledge of their particular roles in the foreseeable future. This truly was a corporate takeover of Citeaux where the entire family handed over their possessions in order to fund the new venture.

Some of the men were married, successful and with small children at home. There was no reason for them to leave their prosperous lives; their motivation for enlistment is a mystery.

They were convinced by Bernard and eventually all followed. The oldest brother, Gerard, was in doubt over his part in the new enterprise as he was a happily married man with two children and well off financially.

He had to be convinced to give up the life he had built to follow Bernard into Citeaux. Bernard predicted that Gerard would follow him into monastic service but not without travail. "Ah! I know that tribulation alone will give thee understanding," according to legend he then placed his hand on his brother's side, "the day will come, ay, and quickly come, when a lance shall pierce thee here, and make a way to thy heart for that counsel of salvation which thou now despises. And thou shalt fear greatly, but shalt in no wise perish."

A few days after, Gerard was surrounded and attacked by enemies, and held captive, having been wounded by a spear in his side. "I turn monk," he exclaimed, "monk of Citeaux!" a vow which, on recovering his liberty, he hastened to fulfill. 1.

Gerard was sainted as well having become noted as a gifted builder and craftsman across many disciplines. After quitting military life his younger brother put him in charge of overseeing Clairvaux Abbey.

Many such legends regarding Bernard's foresight and 'other' gifts are disregarded as being posthumous; however I argue that it may indeed be authentic due to his intuitive abilities gifted at the feet of the Magna Mater.

The early meteoric success of the Cistercian Order is a testament to Bernard's leadership skills at an astonishing young age, convincing men of greater years and experience to change their entire lives for what may only be termed as a multifaceted Grail Quest. There was certainly an extra 'something' about Bernard.

Abbot Harding found himself overwhelmed with new numbers and soon faced the problem of over population. It was never in the plans of the original founding of 1098 that there should be such extensive growth into the world but that the Cistercians of Citeaux should rekindle the monastic ideal set out by Saint Benedict of Nursia at Monte Cassino in 529 AD. However the sudden influx was welcomed as his Cistercian Order was crumbling. It was evident to Harding that unless he allowed this new youthful vigor, his beloved monastery, if not the actual order, would soon disappear forever.

Is it possible that the novice Bernard brought him into the esoteric tradition or was he a member himself? Harding was a well-travelled scholar and monk prior to joining the Abbey of Citeaux. His contributions are of historical significance. He maintained the scriptorium at Citeaux to a high standard, consulting rabbis (despite prejudices that were rampant against Jewish society and those fraternizing with them) in order to gain access to the earliest sources of the translations of the bible.

Harding was certainly intelligent and is considered an early leader of the Cistercians and later became a saint in 1623. Bernard's charisma was infectious and I doubt that Abbot Harding would have retained a bulwark against the personable younger man who would succeed him and lead the Cistercians into the future. Change was on his doorstep and there was no going back.

In a few short years four daughter houses were created at La Ferte, Pontigny, Morimond and lastly Clairvaux. In 1115 AD and only in his early twenties, Bernard de Fontaines became Abbot Bernard de Clairvaux, a name which he himself chose.

The Abbot dubbed his new home Light Valley or Clair Vaux, changing its prior name of Val d'Absinthe also known as Wormwood, which was a wild, inhospitable tributary of the Aube River.

The transformation of Wormwood to Clairvaux is reminiscent of Saint George slaying the dragon - a reference to light overcoming a dark serpent, albeit with a name change. The date of founding is significant as it was June 24th, the feast day of John the Baptist who would become the patron saint of the Knights Templar.

The shrewd young man had other options for the site of the new abbey but chose Clairvaux for a very good reason. The land was protected by the Counts of Champagne and also the property was situated on the ancient Agrippen Way from Lyon to Reims and the main link from Italy to England. It is clear that from the outset Bernard had a master plan.

The land was gifted by the first count of Champagne, Hugh of Troyes who left his pregnant wife to become one of the initial nine members of the Poor Fellow-Soldiers of Christ and of the Temple of Solomon! Obviously there was a large scale plan in place to affect great change for Europe and the Middle East and by all accounts, regardless of the final outcome in the Holy Land of the Middle Ages, they succeeded.

The two men were close. There is a deeply affectionate letter remaining from Bernard to Hugh in 1125 AD. 2. Hugh generously gave the Abbey of Clairvaux and its dependencies many resources such as fields, vineyards, woods and water.

The Rise of Abbot Bernard

At breakneck speed Clairvaux was transformed and enlarged - out of necessity as a political residence. It soon exceeded that of Citeaux (though unofficially) in prominence as Abbot Bernard gained popularity amongst the poor, who sought his protection, the wealthy who sought his advice and clergy who sought after him to become their own bishop.

Abbot Bernard would have been happier living in the original wooden buildings of Clairvaux but it was soon apparent they would not suit the demands placed upon them. The charismatic new Abbot soon drew some 700 novices to Clairvaux! The overcrowded conditions were relieved by further growth into other European countries such as England, Ireland, Italy, Germany, Portugal, Sweden and Switzerland. 3.

The Abbey of Clairvaux would rival Rome during Bernard's lifetime as his unequaled political power surged. He was the most famous man of his age when kingdoms were unstable and trustworthy leaders were thin on the ground.

To Bernard political action and spirituality were the same, therefore his initiative into the wide world at the expense of his vows to remain in the abbey were necessary. Indeed it was his mission to be an active man in the public eye.

He travelled only with a secretary who took dictation, was painfully thin and wore the characteristic undyed wool of the Cistercians that marked them famously as the White Monks. Amongst the well fed, prelates in purple finery and secular lords in armor, he stood out as clearly recognizable and the people loved him for it. 4.

Bernard's ascetic life, expressed in his attire and eating habits is recognizable today in one of India's most famous sons. Gandhi left his marital bed, wore little more than a loin cloth and ate sparingly eschewing material possessions and changed the course of history as had Bernard.

The Cistercians would follow the model of Clairvaux by choosing inhospitable and forested lands in the wilds away from population centres. Settled into protected valleys, there would also be a river nearby, necessary for the cultivation of the land. Their abbeys always stood near water, having a special relationship with it; symbolic of baptismal initiation and the primordial energetic waters of Genesis in the beginning of the world. The choice is a spiritual one which reflects etheric energy, the Virgin as a flowing river and the Son as a fountain, and of course, practicality. The Virgin is as important to a flowing Cistercian river as Isis is to the Nile.

Reverence for the higher dimension of water is reflected in the names chosen for their abbeys such as Fontenay, Trois-Fontaines, Fontfroide, Aiguebelle, Belaigue, Auberive, Haute-Fontaine, Aubepierre, Bonnefontaine, the list is extensive.

Where needed their use of hydraulic engineering was singular and one example can be found on the hillside at Obazine where a community of hermits associated themselves with the Order. The original, though ill placed buildings were kept, but water was an issue. They harnessed the resource from a mile away, carving a canal and redirecting the water to the hillside. The abbeys were protected from floods by many clever means such as building terraces. 5.

They drained marshes turning them into fields of golden cultivation and in England grazing land for the profitable wool trade that would explode the economy

The Secret Dossier of a
Knight Templar of the Sangreal

of the British Isles.

They were the industrial revolution of their day, equaled only by their sister order the Knights Templar. There was no economic sector that they were not involved with. From forestry, cereals, wine, fruit, fisheries, sheep, mills, tiles, tanneries, brewing ale, pottery and trade. They even extended their hand to mining and metallurgy. The monks also had access to a pharmacopeia where extensive use of herbs was promoted as healing was a vital aspect in their communities and lives.

The abbeys were key to the economic development of medieval towns as the individually poor monks traded their quality products for items that they could not manufacture. Self-sufficiency however was a vital part of their way of life. Abbot Bernard set the example that the Cistercians would follow, acquiring land that others deemed unusable, persuading owners to gift it to their cause. Clairvaux went from strength to strength and had storehouses dotting the country side. By the 13th century it had acquired thousands of acres!

William of St. Thierry was a constant companion of the energetic Abbot and would eventually become an abbot himself. Of the new monastery at Clairvaux and his mentor, Bernard, he states:

"I tarried with him a few days, unworthy though I was, and whichever way I turned my eyes, I marvelled and thought I saw a new heaven and a new earth, and also the old pathways of the Egyptian monks, our fathers, marked with the recent footsteps of the men of our time left in them. The golden ages seemed to have returned and revisited the world there at Clairvaux.... At the first glance, as you entered, after descending the hill, you could feel that God was in the place; and the silent valley bespoke, in the simplicity of its buildings, the genuine humility of the poor of Christ dwelling there. The silence of the noon was as the silence of the midnight, broken only by the chants of the choral service, and the sound of garden and field implements. No one was idle. In the hours not devoted to sleep or prayer, the brethren kept busy with hoe, scythe, and axe, taming the wild land and clearing the forest. And although there was such a number in the valley, yet each seemed to be a solitary." 6.

Though it sounds idyllic it was far from simple initially. The monks willingly engaged in back breaking work to change their landscape and build the new monasteries.

This type of focused effort is needed for any worthy vision. A modern example of this fine attitude is that of a family living together, pooling their resources to start a successful business for the benefit of the entire group. We've forgotten how to live communally in our Western world of single home ownership, leaving our wise elderly folks to sit outside of the younger generations, losing the supportive beneficial effects of all age brackets upon each other. As the economy has worsened through the Recession of 2008 many families are being forced to live with one another. Perhaps as a result we will become wiser as a society recalling the benefits of living together and do so out of choice and not financial need.

His organizational ability has been likened to the equivalent of the modern corporate structure hundreds of years ahead of his time. Modern life has been made less human and very stressful in many ways by large massive business models. I prefer to view Bernard's plan as being akin to organized sustainable communal living with an easily repeatable formula instead - with imposed size limitations due to the cookie cutter model of abbey building the Cistercians rolled out repeatedly. Once overgrown the next obvious choice was to split off to form a new community. A business model advocated by the book The Tipping Point which bases its formulas on the needs of the human psyche rather than bottom line.

An enlightened mind does not necessarily come with an encyclopedia of knowledge. Science must still be an ongoing quest. However an initiate such as Bernard has a special perspective of the material world which allows for innovative lines of thought with the potential to seriously impact history.

The young Abbot insisted upon a fiercely strict monastic observance and such extreme self-denial that his men were suffering from lack of food. Only the influence of his good friend Bishop William de Champeaux, who was professor of theology at Notre Dame of Paris and the concern of the General Chapter, managed to sway him to lift his restrictions.

Seeing the wisdom of their words Bernard did make changes which eased the life of his followers though he did not spare himself. The health problems he suffered in his entire life may have partly been through lack of nutrition. If he had our understanding of nutrition today it is possible he would have lived well past the age of sixty-three which was still very advanced age for this era.

Regardless of this lack of nutritional knowledge the reformations he would instigate has withstood the test of time and is the model for monastic life into the 21st century.

What this episode does show us is his ability as a leader to listen to the good advice of those around him and respect their council. It indicates a level of humility required in true leadership which engenders respect. This episode in Bernard's life also gives us a glimpse of his humanity. That none of us are perfect and all are on the same path towards 'understanding' as soft organic beings with peaks and valleys. The shining star in any life is made brighter for the personal obstacles that have been overcome.

A Constitution

The contributions of the Cistercians do not end with reclaiming unusable lands, advanced spiritual architecture, engineering and economics.

Abbot Stephen of Citeaux convened the first governing body in which its unique parliamentary style was developed into the General Chapter of the Cistercian Order in September of 1119 AD.

It dealt with internal legislation, public relations and policies. Should a debate at the General Chapter meeting be left undecided it would defer to the Abbot of Citeaux for the final decision of a contested issue.

The Cistercian Constitution rejected feudal inefficiency and pyramidal-hierarchical rules. It stated that each monastery was independent having autonomy over their affairs, electing its own abbot and without financial obligation to the Mother House or to other abbeys.

There would be 'federal control' from the top to ensure that the independent abbeys were maintaining the unity of the Cistercian Rule. The original Four Daughter houses were expected to visit their own priories once a year as they in turn were visited once a year by the ruling Abbot of the day from Citeaux. 7.

Bernard was invited to speak during this inaugural event. By this time at the young age of twenty-nine he had already helped to found the Knights Templar.

As a key speaker he was welcomed with respect and avid attention. During this General Chapter the basis was formed for the constitution of the Cistercians and the regulations of the Carta Caritatis also known as the "Charter of Divine Love" and the "Charter of Charity".

It was drafted by Abbot Harding and finally confirmed by Pope Callixtus II on December 23, 1119. This is therefore one of the oldest constitutions in the world! It predates both the Magna Carta of 1215 AD and the Declaration of Arbroath in 1320 AD.

The English Charter of Liberties in 1100 AD was chiefly ignored by monarchs until 1213 AD. The speed in which the General Chapter came about was stunning. This was unprecedented in religious organizations at this time and is just as revolutionary as the Knights Templar would become. Was there a pre-existing invisible 'nation state' without borders where such an advanced form of governance sprang?

So many of the contributions of the Cistercians and the Knights Templar have seemingly no prior groundwork yet their revolutionary tactics have echoes in the ancient past. The Cistercians were quite simply the precursors of Republicanism and European Unity. The Cistercian Order itself still exists but it is the Knights Templar that took these concepts into the New World to the Americas and eventually introduced democratic forms in Europe and America.

The Cistercian Order was granted a rare tax exemption status in 1122 AD until jealous rivals forced a change in 1215. Tax exemption was a device that was an important factor in their growth and identical to the situation which also allowed the Knights Templar to prosper. The connections between the two Orders never seem to end.

The Rise of Abbot Bernard

The Great, the Poor & Self Realisation

The Abbot was a staunch supporter of the poor who were fed by the hundreds outside his abbey gate. His words from the famous Apologia ad Guillelmum of 1124 AD have a revolutionary zeal:

"The Church shines with splendor on all sides, but the poor are hungry...The walls of the church are covered with gold, but the children of the church go naked...Ah Lord! If the folly of it all does not shame us, surely the expense might stick in our throats?...You will seal my lips saying that it is not for a monk to judge, please God that you seal my eyes also so that I may not see. But if I held my peace, the poor, the naked, and the starving would rise up and cry out..."

Bernard had great insight and compassion for humanity. Perhaps he would have agreed with fair distribution of wealth and economic justice if he had been alive today?

Bernard was chosen by his colleagues to preside over a dangerous schism in 14 February 1130 AD which set powerful political forces against each other. During the process of election two popes had been chosen through a then existing loophole which has since been rectified, Pope Innocent II and Pope Anacletus II.

Abbot Bernard's deliberations culminated on Innocent II, thus raising him to the Throne of St. Peter. The task did not end there as the Abbot had to use his diplomatic skills to encourage the supporters of Analectus II to accept the final decision and stand down on any possible military action. The situation continued to be a potential powder keg until Analectus II died eight years later.

Over the Abbot's lifetime he would see six more of his own Cistercians become cardinals and over thirty bishops.

Bernard's hand stretched to the election of a second Pope, his own disciple and close friend became Eugenius III in February 1145 AD, thus placing a Cistercian in the highest ecclesiastic role in Europe.

Bernard's spiritual son, Eugenius III asked his mentor for words of wisdom before embarking upon his new role. The singular work, "De Consideratione" ("On Consideration"), is still relevant today to the Roman Papacy.

The book covers the vital topics of how to be a wise leader. It is a 12th century self-help manual for the head of the Catholic Church. The ultimate goal of the book explores the mystery of the trinity culminating in the concept of one god.

He stresses the need to search for God through contemplation and meditation over mental discussion. The Abbot understood the need for 'Being' and 'Knowing' versus the state of intellectualism which prevents transformation.

His original plan of infiltration and takeover of Catholic Europe had succeeded. The Cistercians and the Knights Templar were here to stay.

However there would be a third branch to the Abbots intentions - a woman and leader within the Benedictine Order from whence the Cistercians rose.

Divine Union of Sol and Luna

1. Morison, James Cotter. The Life and times of Saint Bernard, Abbot of Clairvaux: A. D. 1091-1153. London: Macmillan, 1868.
2. Greenia, Conrad. Number Nineteen ed. Vol. 7. Kalamazoo: Cistercian Publications, 1977.
3. Gildas, M. The Catholic Encyclopedia. New York: Robert Appleton Company, 1907.
4. Gaud, Henri, Jean-François Leroux-Dhuys, and John Crook. Cistercian Abbeys: History and Architecture. Köln: Könemann, 1998.
5. Ibid
6. Schaff, Philip. History of the Christian Church, Volume V: The Middle Ages. A.D. 1049-1294. 1882.
7. Gaud, Henri, Jean-François Leroux-Dhuys, and John Crook. Cistercian Abbeys: History and Architecture. Köln: Könemann, 1998.

Nine

The Abbot: Early Medieval Feminist?

Bernard did not deal strictly with men though it could be argued that he dealt with powerful women out of necessity, as they could not be ignored. The rules of the day regarding men and women were strict beyond our comprehension as to be an alien landscape and though he was extremely vocal, even Bernard would have fallen afoul of the system if he were too bipartisan regarding the Divine Feminine.

However we must ask - is the traditional religious-academic viewpoint of misogynistic thought regarding this leading light of the Underground Stream truly accurate?

The frequent correspondence and meetings with influential women of his day and the bold knight of Mariology could be construed as underpinning an alternate stance on all things feminine.

The core belief that womens' souls were equal to men and were therefore brothers in spirit as far as Bernard and the tradition were concerned was certainly a dangerous heresy and not one to speak of publicly.

Indeed this is still a contentious issue in many conservative corners around the world. Nor has this anti-estimation of women's souls shifted in the world, costing Christianity a drop in church numbers in the west and a continued excuse to relegate women as second class citizens in the secular world through such gender issues as unequal pay and an overt apathy of domestic violence and rape convictions.

The Abbot was involved with every strata of life, male or female. He was not a feminist by the strictest of modern standards as the concept did not exist until very recently; but he was certainly ahead of his time and ahead of many men of our own age.

It was not the norm for a woman to ascend to great social heights in the middle ages but there were those of strong character that would not remain in the background to let their male counterparts exist in the sun alone.

Indeed when men went to war, it was up to the woman to step in as head of household and take over his duties. She would need to be capable of running all aspects of a household from the small farm to noble estate. Physical protection would also fall under her direction if not actual practice. There are accounts of women donning armour and holding off marauders with other household staff.

European women were secondary in society but their husbands needed a strong feminine counterpart regardless and not a wall flower that might lose the family home. Even in today's world, male or female must be aware of being taken for a financial ride by unscrupulous business practices from small time operators to large corporate fraudsters. Women were out of necessity far more assertive during this time period than we give them credit for or their men folk in 'allowing' feminine assertiveness. They had to be assertive – it was life and death.

It is said that Eleanor of Aquitaine appeared at a field nearby the Basilique de Madeleine in Vezelay France (where Bernard preached the Second Crusade) dressed as an Amazon warrior along with her female vassals.

The Secret Dossier of a
Knight Templar of the Sangreal

Though this story is disputed by scholars it is a colourful way of expressing her outgoing character, strong will and liveliness. The legend was started by comparing her to an Amazonian queen by an admiring contemporary Greek historian who also lauded her as a great beauty.

Eleanor travelled to the Holy Land with her own military resources at her disposal alongside Louis, her husband, King of France. She bitterly opposed him upon his insistence of attacking Islamic and Christian-friendly Damascus whom the crusader states actually had an alliance, instead of retaking the fallen Edessa.

Their marriage, having been tested to the extreme on their journey from France, finally broke down. He arrested her, taking her back to France and of course this action was the death knell of their marriage which she would eventually have annulled. 1.

Queen Melisende of Jerusalem was no less a stunning creature of great courage and similarly suffering from power struggles within her marriage. Melisende's husband, Fulk IV, tried to have her active political role withdrawn upon the death of her father the King of Jerusalem, Baldwin II. However she had been crowned equally beside Fulk IV. I feel some sympathy for Fulk as he'd given up his role as the powerful Count of Anjou, lured to Jerusalem by Melisende's father with the promise of sole kingship which Baldwin II revoked upon Fulk's arrival. 2.

Baldwin II was very aware that the delicate balance of the crusader states needed an experienced, intelligent military man at the helm. He set his eye on Fulk hoping to add his strength to that of his strong willed daughter.

The pressure to have a man as head of state was of gravest concern for Baldwin II and those of the male nobility around him, hoping for a warrior king to hold the Christian states together.

Baldwin II did not want his own line to be set aside if Fulk chose to make his own son by his first marriage his heir apparent in Jerusalem. He was not about to sideline his daughter and declared on his death bed that Fulk, Melisende and their young son would govern equally as a triune.

He wanted his line to be remembered through his daughter and not Fulk causing great embarrassment for the recently resigned Count of Anjou. Fulk's autocratic style of rule was deeply counter to the collegiate culture in Jerusalem. 3.

Interestingly enough, Fulk had joined the Knights Templar in 1120 as a married brother and thereafter supported them with a yearly stipend and also financially supported two knights in the Holy Land throughout his life. 4.

Melisende also had powerful ecclesiastic allies who supported her claim against Fulk. He was not successful in his attempt to become the sole ruler. However this storm would pass and they would actually become fondly reconciled with each other before his death and had a second son together.

Upon this and other critical moments the Abbot wrote giving her his strength and not conspiring to usurp the queen by virtue of her gender. She was the ideal queen and widow, including her as a prototype in his written work the Epistolae. He implored her to protect the poor and the Templars within her Kingdom of Jerusalem.

Bernard requested that she remain unmarried after the accidental death of her husband. The Doctor of the Church understood that another marriage for Melisende and her son could result in an unstable political situation as did the Queen.

The Abbot: Early Medieval Feminist?

Is it possible that he sent a hidden message to her? The state of widowhood is directly related to Isis upon the death of Osiris and is today held within the mystery of Freemasonry. As Mary Magdalene was a widow through the sacrifice of Jesus, Melisende is her descendant and inheritor.

On his deathbed in 1153, Bernard wrote just three letters, illustrating what was foremost in his mind and heart; One to the patriarch of Antioch, a second to his friend – Brother Andre de Montbard and also the following to Melisende.

Bernard wrote to Melisende:

"....you hold yourself peacefully and calmly, rule yourself and your things wisely and by counsel of the wise that you love the brothers of the Temple and keep them close to you, and prudently and wisely meet the imminent dangers of the world according to the wisdom God gave you, with salutary counsels and aids. Such works, truly, are suitable for a strong woman, a humble widow, an exalted queen. Not is it unworthy, as you are a queen, for you to be a widow, which you would not be if you did not choose to be. I think that it is your glory, especially among Christians, to live a widow no less than a queen. This is a matter of succession, that of virtue; this from birth, that from the grace of God; this you were felicitously born, that you attained virilely. It is a double honor: one according to the world, the other according to God, both from God. Let the honor of widowhood not seem small to you, about which the Apostle says: honor widows who are true widows." 5.

He literally councils her to act as though she were a man in all ways except for the task of riding into battle. Melisende is remembered today as a wise and incredible medieval queen. Interestingly enough Freemasons today often identify themselves as the 'son of a poor widow' or the son of Isis.

Benedictine Abbess - Hildegard von Bingen

If Bernard had a female counterpart then that surely would have been the Jewel of the Rhine, Hildegard von Bingen. They were two faces of the same coin. Their few differences were that she did not attain the financial widespread growth for her abbey that Bernard had achieved for the successful Cistercians.

She is as self-deprecating as the Abbot and also as charismatic. In one letter she alludes to having precognition of him and there is evidence that she had influenced his life as well.

Bernard brought her to the attention of Eugenius III and it was declared upon the reading of her channeled but unfinished work, Scivias, before Archbishops and Cardinals that she was divinely inspired. She was at this point encouraged to continue with her prophetic work. Bernard had advanced her career greatly.

The Abbess did not shrink from harshly challenging Popes, Emperors or kings and even came close to being excommunicated for her outspokenness over dress codes.

She believed that cutting nuns hair was wrong as virgins were pure as a created being and no alteration such as a haircut was needed. She also celebrated May Day with her nuns without the normal Benedictine habit and veil with their hair loose around their shoulders which had caused threats of excommunication.

Hildegard was truly a Renaissance woman having left us a legacy that spans multiple disciplines. Lynn Picknett and Clive Prince in the Templar Revelation suggest that her unusual level of education and knowledge may be the product of a hidden mystery school and that her writings were in sympathy with the troubadour cult of love. 6.

I would certainly add that Bernard's gifts were the product of the same school which he was literally born into. Indeed she wrote unabashedly of the divinity of sexual union as a means of transcendence. She wrote extensively on a holistic approach to healing that was centuries ahead of her time in the west.

The Abbess preached, touring the Rhineland at a time when women most certainly did not speak publically. "Who is this woman" Asked Pope Eugenius III, "*who rises out of the wilderness like a column of smoke from burning spices?*" 7.

This is an almost sensual accolade and certainly complimentary. She had mastered theology, contemporary philosophy, was well versed in natural science and husbandry.

Like Bernard, her view of nature was an expression of the divine in the physical and she reveled in it! Heinrich Schipperges, an emotive expert says of the Abbess:

"Wisdom and beauty, light and love are the sources of Hildegard's language and its ability to affect us. Her poetic sensibility reinforces her keen intellect and far-ranging imagination to the point at which the joy she felt pierces through the centuries in between. We best appreciate Hildegard when we look at nature, human and extra-human, in her spirit, and see that all things are potentially joyous, as they were meant to be." 8.

Researcher Marsha Meskimmon describes Hildegard's art as upholding the Divine Feminine as the divine source of all:

"Arguably, Hildegard's visions constituted a form of 'feminine' theology, an exploration of the divinity of humanity, conceived not as 'men', but as more fluid, androgynous subjects. Within the text she consistently used pronouns which defied gendered categories (e.g. 'person' rather than 'man') and her figural style is markedly open to interpretation. The figure of Christ, for example, is an unbearded youth, angels and saints are androgynous, choirs of feminine figures abound and the Ecclesia is a female deity." 9.

The popular Abbes was a good listener, loyal friend and excellent administrator. She believed in the power of music to transform a human being which is as important as the soaring hermetic heights of a cathedral and its mutual spiritual effect on the body and soul.

Her dozens of lyrical musical compositions and songs are still being performed and recorded today. Hildegard was an amazing artist who left illuminations of her visions as they took place, some of which take on an eastern feel as if they were inspired by meditative mandalas. Many of her images have a great deal of strange geometry encoded within them.

Hildegard left us a legacy of music, lyrics, art, healing and inspired Christian mysticism. One of her paintings is a direct precursor to Da Vinci's Vitruvian Man and filled with enigmatic geometric alignments, the forces of nature and divine winds, all surrounded by the energizing colour red. Geometry is key to the tradition and is coded evidence of their existence in art and architecture. The letter 'G' in Freemasonry stands for geometry but according to Brother Bernard God *is* Geometry! Hildegard's natural visions give testament to this view of nature as divinely mathematic.

The Sun and the Magdalene

Regarding Vezelay and Saint Bernard, Ean Beggs writes:

"He encouraged the pilgrimage to Compostela, sometimes called the Milky Way, star-studded with Templar commanderies, Benedictine or Cistercian hostelries and churches of the Black Virgin. From one of the four great starting points, Vezelay, centre of the cult of the Magdalen and subsequent Black Virgin site, he preached the Second Crusade." 10.

The Abbot Bernard's choice of Vezelay's the Basilique de Madeleine (Cathedral of Mary Magdalene) is interesting as it had been the plan of Pope Urban II also to announce the First Crusade at La Madeleine in 1095 but changed the venue to the Council of Clermont instead. It was again the choice of staging for the Third Crusade.

Since the famous fictional book the Da Vinci Code was published, tiny Rennes le Chateau has become synonymous with the Magdalene bloodline but in the Middle Ages the impressive Vezelay was her centre of pilgrimage.

The great basilica was begun in 1096 when Godefroy de Bouillon rode forth to claim the Kingdom of Jerusalem as a Merovingian descendant of Christ.

Ean Beggs continues:

"Although it is not explicit in his writings, it is plausible to deduce from his actions that Bernard cherished the vision of a new world order based on the three pillars of the Benedictines, the Cistercians and the Templars, under a King of Kings. Thus the theocratic ideal of Godefroy de Bouillon would have found fulfilment." 11.

Indeed this may be a fair assessment of Bernard's thinking and certainly springs from the widespread religious culture of the day. An enlightened and intelligent descendant of the bloodline would indeed be any country's hope for a fair and equitable future for all its inhabitants.

Failing this hope, democracy has sprung up as a viable way to enforce political accountability which lacks within an absolute monarchy. There is a saying 'the only thing democracy has to fear is a benevolent king' – true if there were a way to guarantee this benevolence from one Priest King to the next; however history is riddled with kings and queens who were tragically less than messianic in their behavior - Hence the push for democratic forms out of the grace of feminine France in the 18th century.

The choice of Vezelay was therefore no accident as a rallying point to the Holy Land. It was a statement of homecoming for the descendants of Jesus and their hope of returning and maintaining a Christ on the throne in Israel.

According to legend the Magdalene spent the remaining thirty years of her life meditating in a sacred grotto at Saint Baume in Southern France. She was seen to have levitated while in prayer and miracles of healing were many.

People would sit outside her cave in hopes of a blessing from the exiled Queen of Israel. Legend tells us that upon her death she was buried at Saint Maximin where from the fifth century her tomb was protected by Cassianite monks from Marseilles.

Her relics were removed to Vezelay by a monk named Baudillon for safekeeping during the Syrian invasion in 719 AD by the Emirate of Córdoba. It would take a series of battles over three generations from 732 AD to 759 AD to free the Magdalene country.

French hero Charles Martel and his son Pippin the Younger pushed the Moors back. Charlemagne struck the final blow by invading the mountains of north Moorish Spain in 778 AD where he made land grants to the impoverished war weary Visigothic refugees and also founded several monasteries for their protection. The Saracens tried again to invade France in 792 AD but were repelled by Louis, King of Aquitaine.

Pippin and Charlemagne had one very important dynastic link in common. The Carolingian men had married Merovingian Princesses in order to solidify their claims to the throne.

The Carolingians had usurped, in collusion with the Church, the sacred line of the Merovingian long-haired sorcerer kings. This is why Charlemagne is so important to the modern researcher tracing his/her ancestry. If one may trace a line of descent back to Charlemagne, then you are of the bloodline of Christ.

The Pope confirmed that the relics of Mary Magdalene were genuine in 1058 which lead to an increase of pilgrims to Vezelay Abbey, a major embarkation point on The Way of Saint James towards Santiago de Compostela.

Medieval relic hunting and showcasing for pilgrimage was serious business. It was not unusual for there to have been so many pieces of the true cross or of saint's body parts for there to have been multiple versions of either!

Today we view relics with a different perspective but to medieval culture they made sense as faith was the driving factor in their lives. Indeed faith was also expressed as their entertainment such was its importance. The church knew how to captivate the imagination and they were masters of ritual, theatre, light and colour.

Touch relics which were worn as badges on the shoulder and sold at the location of saint's tombs. Touching the badge to the tomb or relic caused a symbiotic bond to take place. The pilgrim could then travel home and always have a spiritual connection with the saint through the physical touch relic which would bring to mind the qualities embodied by the saint or spiritual being.

The Abbot: Early Medieval Feminist?

It is a method for focusing the mind into a state of meditation which is still highly useful today regardless of one's religion, object of veneration, tradition or practices. The veneration of relics allowed churches to be built and brought prosperity to local merchants which spilled out into the local population. There was no separation of the spiritual and the economy in the medieval mind. Spirituality was life in action.

Some may take a vacation or holiday in order to relax, whereas these individuals would go on a pilgrimage to increase their spiritual understanding and ask for healing, should that be the need of their journey.

In Washington D.C. modern pilgrims wait in line for hours whilst hoping to stand in the presence of the Declaration of Independence enshrined in a building designed to look like a Roman temple. We still bear much in common with our medieval ancestors.

When faced with an object heavy with the weight of centuries one can almost sense another level of life infused within it by the original bearer and added to this the focused attention of pilgrims through time.

The object in question takes on what could be crudely termed a magical dimension that is highly moving. It leaves one with a palpable sense of an extra quality regardless of the belief system of the witness. The Mona Lisa's smile enigmatically pulls millions to her altar yearly in homage to her unfathomable mysteries.

The Magdalene's presence was crucial to the growing economy of the town of Vezelay. The Abbey would later decline when the 'real' tomb of the Magdalene was discovered in 1279 AD in Saint-Maximin-la-Sainte-Baume.

King Charles II of Sicily erected a Dominican convent on the apparently miraculous and perfectly preserved ancient shrine. The attention was now turned back on St. Baume and Vezelay slipped as the main focus for the Magdalene.

The shrine of the Magdalene in Saint Baume has a rather eerie visage that is both compelling and disturbing at once. The skull is encased in a reliquary of gold formed into the graceful neck and head of a woman with flowing golden locks. As a work of art it is beautiful and perhaps could be called lovely if not for its rather macabre visage of the skull encased within.

During the 16th century the Huguenots sought refuge in Vezelay and took it upon themselves to destroy their host's relics, causing Vezelay to lose her major connection to the Magdalene in the public eye.

The current relics were gifted to la Madeleine in the 19th century by the Archbishop of Sens and are contained in a reliquary of the same era which appears to be that of a stylized Ark being carried by six angels. The supposed Magdalene relic had been held by the Diocese of Sens since 1281 AD, having been given to Sens by Pope Martin IV. Still, it was not enough to call the faithful back to Vezelay.

It is highly possible that the Magdalene could yet be secretly buried elsewhere. Dan Brown's fictional tale suggests that she is buried in the Louvre beneath an inverted pyramid under the seal of the Arago monument – frankly it is as good a guess as any and certainly befitting the Divine Feminine nature of Paris.

Treasure hunters have delved Rennes le Chateau in recent decades looking for lost Templar treasure, the Magdalene tomb and other Holy Grails. The scale of the problem caused such disturbances and damage to property and ancient sites that it is now against the law to turn up with a bucket and spade looking for Grails in the French countryside.

The Secret Dossier of a
Knight Templar of the Sangreal

The mystery is still as captivating to us today as in the 12th century but there are other treasures hidden in plain sight that have been forgotten.

The cave of Saint Baume itself is a thing of beauty overlooking a vista that seems to remain unchanged in the 2000 years since Mary Magdalene called it her home.

However, Vezelay deserves to be examined as a potent Magdalene Basilica for another very important reason that yet again brings to mind her worshiper Saint Bernard - The Lady Vezelays' architectural glory.

"What is God?" Bernard asked, "He is length, width, height and depth."
Bernard de Clairvaux

The fine example of Romanesque architecture evident in the abbey of La Madeleine, which began construction by one of Bernard's three arms of his new world order, the Benedictines in 1096 AD.

Eight pools of light lead straight to the first step of the main altar and perhaps the prior resting place of the Magdalene. The high altar faces east towards the Holy Land.

This light event occurs on the summer solstice, the 21st of June which is marked by John the Baptists day of 24th of June. The number eight is of infinity and the secrets of time.

It is the number that the Templars would use in their own sacred spaces and eight pointed cross. The octagon or circle was chosen for their temples.

Some researchers state that the circular form is a reminder of the Dome of the Rock where they first were ensconced in Jerusalem. There are however deeper levels of meaning attached to the number eight, the octagon and the circle.

(Photo opposite by François Walch and uploaded to Wiki by Francis Verillon – August 2008 (Wiki Creative Commons)

Photo credit explanation opposite via Francis Vérillon: "I created this file by scanning the hard copy of a film photography made by François Walch who authorized me to publish it in Wikipedia by email of 28 August 2008. This photograph was given to me by Hugues Delautre, OFM, Sponsor of the work and cited in the Wikipedia article on "Vézelay Abbey", section "Vézelay and light" has four references. - Personal work (own work). I created this file by scanning the hard copy of a film photography made by François Walch who authorized me to publish it in Wikipedia by email of 28 August 2008."

The June 23, 1976 at 2:27 p.m. in the nave of the Basilica of St. Mary Magdalene Vezelay, Father Hugues Delautre OFM gave appointment in the sun, at this precise moment in culmination with respect to the earth, he shows him the secret of the building.)

Please see article under heading: Alignment With The Sun at:
https://en.wikipedia.org/wiki/V%C3%A9zelay_Abbey

The Abbot: Early Medieval Feminist?

The Order expresses this mystery, simply and beautifully at Vezelay. It is a marriage of uncreated light and form giving breath to new life. Vezelay is symbolic of the Chemical Marriage, a fitting monument to the Bride of Christ.

The light event channeled through the vessel of this architectural wonder would not have been lost on Abbott Bernard as it is the natural feminine and holy magic of the earth and sun in constant embrace and ancient dance measured by the massive

La Belle Dame Sans Merci, Francis Bernard Dicksee, c 1901

time piece that is Vezelay. The Golden Light of the Universe embraced by His counterpart, Gaia the Mother Earth. Male and Female Divine, created equally in sublime embrace.

1. Hodgson, Natasha R. Women, Crusading and the Holy Land in Historical Narrative. Woodbridge, Suffolk, UK: Boydell Press, 2007.
2. Mayer, Hans Eberhard. Studies in the History of Queen Melisende of Jerusalem. Cambridge, MA: Harvard Univ. Pr., 1972. p. 26
3. Oldenbourg, Zoé. The Crusades. London: Phoenix, 2001.
4. Addison, C. G., and Robert Macoy. The Knights Templars. New York: Masonic Pub., 1842.
5. Ibid
6. Picknett, Lynn, and Clive Prince. The Templar Revelation: Secret Guardians of the True Identity of Christ. London: Corgi, 2007.
7. As quoted from - Schipperges, Heinrich. The World of Hildegard of Bingen: Her Life, Times, and Visions. Collegeville, MN: Liturgical Press, 1998 p. 11
8. Ibid. p 48
9. Meskimmon, Marsha. "Hildegard of Bingen." Grove Art Online. Oxford Art Online. 30 Mar. 2010 http://www.oxfordartonline.com/subscriber/article/grove/art/T2021730
10. Begg, Ean C. M. The Cult of the Black Virgin. 2nd ed. London: Arkana, 1996. p. 26
11. Ibid

Ten

Conflict and Mystical Legacy

'The honey-tongued teacher' and the Second Crusade

The disaster of the fall of Edessa on 24 December 1144 AD was a major blow to the Christian Kingdoms in the Middle East. It fell to Imad ad-Din Zanghi, the Turkish *atabeg* of Mosul, and was the least protected, most northerly county held by crusaders. The city's Frankish inhabitants were massacred. Baldwin of Boulogne had founded the county during the First Crusade only forty six years prior in 1098. 1.

The Queen of Jerusalem, Melisende, sent an army to the defense of Edessa but they were unable to save the city. Concerns for the safety of Antioch and then Jerusalem were very real. She sent word along with other ambassadors from the Holy Land to Rome calling for assistance. It would be almost a year before Bernard would hear of events which threatened to destabilize the entire region, so slow were communications.

Eugenius III issued the papal bull <u>Quantum Praedecessores</u>, on 1 December 1145 calling for the Second Crusade. It stated that if any man were to join the cause he would be given absolution and a sure place in heaven. Along with this divine promise was a more practical article offering protection of property and loved ones. 2.

There was little initial support for the venture and Eugenius called upon the persuasive Abbot Bernard to convince the faithful. One doubter was King Louis of France who had actually been planning a pilgrimage to the Holy Land. The proposed military expedition became an extension to his current plan and he was reconciled to the Pope by Bernard.

The honey-tongued teacher addressed a throng of epic proportions supposedly numbering some 100,000 souls. The location of his appeal was of sacred and architectural significance as we have seen in the last chapter: Vezelay, Mary Magdalene's cathedral.

The Abbot's eloquence was such that King Louis, his famous troubadour queen, Eleanor of Aquitaine and other nobles present fell prostrate before Bernard, followed by peoples of all classes.

So many had taken up the cross that the fabric ran out and all were shouting, 'Crosses, give us crosses'! The Saint famously gave his own outer garments to the throngs for the fabric cross that would be sewn onto their shoulders. He had certainly turned the tide of a lukewarm reception into an inferno with the force of his will.

Unlike the First Crusade, the Second included many of Europe's aristocracy through the inspired Bernard, but the greatest support came from ordinary people.

The Secret Dossier of a
Knight Templar of the Sangreal

This was a highly dangerous undertaking as even the journey to the Holy Land could cost one's life. This was not an exercise in cynical greed, with some exceptions, but one of faith and altruism however it might be viewed with today's lens.

Many sold their properties in order to participate in the costly affair. The modern myth that only second sons without a future in Europe went on Crusade is not entirely true. Married first sons left their families and homes in order to enact what they believed would be a rescue of Edessa from hostile oppressors.

Female Crusaders were not unheard of but were officially discouraged. Entire families travelled together rather than part as the Holy Land was often a lifetime commitment and one way ticket. Some women actually fought alongside their men as has happened through history. If the battle were lost however, they faced either slavery or death at the hands of the Muslims.

The historical background for the crusades is complex and there is a danger to over-simplify the conflict. It is a separate subject unto itself so large is the field of content. Acts of depraved barbarity were committed by both sides. The leonine valor of knights and their nemesis have also echoed down the centuries. Countless books and films have been inspired by the deeds of the past.

Many researchers have suggested, and I quite agree, that the Templars became involved in the Middle East to retrieve what they considered to be spiritually charged family heirlooms from the time of Christ and to be closer to god, and by all accounts they accomplished their mission. It may very well be that Abbot Bernard himself would have gone with them if he had been in good health. He must have waited with baited breath for news of their success and was joyful indeed when they returned to Europe with newly uncovered mysteries.

As far as the Templars were concerned – they were going home to the seat of their most famous ancestors – Moses, David, and Solomon, John the Baptist, Jesus and the Magdalene.

A Tale of Hope For Edessa: Prester John

Rumors had circulated for years of a legendary priest king named Prester John of India. There were those in Europe who hoped the king would come to the aid of Jerusalem as his bravery as a spiritual warrior was renowned.

As time went on his glamour rose at the hearth side with each retelling of his deeds. As had Melisende, Prince Raymond of Antioch fearing the Turks now at his border in Edessa sent his own emissary, Bishop Hugh, to Pope Eugenius III to entreat him for assistance.

When Hugh arrived in November of 1145 he found that there was already a great swell of men making preparations-having been stirred to action earlier that year by the Abbot Bernard. The meeting between the bishop and the pope was chronicled by learned historian Otto, Bishop of Freising and half brother to Conrad III ruler of Germany.

Otto wrote of Hugh:

"Not many years ago a certain John, a king and priest who lives in the extreme Orient, beyond Persia and Armenia, and who, like all his people, is a Christian although a Nestorian, made war on the brothers known as the Samiardi, who are the kings of the Persians and Medes, and stormed Ecbatana, the capital of their kingdom....When the aforesaid kings met him with Persian, Median, and Assyrian troops, the ensuing battle lasted for three days, since both sides were willing to die rather than flee. At last Presbyter John-for so they customarily call him-put the Persians to flight, emerging victorious after the most bloodthirsty slaughter...

He [Bishop Hugh] said that after this victory the aforesaid John had moved his army to the aid of the Church in Jerusalem, but when he had come to the river Tigris he had not been able to take his troops across it in any vessel. Then he had turned to the north, where, he had heard, the river sometimes froze over in the winter cold. He had tarried there for some years, waiting for the frost, but on account of the continued mild weather there was very little, and finally, after losing much of his army because of the unaccustomed climate, he had been forced to return home.

He is said to be a direct descendant of the Magi, who are mentioned in the Gospel, and to rule over the same peoples they governed, enjoying such glory and prosperity that he uses no scepter but one of emerald. Inspired by the example of his forefathers who came to adore Christ in his cradle, he had planned to go to Jerusalem, but was prevented, so it is said, by the reason mentioned above. But that is enough of this." 3.

It may well have been the concern of Bishop Hugh and Pope Eugenius that Europe might wait for Prester John to save Jerusalem himself and they had to quell this immediately.

They were successful in this but it would open up another mysterious chapter in the history of the Knights Templar. Abbot Bernard would ask the knights to seek out the mystery of this unknown king. Their clandestine journey would entail nothing less than the Ark of the Covenant and the progeny of Solomon and the Queen of Sheba.

It was time for the good Abbot Bernard to take his message to Germany and to the previously mentioned Conrad III who refused to take part in the endeavor. Bernard gained recruits as he passed through Germany into Switzerland and on the way back spoke at Speyer Cathedral. In the emotionally charged sermon he asked of those present, using Christ's words, "Man, what ought I to have done for you that I have not done?" Instantly Conrad melted and he joined the crusade with many of his nobles.

Jewish Suppression

Sadly, as in the First Crusade, anti-Semitism reared its ugly head. A fanatical Cistercian monk named Rudolphe began preaching hate with horrible effect about Jewish communities. There are always a few rotten eggs in any organization regardless of the idealism and nobility of the total group. He was urging massacres in Cologne, Mainz, Speyer and Worms. He claimed that the Jews were not contributing financially to the relief effort in the Holy Land.

Fortunately the Archbishops of Cologne and of Mainz opposed the attacks and appealed to Bernard for help in calming the perpetrators. Bernard caught up with the monk, brought him to heel and sent him back to his monastery in silence.

Abbot Bernard showed remarkable tolerance of other religions and peoples during a time when death followed difference.

I do not think he believed his own words to his Christianized general public that the Jews deserved god's punishment for the crucifixion of the Christ en masse or due to their denial of him as Savior.

Once again we are looking at a misunderstanding of the bible and its corresponding historical events by all three Judaic religions involved. This has resulted in centuries of misguided hate which is still in existence.

An important clue may be found in the remaining open letter from Rabbi Ephraim of Bonn as he recounts the potential genocide from the age of 13 when St. Bernard appealed to the public and brought Radulphe to heel:

"God heard our cries and had mercy upon us. He sent after this ungodly monk another, who was a respectable priest, one of the greatest and most honoured. He knew their laws and was a person of understanding. His name was Bernard, Abbot of Clairvaux in France. He also barked, as is their custom, saying, 'It is good that you march against the Muslims, but anyone who touches a Jew to take his life, is as touching Jesus himself." Rabbi Ephraim continues saying: "For if our Creator in his mercy had not sent us this Abbot Bernard and his subsequent letters, then no remnant or vestige would have been left of Israel. Blessed be our redeemer and saviour, blessed be his name." 4.

Bernard's comment, *"but anyone who touches a Jew to take his life, is as touching Jesus himself"* - is incredible. Jesus was part of a large extended family with as many as seven further siblings not including cousins, many of whom would have had children. Some of their names are listed in the Bible in the book of Mark.

It is even stated by some researchers that John the Baptist, as a Rabbi himself, had children. There are those that escaped to France and others who remained in the Middle East and with later generations migrating to Europe.

This does not take into consideration Jesus' forebears and their children either. The exponential growth of the line by Bernard's time would have been innumerable accepting that children survived warfare, famine, diseases or other calamities which many did.

Holy Grail composer, Adrian Wagner, estimates that the children from Jesus and Mary Magdalene alone, over 2000 years, could produce a population base of approximately 25 million. One researcher thinks that there are as many as two million descendants of Christ in the USA alone and most likely more.

There would often be no way of knowing one's history as over time junior lines lost the information of their heritage. How many ignorant Medieval Christians killed descendants of Christ of either the Jewish population or in the Albigensian Crusade?

It could be said that there were some who did know and committed murder hoping to wipe out any threat from a Davidic bloodline. A Catholic commander named Arnaud, is reported to have said, "Kill them all, the Lord will recognise His own." - Which is indeed what happened at the siege of Beziers France where the entire population of 20,000 were wiped out in one day, regardless of sex or age. 5.

This was completely anathema to Abbot Bernard's desire to protect his distant kin. I am not saying that the entire Jewish population of medieval Europe is of the Davidic line of Jesus but the Abbot did not wish to see *any* Semitic blood spilled. He did not seek the exclusive protection of his distant cousins. He worked hard to prevent the genocide of the Jewish peoples using the commandment from the bible as reason to preserve life as the general population would never have understood there was perhaps another riveting reason to stay their hand aside from human decency.

Bernard de Clairvaux,thought to be a true likeness by Georg Andreas Wasshuber
(1650–1732)

The Secret Dossier of a
Knight Templar of the Sangreal

As had his predecessor, Harding, he sought out the educated rabbis for help in translations, forming alliances with them. He appreciated their knowledge, skills and their fine culture as we should also respect differing peoples today whilst perpetuating our own traditions in joy and honour.

Christians forget that Jesus was born into a Kabalistic *Jewish* tradition and was a Semitic Rabbi who would have had a Bar Mitzvah. Jesus was not a Christian as it is understood today or even in Bernard's time; which was a different form of Catholicism than exists now, as it has been crafted by men over centuries to suit cultural, economic and political views through time.

Today the varying Christian movements around the world are as diverse as the languages spoken and includes 1.2 billion people. Some ignorantly calling Brother Christians heretics even in our modern world, from America to Africa.

It brings to mind the ongoing conflict between the three Abraham religions. All three at their heart are extended family, springing from the *same core* with many similarities and values. Palestinians and Jewish peoples even share a common DNA bond. They are literally cousins. In this world of ever increasing nuclear threat it is time we all start speaking to each other about our common links in our spirituality versus our differences. We may be shocked to find we have more in common than not. If we cannot love our neighbor, then let us have empathy for him and in this fair aspect we will achieve cohesion as a global and golden civilization.

Eventually the ethos of cooperation in religion would flower into Freemasonry where one is admitted simply if you have a belief in a higher power, but religion and politics is a forbidden topic of discussion and the well-being of the broader community is the priority.

The Freemasons were at the early forefront of charitable works from the very start exemplifying the concept of service to others. This ideal is reflected in the creation of The United States and eventually European democracies where freedom of religion is a human right and dignity. The organization was the first outside of a church state to foster the philosophical and psychological potential of a human being.

1. Runciman, Steven. A History of the Crusades. Vol. II. London: Penguin, 1952.

2. Setton, Kenneth Meyer. A History of the Crusades. Vol. I. Philadelphia: Univ. of Pennsylvania Pr., 1958.

3. Silverberg, Robert. The Realm of Prester John: With a New Afterword. London: Phoenix Press, 2001. p. 7

4. Hallam, Elizabeth M. Chronicles of the Crusades: Eye-witness Accounts of the Wars between Christianity and Islam. Godalming, Surrey: CLB, 1997. Pgs. 126, 127

5. Martin, Sean. The Cathars: The Most Successful Heresy of the Middle Ages. Edison, NJ: Chartwell Books, 2006. p. 49

Eleven

The Saint and The Cathars

The Albigensian Crusade is a historically complex event. I may only give it passing comment due to space but not due to the triviality of the subject. In fact it was one of the most shameful heart rending episodes of Catholic history.

The Church lost its moral authority during this time, carrying out this act of aggression which also changed the very fabric of the institution itself with the onset of the Inquisition. The Inquisition has never been called off but the name has changed to something approximating political correctness which hopes to portray a less physically threatening purpose - a fist in a velvet glove. In recent years this department has released pamphlets instructing the faithful on how to spot a vulnerable woman and prevent her from becoming a pagan. Surely their time could be better used eradicating poverty and war?

The Congregation For The Doctrine Of The Faith was given its public make over in 1965. Pope Benedict XVI is its former head. One wonders why this institution, which should never have been given life in the first place, has life now in the 21st century when freedom of religion is an internationally held human right and dignity.

Rome in the 13th century would call upon the faithful to declare war on fellow Christians accused of heresy, having underpinned the battle cry with that of political, monetary and forgiveness of sins-known as an Indulgence.

A vocally aggressive papal legate named Peter had been sent to southern France to force the regional leaders to quell the supposed heretical activities taking place under their auspices. Leaving empty handed from the fruitless and heated discussion, the man was murdered near the river Rhone on his way back to Rome by a frustrated knight of Toulouse possibly acting independently of his lord. The so-called heretics having nothing to do with the murder, but nevertheless were blamed by Innocent III, who wasted no time in fanning the flames of righteous indignation.

Author Laurence W. Marvin states:

"The assassination and indulgence triggered earnest men to take the cross, move south against other earnest men and begin a terrible time of war, massacre, repression, and conquest. The underlying causes for military intervention, the heresy and noble support or acquiescence for it, had existed for over half a century, but it took the killing of Peter of Castelnau to initiate the conflict." 1.

Tensions between the Languedoc and Rome exploded, culminating in the Albigensian Crusade of 1209 which lasted some twenty plus years; however the survivors would be cruelly monitored by heretic hunters who travelled the countryside in pairs almost as a macabre version of the Cathar Perfectae who had previously walked the land in the same manner.

The sect was thought to have finally been snuffed out in the 14th century, however there are claims that the Cathars still exist today. Since I advocate the continuation of the Templar Order today, it is not up to me to comment on whether or not one wishes to consider themselves a Cathar in today's world.

Their survival is a distinct possibility and if so had a direct influence on later streams and Reformationists such as the Lollards. A human being may be murdered but one cannot murder an idea, or further yet, a dearly-held belief. Whilst one individual can be cut down – many are often left in their place such was the Templar experience.

The Albigensian Crusade turned into a land grab of a rich fruitful region by northern aristocracy and spawned the Dominican Order sent to eradicate a truly peaceful people.

The Dominicans would become synonymous with the horrors of the Inquisition which would shine its greedy eye on the ill-fated Knights Templar as well as the hapless Cathari. An estimated 200,000 to 1,000,000 Occitanians were massacred during the crusade having once lived in independent principalities which were then absconded into French soil.

The fortress of Montsegur was the last to fall into the hands of the northern aggressors. Many of the starved and battle weary survivors that had sought shelter within the castle walls were spared as they had been forced to accept Catholicism in exchange for their lives, at least publically.

It is thought that between sixty to two hundred or so Cathar Perfectae were condemned to the pyre. The Pure Ones, men and women, walked out of the fortress straight onto the waiting fires rather than accept, to their eyes, a false dogma. Their dignity and courage in the face of such a horrific death remains one of their most inspiring legacies.

It was reported that they were so mentally prepared through spiritual meditation practices that they did not experience pain inflicted by the flames. Curiously, upon the surrender of the fortress, the inhabitants were granted 15 days to prepare for their fate.

Upon their impending defeat, apparently two to four of their numbers scaled down the dangerous rear cliff face. The identities of these people are a mystery and include women to just the brave knights themselves.

It is an almost impossible feat and escaping with no less than the Holy Grail, according to speculation. What they carried with them has long been commented upon and may indeed have been one of the reasons they were so brutally attacked.

The search and acquisition of ancient source materials and sacred objects has long been a secret battleground since the early church has tried to alter the actual history and content of Jesus and Mary Magdalene's teachings and destroy their descendants or eradicate knowledge of their lineage.

If they viewed this object as a spiritual weapon akin to the Ark or equally dangerous information and teachings, using the cover of a false crusade to gain the Holy artifact/documents is a high probability.

The Saint and The Cathars

The Cathars included populations of the Languedoc, northern Spain and those existing in some cities of Italy. It is difficult to piece their history together as much of their written sources were burned by the Inquisition which leaves much guesswork for authors and researchers.

We can however look to a special woman who I believe to be an inheritor of the Cathars, troubadours and also an author of a book titled: Mirror of Simple Souls. Marguerite Porete, was burned at the stake in 1310 amidst the Templar trials.

She believed that the individual must commune with god and did not have need of priests which of course proved to be a direct threat to the church. Her courage when facing the Inquisition was exemplary. She did not waver when told not to preach from her book or reprint it.

Nor did she recant after a year and a half in prison. So strong was her belief in the transcendence of the soul in a love union with god that she described him as an ideal man and she his long lost princess.

It is of significance that the papers surrounding the trial were lodged with William de Nogaret and William of Plaisians, who were the main prosecutors against the Knights Templar. The episode is another link in the chain of pro-feminine ideals within the priestly sect of the Cistercian and Templar Orders. 2.

Languedoc literally means Language of Oc. Instead of using 'oui' for yes, those in Southern France would have used the positive 'oc'. Their language is now called Occitan and they were culturally and linguistically different from their northern contemporaries. The local dialect still bears witness to their forebears conquered long ago.

The culture literally grew out of the Magdalene community established centuries before though it is evident that the original message took on other elements during the passage of time. It is interesting to note the similarity of names between Mary Magdalene and the Cathar's virgin creator goddess called Mari which translates literally as 'love'.

Under torture the Cathars told of an ancient manuscript by the hand of Jesus and another by the Magdalene both apparently written in Greek. This alone suggests a high education level of the two that outstrips the 'poor' and 'simple' people they have been portrayed as through time.

The book written by Christ, in the hands of the Cathars, was called the Book of Love. The Pure Ones of the Languedoc used it as the basis of their Church of Love or Amor which author William Henry states is the exact opposite of the Church of Roma. The Book of Love and or the knowledge it contained was believed to eventually come into the hands of the Knights Templar for guardianship.

Unfortunately the Church discovered that the Templars had it in their possession as a result of torture sessions endured by the Grail Guardians. Author Kathleen McGowan has used both these mysterious books as the basis for her works of fiction which contain many truths.

Ms. McGowan contends that she has actually seen these books and has met their modern day bearers, though none of this has been put forward into public light as of yet. One may state many secrets in fiction that one may not say in a non-fiction work, including the knowledge of a book written by Jesus and the hand of his companion, the Magdalene.

Author William Henry states:

"Its contents [The Book of Love] were a secret skill (symbolized by the Templar skull) said to grant one the ability to control the forces of nature and to transform ordinary human blood into that of the wise, holy and pure blood of life of the immortal Illi or Illuminati. It is equated with the Holy Grail. -

Webster's says 'Oc' is the root of octo, 8, and ocular, the eye. A related Egyptian word, Ak, means 'light', and aker means 'light being'.

As an investigative mythologist, it is of great interest to me that the Egyptian hieroglyph of the heron/phoenix, , the 'bird of light' (akh), so closely matches the stylized fish glyph of Jesus , though it predates him by millennia. In addition, these two symbols are structurally identical to, the mathematical sign sometimes used for infinity, which spells OC. It is the root for 'octo' or 8. These symbols suggest a continuous transmission of knowledge of the secrets of light." 3.

Bernard did not live to see the Albigensian Crusade take place nor did he meet Marguerite Porete or see the fall of his brainchild the Templars. Late in his life, he was sent to tame the supposed heretical Cathars.

Bernard shared a direct blood tie through his mother with the educated and tolerant Counts of Toulouse who were considered wise rulers by their population. The counts considered themselves Catholics; however they also supported the Cathars and frequently had their Parfaits (male Cathar priests) as part of their retinues.

The Cathars also called themselves Christians, believing that they held an earlier form of Christianity than Catholicism. Transforming the physical body of lead into a worthy vessel of gold, in union with spiritual love, was their goal.

It was a dualist faith with Gnostic leanings and influences from Manichaean's and supposedly the Paulicians in Armenia and the Bogomils of Bulgaria whose movements had merged.

There is some speculation as to the travel of these beliefs as dualism already existed in the area of the Languedoc and actually grew out of the Gnostic thought originally taught by Mary Magdalene as previously mentioned, whose inheritors were the Merovingians.

Author Laurence Gardner states:

"The Languedoc region was substantially that which had formed the 8th century Jewish kingdom of Septimania, under the Merovingian scion Guilhem de Gellone. The whole area of Languedoc and Provence was steeped in the early traditions of Lazarus (Simon Zelotes) and Mary Magdalene, and the inhabitants regarded Mary as the 'Grail Mother' of true Western Christianity." 4.

The Heart Centred Lactation Miracle of St Bernard

Creator:Master I. A. M. of Zwolle - Henk van Os. "The Culture of Prayer," from The Art of Devotion in the Late Middle Ages and Europe, 1300-1500. Princeton University Press, 1994: 52-85. Online source Flickr - The Lactation of Saint Bernard of Clairvaux. Virgin Mary is shooting milk into the eye of Saint Bernard of Clairvaux from her left breast. Bernard described this miraculous healing of an eye affliction himself in the 12th century. the engraving is 32 x 24.1 cm

The Secret Dossier of a
Knight Templar of the Sangreal

The Cathars considered men and women to be equal spiritually, believing that the nature of the soul is androgynous, though the celibate Elect were not even allowed to touch a member of the opposite sex.

The Cathars have been increasingly held up as early feminists. It has been put forward that if the Cathars had survived and grown that equality for women would have occurred sooner than the 20th century.

The Inquisition certainly stalled this process but the inherent problem lies in the interpretation of the bible itself in regards to women as equal, not only spiritually to men, but physically. It is the interpretation of the bible that has held women's rights back, not only in our era, but also in the 13th century.

The Cathars would have had to address this issue for women to have gained equality under their religion as the concept of the secular nation and freedom of religion was not reached by any state until the 18th century with the French Revolution and the American War for Independence.

It is certainly a possibility however, as they did not include the Old Testament in their teachings, but it would still have taken an inestimable amount of time, regardless, for women to have gained equal footing as Perfectae with their brothers. The Cathars mainstay from the bible had been the Gospels, especially the Gospel of John and they also recited the Lord's Prayer numerous times a day.

The Cathar's and Bernard's people were constrained by long held cultural beliefs across a broad landscape that despite their own wishes, held women back as equal beings.

I could be accused of being very rosy in my outlook of the medieval Cathar and also of Bernard. If one studies the Abbot, an individual of futuristic tendencies emerges, but still his life was led within the context of his time period.

I am certain that there could be many written accounts which could be used as evidence of chauvinism either of the Cathars or of Bernard. What intrigues me however is the written evidence *for* tolerance, a shift towards real feminism and also a willingness to consider female counterparts as leadership material and in a time when even considering women - as other than a lesser evil being - was as foreign a concept as a rocket to the moon.

The Abbot did much for women's liberties through Mariology and the Troubadour movement as we have seen. Regardless of how one views the material today, the Cathars and the Abbot were groundbreakers and fanned the early flames of what would one day become possible for women in an equal society.

The main problem the Cathars had as a viable religion with longevity was that they did not believe in procreation. In other words and crudely, they would literally die out if this were followed to the letter.

I am convinced this was a main stumbling block for Bernard who held life as sacred. In a Cathar dualist world, marriage was considered evil. Bearing a child trapped the soul in the downfallen physical, therefore damning it far from the realm of the god of goodness whose powers to intercede were nil on earth.

The Cathar populace was urged to practice forms of coital birth control which drew unfortunate condemnation from Rome. Or rather a very good excuse to add sodomy to the charges of heresy.

The Saint and The Cathars

Should it be true and the Cathar peoples are still in existence today, it is obvious they had to make a decision to pass their faith down through family ties. Some certainly would have taken celibate vows just as the Catholic Church today as an act of devotion to their faith. But the only way to keep a religion alive is to pass it down through converts and more importantly - family.

The Catholic Church and Christian Churches in developing countries still carry the opposite policy on procreation that the Cathars held; but whose own wisdom on the subject should be considered as questionable when taken into consideration the welfare of women and children in impoverished circumstances with the looming threat of sexually transmitted diseases.

One woman dies in childbirth every minute around the globe from preventable issues. But they are still expected to take the risk. Strong leadership exemplifying compassion for women would bring happy converts flocking to their doors, providing a stronger culture socially and economically.

A true example to other nations based upon the practicalities of the human experience. I hope for enlightened policy changes through real leadership and reconciliation between churches (who are in such powerful positions to do good) and their people as a result.

According to the Cathars the world was created by the powerful Rex Mundi, the evil king of the world and therefore all within it was of evil and fallen from grace. Rex Mundi's protagonist, the equally powerful god/goddess of light, had no power on earth as the realm of the spiritual and that of matter did not mix.

This stems from the Kabalistic concept of emanation where matter settles from a higher spiritual plane into the physical and is thought to have become corrupt as it descends.

However this is an underdeveloped concept of emanation and removes the spiritual aspect of life as a school house and accelerated opportunity to learn by simply being alive, let alone the joys of which life may bring. Perspective is everything and life is a goodly gift! Life may be hard but it is the true adventure as we labor under the illusion of separateness from our creator. It is the ultimate thrill ride.

In the eyes of the Medieval Cathar, Jesus was never incarnate as anything other than a spirit due to his high state of spirituality being incompatible with matter. Their denial of Christ having physical form was offensive to Catholicism.

Taken a step further this would mean the denial that the crucifixion/resurrection ever took place which was another basis for the charge of heresy.

There are accounts however of Cathars insisting that the Magdalene was the companion of Christ and that there were children involved. These individuals may have been privy to further information than their fellow Cathars. Like so many belief systems there is a myriad of ideas held under the same umbrella regardless of the status quo.

There are so many differences in the Cathar faith compared to Catholicism that it may be said that it is a different religion altogether and therefore the charge of heresy is ludicrous. Frankly, heresy as a charge is as outmoded now as it was when it was first brought into church policy centuries ago.

I am still amazed that in the 21st century there are those who still use the term. It was merely a political weapon to be used against those who will not bow to a financial and priestly system which had been imposed upon Europe.

The Etymology of the word from the Greek *hairetikos* means simply to be 'able to choose'. It is a value judgment *within* a belief system. Since the Cathars insisted they were Christian they were lamentably labeled heretics.

The Prefects taught that one could be born into the animal kingdom or as a human. As strict vegetarians they would not eat meat or eggs as they are born out of sexual union. They believed they could be cutting short the life of the soul trapped in the physical thus ruining that individual's chance of becoming perfected in life whose ultimate task was to overthrow the cruel wheel of reincarnation. Not unlike that of Hindu or Buddhist thought.

The murdered being whose life was cut short would then be doomed to suffer painful reincarnation yet again in an attempt to reach heaven.

Reincarnation has long been held as fact by more than one religion in the world and is currently practiced by millions around the globe today. The Cathars share this link with Hinduism and Buddhism through the travels of Jesus and his transmission of this concept to his followers. However it must not be forgotten that the Old Testament itself carries intriguing allusions to reincarnation that predate Christ by at least 1000 years.

Reincarnation was determined anathema at the Second Council of Church Fathers, in Constantinople in 553 A.D., where many references to it in the Bible were deleted as they were in direct conflict with many church doctrines such as the newer policy of resurrection and the final Day of Judgment.

The Cathari Priesthood, like Bernard, lived ascetic lives of poverty choosing to serve their communities instead of seeking personal gain. In the face of overweight, corrupt, richly dressed Catholic leaders of the day, the Parfaits were very popular, indeed the bulk of the region were not Catholic but Cathar followers.

The Principality of Toulouse like others in the region protected the Cathars. The churches were empty and the Catholic priests were literally ignored so popular had the religion become in the region. This was a growing problem for Catholicism.

The Abbot Bernard was one of the forerunners of actually preaching to ordinary people. He was able to convert countless numbers as a result of his direct appeal to the population. Bernard's tours were unusual and as a result, a sought after spectacle.

In the village of Abli in southern France the people were dazzled by Bernard and came fully into the church. However he was not to have the same success at Vereil.

Inside the church all raised their right hands professing allegiance to Catholicism. Outside, Bernard tried to persuade those who could not find a seat inside the building.

He was overpowered by the noise of local knights crashing their swords on shields.

He left emptyhanded and angry at the incident. According to author Sean Martin, the Abbot ascribed it more to anticlericalism as to heresy. Who could blame them? Upon returning to Champagne, Martin goes on to note that Bernard said the Languedoc needed "a great deal of preaching". 5.

Obviously the good Abbot thought the wayward Occitans needed serious verbal arm-twisting to see the errors of their ways! Diplomacy is far more preferable than sending in an army which happened after the death of the Abbot.

Though the Abbot spoke out against the Cathar faith, he also asserted, "No sermons are more Christian than theirs and their morals are pure". He admired and recognized in them much of his own way of life and beliefs.

Commonalities included vegetarianism, honesty, vows of poverty and simplicity. Through the differences the tolerant Bernard could identify significant correlations of faith. Of course if he felt sympathy towards them he could never publicly admit it with any strength though he did come close in many statements.

In sharp contrast to the Cathars, Abbot Bernard and Abbess Hildegard were both lovers of nature believing that all the Lord's works were holy and that we are to gain wisdom through the school of the physical.

According to them our doorway to god and the divine *is* the body. In contrast to the Cathars, Catholicism encouraged its members to have large families thus ensuring the next generation of faithful and growing numbers.

All of Europe was officially Catholic at this point in history though there were many minority sects with differing points of view. Perhaps someday we'll have a modern-day brave Cathar come forward and write about their faith as it is today so that we may have a fresh perspective of their lives instead of that of 700 year old legends.

Bernard would have known of the Cathars since boyhood as his Mother's kin were from the Languedoc. Bernard did not take his cohorts to join the Cathari of his mother's land, he chose the Cistercians.

Though there were similarities of thought between Bernard and the Cathars, the differences were insurmountable. Bernard's efforts protected Jesus' physical memory and as his descendant, he would not have been able to view Christ as a purely spiritual being having left no physical imprint on earth. In fact it would have completely flown in the face of all he was trying to accomplish for future generations of Templars and spiritual understanding.

The Saint spent his life building a solid infrastructure within the Catholic community where the Underground Stream could dwell hidden side by side with the unsuspecting and already strong host.

Simply put the numbers of those in the Catholic world were far greater than that of the Cathar and other cults of the day. As an initiate, not to mention a pragmatist, Bernard may have foreseen that at some point in the future hostilities would grow and that the small principalities of the Languedoc would become the target of a much larger and stronger enemy.

Was the writing on the wall during Bernard's life? Very probable. If so, Bernard, as a young man in his teens, had made the right choice of unsuspecting haven in which to safeguard the various streams of the Holy Grail tradition which were near and dear to him.

Bernard was a follower of Augustine of Hippo, the 5th century saint. Augustine taught that in regards to the use of force it must be just and measured with mercy. Pope Innocent III who had called for the crusade against fellow Christians had adopted Thomas Aquinas' stance that the end justifies the means. If Bernard had wanted to use the sword against the Languedoc, he would have.

He was the first to put a sword in the hands of a monk! Many were rocked by the revolutionary concept, they were simply aghast that a monk should be encouraged to be violent.

As upholders of the Ten Commandments, monks were supposed to avoid violence to others, not perpetrate it. If Bernard was willing to implement such extreme change as to create a fighting monk, then he would not have shirked from attacking the Languedoc. He had the influence and could have brought violence to his southern cousins if he had not been an upholder of Saint Augustine's way of life.

Bernard held the Cathars as true fellow Christians, respected their knowledge of esoteric secrets and as co-bearers of Holy Grail traditions. He did not set out to destroy them but to protect them by bringing them into the Catholic Church as part of the Underground Stream in order to preserve their wisdom for the future. His legendary diplomacy skills failed in this instance.

Author Sean Martin suggests that if the succeeding leaders of the church had heeded Saint Bernard's insistence of persuasion over violence against fellow Christians, then the whole horrific episode would have been avoided. Innocent men, women and children would not have been needlessly slaughtered. However as long as the Languedoc held sacred relics and information they were a threat to the political power of Rome.

Left, the Cathar Cross, note the similarity to the Templar Cross Pattee

1. Marvin, Laurence Wade. The Occitan War: A Military and Political History of the Albigensian Crusade, 1209-1218. Cambridge, UK: Cambridge University Press, 2008. p. 4

2. Porete, Marguerite, Edmund Colledge, Judith Grant, and J. C. Marler. The Mirror of Simple Souls. Notre Dame, IN: University of Notre Dame Press, 1999. p. 20

3. Henry, William. "Secrets of The Cathars - Why the Dark Age Church Was Out to Destroy Them." Secrets of The Cathars. http://www.bibliotecapleyades.net/esp_autor_whenry04.htm. Originally Published in Atlantis Rising Dec. 2002 http://www.atlantisrising.com/

4. Gardner, Laurence. Bloodline of the Holy Grail: The Hidden Lineage of Jesus Revealed. Shaftesbury, Dorset: Element, 1996. p. 268

5. Martin, Sean. The Cathars: The Most Successful Heresy of the Middle Ages. Edison, NJ: Chartwell Books, 2006.

Melusine and her mirror of Awareness

Twelve

Death of a Saint

Its achievements were many; Clairvaux Abbey, the rival of Rome, was the jewel in the crown of the Cistercian Order through Saint Bernard's phenomenal life. By 1118, at the beginning of Saint Bernard's career, there were seven successful abbeys which swelled into 351 by 1153 just shortly before his death.

He was termed "The Mellifluous Doctor" in a book about him called The Gallic Bee by Theophilus Reynauld in 1508.

Amongst his many other accolades Bernard, was the Thaumaturgus (miracle worker) of the West. Miracles and healing took place wherever he set foot.

The Abbot was fearless showing unrelenting drive and charisma borne out of passionate belief in his missions, one of which was to safeguard the Western Mystery Tradition within the confines of the Cistercians, the Templars and Benedictines.

He worked his whole life to reform and improve his own church, creating a simpler, uncluttered devotional way with a direct link to god. Bernard is upheld today as the gold standard by reformationists of all Christian movements.

Bernard brought about a love of the Great Mother through direct personal relationship expressed within serenely minimalist and soaring architecture.

His love of the divine reflected in nature was inspiring. He was the gallant knight of the Magdalene through his new religion of Mariology. He did not put the church above the poor, but railed against gold encrusted iconography and greedy clergy.

Contemplation brought about visionary experiences for the Saint that he believed could not be expressed intellectually, as love is not a rational exercise. Modest though confidant he was constantly thrust into the world while striving to maintain a link to his inner solitude. He was the man of the 12th century and his fame was that of a rock star.

Researchers Krstovic´ and Cengage note of Bernard:

"But even while he was alive, Bernard's greatness was assessed not by his writings or deeds but by his life and character. He rejected heresy but did not have a shallow or conservative view of Christian teachings. He believed that faith was to be fostered by persuasion and his eloquent sermons were said to be full of charm and vivacity. Like his letters, his sermons touch on a variety of subjects, great and small, and are addressed to people of diverse stations—evidence of how he could successfully appeal to both unlearned and learned audiences." 1.

Author Christopher Rengers says this of Bernard:

"He seemed to be able to accept a candidate with the worst possible background and yet fashion him into a good monk. Once, he saved a criminal from the hangman and took him to the novitiate. He seized the rope, already around the neck of the criminal, saying: "Give him to me, and I will put him to death with my own hands." He insisted before the presiding Count that he would see to it that the man expiated his offenses by a daily, constant death to self. The criminal became a monk and lived a holy life for some 30 years." 2.

There have been some 500 editions of Bernard's writings published and he was the most read author of his day. His influence was keenly felt by Saint Francis of Assisi, who was an inheritor within the Tradition and just one example of many who took onboard the spiritual model of the famous Doctor of the Church. Bernard's timeless works are relevant today as they are underpinned by a central core of universal teachings and cosmic law.

The Monstrous Chimera

Bernard once called himself a Chimera or the monstrous dual being of his age. On a strictly surface level it would be easy to look no further than to state that people in positions of great responsibility must make difficult decisions at times that are painful and even disliked.

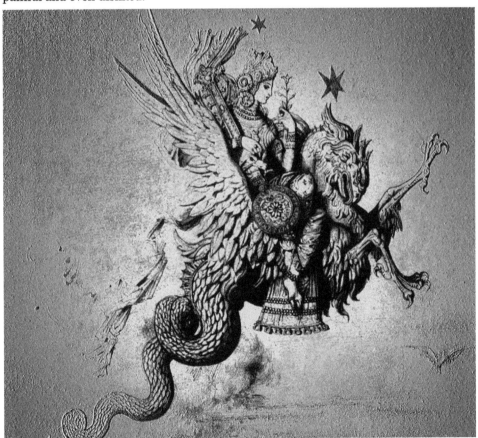

Gustave Moreau Chimera, ink on paper, 1865

The Secret Dossier of a
Knight Templar of the Sangreal

He could be expressing the burden of making choices borne out of a lose-lose situation. Like his female counterpart Abbess Hildegard, Bernard did not shrink from making the unpopular choice even if it upset his own fold, the broader European community and those close to him.

The Abbot was concerned with making ethical decisions as he understood them to be during his lifetime and cultural context. We are talking about no mere politician but a skilled spiritual leader who changed the course of history.

Creating the first fighting monk was as divisive as a modern doctor who had taken the Hippocratic Oath, swearing to protect life and also taking on the mantel of capital punishment.

We must look past the obvious explanation for his cryptic comment on his own personhood as the Chimera is a fearsome ancient beast which is filled with coded esoteric meanings.

The Abbot had undergone the Chemical Marriage of Initiation personified most typically by the Caduceus, which is a staff surrounded by twining dual serpents culminating at the top as both a trinity image and image of oneness and enlightenment. Thus a fully integrated human being is created with both equal but dual parts male and female, with the capacity to use either energy when needed. The Caduceus is familiar to us all as the graphical representation of the medical profession for its healing connotations and connection to the divine.

A Chimera is always female. Homer describes her as an evil fire breathing beast. Her roots predate Roman and Greek mythology with a clear sister figure in the Sphinx, a famous Egyptian wisdom icon and one of the most massive ancient monuments on earth.

The front half of the Chimera's body is a fire breathing lion. The body is that of a goat with the hind of a dragon's tail. This is an alchemical image just as is the Caduceus.

The lion represents great heart-courage needed for transcendence. The goat is associated with the planet Venus which over an eight year period creates a pentagram in the night sky thus implying knowledge of astronomy and that the earth itself was round and travelled around the sun.

Lastly the dragon is a representation of the Serpent Tradition in the west. The tail of the dragon is an allusion to the ability of moving through the etheric planes and mastery over oneself. It is the energy which rises in the body to form the Caduceus.

The feminine and clearly dangerous Chimera is a reference to the hidden mystery school in which Bernard had been born into and became one of its most famous leaders.

Sacred abilities embodied by the fierce Chimera are a double-edged sword of light and darkness, whose strengths must be responsibly used for the good of all and not of personal gain.

Of all the possible figures in history, Dante Alighieri chose the mystic Saint Bernard as the final guiding light in his Divine Comedy in the 14th century. The author was an avid supporter of the Knights Templar even after their persecution when it was dangerous to be associated with them.

Authors Picknett and Prince put forward the case that Dante, Bernard and the Templars were part of a mysterious love tradition embodied by the term Wisdom-Sophia. The initiatic tradition shrouded in terms of sexual union lead the seeker to the attainment of the Holy Grail.

Death of a Saint

Jonathan Black also ascribes a sub-rosa culture to the Cistercian fighting monks:

"The Sufis, the Cathars, the Knights Templar, Brunetto Latini and Dante worshipped the angel-goddess Sapientia, the Wisdom of higher visionary intelligence. They reached a place where the eyesight has another sight, the hearing another hearing and the voice another voice." 3.

Abbot Bernard died at Clairvaux in 1153 AD and was swiftly canonized shortly thereafter in 1174 AD. The speed of canonization is due to the fact he was held as a saint during his lifetime.

He has one everlasting tie to his Black Virgin. Saint Amator was by tradition a servant to the Holy Family, Joseph, Mother Mary and the young Jesus. He supposedly travelled to Gaul and was married to Saint Veronica who is famous for her veil bearing an imprint of Christ's face which figures prominently in Templar reverence.

Saint Amator built the shrine of the Black Virgin in France which became known as Rocamadour where Bernard had visited and worshiped.

Amator's own feast day is held on the 20th of August. This was also the feast date chosen for Saint Bernard and is now erroneously thought to be his actual date of death. He is linked eternally through this date, as the author of Mary Magdalene's religion, under the guise of his beloved Black Virgin the Immortal Isis. 4.

La Ghirlandata by Dante Gabriel Rossetti 1873

1. Krstovic, Jelena, and Gale Cengage. "Bernard of Clairvaux Essay - Critical Essays - ENotes.com." Enotes.com. February 01, 2010. Accessed August 05, 2015. http://www.enotes.com/topics/bernard-clairvaux#critical-essays-bernard-clairvaux. Vol.71

2. Rengers, Christopher. The 33 Doctors of the Church. Rockford, IL: TAN Books and Publishers, 2000. p. 287

3. Black, Jonathan. The Sacred History: How Angels, Mystics and Higher Intelligence Made Our World. Quercus, 2013. p. 272

4. Begg, Ean C. M. The Cult of the Black Virgin. 2nd ed. London: Arkana, 1996. p. 26

The Secret Dossier of a
Knight Templar of the Sangreal

The Shadow by Edmund Blair Leighton 1909

Although the Knight is not a Templar - perhaps he is going to join them as a lay brother as many of the nobility did - leaving their wives behind for a journey to the Holy Land - hoping to return.

Thirteen

In Praise of the New Knighthood

Saint Bernard wrote the Rule of Poor Fellow-Soldiers of Christ and of the Temple of Solomon when he was just 28 years old. The Rule was a manual of conduct by which the Knights of Christ would live out their lives in service of their duties to the Order.

In a revolutionary move, Saint Bernard put a sword in the hands of his mystical white-clad Cistercian monks and created the first professional elite fighting force in Europe. They were known as the Warrior Monks and were unique amongst chivalrous orders; though the solitude of monastic life was not practiced literally as they were squarely engaged in the affairs of the world.

The initial members were already accomplished full-fledged knights with superb skills that would make any fabled Arthurian Knight take notice. Indeed many of the Legends of King Arthur would spring from their mystical and martial adventures as a coded way to pass on their mystery traditions. They were the SAS or Special Military Service of their day and conducted their lives under a highly disciplined and ethical code which automatically excluded those of a less devotional nature.

Bernard practically hijacked the Council of Troyes in approximately 1128 AD, dominating the proceedings and sang the praises of the New Knighthood. Once again the charismatic Abbot was able to sway others in the support and creation of his most famous contribution to history.

Bernard de Clairvaux:

"This is, I say, a new kind of knighthood and one unknown to the ages gone by. It ceaselessly wages a twofold war both against flesh and blood and against a spiritual army of evil in the heavens. When someone strongly resists a foe in the flesh, relying solely on the strength of the flesh, I would hardly remark it, since this is common enough. And when war is waged by spiritual strength against vices or demons, this, too, is nothing remarkable, praiseworthy as it is, for the world is full of monks. But when the one sees a man powerfully girding himself with both swords and nobly marking his belt, who would not consider it worthy of all wonder, the more so since it has been hitherto unknown? He is truly a fearless knight and secure on every side, for his soul is protected by the armor of faith just as his body is protected by armor of steel. He is thus doubly armed and need fear neither demons nor men. Not that he fears death–no, he desires it. Why should he fear to live or fear to die when for him to live is Christ, and to die is gain? Gladly and faithfully he stands for Christ, but he would prefer to be dissolved and to be with Christ, by far the better thing." [1].

A new hero was on the scene as well and spoke of the fledgling Order in an understated manner quite different than the fiery Abbot Bernard's own delivery. Hugh de Payens the first Grand Master laid out his plan for the organisation's activities in Europe and the Middle East, its goals and the rigorous devotional structure.

The Secret Dossier of a
Knight Templar of the Sangreal

No member could have personal wealth and all donations were to the good of the whole. Thus their vow of personal poverty was encapsulated in the famous image of the two knights on horseback who were said to be too poor to own more than one horse. It is also an image denoting accountability. Other early symbols were the famous equilateral Red Cross, the Beuseant flag of a black square above a white also known as the Piebald Standard.

Saint Bernard's friend, Count Hugh de Champagne, did not become the first Grand Master of the Knights Templar but the Count's vassal did! Under what mystifying circumstances does a medieval vassal gain higher rank than his master?

This is an interesting indication of the meritocracy ideal which is a hallmark in all spiritual movements around the globe and true democratic governments. The Templars were hundreds of years ahead of their time politically let alone philosophically.

Laurence Gardner also states that the original group of Templars included the following:

"Hugues de Payens, the first Grand Master of the Templars, was a cousin and vassal of the Comte de Champagne. His second-in-command was the Flemish knight Godefroi Saint Omer, and another recruit was Andre de Montbard, [brother to Bernard's mother the Lady Aleth] a kinsman of the Count of Burgundy. In 1120, Fulk, Comte d'Anjou (father of Geoffrey Plantagenet) also joined the Order, and he was followed in 1124 by Hugues, Comte de Champagne." 2.

The other four knights were Archambaud de Saint Amand, Geoffrey Bisol, Rosal, and Gondemare, though little is known of the latter two individuals.

The original nine Knights were granted use of Solomon's Temple as their base by the Patriarch of Jerusalem. It is now known as the Al Aqsa Mosque which sits on Temple Mount.

The publicly established reason for the formation of the Templars was to protect the roads leading to the Holy Land. This is impractical at best and with only nine knights it is obvious that they could not possibly have policed the roads or sea-ways until their numbers grew. Indeed the original knights spent a great deal of their time excavating Temple Mount and would have had little time for soul searching tourists.

It is quite popular to state that protecting pilgrims was not the actual reason for the Templar's formation but it is actually one very important role that continues to this very day.

As Paulo Coelho says:

"While most of the nobility of the time was concerned only with enriching itself through the labor of the serfs, the Knights Templar dedicated their lives, their fortunes, and their swords to one cause only: the protection of the pilgrims that walked the Road to Jerusalem. In the behaviour of the Knights, the pilgrims found a model for their own search for wisdom." 3.

In Praise of the New Knighthood

We must keep in mind that pilgrimages were paths of initiation, fraught with physical dangers and difficulties if one opted for such a route to inner wisdom such as outlined in Paulo Coelho's book The Pilgrimage.

The Templars acted as guides to chosen initiates who had been gifted with a transcendent mindset, helping novices overcome physical dangers, metaphysical and psychological in nature.

These were not your average pilgrims. This is a very different viewpoint than simply acknowledging that the Templars physically protected all who chose to walk the major Pilgrimage Routes though all did benefit from the strong presence of the Templars as their numbers grew.

Aside from setting up an infrastructure of the Path of the Initiate along the four main Pilgrimage Routes, their activities included excavating the Temple Mount and as Laurence Gardner states:

"They were the King's front-line diplomats in a Muslim environment, and in this capacity they endeavoured to make due amends for the actions of unruly Crusaders against the Sultan's defenseless subjects." 4.

Aside from diplomatic duties the original nine knights spent a good portion of their time tunneling under Solomon's Temple; leaving behind such evidence as discarded sword shards, spurs and other articles used in medieval archaeology.

The date of their inception varies from before 1114 AD with a mention from the Bishop of Chartres regarding the 'Soldiers of Christ' and their activities on Temple Mount, to 1119 AD. Hugh de Payens was leading this small group of chivalrous monks for some time before the Council of Troyes granted their Rule through Saint Bernard in 1128 AD.

The Knights spent the better part of a decade or more in the Holy Land before returning in triumph to Europe and Bernard's glowing reviews. It is highly probable they had discovered scrolls which contained ancient Judaic knowledge, both scriptural and practical along with the Temple's most sacred of holy objects.

It has been speculated that along with Bernard's patronage, their discoveries were the reason behind their success. Much has been written on this subject and interesting clues abound, one of which is carved on the North portal of Chartres Cathedral which of course the Templars assisted in building. The Ark of the Covenant sits on a humble cart in the action of being moved.

The Guardians of the Ark

The wisest of all Kings, Solomon, built a Temple to house the Ark of the Covenant through which god's will was communicated to the High Priest. According to tradition it contained the Ten Commandments also known as the Tables of the Law. It was also said to have housed the High Priest Aaron's rod of sapphire and a pot of manna.

Hebrew lore indicates that the First Temple was built by Solomon in 960 BC standing for over 400 years but was destroyed by the Babylonians in 422 BC.
The Ark may have been taken into captivity but the Babylonians make no issue of it

in their writings or inventories. However there are multiple stories and hiding places regarding the Ark since the Babylonian Captivity which seem to be in conflict with one another.

Ethiopia has an interesting claim. There are medieval stories of its presence in Ireland, the Languedoc, Wales and in England. Even South Africa lays claim to it as does Mount Nebo in Jordan.

These seemingly impossible and multiple resting places may be explained as either advertising for pilgrim trade, or perhaps a more compelling argument is that there was actually were more than one Ark! I am not suggesting that all prior locations are accurate, indeed that would be foolish, but to allow for the concept that if one Ark could be created then surely it had to be a repeatable process.

Moses was raised in the Egyptian Priesthood, mastered their ancient craft and brought with him the technological and sacred information on how to build an Ark along with esoteric lore. This would have been guarded with all due care but as adopted prince he would have been able to gain access to archival material.

It may be that the information was lost to the Order at varying points (possibly during the destruction of the Second Temple in 70AD) but was the knowledge or the sacred object itself retrieved during their descendants' time - the Templars - in the Middle East?

I was told by The Comte de Medici that Hugh de Payens original nine knights discovered secrets and important objects. He said that upon the dissolution of the order in 1307 that the most important items had been taken to Nova Scotia for safe keeping along with valuable staff members and inner Temple sacred treasures including the Ark!

Aside from alternative texts or histories that had been excluded from the Bible and dangerous genealogy documents, it is possible that they also discovered an instruction manual on how to build an Ark.

According to author Graham Phillips, English Templar leader, Ralph de Sudeley brought an Ark back to England in 1180 from Mount Sinai and also retrieved the esoteric scrolls as to how to build these holy objects. 5.

Is this search for the Ark or other such important documents mere fantastical legend or might there be circumstances which allow for the Templars' interest in these holy objects in the first place?

What drove their secret activities under Temple Mount? Why did they go straight to Temple Mount and spend nine years digging? How did the Templars know that any of the Arks were still in existence?

The Second Temple was built in 516 BC and was destroyed, this time by the Romans in 70 AD. It is often stated that the Second Temple did not house the Ark as it had been lost, however Revelations does mention an ethereal Ark being present as a vision.

"And the temple of God was opened in heaven, and there was seen in his temple the ark of his testament: and there were lightnings, and voices, and thunderings, and an earthquake, and great hail." KJV (Cambridge Ed.)

I do think this is coded. It may be that a special Holy of Hollies had been built deep beneath the Temple Mount but it was decided at this time to keep it a secret as the

Ark had been lost to the Israelites more than once. In 1180 BC it was taken from them by the Philistines for seven months but returned to them as it was causing plagues within the Philistine cities.

Moses with the Ark of the Covenant

illustration from the 1728 *Figures de la Bible*; illustrated by Gerard Hoet (1648–1733) and others, and published by P. de Hondt in The Hague; image courtesy Bizzell Bible Collection, University of Oklahoma Libraries

I would put forward the suggestion that the reason we do not have public knowledge of the Ark is that it is simply too dangerous to be known to have possession of it.

The Ark does not need to be displayed in public in order for it to be an effective vehicle for Light in the world. There are legends within Great Britain of esoteric orders and covens that were engaged in astral battles with Hitler, modern Templars being one such group.

It is a well-known fact that Hitler practiced the black arts, having taken Templar symbols, chivalric symbols and those of life bearing ancient cultures, twisting them to his own code of malevolence.

It is a mystery that Hitler never invaded Britain nor for that matter – Napoleon -

who also chose to engage his battles elsewhere, regardless of the fact that Britain would have been easier to conquer than Russia! Yes, Britain was being heroically and physically defended but the lure of Russian resources pulled both Hitler and Napoleon. Occultists of the time insist that this battle of wills between Hitler and the forces of Light were very real with direct physical ramifications.

The Ark was not mentioned on the inventory list made by the Romans upon the Temple's capture and ruination either. Guardians in charge of such valuable sacred objects would have buried them in a protected chamber long before; removal was impossible under the circumstances of siege or occupation.

It is possible that the Tradition lost knowledge of how to make the Arks at this point since the scrolls may have been buried along with the object of Divine Will.

Could the Magdalene have taken an Ark to France? Risking discovery by Romans en-route to France with the Ark would have been too dangerous. I don't think she would have been able to retrieve it under the nose of the Romans or those hostile to Christ in the Temple, even though their enemies may have lacked knowledge of a possible hidden chamber under their own feet!

The priest kings of the bloodline of Christ had fled to Southern France approximately 35 years prior to the destruction of the Temple in 70 AD. The timeframe was within one generation of living memory of Mary Magdalene, whose children were most assuredly alive and with growing families of their own.

In other words, first-hand knowledge of the Ark's hiding place and its transmission to family survivors/supporters seems assured. Some of their numbers had stayed in Jerusalem. Had they managed to get word to those in France that the Ark was still safely buried some time past, and knowledge of this stayed within the priestly order for over 1000 years before they were able to retrieve the articles of their faith?

I would state that the obvious answer is yes and this is precisely the mission and main reason for the Templars fixed attention during their years on Temple Mount. The small carving of the Ark on the portal of Chartres Cathedral remains mute testimony to this possibility.

1. Greenia, Conrad. Number Nineteen ed. Vol. 7. Kalamazoo: Cistercian Publications, 1977.

2. Gardner, Laurence. Bloodline of the Holy Grail: The Hidden Lineage of Jesus Revealed. Shaftesbury, Dorset: Element, 1996. p. 256

3. Coelho, Paulo, and Alan R. Clarke. The Pilgrimage: A Contemporary Quest for Ancient Wisdom. London: Thorsons, 1997. p. 197

4. Gardner, Laurence. Bloodline of the Holy Grail: The Hidden Lineage of Jesus Revealed. Shaftesbury, Dorset: Element, 1996. p. 256

5. Phillips, Graham. The Templars and the Ark of the Covenant: The Discovery of the Treasure of Solomon. Rochester, VT: Bear &, 2004. p. 162

Fourteen

Europe Embraces the Soldiers of Christ

Upon their return to Europe their numbers exploded with noble sons racing to join and others gifting large donations of money, goods and land. Europe had fallen in love with the Templars, through the tireless promotional tours of Bernard de Clairvaux.

This feat is impossible to appreciate today, but communication was almost insurmountable, taking many months for a letter to arrive if at all. People disappeared forever on journeys, leaving loved ones in the dark as to their fate.

Under normal circumstances it would have been conceivable that the growth of the Order would have taken decades but due to the incredible energy of the Saint, it became an overnight phenomenon.

One suggestion is that the new knightly order was holding the church hostage with dangerous documents and that their overnight success was not entirely voluntary on the part of the church.

The Templars were certainly no longer 'poor' nor would they ever be so again during their almost 200 years of public life. Everything was going to Bernard's and Payens' master plan as their Mother House, the Cistercian Order was also going through extraordinary growth as well. The white knights copied much of the Cistercian organisation and adapted it to their own needs quite successfully.

It is indeed a shame that we know so little about the first Grand Master as he would have been in charge of proceedings in the Middle East, quite independently of Abbot Bernard but certainly in concert with the agreed upon goals.

Hugh de Payens would have had to be incredibly talented across a wide spectrum of administration abilities aside from the expected arts of war. Diplomacy, organisational and natural leadership traits would have been highly valued along with his standing as an adept.

His compatriots would have been no less interesting and gifted. These initial nine men were hand-picked for sensitive operations which required a great deal of skill, each bringing their own unique experiences to the table.

The Templars made the Holy Land their prime objective as they were born in the wake of the First Crusade. They were the first to enter a battlefield and the last to leave. They were not allowed to retreat unless given orders to do so and were expected to handle odds of three to one.

They took the heaviest losses in every battle; their bravery was without question, as was their word. Other military forces went into battle with full knowledge that the famous discipline of the Templars could be counted upon under any circumstances.

The Secret Dossier of a
Knight Templar of the Sangreal

A Knight Templar could not be ransomed and knew he would be executed if taken prisoner. If the white knights were ordered to die on the battle field, *they did.* Bernard wrote:

'A Templar Knight is truly a fearless knight, and secure on every side, for his soul is protected by the armor of faith, just as his body is protected by the armor of steel. He is thus doubly-armed, and need fear neither demons nor men' 1.

Amongst one of the more amazing accomplishments of the white knights was the invention of early banking which included charging interest on loans.

It was highly significant as usury was against the tenants of the Catholic faith. Yet they were given permission to charge interest. Only the Jewish population charged interest on loans prior to the Templars.

Many European monarchs found themselves indebted to the Templars and some begrudgingly as the Knights were not such easy prey as the often hapless Jewish brethren.

The Templar treasuries did help protect pilgrims on their perilous journey to the Holy Land or indeed at home in Europe, as roads were not policed and being attacked was almost a certainty. Pilgrims would deposit their wealth at a nearby temple-treasury where they would be given a coded chit that could be cashed in at another temple-treasury when their destination was reached. It was never in doubt that the Templars could be trusted with the life savings of the faithful. If only our modern day bankers that caused the criminal recession of 2008 were of the same ilk.

The Templars launched into building cathedrals, churches, castles, priories, farms and fortresses in Europe, the British Isles and the Middle East. Many of the architectural mysteries of the Middle Ages were built by the Tradition who were masters of code within the Seven Liberal Arts embodied by the spirit of Philo-Sophia.

If they were not building a church or cathedral the Templars were funding and assisting in the creation of the great rose windows across Europe, imbuing them with great beauty and geometrical messages. Author Louis Charpentier of The Mysteries of the Chartres Cathedral suggests that the vivid blue glass of this particular cathedral's rose window cannot be reproduced with our advanced knowledge today. 2.

Indications of the Templar's demise were written early in their career through the destructive emotions of greed and jealousy from those who coveted their wealth and secrets.

King Louis VI (1081 to 1137), also called Louis the Fat, ordered that no further castles or land, regardless of ownership, could be passed onto the Templars; such was their success in France. Louis obviously considered them a political threat from the outset.

These rather hard feelings would fester in the twisted mind of Louis' descendant, Philip the Fair, with disastrous results for the Templars and indeed Europe in the ensuing dark aftermath.

Other monarchs would similarly be disgruntled when King Alphonso I of Spain died in 1131 leaving one third of his kingdom to not only the Templars but to two other monastic orders as well, as he had no other physical heir.

Europe Embraces the Soldiers of Christ

The Moors had been a constant concern for Alphonso and he viewed the Templars and Hospitallers as the only parties capable of protecting his country from another invasion. Though it was contested by other nobles and took years of legal debate the Templars settled for much less than the original will stipulated, however they did maintain significant holdings. The white knights were now a target and watched for every misstep and possible weakness.

The Templars were to a large degree invincible as they were not held accountable to any secular ruler and only to the Pope; nor was a Templar held accountable to the laws of any land but only that of a Papal Curia. Inner discipline was strict, however, and punishment was a public affair, discouraging criminal or anti-social behaviour amongst their numbers. Sadly their good fortune and grace were about to change.

A Day of Infamy

In the summer of 1306 King Philip of France arrested - taking the wealth of the Jewish financiers - and then expelled all Jewish peoples from his country.

But that was not enough, he wanted more. Open greed was Philip's modus operandi. The absolute monarch was facing dire economic problems and his people were starving through mismanagement of finances.

Fleeing an angry Parisian mob he was admitted to the Paris Temple for refuge. Having been rescued, he spent the night enjoying the hospitality of the Templars and it is surmised this is when he discovered the true extent of riches safe guarded in the treasury. 3.

It did not escape his notice – never mind that a portion of it belonged to depositors hoping to retrieve it, after all he had just robbed and forced the Jewish population from their homes and country.

In an effort to gain control of the most feared and respected amongst the monastic military orders, he encouraged the Templars to give him the highest rank of Grand Master for which he was flatly refused. No doubt the Templars did not wish to become another weapon in the King's arsenal for use in his conquests of other neighbouring kingdoms.

Next Philip took an unprecedented move by taxing the French clergy which created strife with Rome. Pope Bonifice VIII responded with a Papal Bull forbidding the acquisition of their properties by the French Crown.

The escalation caused a long drawn out diplomatic battle that ended badly for the Pope. If history has recalled Philip as a villain then surely his most trusted agent Guillaume de Nogaret has been justly given the vilest of accolades through time as that of an evil man.

Fantasy author Katherine Kurtz uses him as an esoteric agent of evil against the forces of light in her Templar novels. Ms. Kurtz was one of the first to write novels about the Templars' well before Dan Brown spurred the genre forward.

Nogaret attacked and arrested the Pope who died of stress four weeks later though he'd been rescued. This was not the only Pope to run afoul of Nogaret.

Less than ten months into his papacy Pope Benedict XI was poisoned paving the way for Philip to gain control of the church. Philip convened with those loyal to him amongst the nobility and bishops, placing Clement V on the Throne of Saint Peter.

Rome at this time was dangerous and it was not uncommon for violence to break out between ruling families who each wanted to place their own son on the Papal Throne.

Philip took advantage of this and Clement agreed to move his new court to Avignon. The new Pope would not be able to stand against the ruthless monarch as his own life was in danger now that the official seat was within physical reach of the King.

Meanwhile support for the Order was dwindling as heavy losses were being incurred by the Crusader States. Ostensibly the Templars' sole goal was the claiming of the Holy Land for Christendom, never mind the growing merchant trade at home which was creating a European boon.

Monarchs were increasingly concerned about having bored armed monks within their kingdoms beholden only to the Pope; basically the Templars had become a State within a State.

There were those of the nobility who were very wary of these Knights who no longer seemed to have a reason for their existence should the foothold in the Middle East be lost. What would they turn their attention to next?

These Templars were free to cross borders at will making them potentially dangerous foes. The white knights were becoming a victim of their own success and paranoia reigned amongst those who were not their friends. However the economic benefits were obvious and it was short sighted not to notice that local economies were being lifted by the Knights activities.

Like their parent Order, the Cistercians, the Templars were immersed in a broad spectrum of businesses. They owned farms, vineyards, stables, armouries, engaged in tile making and animal husbandry, wool and oil. They had shipyards and either built vessels to sail the seas, or in the early days hired merchant ships.

One could count on the Templars to deliver you safely to the Holy Land and not sell you into slavery upon arrival to Muslims as some unscrupulous merchants practiced. They would not throw hapless pilgrims overboard on the way to the Holy Land as some traffickers were guilty.

The Templars actually employed local people and their banking services were of great value including as executors of wills and settling disputes. The preceptories had living quarters for the Templars of course, but often other sections were built for the lay brethren that were employed by the white knights. Europeans of all walks of life and economic standing had benefited by the Templars involving themselves in villages, towns and cities.

Philip knew that the Teutonic Knights and the Hospitallers were discussing forming their own monastic states in Prussia and Rhodes. He suspected that the Templars were considering such a move themselves. His fear was that they would choose Southern France, Magdalene country as their new Templar State. If he could not find a way to bring them to heel then a preemptive strike was necessary as far as he was concerned. He made a last ditch effort to bring the Templars under his control through the new Pope in his clutches.

Grand Master of the Knights Templar, Jacques de Molay, was lured to Paris to serve as a pall bearer at the funeral of Philip's sister in-law Catherine; he'd also made de Molay the godfather of one of his sons! Both were prestigious honours of friendship.

He was also asked to come to discuss the amalgamation of the Templars into the Order of Saint John also known as the Knights Hospitallers, considered by many to be their rival Order.

Jacques de Molay flatly refused this pressure by the Pope and others who wanted to see the Templars broken. Even the Knights Hospitallers were not in favour of what was seen as a hostile amalgamation. The poor excuse given by the Pope was that of the diminished Templar role in the Crusades, which were failing, they were now redundant and needed reorganization.

Friday the 13th has come to mean bad luck which few take seriously today, but nevertheless this particular date has a sinister history. In the pre-dawn hours of Friday the 13th October 1307, almost 200 years after Hugh de Payens and Saint Bernard's successful appeal to the Council of Troyes, many of the white knights were arrested by a power monger in a synchronised raid across France.

It had been in the planning for months, maybe years. Though Philip the Fair may have been a handsome man, the King of France has been remembered by history as the antithesis of 'fair'.

Philip le Bel was involved in expensive wars and had borrowed considerable sums from the Templars whose headquarters were in Paris, his capitol city. In keeping with his true nature, the last thing the King wanted to do was pay back his debts. Upon robbing the Jewish peoples the King had turned his eye on the Templars and after failing to bring them under his rule he unjustly incarcerated all that did not manage to escape.

1. Greenia, Conrad. Number Nineteen ed. Vol. 7. Kalamazoo: Cistercian Publications, 1977.

2. Charpentier, Louis. The Mysteries of Chartres Cathedral. London: Research into Lost Knowledge Organisation; Distributed by Thorsons, 1972. p. 138

3. Butler, Alan, and Stephen Dafoe. The Warriors and the Bankers. Hersham, Surrey: Lewis Masonic, 2006.

Selected Bibliography

Robinson, John J. Born in Blood: The Lost Secrets of Freemasonry. New York: M. Evans &, 1989.

Ralls, Karen. Knights Templar Encyclopedia: The Essential Guide to the People, Places, Events, and Symbols of the Order of the Temple. Franklin Lakes, NJ: New Page Books, 2007.

Vauchez, Andre, and Adrian Walford. Encyclopedia of the Middle Ages. Chicago: Fitzroy Dearborn Publishers, 2000.

Bredero, Adriaan Hendrik. Bernard of Clairvaux: Between Cult and History. Grand Rapids, MI: W.B. Eerdmans, 1996.

Bernard, Samuel John Eales, and Francis Aidan Gasquet. Some Letters of Saint Bernard, Abbot of Clairvaux. London: J. Hodges, 1904.

Fifteen

Trial by Fire

"To appreciate the impact of what happened, think of the President of the United States coming on a State visit to London and staying in the American Embassy. Imagine that the morning after a formal banquet with the Royal family and high ranking officials at Buckingham Palace, the American Embassy is stormed by SAS troops. The President is seized, stripped and tortured, and the Queen appears at the torture scene to gloat in person. This is the nearest modern equivalent to the actions that took place in Paris seven hundred years ago. And it took the whole world by surprise." Robert Lomas 1.

Fortunately the USA and the British Government have a deep friendship making such a scene absurd nor would the Queen's sincere professional character built upon her deep commitment to service ever permit her to be involved in such diabolical machinations. But author Robert Lomas' analogy is absolutely perfect as to the impact and shock this created across Europe and the British Isles.

Philip ignited the flames of rumour that the Templars were heretics who denied Christ and spat on the Cross. They were accused of worshipping idols, engaging in homosexual acts and acts of outrageous depravity.

Honestly none of the charges levied against them were original in the slightest as they were already in use against those who were deemed heretics and were being pursued, tortured and murdered by the Inquisition. Much has been written about the confessions taken under torture and it is very interesting reading though the whole affair is tragically ludicrous.

There are indications they venerated a human head that can only be that of a representation of John the Baptist their patron saint. At some point it was stated that a head in their possession was enchanted and could speak!

The representation of a head was sometimes referred to as the Baphoment (a name which sprung up under torture) which translates into 'Sophia' (meaning feminine wisdom or the wisdom of Christ) using a Judaic form of code called Gematria which was used into antiquity.

A Templar family was also known to have had in their possession the Veil of Veronica. A man's head may be seen on the veil which is said to have been the image of Jesus who had used the veil to wipe his face and gave it back to St. Veronica with the image metaphysically imprinted in the fabric. There is no reference to this event in the bible but seems to have grown out of the 13th century during the Templar period – perhaps out of discovered relics from under Temple Mount?

Templecombe in Somerset held a secret for many centuries. A painted wood panel was found hidden behind a wall to protect it either from Henry the VIII or Cromwell. The panel was discovered upon a restoration project in recent years.

It is perhaps the head of Christ and has similar characteristics to the Shroud of Turin; though most likely the painting could be that of their patron the Baptist.

It has been identified without doubt as that of Templar sacred art and an indication that the Shroud was of importance to the Order and had been in their possession at one time which research bears out. The Order did have a vested interest in the veneration of 'heads' either as a representation of John the Baptist, Jesus or other Saints they held in esteem such as St Catherine of Alexandria. Having a relic on hand was not at all unusual as all churches and monasteries of this time period had the relics of saints on their altars.

The Heroic Jacques de Molay

"The standard nature of the confessions bespeaks the standard application of a questionnaire, which as in most subsequent witchcraft trials guaranteed a remarkable uniformity in details." Peter Partner 2.

Jacques de Molay joined the Order at the age of 21 which is the youngest that a man may enter into Freemasonry today. I have heard of similar esoteric orders in the modern world also holding their minimum age at 21 while others are actually at the age of 40! Jacques de Molay rose to become the   Grand Preceptor of England before becoming the Grand Master.

According to Knight and Lomas the Shroud of Turin was created as a macabre relic using the 70 year old Grand Master as the model. He was literally crucified on a door and then revived. Could de Molay have been a member of the Rex Deus family line and was barbarically mocked as a Second Messiah? 3.

If so it was indeed a miracle that he survived the brutality as evidence of ancient bodily fluids attest to the great physical torture which seeped onto the linen. This is a fantastic theory as de Molay was said to have been near 6'2" and as a Templar wore his hair in the fashion of a Judaic Priest thus matching the visage on the Shroud.

As a good looking man of unusual height he represented the ideal of Christ himself and would have been very striking during his time. That de Molay was barbarically tortured is known, however his part in the making of the Turin Shroud is rightly questioned.

Authors Clive Prince and Lynn Picknett have questioned the authenticity of the Shroud and have concluded that the only individual with the skills to create it would have been that of the master Leonardo da Vinci. 4.

He was the first artist in our history to have dissected the human body to understand in greater depth how a body functions in order to portray its correct form more fully, giving his works a haunting realism. His was the only hand during the Renaissance period that was qualified to have created the Shroud of Turin.

A recent replica of the shroud has been successfully made using a camera obscura and it has been determined that da Vinci knew of the process and used it to create the compelling figure on the shroud.

The master artist da Vinci may have indeed had the last laugh as the face on the Turin Shroud seems to match perfectly with his own profile thus giving us – as the handsome man he was – the most copied visage of Christ down through the centuries.

The Secret Dossier of a
Knight Templar of the Sangreal

According to a forensic scientist working on the project to unravel the mysteries of the Shroud; only a photographed image could have transferred the face onto the shroud.

If a head were to be wrapped by fabric and the imprint remained once the fabric were removed from the face and the fabric flattened out again – the distortion would be rather alien if not ugly in nature as a two dimensional representation had been created and not the three dimensional image that is on the shroud today.

It is simply impossible without the aid of a camera to create the visage on the shroud. I find this the most compelling bit of evidence that the shroud is a 15th century work of art but a fake nonetheless.

The body fluids from the tortured man on the shroud must have come from a corpse obtained at a hospital by Leonardo to fake the blood and other signs of distress.

The de Charney family is a direct relation to Jaques de Molay. They claim to have had the Shroud of Turin since the Crusades. It has been surmised that their copy of it was a rather bad fake which had been later purchased by the Savoys and hidden for 50 years until the services of Leonardo were acquired to recreate the relic. Interestingly enough both Leonardo da Vinci and Jaques de Molay were of a similar height and appearance.

As much as I would like the shroud to be that of Jesus himself or even that of de Molay, I highly doubt it. I have a background in dress design and am familiar with the nature of fabric. It simply does not last long under damp conditions that many European households would have been subjected to prior to central heating.

Fabric simply starts to shatter literally and discolour. A maximum of 500 years is possible at the most when treated with the utmost care and under modern climate control technology.

It may be that in the Middle East a garment or shroud might have a longer life if kept in dry conditions, but certainly not in Europe. If the shroud of Christ existed and was kept, it disintegrated centuries ago even if it came to Europe through Mary Magdalene and eventually found its way into Templar family hands.

It would not have lasted. Is it possible that with the natural deterioration of the original, that a copy might have been made by the de Charney family to keep the memory of the original shroud alive and then again by the Savoy's through the gifted hand of Leonardo da Vinci?

Vatican researcher Dr. Barbara Frale, has determined that the Templars may have had the Shroud in their keeping since the sacking of Constantinople in 1204. 5.

She contends that a young initiate in 1287 was shown a mysterious linen with the visage of what he took to be Christ and was required to kiss the figure's feet three times.

Dr. Frale surmises that this ceremony could have been the origins of the accusation of Templars worshiping a bearded head. However there is rather a large difference between worshiping the total figure on the Shroud, kissing its feet and worshiping a head.

John the Baptist was their patron saint after all, why wouldn't the Templars have venerated a head as a symbol of their connection to Christ? It is an understandable correlation however as she was doing her best to absolve the Templars of any guilt - as if this is even an issue - 700 years after the fact!

Trial by Fire

Of course the Templars had more than one important relic in their care. The Shroud certainly and other researchers have made interesting discoveries regarding evidence of John the Baptist's head and its mystical attributes. The Shroud lays protected in the royal chapel of the Cathedral of Saint John the Baptist in Turin, Italy.

Veil of Veronica by Albrecht Durer 1513
reproduced by FoekeNoppert
The Veil has often been associated with the Shroud of Turin

1. Lomas, Robert. Turning the Templar Key: Martyrs, Freemasons and the Secret of the True Cross of Christ. Hersham: Lewis Masonic, 2007. p. 15
2. Partner, Peter. The Murdered Magicians: The Templars and Their Myth. Oxford: Oxford University Press, 1982. p. 68
3. Hopkins, Marilyn, Graham Simmans, and Tim Wallace-Murphy. Rex Deus: The True Mystery of Rennes-le-Château and the Dynasty of Jesus. Shaftesbury: Element, 2000.
4. Picknett, Lynn, and Clive Prince. The Templar Revelation: Secret Guardians of the True Identity of Christ. New York, NY: Simon & Schuster, 1998. p. 24
5. Frale, Barbara. The Templars and the Shroud of Christ. New York: Skyhorse Pub., 2012.

Sixteen

The Fruition of a Templar Curse

"The inquisitors had orders to 'spare no known means of torture' so they could let their wild imaginations run free. Some Templars had their teeth pulled out one at a time, with a question between each extraction, then had the empty sockets probed to provide an additional level of pain. Some had wood wedges driven under their nails, while others had their nails pulled out. A common device was an iron frame like a bed, on which the Templar was trapped with his bare feet hanging over the end. A charcoal brazier was slid under his oiled feet as the questioning began. Several knights were reported to have gone mad with the pain. A number had their feet totally burned off, and at a later inquiry a footless Templar was carried to the council clutching a bag containing the blackened bones that had dropped out of his feet when they were burned off. His inquisitors had allowed him to keep the bones as a souvenir of his memorable experience. The hot iron was a favourite tool because it could be easily applied again and again to any part of the body. It could be held a couple of inches away, cooking the flesh while the question was asked, then firmly pressed against the body when the answer came out incorrectly or too slowly."
John J. Robinson 1.

The Pope's True Character

Clement has been remembered by history as a very pliant Pope and surely in a very difficult situation but perhaps the sum total of his character has been deliberately lost over time.

The Templars were betrayed by him at the second session of the Council of Vienne on 3rd of April 1312 when the Order was formally dissolved and upon pain of excommunication - no one may ever wear the regalia of the Knights Templar again.

Obviously this has changed and both men and women today don the garb of the Templars quite freely in varying neo-Templar societies and also the upper chivalric Templar degrees of Freemasonry.

The Council of Vienne was attended by King Philip, his three sons in a room full of their armed men. Perhaps enough ready steel was at hand to sway the most stalwart of souls in the Pope's position. However I am not so certain that there was not some measure of cowardice in the breast of Clement V and an unflattering eagerness to comply with Philip's demands.

Though the Order had been disbanded, the Pope had convened another session where the guilt of the Templars was being read out loud to delegates of the Church and also the nobility.

The congregation was gate-crashed however by a handful of extremely brave fugitive Templar Knights:

"Although the order was now broken up, and the best and bravest of its members had either perished in the flames or were languishing in dungeons, yet nine fugitive Templars had the courage to present themselves before the council, and demand to be heard in defence of their order, declaring that they were the representatives of from 1,500 to 2,000 Templars, who were wandering about as fugitives and outlaws in the neighbourhood of Lyons. Monsieur Raynouard has fortunately brought to light a letter from the pope to king Philip, which states this fact, and also informs us how the holy pontiff acted when he heard that these defenders of the order had presented themselves. Clement caused them to be thrown into prison, where they languished and died. He affected to believe that his life was in danger from the number of the Templars at large, and he immediately took measures to provide for the security of his person." Charles Addison 2.

Author Charles Addison goes on to state that some members of the nobility were appalled and demanded to let the men be heard due to the long illustrious career of the Order. The proceedings were immediately shut down by Clement over protests of those nobles not in the pocket of the King.

It is interesting that at the beginning of the Order's existence there were nine knights and at the end there were also nine who magnificently stood to defend the honour of their brothers.

The imprisonment of these nine knights was not the last despicable move on the Pope's behalf. He also wrote letters to the kings of Castile, Leon, Aragon and Portugal complaining that they were not torturing the Templars in their domains to gain the truth.

Addison states that the Pope contained in his letters, *"The bishops and delegates,"* says the holy pontiff, *"have imprudently neglected these means of obtaining the truth; we therefore expressly order them to employ torture against the knights, that the truth may be more readily and completely obtained!"* 3. Not only did he want them arrested, he wanted to destroy them in body, mind and soul as he was in fear of his life from having betrayed them not once but twice.

Clement was worried he would risk a schism within the church by *not* dissolving the Order. But was there a case for a schism and would it have occurred as the Pope was the main mover behind the accusations of Templar heresy aside from the French King.

Without Clement the charges surely would have collapsed. Certainly Philip would have put an immediate end to the Pope's life should he not cooperate with the plan and create another puppet Pontiff. But if Clement had turned about and asked for those loyal to the Templars for protection it is possible their own nation state would have followed.

But frankly outside of France monarchs were slow to charge Templars of heresy and without Philip's dogged insistence the whole affair would have fizzled out completely.

Alas the hoped-for Templar State in Southern France was not to be due to

The Secret Dossier of a
Knight Templar of the Sangreal

Clement's lack of vision and personal courage. Indeed Europe may have had a renaissance far earlier had this choice by Clement V not been made. He could have come back from the brink but chose not to do so. Templar sciences would have continued to flourish regardless of the Inquisition's superstitious malice licking at their defended borders.

The 23rd and last Grand Master of the Templars, Jacques de Molay, had finally confessed under torture to denying Christ and the Cross.

After languishing in a dungeon for almost seven years, living with the ongoing pain of arthritic limbs from the initial crucifixion torture, de Molay, along with three other knights, loaded down by heavy chains, were brought by cart to Notre Dame in Paris on the 18th of March 1314 AD.

A public scaffold had been erected and a crowd had gathered to hear the confessions of the prisoners. According to Charles Addison the Last Grand Master would not save his life by publically accepting the charges as had been planned by their accusers:

"...but the Grand Master, raising his arms bound with chains towards heaven, and advancing to the edge of the scaffold, declared in a loud voice, that to say that which was untrue was a crime, both in the sight of God and man. " I do," said he, "confess my guilt, which consists in having, to my shame and dishonour, suffered myself, through the pain of torture and the fear of death, to give utterance to falsehoods, imputing scandalous sins and iniquities to an illustrious order, which hath nobly served the cause of Christianity. I disdain to seek a wretched and disgraceful existence by engrafting another lie upon the original falsehood." 4.

Philip was so furious that the open confession was not to take place and without any other discussion or authority, he ordered the immediate execution by fire that many 'heretics' have suffered.

Before dusk de Molay and Geoffrey de Charney, the Preceptor of Normandy, were led to a slow burning charcoal pyre and roasted alive while Philip watched from a distant safe window as the flames engulfed the knights.

It has been said that de Molay's last words were that of a powerful curse aimed at Philip and the Pope, that both men would be dead within the year. I don't doubt that if there were some 2000 knights still at large in France then certainly a few of their number would have secretly attended the last moments of their Grand Masters life and brother knights, to hear the final words of their leader.

The deaths of the Pope and King did follow within the year and were surely revenge for the notorious murders of their brothers. A worthy monument to the memory of the knights and their Grand Master may be viewed near the scene on the River Seine; they have not been forgotten by Paris.

The Fruition of a Templar Curse

Clement died on 20 April 1314 and his body was consumed with flames when the church he rested in caught fire. At the time, having one's body decapitated or limbs removed meant that resurrection would be impossible. It may be that fire was the least assault on the body of the Pope by those who took vengeance on him. Philip died of a possible stroke during a hunting accident on 29 November 1314 just months later.

I believe that Jacques de Molay's curse came to fruition at the hands of the warrior monks who witnessed his cruel death.

1. Robinson, John J. Dungeon, Fire, and Sword: The Knights Templar in the Crusades. New York: M. Evans &, 1991. pg. 438, 439
2. Asbridge, Thomas S. The Crusades: The Authoritative History of the War for the Holy Land. Reprint ed. New York: Ecco Press, 2011. p. 290
3. Ibid 291
4. Ibid 294 & 295

Seventeen

The Mystery of Clement's Pardon

The Vatican researcher, Dr. Barbara Frale, has discovered what is being called the Chinon Parchment, named after the castle where the Templars were imprisoned in Southern France.

She discovered it had been misfiled in the 17th century and utterly forgotten. It is a pardon signed by Pope Clement in 1308 after secret interrogations with de Molay and a few other knights on charges of heresy, absolving the Order, declaring them innocent.

He never publicized the document nor used it against Philip. At some point early on he changed his mind and decided to betray those in his charge, concerned it seems more for his own life than the lives of the many.

The Chinon Parchment was brought into public light with all fanfare due a visiting head of state. Though the parchment had been found in 2001 its official debut was 12 October 2007 which marked the 700th anniversary of the arrests. "This is proof that the Templars were not heretics," said Dr. Frale. "The Pope was obliged to ask pardon from the knights."...and continued with...."For 700 years we have believed that the Templars died as cursed men, and this absolves them." 1.

What a shame that no Pope in the last 700 years thought it honourable to absolve the knightly order. Later Popes who knew the Templars still existed made no attempt to clear their name.

Despite my own suspicion over the timing of this weak olive branch I am pleased it was made public for the memory of the supposed 'cursed men' who died horribly. The might of the modern Vatican surely need not rest on a dusty signed document by a Pope who had shown little courage, while bringing down his own knightly order, men who had left such valuable contributions to society and under his protection.

Her book and surrounding pomp and ceremony does seem to indicate broader political interests at heart in regards to the modern day popularity of the neo and real Templar Order. Is this statement by the Church an indication they have a diplomatic interest in bringing the Templars back into the fold?

It seems as if the modern Catholic Church is wishing to be inclusive to the memory of the Templar Order; but at the same time white-washing Clement V's character reducing his part in the knights' downfall as a way of gaining innocence by proxy.

It is a shame that the Church felt it needed to absolve Clement V in order and to give credence to the Chinon Parchment. Many Medieval Popes were deeply flawed and their atrocious behaviour could be seen as par for the course and culture of the time - are we not past this even today?

It seems not, if continued scandals of mismanagement and that of pedophile priests are anything to go by, surely their house is in need of a serious review which takes courage, and courage that I would admire should the powers at be in Rome ever decide to develop.

It is quite simple to see that the Templars were victims of outright greed and false accusations. Was it indeed necessary for the modern church to align itself with

Clement V rather than using a reasonable approach to review the absurdity of the Trial and pronounce the Templar Order as innocent? *At any point in the past 700 years?*

Would this have called into question the still extant Inquisition who hunted Templars? Recently given a soft name change - the Congregation for the Doctrine of the Faith - and their violent role in the proceedings against the Templars?

Perhaps it was easier to absolve Clement V than to raise sticky questions as to the guilt of the Inquisition and the Church's current though obvious outmoded need of this so called Holy Office?

A public apology for the torture and murder of the Templars at the hands of an organisation still in use would be quite awkward indeed. Best to focus on Clement V safely long dead to remove any heat on the heinous and modern Inquisition.

The Chinon Parchment provided a quick and simple way of addressing the issue. It truly is appropriate that the Catholic Church publish the Chinon Parchment and officially absolve the Knights Templar.

It should have been done at least 200 years ago when the West started its road to democracy. They cannot reclaim the Templars however as they've been operating outside the auspices of the church for 700 years, though individual members may indeed have chosen to be Catholic themselves does not mean that the Templar Order wants to have the Pope as their leader once more.

The Templars were so independent that it could be said that their loyalty to their Grand Master was greater than to that of the Pope. Stating that they are innocent is correct but the church cannot offer an open door at such a late date. It is simply insulting and outlandish on every level. It could be a desire to gain converts by publishing the document and reminding the public that the Templars had answered to only the Pope between the 12th and 14th centuries.

Regardless of the recent public support of the Vatican on this issue, intriguing questions remain as to the Templar inner core belief system that cannot be dispelled by bland modern day re-branding. Were the Templars innocent? Absolutely! Did they tow the Catholic line? Yes *and* no. After all, they were truly Christians, but a branch of spirituality that the Catholic Church felt it could no longer be aligned to.

With so many Christian sects in the world today, beyond count, should we not acknowledge someone as a Christian (or any other religion) if they themselves describe their belief as such?!

Truly one man's heresy is another man's faith. If we are to have world peace then we must learn to respect each other. Nowhere in the Ten Commandments does it say to kill others of a differing religion. It says, thou shalt not kill, *period.*

Until a global saviour does arrive - but we mustn't wait, as we are responsible for each other now - we must live with each other neighbour to neighbour and nation next to nation. Tolerance and empathy *is* world peace!

The following thought does tickle me however though I view the Chinon Parchment with a certain amount of misgiving. Within the male-dominated Vatican it is most interesting that a woman, Dr. Barbara Frale, has 'proved' the innocence of the Soldiers of Christ after 700 years of black-listing.

Perhaps in this new era of the awakening Divine Feminine the Vatican has sought to present itself through an accomplished academic woman? Presenting a softer face to the world. Or perhaps the Divine Feminine is asserting Herself irrevocably through Her beautifully subtle but insistent guidance?

After all, it was a woman, Barbara Frale that actually found the document asserting the innocence of the Templars. That same Marion spirit that Saint Bernard (and a myriad of other wise ones) gave himself away to in utter bliss. It was obviously time to put this issue to rest at the hand of the Divine Feminine.

The last Grand Master of the Knights Templar - Jaques de Molay - of the above ground era (1292-1314)
Image By Unknown - Bibliotheque Nationale de France, Public Domain, https://commons.wikimedia.org/w/index.php?curid=2612812

1. Rome, Malcolm Moore in. "Vatican Paper Set to Clear Knights Templar." The Telegraph. October 05, 2007. http://www.telegraph.co.uk/news/worldnews/1565252/Vatican-paper-set-to-clear-Knights-Templar.html.

Eighteen

Continuation of the Order

Escape into the Night

It is a complete utter fairy tale that the real men that constituted the Templar Knights and their retainers simply disappeared in a puff of smoke upon Pope Clement V's dissolution of the Order in 1314.

These were real flesh and blood men devoted to their chosen life built upon centuries of tradition. They did not simply roll over into the earth in despair and vanish as is continually claimed in many circles.

These were hardened warriors, innovators and more importantly they had beliefs worth living for that a greedy king and his puppets could not subdue. There are estimates of 9,000 to 15,000 preceptories across Europe, Ireland, England, Scotland and Wales at the time of the arrests in France.

Each of these locations would have included knights, monks, lay brethren and other retainers. Their numbers were into the thousands. At their height there were estimates of 20,000 Knights *alone* across these kingdoms not including support personnel.

This figure could easily treble if not quadruple the estimate of 'only' 20,000 knights. It is simply irresponsible academically to state that they no longer existed and if there is a cry of conspiracy here it is indeed an academic one.

The conspiracy was originally perpetrated by the Catholic Church who turned on the Knights, but also a few fearful heads of state and by the Templars themselves who were forced underground in order to survive in a world not ready for their wisdom and steel.

Napoleon and the Vatican Archives

It is perhaps an understatement to say that Napoleon had a great interest in the Merovingian dynasty. It is highly possible he felt he was a descendant. He wore 300 golden bees on his coronation robe which had been excavated from the tomb of King Childebert II (570–95). Napoleon wove Templar and Freemasonic symbolism into art and architecture, effectively aligning himself with these ideals.

He is highly regarded as a hero by many in France and has admirers around the globe, though understandably those nations that felt his aggression do not hold him on such a high pedestal. As a sneer, his height of 5'7" is commented upon as 'short man syndrome' – at the time he was above average in height (5'5") and no one commented at that point in history on his stature; it is a modern construct only. Regardless, he had raided the Vatican Archives, moving them to Paris.

The Secret Dossier of a
Knight Templar of the Sangreal

It is probable that important documents found their way into the hands of Merovingian descendants at this juncture and have never been returned to Rome. One document that gained public attention related to the escape of the Templar fleet from La Rochelle:

"After Napoleon conquered Rome in 1809, some files were brought back to Paris from the secret archives of the Vatican. Among these were a few documents relating to the Templar trials. In one of these records was the statement of Jean de Chalons, a member of the Order from Nemours in the diocese of Troyes." - Johannes and Peter Fiebag, The Discovery of the Grail, translated from the German by George Sassoon" 1. As quoted by

http://www.lundyisleofavalon.co.uk/templars/tempic055.htm

Jean de Chalons testified:
"On the evening before the raid, Thursday October 12th 1307, I myself saw three carts loaded with straw, which left the Paris Temple shortly before nightfall, also Gerard de Villiers and Hugo de Chalons, at the head of 50 horse[men]. There were chests hidden on the carts, which contained the entire treasure of the Visitator Hugo de Pairaud. They took the road for the coast, where they were to be taken abroad in eighteen of the Order's ships." 2. as quoted by http://www.lundyisleofavalon.co.uk/templars/tempic055.htm

According to Malcolm Barber, Gerard de Villiers was captured and never made it to the coast. If there had been 50 men with him and three carts of treasure, it would not have been the Ark or other such priceless relics.

He must not have had anything of sacred value other than gold or silver as King Philip would have most certainly put the Ark on display as evidence of his divine mandate to rule. Conversely Philip would have used anything controversial against the Templars and it is certain the King made quiet but fast use of the bounty from the three chests.

We do know that King Philip received a very rude surprise when he found the Paris Temple devoid of any Templar treasure, much to his frustration.

Apparently the skull of a woman covered in silver was found and a few other inconsequential items. False claims of idolatry were already being hurled by the Crown and unfortunately this find did not dispel the accusations.

Certainly this claim could be explained and makes no sense as relics were a part of everyday religious life in the Middle Ages across the board.

However the veneration of the head was a consistent theme through the trial as we have seen. We do not know of course whose head this was purported to be but if it was in the Paris Temple then the Knights would have believed that the woman held esoteric wisdom during her life as a Saint.

Philip's frustration must have mounted to intolerable levels when it was discovered that the entire fleet had also escaped into the night, leaving only empty moorings at La Rochelle the main port for the Templar Order on the morning of the arrests.

Any hopes he had to use the ships to further his campaigns were dashed! Both the vacant Paris Temple and the mysterious disappearance of the fleet can only be construed as evidence that Jacques de Molay knew an attack was imminent.

Many historians have stated that De Molay could not have known as he seemed to be in denial over the losses occurring in the Holy Land and extrapolated that he would also be in denial regarding Phillip le Bel's plans for the Order.

He may indeed have held out too long for his hopes of maintaining Jerusalem but all evidence points to a concerted evacuation of the Paris Temple which could only have occurred under his auspices.

Just how the Paris Temple was cleared is a mystery as it was literally under the nose of King Philip as the palace was nearby and any untoward activity would have been noted by his spies.

The Paris Temple could have been cleared of its esoteric and golden treasures over a period of time, however short, through the careful planning of the last public Grand Master.

We must look at the strategic possibilities in order to reconstruct the legendary disappearance of the Templars from Paris and France. Gerard de Villiers attempted escape may give us an indication as to how the Paris Temple was evacuated.

To assume that his departure at sunset was normal on the evening of the 12th is just too much of a coincidence as all regular travel would have commenced in the morning hours and not the dusk of night.

The noise alone of horses and men would have been unmistakable in the cobbled courtyard of the Paris Temple. It makes no sense for de Molay not to have known that 50 knights on horseback along with three cart loads of gold and silver had left his Temple under Villiers command.

An ostentatious display of 50 armoured knights would have been immediately recognised as soon as they left the confines of the protective walls.

They were allowed to travel some distance from the preceptory as Philip's men would have arrested them out of sight of the Paris Temple so as not to alert de Molay that his men had been intercepted.

There must have been a great many of Philip's men at arms and the location would have been chosen carefully in order to trap the Warrior Monks. Templars were expected to handle odds of three to one and Villiers men would not have gone quietly. An all-out battle must have ensued in order to capture Villiers.

We must accept the possibility that Villiers may have been a decoy with the hope that he would gain the safety of the coast, but sadly ships from La Rochelle had to leave the rendezvous point without Villiers and his company of men who were left behind as casualties.

Overland passage to La Rochelle to the south was almost impossible under the circumstances and heavily patrolled by Philip's men, which suggests that he may indeed have been acting as a decoy with ultimate hopes, however faint, of escape.
La Rochelle was honestly too far south to be a practical meeting point as the fleet had left the night of the 12th, having split up to go their separate ways. Villiers could not have made it that far south in time and would have been aiming to meet a ship on the coast directly west of the Paris Temple.

Any rescue vessel would have had to sail up the coast northward to the estuary of the river Seine. The route out of Paris on the river Seine would have been dangerous for the Templars as well, but if Villiers managed to draw a significant number of Philip's men away from the Temple perhaps this would have gained time for the last of those chosen to flee via the river-route out to sea.

Originally The Villeneuve du Temple of Paris stood between the 'Place de la République' (Republic Square) and the 'Place de la Bastille' (Bastille Square). Nothing now remains of the Templar presence in Paris having been demolished over the centuries. Interestingly enough the original round tower of the church had a circumference of 33 feet. 3.

http://www.templiers.org/paris-eng.php

The most obvious escape route for the Paris Temple was located on the river Seine and would have been the now Port of La Havre which empties out into the Atlantic. Historians debate this endlessly that the Seine would have been watched by Philip for months and any mysterious movements from the Paris Temple would not have gone unnoticed.

However the Seine was a regular trade route to Paris dotted with merchant towns which is why the Temple was there in the first place. It was highly strategic both politically and economically.

The large galleys anchored at La Rochelle would not have been able to access the river but smaller vessels were in common use supporting the economy of the river and the cities and towns out to the coast.

The Order had a minimum of twelve armed preceptories down the river Seine where The Grand Master had time to disguise the Temple treasure amongst mercantile goods and send it out towards the coast and eventually rendezvous with the fleet from La Rochelle carrying personnel and perhaps the most valued sacred objects rescued from the Paris Temple.

Likewise, Philip would not have risked raiding a Templar caravan going over land until the morning of the 13th so as not to alert or spring his trap too soon. It was a gamble he had to take and it most certainly did not pay off as he'd hoped.

How much notice did the Templars have? Six months? One month? We know that de Molay knew of the accusations months in advance and had taken steps with the Pope to clear their name. He was on the alert at least a year ahead of the arrests.

His network of allies would have confirmed the growing danger as the months passed. It's highly probable that when Philip sent out the notices of arrest one month prior, word leaked out and then back to Jacques de Molay.

Philip's orders in sealed envelopes were to be opened on the eve of October the 12th but human beings are curious creatures. I highly doubt that all would have obeyed this unusual order from the King. Once the sealed orders had been opened any Templar sympathiser would have surely alerted the intended victims.

The Grand Master's worst fears were confirmed and he had one month to take action to save his Order from annihilation in France. What actions he took prior to this we do not know but it seems likely that preparations were already in motion as clearing the Temple in Paris would have been a great undertaking and not including those other important preceptories across the kingdom.

Continuation of the Order

It is interesting to note that some preceptories seem to have actually been taken unawares as if some decision might have been made not to alert all of their numbers. If too many were told, understandably word might have found its way back to Philip that his plans were not a secret - however Machiavellian this may seem. Or is it simply that they lacked a sufficient amount of time in which to allow everyone to escape?

This leads again to a strong indication that there was only one month unequivocal knowledge of their fate. By the time de Molay knew of their impending doom, all but the most immediate personnel, riches and holy treasures were given the chance to flee.

We must remember that one month notice in the 14th century was insignificant due to travel and time constraints. It was vital that the bulk of the treasuries be moved along with key personnel and it was stunning just how much they did manage to accomplish.

In order to ensure the best overall success of escape the Order dispersed their men via land, the river Seine and sea. The treasure had been split and the men would have taken varying routes to safety so as not to lose all should they be captured.

Why did he not protect the Order with force of arms? There were simply not enough of them in France to do so and calling upon Templars from other kingdoms may have taken too much time and certainly fully armoured Knights pouring into France would have been hard to disguise let alone welcomed by Philip.

It is clear that Jacques de Molay sacrificed himself to save the Order. He knew through his own intelligence network that King Philip was going to strike. Jacques de Molay gave his people time to escape by handing himself over to King Philip along with a few other brave officers. De Molay chose to stay to protect the name of the Templars and perhaps even to rescue it through legal means with the help of the Holy Father, the only man they officially answered to.

Records have not survived regarding the actual numbers of the Templar fleet in total. However based on the extensive maritime activities of the Knights, 18 galleys moored at La Rochelle could be considered a humble figure and must not be thought of as the entire fleet. There would have been ships in the Mediterranean and with trade to Britain and Ireland we can assume that there were further galleys in the Atlantic and the North Sea. Not to mention those of the Scandinavian countries. History is littered with the accounts of safe harbours where the Templar inheritance thrived.

1. as quoted by http://www.lundyisleofavalon.co.uk/templars/tempic055.htm
2. as quoted by http://www.lundyisleofavalon.co.uk/templars/tempic055.htm
3. http://www.templiers.org/paris-eng.php

Nineteen

Safe Harbours

One need not travel far to find immediate hard evidence for the continued survival of the Knights Templar. Existing trade with the British Isles, sympathetic Flanders and the Hanseatic League opened escape routes from France. English and Scottish Templars welcomed their French brethren, as did kingdoms to the south, north and east of France.

All Templar properties and wealth were to be conferred to the Hospitallers though in England it took up to the 1340s for some properties such as the London Temple to legally pass into their hands. During this interim, who was minding supposed ex-Templar preceptories? It seems the Templars themselves were and did so until the existing generation passed.

Templars remained in these properties, living out their lives under the protection of individuals attempting to hold on to the preceptories, safeguarding them from either the crown or the Hospitallers.

Descendants of those who originally gifted the property to the Templars tried taking them back in order that the lands not fall to the Hospitallers, others managed to tie up the issue in legal proceedings lasting years.

Some land holdings were completely derelict by the time the Knights of Saint John acquired them. In a few instances the Hospitallers actually vandalised or tore down Templar churches.

A number of Templars had no choice but to become Hospitallers, others changed their names, shaving off their beards. They simply remained within their chosen communities while becoming part of the population. Some older Knights were actually pensioned off quite fairly, some into lives of poverty. Significantly many actually fled to other countries as we shall see.

According to Alan Butler and Stephen DaFoe, Templars had an existing alliance with small fiefdoms beginning in 1291 which eventually bore the nation of Switzerland.

Legends circulated of white knights on horseback, helping to protect these small kingdoms from the aggressions of the Holy Roman Empire.

Switzerland developed into a banking nation with very independent characteristics to other banking systems. Their flag is also a testament to their Templar heritage. It is simply reversed with a white cross on a red background. Though neutral, their military prides itself on their bravery and professionalism and to this day the Swiss Guard cares for the security of the Pope.

In June of 1317 Spain's sympathetic King James II gave refuge to the Knights Templar through a new military Order. He persuaded Pope John XXII to acknowledge them as the Order of Montesa and based on the Cistercian Rule and dedicated to Our Lady and also Saint George of Montesa. Their principle task was to protect the area from the Moors which of course they managed with great success.

Interestingly enough the Master of the Order of Calatrava, begun by a Cistercian monk in 1158, had strong links to the Templars, was given the right to visit the fledgling Order of Montesa to settle disputes. Some of the original knights were volunteers from the Order of Calatrava. This right of the Master of Calatrava to officiate over disputes was granted on 22 July 1319 which is the feast day of Mary Magdalene.

A similar story could be told in Portugal where King Dinis refused to hand over Templar properties to the Hospitallers and told the Pope those lands were indeed his since he was king and the Templar holdings were in his kingdom.

If the Pope thought he had enough military might to challenge this he was certainly welcome to try his hand against the newest recruits to Dinis's army, the well-armed and double-crossed Templar Order!

King Dinis then created his own military order called The Order of Christ. The Pope in 1319 granted the new order the use of the Rule of the Cistercians. This is no accident and a blatant indication that the Templars were indeed still very much alive and just as involved in affairs of state.

Some Templars were invited to join their cousins the Teutonic Knights where they were free to be open about their practices.

| Knights Templar Cross Pattee | Swiss Flag | Order of Montesa | Montesa Spain |

Survival in England

Edward I is counted by some to be England's greatest king, depending on one's nationality of course! He brought the Welsh nation brutally under his banner in an attempt to create one nation out of the British Isles using the fabled King Arthur as his example.

The dream of one great kingdom of the British Isles is ancient, but Edward I did not ask nicely, he was ruthless. Scotland had long been a target of Edward I and he was dubbed Hammer of the Scotts for his cruelty.

Whatever one may think of Edward I he was a brilliant, tall warrior who lead from the front and continued down the road towards a legal system begun with the Magna Carta; conversely France was suffering under an absolute monarchy, ever tightening its grip on the populace over three generations up to Phillip le Bel's time.

The ageing Edward I died in July 1307 leaving his feckless and useless son to inherit the throne. Edward II was the antithesis of his brave father and one of the worst kings in English history.

John J. Robinson of Born In Blood does not think that Phillip le Bel would have struck the Templar Order if Edward I had lived. A combined Templar Order with the strength of Edward I may very well have put the French King off from taking such action. It may have given Edward I all the excuse he needed to invade France with the Templars eager to rescue their French Brethren.

To his credit and fortunately - Edward II was not the least interested in the Templar's dissolution reacting very slowly to the arrests and making a half-hearted attempt to please the Pope from the safety of his near impenetrable island home.

The papacy would complain to Edward II that Templar lands now belonging to the Order of Saint John were being absorbed by the Crown of England.

Edward II seemed genuinely shocked that the Templars were guilty of anything which was quite right. His own hesitation was echoed by the peoples across Europe in a complete state of horror over the events and demands out of France.

As far as Edward II was concerned, as long as one did not wear the Templar regalia and took up civilian life, he turned a blind eye. He was slow to issue arrest warrants, taking anywhere from one to three months to respond to the Pope in France.

The Inquisition was not granted carte blanche in the British Isles though they were allowed to enter; they were not allowed to torture their Templar prisoners. As a result the 'confessions' were far less colourful than those obtained under torture in France.

However torture of a different nature was employed such as solitary confinement with meagre bread and water. According to Charles G. Addison, Templars were shifted from cell to cell and dungeon to dungeon whilst being 'treated with rigour' in an attempt to extract damning information. Though they fared better than their French brethren it could not have been at all easy to be a Templar in custody in England. 1.

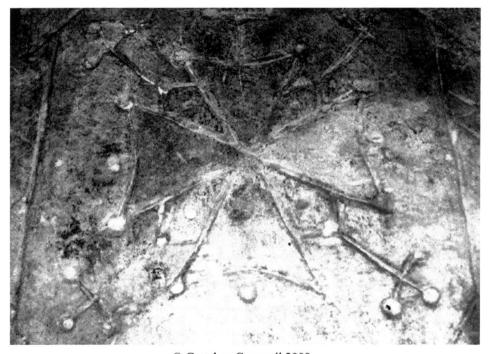

© Gretchen Cornwall 2009

I photographed graffiti in the Martin Tower within the Tower of London complex. It had been a place to hold prisoners but is now a gift shop. The last Grand Master of England, William de la More had been arrested along with many others in solitary confinement within the Tower of London. But had he been placed in the Martin Tower? Was the work of the Templar cross his hand?

The corners of the equilateral cross are marked with upright swords over what could be a shield; pointing toward the centre with a fifth sword above the top of the central cross. The corners of the border have been 'cut' off to create an eight sided frame which includes a chevron design and what could be an exaggerated 'X' in the lower right hand corner. It is clearly Templar. Are the chevrons part of the heraldic device of the man who carved it? Chevrons were often added to the shields of coats of arms. The five swords form an oddly shaped five pointed star over the cross pattée. This work could not have been swiftly done – the prisoner had to have been incarcerated for some time.

The Great Society, according to John J. Robinson, could only be of Templar origin, made itself known through the Peasant's Revolt of 1381 and had widespread support throughout England. In York, Scarborough and Beverly, Robinson points out that some 1500 'rebels' had been led by an ex-mayor of York all wearing white woolen hoods with red tassels.

The rebels were publically announcing their Templar and Cistercian heritage through this highly organised, egalitarian act of donning white and red wool as a uniform. Bleached wool and red dye were expensive and affordable only to those at the Merchant class and above. This was not a 'mere' peasant revolt by illiterate masses.

The uprising was the direct result of cruel taxes and harsh conditions which made life almost unbearable for the general populace of feudal England. Interestingly enough Robinson also points out that amongst the property damage inflicted by the so-called rebels, the holdings of the Hospitallers bore the brunt of the destruction.

They swore an oath of fraternal bond, "all for one and one for all" 2. The slogan was picked up by Templar sympathiser and author Alexander Dumas the French author of the classic story The Three Musketeers.

Those Templars that were unable, or chose not to go north to Scotland, shifted into their cousin society within the Guild Halls, through existent and ancient Freemasonry a branch of Templarism. This was a natural progression as the Templars and Cistercians were trading partners with the merchant class and Guild Halls across Europe and were indeed already enmeshed partners.

The Secret Dossier of a
Knight Templar of the Sangreal

The Celtic King Robert the Bruce was excommunicated at the time of the Templar arrests in France and by proxy so was the entire kingdom of Scotland.

Having strong ties with the Templars and sympathies that extended deeply into the realms of the esoteric it was a natural for Bruce to embrace armoured knights fleeing the clutches of the Inquisition and French Monarch.

The battle of Bannockburn fought on St. John the Baptist's day of 23rd and 24th of June in 1314, left Edward II's army reduced to a tragic nothing, having eventually lost more than half his entire army of 20,000 men and leaving Scotland with its sovereignty intact and his father Edward I rolling in his grave! Fantastic legends exist of white knights on horseback, striking terror into the hearts of the English and dealing them a crushing defeat.

The famous cavalry charge being of Templar origin is often dismissed as a romantic tale, however there is mundane evidence to suggest that the Templars were alive, well and thriving in Scotland. The real question regarding their cavalry charge at Bannockburn should be rephrased to - how could they *not* have been there? 3.

Baigent and Leigh's Temple and the Lodge unearthed magnificent information pertaining to Templar holdings in Scotland. Bruce had acknowledged via a charter in 1314 the properties of the Hospitallers.

The authors point out how interesting it is that the charter simply acknowledges the holdings that were already in the possession of the Order of St John and *not* Templar holdings which did not pass to the crown nor to any secular lord as it seems to have in England. Indeed it appears that the Templars simply stayed in their own preceptories and continued running their estates as per usual.

The Grand Master of the Hospitallers ordered an inventory of all preceptories for the Order of St John around the world in 1338. Notably it was claimed that every single last Templar holding in Scotland had been destroyed in the wars with England which was a polite way of stating that the Templars denied the Order of St John any possibility of acquiring their Temples.

However a very odd situation had occurred directly after and seems to have been a very open secret that literally became forgotten as the centuries rolled forward.

"Notwithstanding the obscurities, a certain pattern does emerge: after 1338, the Hospitallers began to acquire Templar holdings in Scotland, albeit in a decidedly equivocal way; prior to 1338, however, no Templar property was passed on, yet with the exception noted above there is no record anywhere of anything else happening to it. What is more, the Templar lands, when the Hospitallers did eventually receive them, were kept separate. They were not parcelled out, integrated with the Hospitallers' other holdings and administered accordingly. On the contrary, they enjoyed a special status and were administered as a self-contained unit in themselves. They were handled, in fact not as if St John actually owned them, but were simply in the capacity of agents or managers, holding them in trust. As late as the end of the sixteenth century, no fewer than 519 sites in Scotland were listed by the Hospitallers as 'Terrae Templariae'-part, that is, of the self-contained and separately administered Templar patrimony!" Baigent & Leigh. 4.

Safe Harbours

Baigent and Leigh had uncovered the work of James Maidment's Templaria, who was a genealogical lawyer and antiquarian from the 19th century. Maidment's findings revealed that the Templar holdings in Scotland amounted to 579 locations! The Maidment research is held at the National Library of Scotland.

In other words, the Templars were operating freely in Scotland up to the 16th century under the most curious of circumstances. They had not become absorbed by the Hospitallers but were operating under the name, Order of the Knights of St John *and* the Temple! Two separate entities.

Due to the distance from Rome and Paris, allotting for the military strength of the Templars in Scotland and the support of the Scottish Crown, there seems to have been no alternative but for a secret agreement to have been made between the Templars, the Order of St John and Rome as they simply could do nothing to stop the Templars in far flung Scotland!

The Church hoped for reconciliation at some point barring political pressure from France and its then ruling house of Capet. Why wouldn't they? The Templars had knowledge, power and resources which the church wanted to leverage under their own umbrella. The potential plan never culminated in a public resurrection for the Templars in the last 700 years, as an official body recognised by the Catholic Church. The Templars recognized themselves without the need of external validation. They have no incentive to do otherwise.

Today the Catholic Church forbids any of its members to join the Freemasons which is an important doorway to Templarism.

Written and artistic evidence of every nature from paintings to architecture and song, let alone the verbatim testimony of those involved over time, has been provided though not in its entirety in this volume. Academic rigor is vital and must be upheld but it is irresponsible to state that the Temple dissolved and no longer exists.

Mount Heredom

I would like to offer up the legend of Mount Heredom as subtle and evidential proof of the continuance of the Templars - and informational gift by the alchemist John Temple.

The Royal Order of Heredom (Rite of Heredom) in Scotland was revitalized out of the ashes of the Templars by King Robert the Bruce in 1314. It had been created originally by Kind David I and coexisted with the Templars.

It has been stated that the rite of Heredom is an 18th century invention, however I was told that it had been practised in the 14th century with each degree matching that of a year of Christ's life. It is an oral tradition without a paper trail which was finally written down many centuries later.

C.W. Leadbeater tells us, 'there is nothing whatsoever of any high degrees in the extant Minutes of Mother Kilwinning, No. 0 upon the roll of the Grand Lodge of Scotland, which dates from 1642. 5. He goes on to say that regardless there was proof of the Templars in Scotland and that the rhymed ritual of the Royal Order 'bears internal evidence of age, and although its Christianity has been ruthlessly

The Secret Dossier of a
Knight Templar of the Sangreal

edited in protestant interests there are yet traces of the old mystical ideas of the Celtic Church'. 6.

Legend places Heredom's origins as the Celtic Church on Iona but then it is moved 60 miles northwest of Edinburgh in the inhospitable mountains. The sanctuary protected by the mountain is Kilwinning Abbey. 7. The legend of Heredom would indicate a Templar precursor, that of the Kingdom of Rheged in Cumbria and of Arthurian lore.

Certainly a physical location is acceptable as a practical metaphor for the inter-dimensional sacred mountain of initiation and its holy house, temple or cave.

The sacred mountain of alchemy was recreated out of the ancient past of Mount Sinai/Horeb, Mount Moriah, and Jebel Uweinat which straddles the borders of Egypt, Libya and Sudan. That it should reappear across the Gaelic and Cumbric landscape culminating in Scotland is born out of the understandable human desire to replicate one's faith in the back garden. That it appears to move its address is also practical due to changes in circumstance.

The alchemical sacred mountain becomes the Great Pyramid as the centuries roll forward. Knowledge from Hermetic Egypt became part of the European tradition. The alchemical mountain and Great Pyramid are one and the same. Both contain hidden sanctuaries where experiential knowledge is imparted.

Stephan Michelspacher, Cabala, Spiegel der Kunst und Natur: in Alchymia 1663 AD

117

Safe Harbours

The Temple and the Spy Master

Though hotly contested, the plethora of evidence that the Order survived speaks for itself. Evidence can be found in plain sight and also hidden into modern times, including paper trails, architecture, familial history, garden landscapes, city planning and of course Masonry. The Knights Templar has an unmistakable feel and fingerprint. It is not too difficult to detect once the surface has been scratched.

While researching for this work I came across what might be considered circumstantial evidence during the reign of Queen Elizabeth I – A series of letters between her spymaster Walsingham and an agent in Bruges named Davison. The surviving letter has the curious phrase that there were '...two companies of 'Temple's' regiment, in garrison at Brussels that were enroute to Dendermonde to support a mutual cause. 8.

The letter speaks of the many people involved in the conflict, places and the negotiations that Davison was undertaking on his queen's behalf. They were all very specific in the lengthy letter to Walsingham. The word 'Temple' is in quotations in order to highlight it.

My contact told me unequivocally that the Order was active during this time. Have I just found confirmation of this between England's most famous spy master and one of his agents?

Invisible College within the Royal Society

James I, son of Mary Stuart Queen of Scotland, was initiated into the Lodge of Scoon and Perth in 1601. His court moved to London on the death of Elizabeth I, becoming James VI and the first king on written record to have become a Freemason.

Charles the II would be the inheritor and protector of the Invisible College publically known as the Royal Society and was one of their most influential patrons. He was famously moderate when it came to the subject of religion, choosing to let his people and courtiers decide their own spiritual life. Science, reason and a life devoid of dogma were his calling. Charles the II was one of the most spiritual and esoteric kings the world has seen, he was another Solomon. Charles died without legal issue but remained steadfastly loyal to his Queen all his life, choosing not to divorce her though he had many children by other women.

He did not want to plunge the country into civil war by passing the crown to one of his legalised sons as he'd lived through the dreadful years of civil war and suffered the beheading of his father by Cromwell. He gave the throne over to his Catholic brother James. Sadly, his brother and successor did not have the same mettle and was quickly replaced by William of Orange whose own dynasty brought many Teutonic-Masonic gifts and a yearning to discover the secrets of nature.

Charles II's legacy, The Royal Society, sought to uphold reason over superstition above the political and economic intrigues of organised religion. Even though their numbers included clergy and men who were anti-monarchy the Royal Society also included those who were loyal to the King.

What an incredible situation to have such an inclusive monarch who placed knowledge above that of political loyalties and respect over beliefs. This is an echo of Freemasonry and true democracy as the only prerequisite to joining is the belief in a supreme being regardless of one's religious background or political leanings.

The importance of belief in a supreme being may take many forms (such as love of any of the Seven Liberal Arts or becoming a master of a sport) unrelated to deity but instilling a sense of accountability/honour and fostering a life-long need to progress as a better person.

The discussion of religion and politics is forbidden in Lodge meetings. In order for the scientists of the Royal Society to progress they would also have to adopt the same rules of order.

Dr. Robert Lomas quickly harnesses the importance of Templarism to the Royal Society as he quotes a summation from the Second Degree:

"You were led in the Second Degree to contemplate the intellectual faculties and to trace them through the paths of nature and science even to the throne of God Himself. The secrets of nature and the principles of intellectual truth were then unveiled to your view."

And:

"This antient ritual sums up the inspiration that drove Sir Robert Moray to create the Royal Society. Modern Freemasonry may be eccentric, old-fashioned and slightly out of touch but its principles are sound. I have come to believe that it was these principles which inspired Sir Robert Moray to found the Royal Society. The scientific developments that have flowed from that act have benefited the whole world". 9.

The effect of the Templar mindset is exemplified by the Royal Society and its continued benefits for our world today and into the future.

One of the oldest documents in Masonic British history is a charter dated 1601 recognising the Sinclairs as the hereditary Grand Masters of Scottish Masonry.

According to Lodge sources the honour was conferred on the Sinclairs by James II of Scotland who reigned from 1437 to 1460, which irrefutably dates continued Templar activity in Scotland. It is clear to see that the Templars survived, continued in the Merchant Guilds and eventually became public as the Freemasons. A similar story is evidenced across Europe. 10.

The Scottish rite of Heredom ensured that a man moved through 33 degrees to reach 1st degree Templar. Mark masonry is considered the 'short cut' towards the same peak.

I have put forward a fraction of evidence in writing for the Templar presence in Scotland up to the 16th century which is not at all too far off the mark from the initial whispers of Freemasonic activities in the 17th century.

On 24th June 1717 the United Grand Lodge of England was consecrated at the Goose and Gridiron alehouse in St Paul's Churchyard. The significance? The Templars of England had to attend a church service at the old St Paul's Cathedral to accept their fate disbanding their order in public five centuries earlier. It does seem that they had announced their public return with the full support of the new king, George.

Safe Harbours

By the 1750s we have written documentation of Lodges across England and Scotland also that of France and other European nations. An organization of this depth is not born overnight and is a clear transmission from the past.

The Templars no longer needed to hide their presence from the world as enough time had slipped past. The Templar Order continued to initiate and grow their numbers across the British Isles and Europe passing down their wisdom from Father to Son. But from the 18th century onward, women were now being openly admitted.

The Damsel of the Sanct Grail 1874 by Dante Gabriel Rossetti

1. Addison, C. G., and Robert Macoy. The Knights Templars. New York: Masonic Pub., 1842.

2. Robinson, John J. Born in Blood: The Lost Secrets of Freemasonry. New York: M. Evans &, 1989. P. 31

3. Mackenzie, Agnes Mure. Robert Bruce, King of Scots. Edinburgh: Oliver & Boyd, 1934. Chapter XI

4. Baigent, Michael, and Richard Leigh. The Temple and the Lodge. New York: Arcade Pub., 1989. p. 139

5. Leadbeater, C. W. Freemasonry and Its Ancient Mystic Rites. New York: Gramercy Books, 1998. p. 124

6. bid

7. Corbin, Henry. Temple and Contemplation. London: KPI in Association with Islamic Publications, London, 1986. p. 352

8. 'Elizabeth: December 1578, 1-5,' in Calendar of State Papers Foreign, Elizabeth, Volume 13, 1578-1579, ed. Arthur John Butler (London: His Majesty's Stationery Office, 1903), 318-327, https://www.british-history.ac.uk/cal-state-papers/foreign/vol13/pp318-327

9. Lomas, Robert. The Invisible College: The Royal Society, Freemasonry and the Birth of Modern Science. London: Headline, 2002. p. 422

10. Baigent, Michael, Richard Leigh, and Henry Lincoln. The Holy Blood and the Holy Grail. London: Century, 2005. p. 152.

Twenty

The Templars of Rosslyn, Portugal and Nova Scotia

We cannot speak about the Templars without discussing Rosslyn Chapel located just outside of Edinburgh Scotland, ingeniously created by an enlightened prince.

The topography of the Village of Roslin is surrounded by steep rolling hills and therefore naturally protected. Rosslyn Chapel sits on one little hill and across from it is another steep hill where the castle sits taking strategic advantage of its position.

It is a gorgeous lush, green and growing place. Upon visiting the nearby Rosslyn Castle and walking around the base of the hill upon which it sits, I was struck by the wild white flowers of garlic that had multiplied to surround the hill and the castle remains. Had the plant escaped from a garden in some distant past? It was a lovely gentle sight however the odour of garlic was rather discernable.

I could not help myself thinking that the garlic with its white flowers and pungent scent warding off the things of the night which Bram Stoker found so menacing. I was to learn at a later date that the garlic was wild and natural, apparently not planted by anyone.

I encountered no such vampiric ghouls whilst walking through the forested valley and the hill of Rosslyn Castle; however the Chapel has its ghostly remains.

I could hardly contain myself as I approached the entrance to the Chapel a bit surprised at its bijou size compared to its reputation and to the size of the great cathedrals of Europe; though by contrast it is one of the most highly decorated churches in the world.

I had been within the chapel for some time. While near the heart of the altar, I saw out of the corner of my eye a vicar in his black robe standing opposite by the entrance door. His hair was white, parted on the side and he was of trim build, high cheek bones and a handsome demeanour. I turned to look thinking to see a live human being but the man had disappeared. The impression I was left with was that of a man doing what he enjoyed the most, welcoming parishioners to the service. I was pleased to have seen him still looking over his flock.

Oliver Cromwell destroyed the castle nearby but left the chapel intact using it as his stable. It may be that as a man with Masonic leanings he recognized the purpose of Rosslyn Chapel and decided not to destroy it, which he certainly could have done as he had so many other works of religious art and architecture.

The Sinclairs

Certain families have been linked with the Templars and their survival through the centuries in Scotland. The most famous are the Sinclairs due to popular fiction and of course its book in stone, Rosslyn Chapel. Their name is ancient and derives

The Templars of Rosslyn, Portugal
and Nova Scotia

from the Latin, 'Sanctus Clarus' meaning 'Holy Light'. 1.

Sir William St Clair III and last Earl of Orkney (1410–1484) was descended from the Earl Rolf of Norway of the 10th century who invaded Normandy (Nuestria) and through a series of skillful family marriages and sheer brawn, set up a mystical dynasty with many notable descendants including the Counts of Champagne, Gisors, Blois and of course William the Conqueror.

Hugh de Payens original Grand Master of the Templar Order was married to Lady Catherine Saint Claire.

William the Seemly Saint Clair was gifted the land of Roslin by King Malcolm Canmore for the safe delivery of his bride and future queen, Princess Margaret in 1057.

He was accompanied by the Hungarian knight, Sir Bartholemew Ladislaus Leslyn (the ancestor of the Leslie family); the event is commemorated by a carving of Sir Leslyn and the Merovingian Princess Margaret in the chapel.

She is riding pillion behind him while holding an equilateral cross symbolic of the Holy Rood of Scotland. The carving seems to echo the Templar Seal of two poor knights on horseback.

Earl William, architect of Rosslyn Chapel, had been a member of at least two Orders of mystical merit. 2. The Order of the Knights of Santiago represented by the cockle shell (with its association with the human heart) and the Order of the Golden Fleece, founded by the Duke of Burgundy.

"...he was the patron of craftmasonry throughout Europe, a Grand Master and an adept of the highest degree. Records later confirmed that Sir William was appointed not only hereditary Grand Master of the Craftmasons but also of all the hard and soft guilds in Scotland, such as the shipwrights, paper makers, tanners and foresters." Wallace-Murphy & Marilyn Hopkins 3.

The man was a powerhouse and inherited a tradition and skills from his own father and grandfather who were responsible for the botanical specimens exemplified by the carvings in the colligate chapel.

The foundation was laid for the large church dedicated to Saint Matthew in 1446. The current Chapel was meant to be the choir but only the roof was completed by his son after Prince William's death in 1484, leaving the rest of the church incomplete and its larger foundations exposed due to lack of funds.

I've shown written documentation for the survival of the Order and here in Rosslyn Chapel we have one of the finest examples of the continuation of the Order in Medieval architecture. It is not the only Grail structure in the world but surely one of the boldest, lacking any subtlety of its artistic content. Though small in size the explosion of carvings and flying buttresses lends it an otherworldly air, as if the master builder were creating life out of stone. The chapel's beauty asks to be studied by the inch, but it also demands one's respect. Nothing was left to chance and all carvings have meaning.

It is replete with flowing vegetation, Templar symbols that Freemasonry recognises easily with angels and green men.

Laurence Gardner notes that:

"There are swords, compasses, trowels, squares and mauls in abundance, along with various images of King Solomon's Temple." 4.

The Secret Dossier of a
Knight Templar of the Sangreal

He goes on to state that: "Apart from the Judaic and esoteric carvings, the Christian message is also evident, with an assortment of related depictions in stone. Amid all this there are constant traces of Islam, and the whole is strangely bound within a pagan framework of winding serpents, dragons and woodland trees. Everywhere, the wild face of the Green Man peers from the stone foliage of the pillars and arches-symbolizing the constant earth forces and the life-cycle" 5.

The Apprentice Pillar

Hiram Abiff is the legendary architect king who built King Solomon's Temple to house the Ark of the Covenant and is accredited with inventing the all-important keystone which prevents the structure of an arch from collapsing.

He was murdered by three jealous underlings who wanted his secrets of engineering. His assassination is commemorated in Freemasonry today. His face is amongst one of the many mysterious stone carvings of Rosslyn Chapel and the legend is wrapped in the Apprentice Pillar a column of incredible beauty.

Green boughs spiral up the column giving its softly squared edges an illusion of being rounded, hence its genius of carving.

An angel sits atop amidst more greenery holding an open book. The famous column is supported by salamanders, an alchemical icon of fire. The four 'corners' of the pillar and the spiral boughs represent the number eight.

The Secret of Bees

I was rather sad on approach to the chapel to see the protective scaffolding and metal roof, however it allowed for a chance to view the verdant panoramic from the top of the chapel.

The finials on the roof were remarkable with a high degree of detail one cannot see from the ground. The scaffolding was a rare opportunity for visitors as it of course would be taken down in June of 2010.

Rosslyn Chapel continues to reveal its secrets even after 600 hundred years. Two stone beehives were exposed in March 2010 during restoration work on pinnacles on the roof of Rosslyn Chapel.

It is believed that they were built as a mark of respect for wild bees and not obviously a place where they could have harvested honey easily.

Harvesting honey was already a long established practice in Europe during the 14th century. The Chapel is a wild homage in stone of the divinity of nature with the bee hives so elevated as to be unreachable by human hands.

The bees enter their stone home through a flower in order to build their honeycombs the perfect symbol of sacred geometry in nature. It is almost as if Prince William placed a 'G' atop the Chapel as bees are the only creature in nature to build in a geometric pattern and are thus considered to represent God. 6 .

The Templars of Rosslyn, Portugal
and Nova Scotia

The act rings of Bernard de Clairvaux's own quote that *"God equals length, height, width and depth!"* If there is a further secret to the bee as a symbol perhaps we should consider that the hive functions around a single Queen? I think this would have appealed to Bernard.

The New World

What are we to make of the explicit carvings of maize and Aloe Vera in Rosslyn Chapel? Since it was unknown in Europe we have to conclude that Prince Henry travelled far enough south into the warmer climes of America in order to have discovered it! As proof of this discovery his grandson would immortalise the exotic plants in stone.

The sea voyage made by William Saint Claire's' Grandfather, Prince Henry, in 1398 predated Columbus by some ninety years.

Columbus was not the first to visit the Americas but did so due to having married into the Sinclair family and acquiring their maps.

Columbus was also sponsored by Leonardo da Vinci, another recognised leader in the tradition. He was also a member of the Order of the Crescent founded by Rene d' Anjou, a Grail Prince and Grand Master.

It is accepted that the historic Templars had the most sophisticated libraries of maps of any Order of their day; it appears this trend did not alter into later centuries.

How did Henry Sinclair come to know of North America? Perhaps he was bringing relief to a Templar colony? Perhaps he'd been liaising with them as his family had since Templar vessels retreated to their Nova Scotian preceptories? We need look only to the Vikings - his ancestors from Norway - for precedence.

It appears that trade ensued for almost four hundred years from 1000 AD with the Inuit tribe and the Norsemen looking for lumber which was needed in deforested Greenland. The Orkneys were also deforested and would have benefitted by the tall pines of North America.

A Norse settlement was found at L'Anse aux Meadows in Newfoundland by archaeologist Anne Stine Ingstad 7. Proving once and for all that the discovery of the America's was indeed Norse and not Spanish-predating the Spanish claim by some 400 years if not more.

According to legend Prince Henry Sinclair took a fleet of twelve vessels and some 300 colonists, knights and men at arms to Nova Scotia, their New Jerusalem in the New World, perhaps to reseed an earlier colony. 8.

There is archaeological evidence that Prince Henry built a 'Grail Castle' in central Nova Scotia in an area reachable by a river to either side of the peninsula. The ruins are rubble work consistent with 14th century fortifications typical of Northern Scotland and Scandinavia. 9.

Oak Island

Oak Island is the home of the Oak Island Money Pit and not too far from the coast of Prince Henry's Grail Castle remains now called Ross Castle.

The Money Pit is a man-made shaft of 31 meters or approximately 101 feet that has refused to give up its secrets.

Millions of dollars have been splurged trying to pry loose its treasure and has caused the death of at least six men who have paid the price for underestimating the master builders.

Core drilling has brought up mysterious finds such as coconut fibres which had been imported from the Holy Land and dated 1200 AD to 1400 AD.

It is a phenomenal discovery as only Templars would have had the capacity or the interest in bringing sacred palms to the New Jerusalem in order to consecrate the burial of a mysterious treasure.

In 1795 a teenager named Daniel McGinnis discovered the pit, having noticed a circular depression; with the aid of two friends over several days they were able to dig down 30 feet.

Two feet down they were rewarded with flagstones covering the hole and noticed that every ten feet there had been a layer of oak logs and coconut palms.

In all it took them an eight year period with interruptions to gain 90 feet in depth where they discovered the most astonishing stone with runic inscription that has been deciphered as saying that there is 2 million pounds worth of treasure below.

Was the stone left by Norse Templars with aid from their brothers in Roslin? Was it an advanced red herring? If so, why? Recently it has been discovered that the entire beach where the pit is located is actually man made and all without the aid of heavy earth moving equipment! The beach disguises the array of tunnels used to flood the pit to prevent it from being looted. It is an engineering marvel of great skill and tenacity.

Marty and Rick Lagina are the current owners of the island. Their personal wealth has been added to the string of efforts over the centuries in an attempt to understand the mysteries of the pit and has been recorded in the History channel programme, The Curse of Oak Island. Authors Alan Butler and Kathleen McGowan joined the brothers in their search to pry loose the secrets of the centuries old mine.

Glooscap

Prince Henry is also mysteriously linked to the Glooscap legend, the creator god of the Mi'kmaq peoples; meaning to come from nothing with abilities to change his environment. Certainly moving great amounts of earth to create the Oak Island Money Pit and the building of the Newport Tower, could be construed as god-like activities.

The extraordinary architect Prince Henry may have been the impetus for the creator god. The tribe assisted the Grail Guardians from Roslin and named him Glooscap as a mark of respect and friendship with their new allies.

It has been suggested that three of Prince Henry's daughters may have married into the tribe which indicates great trust and longstanding relationship with the Mi'kmaq peoples.

Glooscap was able to control the seas and the remarkable fleet of Templar ships would have reminded the tribe of a man-god's ability to magically harness the waves.

The Mi'kmaq's were also skilled mariners and were exploring the deep waters into ancient times as well as the Norse and the Sea Peoples of the Middle Eastern legends. Steven Sora suggests that the North American tribes had contact with the Picts and other Celtic peoples long before Prince Henry and the Vikings sailed to their shores. 10. It is natural then that their god had sea connections. If Prince Henry was not Glooscap then certainly they recognised in him a remarkable individual.

The journey of Prince Henry may have been assisted by the Mi'kmaq tribe whose legends tell of the knights from afar. They recall the death of an important companion to the Prince.

The Westford Knight

Sir James Gunn is documented to have been the trusted aid of the Prince. His effigy is said to be that of the Westford Knight burial slab found in Westford Massachusetts, carrying a broken sword, the symbol of death and many symbols relating to points on the compass and stars.

The tombstone has left us with the intriguing question as to its purpose. Most Templar burials are anonymous, yet here is one that is replete with symbols which could be a map detailing hidden sacred relics. 11.

Scott Wolter, geologist and investigator of the History Channel's popular documentary series, America Unearthed, was asked to verify a newly discovered carving on the stone effigy. With his background in geology, specializing in techniques of stone carving and the components of mortar, he has increased the level of scientific evidence for the case of the Templars in the New World before Columbus.

Wolter determined that the 'X' carved into the stone was indeed a Hooked X – a Cistercian cipher which he had been researching for over 15 years.

The exciting find was released in January of 2015 in the two part programme The Templars Deadliest Secret: Evidence Exposed & the Chase. 12.

According to Wolter the Hooked X is the symbol for Mary Magdalene and her spouse, Jesus. The 'hook' within the upper part of the 'V' signifies their children – the bloodline of Christ. 13.

Hooked X Graphic by © Gretchen Cornwall

The Secret Dossier of a
Knight Templar of the Sangreal

Kensington Rune Stone

In our whistle stop tour of the North American Grail Colonies we cannot miss the Kensington Rune Stone found in Minnesota in what appears to be a European colony from 1362 (pre-dating Prince Henry's journey by 36 years) as the date on the stone attests.

In his book, the Hooked X, Wolter investigates a mysterious large stone with odd runic markings found in 1890 by a Swedish immigrant not far from Kensington, Minnesota. The runes appear to be Norse comprised with Cistercian codes of the 14th century.

Wolter maintains the stone's authenticity of Templar origin which means that it is highly probable the Templars were already in the New World by the time relief ships came from Roslin.

Their purpose for being there may have stretched back to their earlier days of Templar public life and is by some historians the reason for Templar wealth due to mining activities in the New World.

Had the Templars been visiting North America and South, as early as the Vikings? Scott Wolter thinks this is the case and that the two groups were synonymous. Again we have evidence for a continuing tradition predating the public life of the Templars.

Niven Sinclair wrote a compelling forward to Wolter's book:

"History needs to be rewritten. The North American Continent is awash with evidence of pre-Columbian visitors who left their imprint on the landscape and their writing on stones and boulders as markers for those who followed. Ogham and Runic inscriptions tell a story of Celtic and Viking penetration into the very hinterland of the New World."

He goes on to state:

"Historians have been singularly slow in explaining the presence of runic inscriptions; they describe them as "fakes" which is a convenient excuse to hide their own ignorance." He describes The Hooked X: Key to the Secret History of North America by Scott Wolter as "...a masterful combination of science and logic as well as being a gripping detective story that leaves no stone unturned (literally as well as figuratively)." Niven Sinclair 14.

Newport Tower

Another controversial location, the Newport Tower in Rhode Island, does not sit comfortably with the academic world regardless of the mortar dating to approximately the early 15th century.

William F Mann has this to say about the round tower with eight arches:

"Over the years the construction of the tower has been attributed to a virtual who's who in medieval and early colonial construction, including the Templars, the Norse, the Irish, the Portuguese, and even the colonial governor Benedict Arnold. Yet never have the Cistercians – who may have accompanied Prince Henry on his journeys –

received any credit for this building in spite of their obvious relationship with the Templars and similar knowledge base. The Templars and Cistercians were known to have been connected through their religious beliefs, business acumen, and engineering skills. Over time, in fact, the Cistercian order developed a virtual monopoly on mining and milling operations, became experts in the construction of waterworks, and, because of both of these skill bases, controlled commerce. What is more revealing is that within two hundred years of the establishment of the Cistercian order, at a time when the Templars were being forced to move underground to survive, the whole of Europe from Norway to Portugal was blanketed with Cistercian monasteries and convents." William F. Mann 15.

Scott Wolter has also surveyed the Newport Tower and concludes it is Templar in origin and that the prototype may be found in Tomar, Portugal.

"Inside the Knights Templar castle overlooking the city of Tomar, Portugal, is a church with an ornately decorated altar that is a near exact architectural replica of the Newport Tower. The eight-columned, two story octagonal stone tower with rounded arches is the most sacred part of the church and is consistent with the claims of many researchers the Newport Tower was built by circa 1400 era Knights Templar as an observatory and a church." Scott Wolter 16.

The blog he has written on Google shares stirring photos of the church and other locations from his journey to Portugal and Paris.

The Newport Tower includes an egg-shaped keystone which aligns to Venus and also a notched keystone which bears a striking resemblance to that held by the great Statue of Liberty. Wolter concludes that the tower was an observatory and a holy place of worship.

Wolter also noted the rising sun of 9:00 am struck the egg shaped stone and was being used as a keystone above one of the arches. He discovered that it corresponded with the time of morning when Christ was crucified.

Religious monastic hours of prayer are conducted from sunrise at 6am, 9am, 12 pm, 3 pm and 6pm or Vespers/sunset. He had found one solar office of prayer, were there more indications that the Newport Tower was a holy observation structure? 17.

Wolter continued his study of the Newport Tower into the day and found that the sun had indeed expressed itself on another keystone at 3PM. This confirmed the theory that the tower was aligned to the Benedictine daily monastic prayer cycle. 18.

Ross Castle

Ross Castle in Nova Scotia was investigated by Scott Wolter and found that its rubble was consistent with those of castle remains in Europe. During a filmed documentary for his programme, America Unearthed, he excavated its remains and found a subterranean chamber within its confines that had been backfilled. Any possible treasure that had been there was moved and the chamber destroyed long ago. The castle is in a ruinous state and sits on private property.

The Secret Dossier of a
Knight Templar of the Sangreal

The Templar colonies did not seem to survive in the harsh wild environment despite evidence to suggest that they and their allies were visiting the Americas over several hundred years.

What befell the colonies is a mystery. There are those that think they survived, having married into the tribes and others that believe they died out or went back to Europe. Perhaps all of the above? Others claim they were killed by incoming colonists who might have been shocked at seeing Caucasian faces already on shore or perhaps even their mixed-race descendants.

It is known that Prince Henry returned to Roslin leaving many of the colonists behind, but he was assassinated shortly thereafter. Although it is equally possible he died defending Scotland from an English invasion but records do not exist to corroborate or dispel either scenario.

Needless to say the initial Templar search for freedom was successfully met by those following George Washington several hundred years later.

The Order of the Garter

I will seemingly digress for a moment to introduce the Order of the Garter to better understand one of its members, Prince Henry the Navigator of Tomar in Portugal.

The Order of the Garter was established in 1348 by Edward III of England under unusual circumstances. He is viewed as one of England's greatest kings out of the ashes of his father, Edward II's disastrous reign. 19.

It is probable that secular Templar priests advised Edward III upon the formation of the Order of the Garter and its associations with the Round Table of King Arthur. Supposedly, Joan the Countess of Salisbury lost her garter during a ball. The Countess was duly embarrassed until the King came to her rescue. He put on the lost garter and told the snickering crowd, 'evil to him who thinks evil of it', which became the motto for the Chivalrous Knightly Order whose patron Saint is the dragon slayer Saint George.

There is hidden magical meaning behind this event and the actions of the King. The circular garter is a representation of the Round Table itself along with the English flag which bears strong links to the Templar Order, literally mimicking the Red Cross on the white background. That a woman seemed to be the centre of the controversy puts the subject of the Divine Feminine back on the map as a continuing theme.

Much has been made of the timing for the formation of the Order of the Garter and its Gnostic imagery of the dragon slayer and the Templar cross in the defence of a lady meant to represent a hidden goddess or priestess.

The Order of the Garter is the highest honour of Great Britain with lifelong membership and only numbering a total of 24, twice the number of a coven or discipleship.

The Templars of Rosslyn, Portugal and Nova Scotia

The Other Prince Henry-The Navigator

Prince Henry the Navigator was a member of the most prestigious English chivalrous order ever formed, the Order of the Garter. His presence in the order was indicative of the close ties between England and Portugal, based on mutual Templar and family interests. The political friendship exists today, remarkable considering it has been an alliance which has lasted 700 years.

Interestingly enough, Columbus' father in law was actually a relative of Prince Henry the Navigator of Portugal. Philippa of Lancaster was his mother and sister to King Henry IV of England. She inspired the initial search for a trade route with Christian Ethiopia across Africa as the Muslims blocked access via Egypt and the Mediterranean. Her hopes were with the legendary King of India.

"With Prester John's cooperation, perhaps, a new spice route could be established, with caravans crossing Africa to the Red Sea and bringing pepper and cloves to Lisbon. Philippa herself organized the expedition, devoting three years to arranging the financing and assembling the arms, ships and men. Three of her sons took part...." Robert Silverberg. 20.

One of which was of course Prince Henry, her third son, who carried on the mission set out by his mother. Prince Henry the Navigator was born in 1394 and became the Grand Master of the Order of Christ in Tomar, Portugal at the age of 23 until his death in 1460. From this point on the Kings of Portugal would be the titular heads of the Order.

He had distinguished himself militarily in battle against the Moors and Barbary Pirates and was well respected in his leadership capabilities. His impact on the world was great, sparking an organized exploration of the world and pushing the science of navigation forward affecting the next four hundred years of European colonisation.

As history attests, the route to Ethiopia across land proved too perilous for the Navigator's time. He focussed instead on circumventing Africa in order to reach the Indies. This also proved a monumental task taking many decades and one which he would not live to see himself.

The Portuguese navigator Vasco da Gama, who had links to the Order of Christ, directly benefitted from Prince Henry's knowledge and pioneered the Cape route to India in 1497. He carried with him letters of introduction to Prester John and a white flag with the double red cross of the Order of Christ.

As a foremost maritime innovator and true to Templar tradition, Prince Henry sought out the best technology and information regardless of its provenance. He engaged Christian, Jewish and Muslim experts in a broad range of fields, specifically navigation and cartography.

True to the life of a priest, he never married and lived an austere life that Bernard de Clairvaux would have approved. He set up his own school of navigation and an observatory. He himself never travelled, preferring to direct the exploration from afar, spending his time on gathering information from his captains and others engaged in the mission to find a way through to Ethiopia around Africa.

Prince Henry also spent a great deal of attention on his ships, developing the lighter, faster Caravel. Though small it was swift with the capacity for sailing further and with greater efficiency.

Regardless of the fruit borne out of his navigational studies there is a shroud of secrecy around the Prince and his activities. Secrecy was so great that information gathered during any voyage was held close upon pain of death. One could speculate that the monetary gain from his increased knowledge would be worth the suppression of information in itself; but for one important clue - Prester John.

Therefore we may indeed have evidence for the real motivation behind the push to Ethiopia besides the riches to be gained through new allies and possible trade routes.

We cannot assume that the English crown had the Ark at this time, simply because they seem to have launched a great effort to locate it through Philippa. If we accept that the Order of the Garter was Templar in origin then it presupposes they had knowledge of Prester John as a guardian of the Ark of the Covenant.

True it was widely accepted in Saint Bernard's time that Prester John existed and the Templars of the 12th century took it quite seriously, eventually placing his kingdom as being that of Ethiopia.

The Templars closest to the English crown of the 15th century may have lost the knowledge of the other Arks that had been in the possession of their fellow brethren 300 years prior.

It may be that they sought the knowledge to build an Ark and to gain access to the information via its guardian, Prester John of Ethiopia. The information of the Ark seems to have flowed from the Order of the Garter to Philippa. She then engaged her Portuguese husband and son Henry who acted upon it with the greatest of passion.

Author Graham Hancock points out that an interesting link to the Templar Order may be that of Prince Henry's will which was dated by him as 13 October 1460, an echo of the date of the arrests in Paris 153 years earlier. Graham Hancock 21.

Hancock also points out that a decade prior to Vasco de Gama's successful voyage, the Grand Master of the Order of Christ sent Pero de Covilhan on a secret mission through difficult Islamic-held territories in an effort to reach Ethiopia.

Covilhan succeeded in reaching his objective but was held under comfortable house arrest all his life by the emperor. Hancock surmises he was searching for information regarding the Ark. He was alive when the first official Portuguese ambassador set foot in Ethiopia.

The author goes on to say:

"...One of the members of this embassy was Father Francisco Alvarez – and the reader will recall that it was Alvarez who had been told by priests of the ancient tradition that the rock-hewn churches of Lalibela had been 'made by white men'." He goes on to say, "...I now turned back to the English translation of the length narrative that Alvarez had written after leaving Ethiopia in 1526. Re-reading his chapter on Lalibela I was struck by the description he gave of the church of Saint George. Carved into the roof of this great edifice, he said, was 'a double cross, that is, one within the other, like the crosses of the Order of Christ'." Graham Hancock 22.

The Templars of Rosslyn, Portugal and Nova Scotia

The Templar Knights carved out the church of Saint George a few centuries prior to the official visit by their Portuguese inheritors, who came bearing an identical cross on a white silk background to the Emperor of Ethiopia, Lebna Dengel.

The Emperor would soon be plunged into war by an invading Muslim army bent on wiping out the Christian country. He held off any acceptance of help from the Portuguese during six years of constant incursions by the Muslims.

His hesitancy to include Portugal in Ethiopia's defence may have been brought about by his concern over their interest in the Ark. Eventually weakened he had to concede that his country would not stand unless the Europeans stepped in.

Exhausted and brokenhearted, he died before that help could arrive, leaving his son who was only in his early 20s to lead their diminished army.

In 1541 rescue came as 450 Portuguese musketeers landed at Massawa.

"The British Historian Edward Gibbon was later to summarize their achievements in just nine words: 'Ethiopia was saved by four hundred and fifty Portuguese." Ernesto Frers 23.

They were led by none other than the son of Vasco de Gama a Knight of the Order of Christ. Two years later the Muslims gave up their ambitions to harness the Ethiopian nation suffering great losses under the forceful musketeers who fought with leonine heroic proportions. Their efforts to secure the Ark or to gain its secrets seemed to have failed, however. Some one hundred years later Emperor Fasilidas deported all Portuguese settlers and ordered any who attempted entry into the country to be beheaded.

The story does not end here however....

1725 woodcut of Stede Bonnet with a Jolly Roger inCharles Johnson's
A General History of the Pyrates

The Secret Dossier of a
Knight Templar of the Sangreal

We take for granted the menacing flag of the pirates known as the Jolly Roger as a common every day image of violent times past, fancy dress parties and the poison to be avoided under the kitchen sink.

The Templar fleet split and went separate directions, some becoming pirates whose emblem of the Skull and Crossbones is well known to Freemasonry and modern 'pirate lore'.

Why they took to the sea is easily understood. Those who served the Order on vessels as Templar Knights and retainers were simply good at it and were not going to dispense with their knowledge of the seas as well as their vital resources - ships and men at their disposal - already trained, ready and eager to strike a blow against those who had betrayed their Order.

They simply continued serving the Order as the most experienced mariners of their time. It is theorised that the 'pirates' terrorised Catholic vessels, engaging in a secret war on the seas lasting hundreds of years after 1307 with a navy that should not have existed.

Eventually these mariners and their descendants would meld into the various countries in which they found themselves, their battles turning into the political concerns of nations in which they were loyal. One such would become the United States of America.

The Skull and Crossbones is a deep esoteric reference to inner transformation as well as being a blatant demand on the high seas to 'stand and deliver' or face your maker!

When shifted, the crossbones serve as a hidden Star of David and also the equal lateral cross of the Templars when in a straightened position.

The skull is emblematic of John the Baptist their patron Saint. Many variations on the Flag developed over the years with quite blatant symbolic messages hidden in full public view striking terror into the hearts of the intended victims who never realised the full impact of what they were witnessing.

The flags colouration is curiously close to the Templar flag the Beasant and the classic black and white marble flooring of Masonic Halls first seen in Solomon's famous Temple.

Those ships that fled to Portugal flew the flag of the country that adopted them whereas the English and French Templar galleys had to fly another flag, adopting the Jolly Roger already in use a few centuries before by a maritime King.

The image first appeared under the reign of Roger II of Sicily (1095-1151) who enjoyed connections with the Templars. Though it has to be said the affiliation was not always an easy one as he ran afoul of Saint Bernard, choosing to support Pope Anacletus II over Bernard's choice of Innocent II.

There are always disagreements when human beings are brought together regardless of their fundamental and shared belief systems. Roger II was a patron of the arts and cultivated a shinning educated court where his subjects and guests named him *le joyeux Roger* or Roger the Jolly. 24.

The Skull and Crossbones can be clearly seen on Templar tombstones in Scotland and naturally were continued to be used by a branch of their descendants, the Freemasons.

The Templars of Rosslyn, Portugal and Nova Scotia

1. Laurence Gardner: Bloodline of the Holy Grail, Element Books, 1996 p. 296
2. Tim Wallace-Murphy & Marilyn Hopkins: Guardian of the Secrets of the Holy Grail, P. 7.
3. Ibid
4. Laurence Gardner: Bloodline of the Holy Grail, Element Books, 1996 p. 296
5. Laurence Gardner: Bloodline of the Holy Grail, Element Books, 1996 p. 296
6. http://www.timesonline.co.uk/tol/news/uk/scotland/article7080735.ece
From The Times March 30, 2010 Rosslyn Chapel discovery is causing a buzz Melanie Reid
7. http://en.wikipedia.org/wiki/L%27Anse_aux_Meadows
8. David Hatcher Childress: Pirates and the Lost Templar Fleet, p 158
9. David Hatcher Childress: Pirates and the Lost Templar Fleet, p 158
10. Steven Sora: The Lost Trasure of the Knights Templar, p 69
11. William F. Mann: The Templar Meridians, p. 42 & 43
12. http://www.history.com/shows/america-unearthed/episodes)
13. http://scottwolteranswers.blogspot.co.uk/2015/01/two-brand-new-medieval-hooked-xs.html
14. Introduction by Niven Sinclair, The Hooked X: Key to the Secret History of North America by Scott Wolter, ISBN: 0-087839-312-9 William F. Mann: The Templar Meridians, p 67
15. William F. Mann: The Templar Meridians, p 67
16. http://scottwolteranswers.blogspot.co.uk/2015/01/two-brand-new-medieval-hooked-xs.html
17. Pg 209, Scott F. Wolter, The Hooked X, North Star Press of St Cloud Inc, 2009, ISBN -13-978-0-87839-312-1.
18. Pg 210 Scott F. Wolter, The Hooked X, North Star Press of St Cloud Inc, 2009, ISBN -13-978-0-87839-312-1.
19. Elizabeth Hallam, Editor: Chronicles of the age of Chivalry: ISBN 0-297-79220-2 Page 262
20. Robert Silverberg: The Realm of Prester John ISBN 1-84212-409-9 Page 194 195
19. Graham Hancock: The Sign and the Seal ISBN 0-671-86541-2 page 170
20 Graham Hancock: The Sign and the Seal ISBN 0-671-86541-2 page 171
21 Graham Hancock: The Sign and the Seal ISBN 0-671-86541-2 page 173
22. Ibid
23. Ernesto Frers: The Templar Pirates: The Secret Alliance To Build The New Jerusalem, ISBN 10-1-59477-146-4 Page 44
24. Ibid

Twenty One

The Templar Matrix Map of the World

Matrix Definition

"A substance, situation, or environment in which something has its origin, takes form, or is enclosed" The Free Dictionary

During the Introduction, I explained that I'd been contacted by a modern day Templar descendant and was given a map for inclusion in the book. I've subsequently named it the Matrix Map. The definition of 'matrix' describes the supportive qualities of Gaia-Earth which allowed for the natural creation of the magnetic lines found on the map.

Through years researching the map, its properties became more apparent as multiple scientific, historic and intuitive disciplines led me from one discovery to the next in a seemingly never-ending line of exciting revelations. If my tone seems overtly positive, I can only state in my defence that there are simply too many connections to be ignored or brushed aside as coincidental.

During the meeting, the Comte de Medici (aka John Temple) gave many clues to the map's significance, but I was certainly not handed all the relevant information. He was deeply taken with the map and very proud of it with the bearing of certainty that could only come from experience and the knowledge of hope that it would bring for the future.

He actually stated that his order was surprised no one had discovered at least some aspects of its secrets, hence the need to give the map to a member of the public. I have to admit, after wrestling with it over the past few years, I had some sympathy for my fellow members of the public.

This was an interesting comment he had made however and has led me to suspect that the Tradition has over the centuries given intuitively divined theories to the public to develop, or to 'discover' them and to a 'timeline' which suggests an overall beneficial plan for society as a whole.

I do not wish to belittle actual scientific research and the hard-won theories or inventions which spring from highly intelligent and fevered brows across the world in any era, but that there has been guided-intuitive precedence for some forward leaps from those capable of inner-space travel or remote viewing, and those capable of recognizing the potential of that imparted theory or knowledge. Even so an inspired theory still must be broken down by hard work on the physical plane to bring it into fruition. After all, Leonardo di Vinci envisioned a helicopter but did not have the technology at the time to develop it further.

The Templar Matrix Map of the World

How did the Matrix Map function? What is its purpose? Could a human being interact with it? In other words, I had to break the code of the Templar's secret Matrix Map of the World.

Conversations with a Templar

I was to discover through my own research that there are five aspects to this mapping system that had been put into my hands as a puzzle.

One is of magnetic lines which span the earth, secondly creating geometric shapes and third its odd ties to the British Ordnance Survey Map. The fourth element is related to latitude and longitude. The fifth element explores mysteries of 'pre-history' and current historical episodes and personages. All five aspects overlap with one another in an eerie synchronistic manner.

John Temple also brought up the importance of that infamous date of 21 December 2012. The highly-debated date has spurred an industry of careers, books and films all culminating on what many thought could either be the end of the world or the beginning of an enlightened era or a combination of both.

I have always hoped for a positive outcome to humanity's fate myself. The seeds of which are seen all around us in the good works of empathically-driven individuals and groups around the world.

The more empathy we have as a race the better our chances of survival are as a species and the happier we will be as a whole. Many researchers have noted the changing energy of earth herself, and as she is our mother, the effect on us as electromagnetic beings must be significant.

The Comte believed that the date was highly important and that the changes wrought by the approach of the date and also the aftermath would be felt for years to come. He spoke of a fifth world and a new age of enlightenment and peace on earth.

This book will be released well after 2012 so I will not develop this event further here except to say that our sun aligned with the central sun of the galaxy. It is a massive event which takes place every 26,000 years and known as Precession. We are experiencing an ever increasing brightness over a period of time as if in a room with a galactic dimmer switch.

As the date wanes and we pass 21 December 2012 the effect will be with us for another two hundred years. Therefore we will see continued heightened change in a similar burst of social, political and technological marvels and upheavals.

Noted 2012 author Walter Cruttenden, who was the guest author in September 2012 on Graham Hancock's informative site, suggests that the effects of Precession actually started a few hundred years earlier than my own reckoning and also have a positive outlook on humanities overall fate:

"This means we are now awakening from a time when individual consciousness perceived itself as purely a physical form, living in a strictly physical universe, to a time when we begin to see ourselves and the universe as more transparent and mostly made up of subtle energy. This began with the discoveries of the Renaissance (principles of electricity, laws of gravitation, microscopes, telescopes, and other inventions that expanded our awareness) and has accelerated since with the emergence of quantum physics, which shows us that matter and energy are interchangeable and proves Einstein's concepts that even time and space are relative. In short, we are back on the upswing, just beginning to "re-member" ourselves as pure consciousness living in a world of undreamed of possibilities."

According to Paramahansa Yogananda, author of Autobiography of a Yogi, by the year 4100 AD (when we cross into the Treta Yuga proper):

"telepathy and clairvoyance will once again be common knowledge." It may seem far-fetched, but according to myth and folklore, there was such a time on Earth before, in about 3100 BC, the last Treta Yuga. Genesis would designate the Treta Yuga the pre-Babel age, when mankind communed freely with nature before God "confused the tongues." 1.

I was literally told that my book was meant to assist the future and I could only conclude that he and the modern Templars also thought the world would certainly continue in hope and not disappear in a flaming field of broken asteroids as predicted by many 2012 doomsayers. Certainly he was trying to impress that human beings are linked with the earth's energy patterns and that we must as individuals become more aware of interacting with earth and also becoming more responsible for our own thoughts as their impact on the environment and each other is profound.

Further I can only extrapolate that the timing of release for the Matrix Map is due to public heightened interest in quantum mechanics and intuitive sciences. Why the Templars want to share this with the world now might only be explained by this shift and acceptance of these scientific ideals in cultural thought.

As far as 'standard' maps are concerned the world is very well measured and continually plotted by satellites. Maps were guarded as state secrets in the past for many reasons but this has completely changed. Currently with the progress of the computer era, Google Earth software and many other programs are freely available. Our knowledge of the globe is complex and available to the average person and with growing accuracy.

Illustration One (opposite) is of the whole world. I found it curious that there were more intersecting lines across the Middle East and Europe than the Americas, China, Russia or Asia - except one point off the western coast of Peru and that of Nova Scotia. The later certainly makes sense as Nova Scotia has long been connected with the Templars.

The modern map I was actually given is – (AA Map of the World–ISBN 0-7495-4603-4 – Scale 1:32,5000,000-1 CM = 325 KM – 1 inch = 512 Miles) The original map I was given is online at

http://thesecretdossier.co.uk/maps-stars/

Due to copyright laws I am not able to reproduce the actual map here but developed my own illustration for the purposes of this book.

© Gretchen Cornwall

The Templar Matrix Map of the World

The Secret Dossier of a
Knight Templar of the Sangreal

It almost appears as if the lines correspond to areas that the historic Templars would have been able to visit or had knowledge of through their antecedents.

However this does not explain their knowledge of Peru, or the fact that there are singular lines running through, however sparsely, to the other nations mentioned.

Unless they were physically visited or Remote Viewing was employed centuries ago. He has said that the historic Templars could follow these lines to where they intersected, which is evident at important locations such as Malta, Geneva, Dover and Bornholm and also to the major energy centres of multiple energetic crossings. However the provenance of the map is modern and by a 'sighted' Templar.

He was quite emphatic about the importance of a very large mountain which straddles the borders of Egypt, Sudan and Libya, indeed Jebel Uweinat is one of the least explored mountains in the world. Egyptian hieroglyphs of the Pharaoh Mentuhotep II which date back 4000 years were discovered in 2008, other pre-historic glyphs have been found as well and are in need of protection. 2.

He did make the comment that he believed these massive magnetic lines actually helped to form continents and that human beings were responding to the energy lines and forming the borders of countries around the lines.

Examining Portugal and the vastness of North America one could see his point. Does this statement answer the question as to whether or not this was a completed energetic global map and a matrix that was formed when the world was new?

Have the lines changed over the long passage of distant time? Or have they remained constant and their subtle energies eventually the cause of Continental Drift?

The nature of our magnetic earth shield changes and we have experienced magnetic pole shifts approximately every hundred thousand years. How this has affected the Matrix Map in our distant past I am not certain. Anything is possible, but when did the Templars become aware of the energy lines and their significance? Had they known of it during their historic period and then forgotten? Is this a recent rediscovery?

On the face of it – I concede that the map does not look inspiring at all until one delves into its substance which is one reason I trusted it as there was no attempt to dress it up and make it appear to be something other than straightforward.

It was up to me to figure out why it was important as he already knew it was. Basically I was given a series of lines drawn on a modern map and without any knowledge of the date when this was in use or when its properties were discovered – possibly lost and rediscovered.

Even with these caveats, it has proved to be worth studying and has led me to discover interesting historical links between S.E. England and a seemingly disconnected area in the north of the country with some rather amazing historical personages that I would never have heard of otherwise. The map has proven to be a golden thread linking, churches, people and history together.

Interestingly enough, during the meeting with the Comte, he did not refer to the lines as ley-lines, only calling them magnetic lines. However the properties he describes these lines as having, run parallel to ley-lines. He was insistent that the lines could be perceived intuitively by both animals and also a trained navigator.

Since the Matrix Map stretched across land as well as sea, its sacred purpose would not have been limited to the Templar navy as we will explore. The Templars were masters of the sea almost from day one, and as I have shown in prior chapters had been visiting North and South America at least from the 9th century. But there are other clues which indicate that Templar awareness of this map may be far older and visits to far flung places of the earth by the Tradition could go back millennia.

The Feathered Serpent

In answer to my question during our conversation regarding the Templars' ability to travel afar, I was reminded of the legendary Quetzalcoatl. I was rather pleased the subject had been raised.

The Aztecs claimed that their culture was given to them by a pale god and that they had built the main tenants of their civilisation on his teachings. This foreign god from across the sea taught their ancestors geometry and the arts of peace before returning eastward from whence he came. He was called the Feathered-Serpent.

"...the tradition of the white god who came from over the seas and brought civilisation with him was common to Mexico, to Yucatan and to Peru alike. His title was Quetzalcoatl in Mexico, Itzamna or Kukulcan among the Maya of Yucatan and Vira-Kocha or Tiki in Peru." James Bailey 3.

The importance of Quetzalcoatl cannot be over stated. The pyramid dedicated to him at Cholula has a base of 45 acres alone, far larger than that of any Egyptian pyramid.

Authors James Bailey and Graham Hancock both came to many of the same conclusions as that of the brilliant Victorian writer Ignatius Donnelly who asked the following question, "On the monuments of Central America there are representations of bearded men. How could the beardless American Indians have imagined a bearded race?" 4.

Hancock, author of Heaven's Mirror, also asserts that this individual remembered as the god-man Quetzalcoatl was part of a pre-existing civilisation that had, as explorers and pioneers, brought their skills with them to South America. According to Hancock these long-ago explorers and settlers may have travelled much further north. 5.

The Kennewick Man found in Washington State, USA, was shockingly dated in 1997 as being over 9300 years old, having been mummified by the elements. He displayed physical features consistent with Europeans. Similar remains have been found as far east as Minnesota much to the surprise of archaeologists. 6. Caucasians were not supposed to have visited this part of the world prior to Columbus. But as we have seen with the Vikings and the Templars that this assessment is not accurate and has been overturned in recent years.

Geneticist and Mitochondrial DNA expert, Douglas Wallace, postulated that Europeans had migrated to North America as early as 15,000 years ago! DNA mapping of great Diasporas have overturned many preconceptions of history. This particular discovery is a great example of true science overcoming past misconceptions and is supported by ancient finds thus giving credence to revisionist historians. Native Americans living around the Great Lakes and also the Iroquois have within their genetic heritage strong links to Europe. 7.

Evidence of the worship of the feathered-serpent precedes the Aztecs through three prior cultures and having existed at least 3500 years ago *and more*. Scholars tend to overlook the evidence found in South America as it does not suit the historical record. The Aztecs said these early settlers 'seeded' the area and were the 'first' peoples.

Many engravings dating back to 1000 BC have been uncovered in Mexico with Caucasian features. Graham Hancock asks, "How old are the myths of Quetzalcoatl? Could they go back to these prehistoric Caucasians, 'similar to Europeans', who were in the Americas in the Stone Age, at least 9000 years ago?" 8.

An interesting question to ask: were these South & North American cultures being 'reintroduced' at various points in history to the same ideas such as advanced stone masonry, spiritual ideals and astronomy - via representatives of the ancient Tradition - especially since we are looking at such vast spans of time in major building works whose purpose was identical? Communion with the stars within and without.

South America may have been repeatedly visited by a culture which had a vast political outreach and indeed had outposts or colonies in the Americas, Asia, Africa and Europe.

During the interview with the Comte the controversial subject of Atlantis was broached.

He stated that it most certainly *did* exist. It became an exciting meeting to say the least!

As for myself I appreciated hearing this from a man who I considered to be a credible modern Templar descendant with knowledge. In the following years since this meeting I have not had cause to repeal my initial assessment. Though I've only had a few further brief conversations, the information I was given is strong enough to verify itself, therefore my impression has remained positive.

As an Atlantis proponent myself, its existence as discussed by the Templar Knight was not a difficult concept to embrace. I was however always willing to take on new ideas as to its location which cannot be 'proved', but its existence in my estimation is without question based upon the extensive myths, geological and climate changes of the past – which actually *allow* for Atlantis, along with archaeological evidence in other countries that does not fit the current historical time-line.

Graham Hancock states that Plato's Atlantis was given a date of 9600BC for its demise. Other legends never assert a date for catastrophic events, but may only be extrapolated loosely, based on the date the culture in question wrote their legends, which are in *their* distant past beyond their own memory and supportive archaeology. His point is highly significant lending an intriguing historical context to the date of the Atlantean cultures supposed demise. 9.

Continental Drift has been cited as the reason why Atlantis could not have existed in the Atlantic and must surely be only a morality tale invented by Plato about the destruction of Santorini and the Minoan civilisation which are the current favourite locations of the academic world for Atlantis.

But Plato was exact about the date and location which means that the Greek island of Santorini's destruction is far too recent, not to mention it is simply in the wrong place. Santorini is within the Mediterranean Sea and not beyond the Pillars of Hercules – the Straits of Gibraltar. We must look elsewhere and in the Atlantic which is where Plato gave us as the location of the fabled civilisation.

Plato's source for Atlantis came from Egypt. What credibility can we allot to the Egyptians for this story? A quick glance at their culture may provide a valid point. We cannot replicate an Egyptian pyramid today, even with our 'advanced' technology such was the high state of their precision building.

The Egyptian interest and ability to accurately record history is well known, along with their ability to travel the seas and trade with other cultures. Indeed Egypt was at war with Atlantis at one point according to the Greek scholar. It seems as if differences of opinion had sprung up between these far flung family member states. If Plato, by way of the Egyptians, were so exact about the date, why would Plato have misplaced a civilisation in the wrong sea?

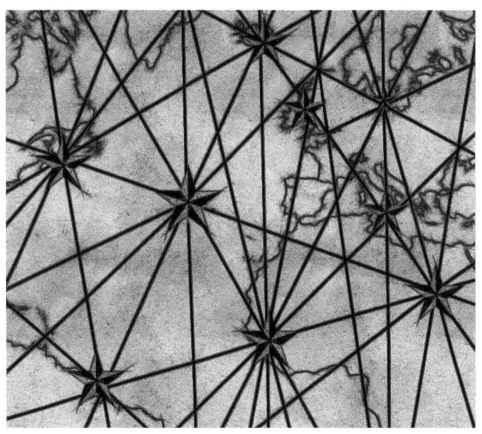

Map of the Atlantic, Nova Scotia & Western Europe & Africa by © Gretchen Cornwall

The Secret Dossier of a
Knight Templar of the Sangreal

My Templar contact exonerates Plato's location for the capitol by stating that the Azores were the remains of the lost Atlantis. One can see multiple crossings of the magnetic lines over the Azores marking - it as a site of significance and high energy.

The German Jesuit scholar and cabalist, Athanasius Kircher (1602 1680), wrote his magnum opus, Mundus Subterraneus in 1665 – replete with alchemical imagery and philosophy. He is the father of modern geology and is considered of equal stature to Leonardo da Vinci, such was the importance of his work across a plethora of volumes.

The adventurous spirit once had himself lowered into Mt. Vesuvius to explore the active volcanoe's inner workings! He was also the spiritual mentor of the painter Nicholas Poussin whose famous painting Et in Arcadia Ego has been the subject of many recent books and thought to hold the secret of Rennes Le Chateau.

He discusses the location of Atlantis as being what appears to be a large Island in the Azores. He maintains that it is a copy of an ancient Egyptian map, thus making it on par in importance to Plato's own work on Atlantis and giving further weight to Plato's claims as the two original sources are both Egyptian.

As far as we know, Plato did not include a map of Atlantis in his work. Is it possible that he had the map and original manuscript but they became separated? How Kircher came into possession of the map is a mystery, but it is conceivable that it was rescued from the infamous burning of the Alexandrian Library or the Romans had taken it from Egypt on the fall of Cleopatra's reign in 30 BC, thus eventually bringing it to Italy and European hands where it was copied through the centuries and survived long enough for the scholar to utilise in his theories on geology.

The map is clearly 'upside down' as North is actually in the South. But it could be suggested that this is what gives credence to Kircher's claim of its Egyptian origins, as the Egyptians viewed their own country in this very same fashion.

The Upper Nile was considered to be in the south by their accounts and placed the Lower Nile in the North. Upside down to the way we view the world today. Turning the map upside down places Atlantis in the Azores with the names of current countries and continents clearly marked by the German scholar. America, Atlantic Ocean, Atlantis, Africa and Spain are named by Kircher and in their correct location.

The Templar Matrix Map of the World

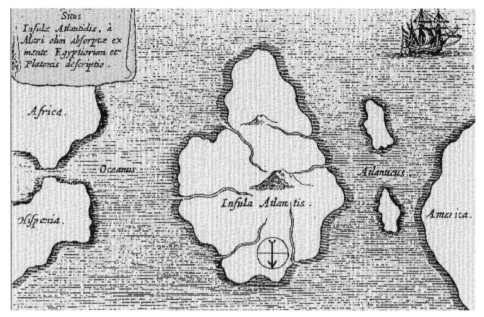

Athanasius Kircher, Mundus Subterraneus, 1665 10.

The Latin translation from the upper left hand corner reads – "Site of Atlantis now beneath the sea according to the beliefs of the Egyptians and the description of Plato."

What I find interesting about this map are the two smaller islands off the coast of America. Could these two smaller land masses shown on the map be the remains of Atlantean satellites and solving the riddle of the Bimini Road in Florida? Might we view the lower island as Saint John's of Nova Scotia and the upper island as once having existed off the coast of Florida?

The enigmatic underwater structures called the Bimini road, thought by many to be submerged ancient architecture and just off the coast of Florida, have been cited as possible Atlantean remains.

This has caused many to place Atlantis just near Florida and not in the Azores. However I would suggest that the Bimini structures are most certainly related to the civilisation on the Azores as Kircher's interpretation of the Egyptian map indicates.

Modern geologists dismiss these very regular, large blocks on the sea bed as being a natural formation and scoff at the idea that they are the remnants of an advanced past.

Of course the Bimini Road is within the infamous Bermuda Triangle which raises another topic of great interest. John Temple made the comment that he was looking forward to hearing what the UFO community had to say about the map in connection to the Bermuda Triangle, and the many disturbances and disappearances of flights and ships in the area, and the odd effects it has had on human beings caught within its domain.

The Secret Dossier of a
Knight Templar of the Sangreal

The Cuban Subsea Pyramid Complex was discovered within the last few years by Pauline Zalitzki and her colleague and fellow scientist Paul Weinzweig. The pyramids are larger than Egypt's monuments and the city is unmistakably of human intention. Streets laid out, temples, dwellings all that is needed for human habitation sunken beneath 600 feet of water. The area has been painstakingly mapped by submersibles and reproduced in 3D imaging by the pair and their team. The end of the last ice-age took the city state leaving its legends to baffle historians. 11.

The city in the Atlantic near Cuba validates both Plato and Kircher. At this point we have Plato's account and Kircher's map as evidence for Atlantis having existed along with what we might call cultural anomalies across continents.

It has been stated that the Azores could not have been Atlantis due to the lack of archaeological finds and seems to have been uninhabited until the Portuguese claimed it in the 15th century. Prince Henry the Navigator initiated the first settlement and the legend of Prestor John also became entangled with the Azores.

There is an explanation as to the lack of major finds. Perhaps anything mankind had built was literally levelled and washed away? Most capitols are not on the apex of the tallest mountain peaks (as the Azores are seen today) as it makes transport of goods needed to sustain commerce quite difficult.

There may very well be the remains of ruins deep underwater and further down the sides of the massive mountains that form the Azores today. A decayed underwater pyramid could look like a rounded mountain or hill. A ruined temple or town covered by meters of mud flow and sediment would have a softly rolling appearance and very difficult to detect. Constant quake activity through the millennia could have caused further displacement of significant archaeology that one would expect of a world capitol.

We are left with a modern impression of the Azores as some distant remote set of islands not having seen human habitation prior to the very capable Prince Henry the Navigator. However this has been recently overturned by Portuguese archaeologist Nuno Ribeiro (president of the Portuguese Association of Archaeological Research) who had been studying the larger island of Terceira since 2010. 12.

The search broadened out to reveal activity across four islands. It seems that Romans had left inscriptions, the Greeks and Carthaginians had left coins.

Carthaginian temples dedicated to the goddess Tanit and many hypogeums (vaulted burial chambers) have been discovered. There is evidence of habitation going back to the Bronze Age which includes ancient rock carvings in caves.

Certainly this is not definitive proof of Atlantis as most of the activity is too recent but it is an indication that the islands were *not* cut off from curious human beings with the capacity to travel the seas going back millennia. It is possible that the Bronze Age rock carvings may be of interest to us in the future in regards to Atlantean remains.

The Azores are a series of nine volcanic islands of such height that they are amongst the tallest mountains in the world with much of its land mass under water.

Atlantis may not have been a large continent but very well could have been a series of islands of varying size along the imposing under water Mid Atlantic Ridge which is the longest mountain range in the world and seismologically active today.

It is also possible that the more this area is explored and technology advances we may find that the island was actually as large as Kircher and Plato state.

As I am trying to be true to Plato's account regarding the information of Atlantis, can I really 'cherry pick' what he has put forward? Taking on board a few ideas and leaving others out? Perhaps the main island was as large as he stated? Currently the geological data does not support this; we shall see. But science is constantly overturning prior theories.

It is also easy for errors of translation to occur over time. So it is possible Plato had the correct location and the timeframe for Atlantis as being an ancient culture that may have lasted millennia; but that he had the size of the island wrong?

The theory of Continental Drift actually *does* support the Azores as the location of Atlantis. There is a mini continent in a triangular form where the Azores 'fit' using the accepted theory of plate tectonics of the original and ancient mass continent of Pangaea.

"It is evident that any search for Atlantis must focus its attention closely upon the Azores. The evidence that these islands form but the mountain peaks of a recently-submerged landmass becomes more extensive with every passing year. It is now freely admitted that the archipelago sits upon a continental plate composed largely of granite and sedimentary rock, described as the Azores Microplate. The Mircroplate, of triangular shape, encompasses an area roughly the size of Ireland, and it is obvious that this mini-continent must at one time have been conjoined to the African and Iberian plates. A glance at a map reveals that the Microplate forms a rather neat 'fit' into the triangular Atlantic indent between Spain and Morocco." Emmet John 13.

Opponents of the Azores as the home of Atlantis state that the M.A.R. could only have produced a series of islands and it certainly could not have supported a global capitol due to their comparable diminutive size. As we have seen, a micro-continent the size of Ireland would suffice for our capitol of Atlantis though it certainly is not the large landmass that Plato puts forward, unless a discovery overturns this assessment.

I would like to remind readers that Britain, even with its much smaller landmass had colonized vast reaches of earth. The phrase, "The sun never sets on the British Empire" was actually true at one point. The size of the island should not be a barometer for Atlantean ambition or an indicator as to their technological ability.

Devastating earthquakes, resulting from slipping tectonic plates, could have levelled the capitol. This is not such an outlandish concept, as today those living on the 'Ring of Fire' on the West Coast of the USA know that they face an imminent earthquake on the Richter Scale of 9 which would cause liquefaction of the soil in the N.W. city of Seattle, Washington and surrounding area through which no building or structure would be able to withstand. The inland sea of Puget Sound and the lakes Washington and Sammamish would become sloshing giant bathtubs of Tsunamis wiping out any remaining life unlucky enough to be nearby.

Washington State is also home to five active volcanoes, one of which spectacularly erupted in 1980 wiping out the nearby forest for miles around and forcing those living in nearby towns to evacuate.

California has long lived under the same threat of the Ring of Fire, the San Adreas

Fault is very unstable causing small quakes almost daily.

We are all familiar with the great loss Japan suffered during the Tsunami of 2011 caused by an earthquake at sea which levelled villages and towns, hoisting sea-going vessels about as if they were toys; and that of the 26th December 2004 Indian Ocean Tsunami resulting in such tragic loss of life.

Our world is a dramatically and constantly changing landscape. Geologists know this but to the lay person this is a distant concept as we go about our daily life. We must not be naive that large scale catastrophic events never take place either now or in the ancient past. Our current world was created out of the turmoil of geological violence.

The second issue affecting the Atlanteans is a concern today. If climate change continues, we are facing the possible disappearance of the Greenland and Antarctic ice sheets which would result in sea levels rising from 30 to 40 feet.

Seaports and cities on coast lines would have to move miles inward and billions would be displaced the world over should this current trend continue. Tragically, scientists have calculated that half the population of the world is estimated to perish from water and food shortages, social upheaval and through loss of land mass should the trend not reverse or halt.

Approximately 11,000 years ago sea levels rose dramatically at the end of an ice age referred to as the Pleistocene epoch, causing flooding worldwide with devastating results. This event was recorded in all the religions the world over as the flood.

Atlantean author, Otto Muck, also offers the possibility of a massive meteor hitting the Carolinas 12,000 years ago which would have caused a tsunami in the Atlantic with devastating effects to the Azores and certainly any land near Florida.

A significant sea level rise 11,000 years ago due to the end of the ice age along with shifting tectonic plates could have brought the Atlantean era to an end, forcing its colonies to fend for themselves with remnants of the civilisation to continue separated by rising waters and with its centre of cohesion gone.

Let us recap some possible human remains and archaeology as supportive evidence for Atlantis. Is it possible that some of the Stone Age pioneers' remains found in the Americas might have actually been Atlantean and/or their descendants? Were the early cultures of Mexico on up to North America influenced and seeded by Atlantis?

Ignatius Donnelly and James Bailey have noted that ancient carved reliefs and statuary in Mexico bear strong resemblance to people of African origins, European *and* Semitic! Later carvings actually show what we consider to be the indigenous peoples of Mexico today – as wearing false beards copied from the memory of visiting Europeans and Middle Eastern men. 14.

What could be the reason why seemingly disparate cultures, separated by centuries, let alone continents, would worship the same god, principles and also be master builders of pyramids with astronomical knowledge other than a single point of origin?

Case in point - that of the Olmecs which had clear African heritage and those of European characteristics both successively settling into Mexico worshiping the same god of peace with the same incredible skills in engineering and with messages of love. If these races with the same belief system were from surviving Atlantean satellites that would be interesting indeed.

When the British Empire shrunk, many Asians, Africans and peoples from around the world sought refuge on a small island that they considered to be their real cultural home versus the place of their genetic origins. Hence they moved to Britain as they themselves *were* British and were no longer welcome in their native land for varying political reasons. The United Kingdom is one of the great melting pots of the world as a result.

The map by 19th century American Congressman, Ignatius L. Donnelley from his book, *Atlantis: the Antediluvian World,* shows what he considers to be the political outreach of the Atlantean culture and may shed a new light on the mummified remains of the Kennewick Man found in Washington State in the N.W. of America with further 'European' remains being discovered further east.

I would like to also point out that Peru is also indicated in Donnelley's insightful map which may be the reason why there is an energy hot spot on the Matrix Map.

Did the energy vortex off the coast of Peru inspire the culture behind the creation of the mysterious Nazca Lines? Created between 400 and 650 AD the lines depict a hummingbird, monkey, a giant and a spider which can be seen from the heights of surrounding hills and clearly from the air.

Peru is also home to one of the most extensive pyramid building programs in the world of over 250 behemoth structures across the Lambayeque Valley spanning 3000 years.

An interesting anomaly is that of Francis Bacon's utopian novel New Atlantis, published in 1627. Bacon envisioned a fair civilisation where all acted in the public interest. His vision of scientific exploration mimics that of the modern university and was named Solomon's House. He placed his idyll on an island just west of Peru.

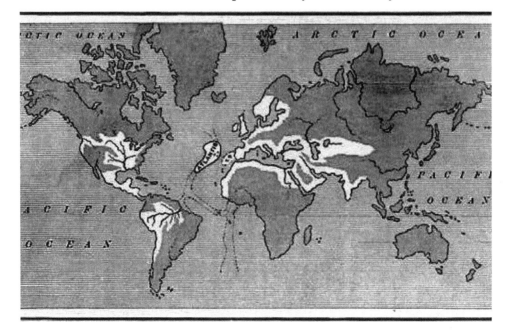

The Secret Dossier of a
Knight Templar of the Sangreal

Prior Page - Atlantis: The Antediluvian World, Ignatius Donnelly 1882 15.

Donnelley's book of 1882 is a worthy read even today. It is easy to see where many modern authors draw their inspiration for their own careers. Donnelley was the father of the Crypto History or the Revisionist History genre.

The Aztec civilization fell due to their collective belief that Cortez was their returning god, thus opening the front door to a hostile force who took an interest in the large amounts of Aztec gold. The Spanish Conquest of 1522 ended the culture of pyramid builders across South America forever. Though the Conquistadors did not set foot in Peru, fear alone caused the pyramid builders to destroy their heritage by fire as they left their geometric cities.

Quetzalcoatl has similarities with what we term today as Christ Consciousness. He was known as the morning star by the Aztecs. The Aztecs claim that the god-man was ruddy in complexion, tall with a long beard and fair haired. He was strong in body and with a broad forehead. His eyes were large and he came across the waters in a boat with no oars. Could they have witnessed sail power for the first time or some other form of technology?

"He wore a mitre on his head and was dressed in a long white robe reaching to his feet, and covered with red crosses. In his hand he held a sickle" Ignatius L. Donnelly 16.

If it were not for the fact that this individual supposedly predates the Templars, and apparently by thousands of years, I would say they were describing a Templar or Cistercian of the early middle ages! Possibly even a Druid priest if we must go back 2000 years - as the sickle seems to indicate - but we know the Cistercians were also master herbalists.

Is it possible that the Templars and Cistercians from the 9th to the 14th centuries did visit Mexico as the returning feathered serpents hence the clear description and inspiration of the false beards shown in many Aztec reliefs?

It is well known that Templars did not shave their beards in memory of priests of the Judaic Temple in the Holy Land. As the Templars claim ancient heritage and a *continuing* tradition (across peoples and borders) that has been transmitted since the dawn of history it would only make sense that there was more than one Feathered Serpent, and that indeed he was a man imbued with intuitive Christ-like gifts, let alone the arts of peace.

There is no reason that they would not have continually visited both Americas and exchanged culturally-helpful information in exchange for useful goods such as gold or even as a sheltering safe haven.

Durham Cathedral has the distinction of being one of the earliest Norman cathedrals built in England. I had visited the Cathedral which is dedicated to the Virgin and St. Cuthbert and took this photo of what appears to be a fiery, solar being and magnificently large door knocker. It is an eerie image and oddly out of place even as an example of the 'grotesque' form of art which mysteriously covered churches and cathedrals of this time period across Western Europe. It has an air of the exotic about it and is very unlike the green-men or gargoyle visages of the day.

At the time I could not help but consider the corresponding image of the feathered serpent god Quetzalcoatl and the legends of Templars having visited Mexico.

I was struck by the haunting images of the Aztec dragon while standing in front of the imposing Durham door knocker prior to entering the cathedral. Could the door knocker of Durham Cathedral be testament to an eyewitness account of the massive complex which is the ancient city of Teotihuacan whose builders remain a mystery? Could a Cistercian or Templar have sailed to the Pyramid of the Sun and had this door knocker commissioned in memory of what he had witnessed? The World Heritage site was initiated during 100 BC with the Pyramid of the Sun completed in 200 AD.

Photo by Jami Dwyer 2008 17.
http://en.wikipedia.org/wiki/File:Teotihuacan_Feathered_Serpent_
%28Jami_Dwyer%29.jpg

The image taken by Mr. Dwyer is from the Temple of Quetzalcoatl of Teotihuacan. Archaeoastronomers believe Teotihuacan may have been built to acknowledge the spring equinox. Interestingly enough, some researchers think the layout of the temples accurately matches that of the planets in our own solar system.

The Aztecs believed the god-king instructed them not to practice human sacrifice except that of fruits and flowers and was known as the god of peace. He was a great civiliser, astronomer-builder, teaching a religion of intelligence and compassion. Sadly the Aztecs did sacrifice great numbers of people for which they suspected that when their god returned they would be punished for disobeying his commands. The gruesome acts would be the only excuse the Spanish needed to overcome their civilisation. 18.

The Secret Dossier of a
Knight Templar of the Sangreal

My contact seemed very certain that Quetzalcoatl was a Templar Master and that they had indeed sailed to many far flung places of the world. His seemingly inaccurate timeframe for the god-king visiting Mexico during the Middle Ages has its explanation in repeated visits over millennia by the Order.

© Gretchen Cornwall – Durham Cathedral

1. Cruttenden, Walter. "An Ancient Message for the Future - Graham Hancock Official Website." An Ancient Message for the Future - Graham Hancock Official Website. August 26, 2012. http://grahamhancock.com/cruttendenw2/.

2. "Fliegel Jezerniczky Expeditions." Fliegel Jezerniczky Expeditions. http://www.fjexpeditions.com/frameset/uweinat_inscription.htm.

3. Bailey, James. God-Kings and the Titans: The New World Ascendancy in Ancient Times. S.l.: Hodder and Stoughton, 1973. p. 31

4. Donnelly, Ignatius. Atlantis: The Antediluvian World. New York: Dover Publications, 1976. p. 165

5. Hancock, Graham, and Santha Faiia. Heaven's Mirror: Quest for the Lost Civilization. London: Penguin, 1999. p. 19

6. Ibid

7. Wallace, Douglas. "Native American Haplogroups: European Lineage." DNA Learning Centre. http%3A%2F%2Fwww.dnalc.org%2Fview%2F15188-Native-American-haplogroups-European-lineage-Douglas-Wallace.html.

8. Hancock p. 19

9. "Graham Hancock on Plato and Atlantis." YouTube. http://www.youtube.com/watch?v=TdQ0P6k8inc.

10. Athanasius Kircher, Mundus Subterraneus, 1665

11. Weinzweig, Paul, and Pauline Zalitzki. "Humans Are Free." Atlantis Discovered in the Bermuda Triangle: The Sunken City Features Giant Pyramids and Sphinxes [Complete]. http://humansarefree.com/2014/02/atlantis-discovered-in-bermuda-triangle.html.

12. Matos, Carolina. "Archaeology: Prehistoric Rock Art Found in Caves on Terceira Island – Azores | Portuguese American Journal." Portuguese American Journal. August 27, 2012. http://portuguese-american-journal.com/archeology-prehistoric-rock-art-found-in-caves-on-terceira-island-azores/.

13. Sweeney, Emmet John. Atlantis: The Evidence of Science. New York: Algora Pub., 2010. p. 77

14. Bailey p. 55

15. http://en.wikipedia.org/wiki/File:Atlantis_map_1882_crop.jpg Atlantis: The Antediluvian World, Ignatius Donnelly

16. Donnelly, Ignatius. Atlantis: The Antediluvian World. New York: Dover Publications, 1976.

17. Photo Jami Dwyer 2008 http://en.wikipedia.org/wiki/File:Teotihuacan_Feathered_Serpent_%28Jami_Dwyer%29.jpg

18. Furlong, David. The Keys to the Temple: Unravel the Mysteries of the Ancient World. London: Piatkus, 1997. p. 134

Twenty Two

British Atlanteans

"The impression we get is of an indirect connection and perhaps the existence of a third party, whose influence spread to both the Euphrates and the Nile... Modern scholars have tended to ignore the possibility of immigration to both regions from some hypothetical and as yet undiscovered area. [However] a third party whose cultural achievements were passed on independently to Egypt and Mesopotamia would best explain the common features and fundamental differences between the two civilisations." Professor Walter Emery 1.

Professor Emery makes a valid point, that Mesopotamia and Egypt seemed to spring out of the sands as if by no prior local connection.

It takes hundreds of years of stability for a society to gain sophisticated language, writing, art, engineering and political structures. It does not happen overnight. Therefore a prior impetus must be considered.

During my conversation with John Temple, he boldly stated that the Egyptian culture was transmitted from the earlier Atlantean to Mesopotamia-Egypt and via Moses to the Judaic peoples. He also stated that Atlantis survived in Britain.

The tie between Britain and the land of the Pharaohs is strong and saw its fruition within the proto-Druids and their inheritors of Ireland and the British Isles. Examining Donnelley's map, one can easily see the flow of influence from Atlantis to Britain and eastward into Europe.

"The links between Britain and Egypt can also be explained from a derivation from a single cultural origin at the end of the fourth millennium BC." David Furlong 2.

Furlong makes a direct link to Atlantis through the painstaking exhaustive research of geometry in the British Isles and Egypt, claiming them as a repository of Atlantean knowledge.

He makes an interesting point that perhaps not all similarly skilled stonemasons were able to escape to both Britain and also Egypt. The Egyptian monuments have a greater degree of refinement than that of the European impetus, however both exhibit the exact same aptitude for geometry, astronomy and alignment with the stars and seasons, if differing completely in artistic style and ability. 3.

According to Furlong both cultures developed their state monuments at the same time, roughly 3000 BC, coinciding with another massive climate shift.

As well as the disappearance through natural disaster of a lost culture on Malta whose ancient temples date from 5000 BC to 3000 BC when the building work suddenly stopped.

Their society ended beneath 3 to 1 meter of silt when the Straits of Gibraltar were breached by a massive wall of water from the Atlantic in 3000 BC which may have been caused by a cataclysmic earthquake toppling Atlantis, according to David Furlong who places the event much more recently than Hancock and Plato.

Furlong noted that one temple on Malta was in the shape of a half skull. Other temple layouts were in the pattern of the trefoil. The trefoil knot is akin to the Ouroboros and is a symbol of eternity. A shape repeated for its sacred trinity aspect across Europe.

How do we make a logical choice for the fall of Atlantis between the evidence given by Hancock and Furlong?

I would like to propose there may have been two disasters and not just one. It is not inconceivable that in a seismically active area for there to be multiple events, indeed this would be more logical than a one-off catastrophe, anything less must be considered pseudo-science.

Most earthquake hot spots around the world rumble constantly. It is expected there will be events around the Ring of Fire and we know that the M.A.R. (Mid Atlantic Ridge) is very active.

Furlong claims that Hancock could not have been correct to place the timing for the Atlantean disaster in 11,000 BC as there is no archaeology to support a mass Diaspora.

Is it possible that there had been a cataclysm but that the entire land mass had not been destroyed, thus leaving the current civilisation capable of survival in its homeland?

If this were the case the Atlanteans would have rebuilt and continued as a people. However, if a second disaster struck in 3100 BC which was total – the Atlanteans would have had to migrate.

Not only that, but if they already had a global outreach, evidence of a mass Diaspora would be non-existent anyway, as only those from the Azores and Cuba itself would have had to flee if they had had the time and warning to do so.

I do not believe it is a 'stretch' to consider a civilisation to have remained in place for millennia; surely it would have grown and changed as is normal for any large city state.

It may have even fallen, regrouped and rose again under differing names with social changes and languages shifting, but with the central themes still in place.

Using our own culture as an example and perhaps more conventionally, are we not directly influenced by a 2000 year old culture called Rome which has been held up as the model of civilisation to be striven for over millennia?

The Old Testament dates back approximately 2700 years, are we not still affected by this ancient text across a large swath of our population? There are some 1.5 billion Christians in the world today and 13.5 million Jewish souls and their Muslim cousins.

The resurgence and knowledge of Sacred Geometry, which were pervasive in millennia past, has become a commonplace theme in the last forty years amongst the revisionist genre and mainstream science under the auspices of quantum mechanics.

A medieval custom, hand-fasting, has seen a surge in popularity. We are a direct product of our long ago past; even millennia ago historical events, customs and practices affect us today, some of them enjoying growing favour as a push towards a society which holds wellness and whole-being with high regard.

The Secret Dossier of a
Knight Templar of the Sangreal

I admire Furlong's theory but we do have evidence for possible Atlantean colonies during 11,000 BC.

The Vedas are India's very earliest written spiritual works and creation story which may be traced back 5000 years and more likely 10,000 years of age, putting us into the period of 11,000 BC.

This is not meant as disrespectful to the ancient culture of India as being incapable of spawning their own spirituality and heritage, but I am a proponent of the theory that there once was an ancient global civilisation.

Local derivatives would have their own flavour but would still retain the overall belief system (as most creation myths around the world attest to) if not political and social.

It is human nature to copy prior religious ideas. No religion springs out of the ground fully formed and brand new. There is always a prior inspiration regardless of how any one particular religion claims to be original usually with the added benefit of being 'better' than a rival system, but it simply is not true.

If one wishes to split hairs I recommend the author Jonathan Black, who has outlined a spiritual history of the world which explores the progression of ideals and thoughts through the beings that incarnated and brought major change with them such as the Buddha, Christ and Saints. I highly recommend both his books on the subject but wish to make a broad overall statement of my own as to our human spiritual commonality and the possibility of a first cause state such as Atlantis.

As we are all human beings there is only one source of spirituality regardless of how it is clothed and regardless of the social constraints of human frailty in understanding the divine nature of men, women and our shared destiny.

In the case of the Vedas I believe we must look to Atlantis. It is claimed that the Asians of India were the first peoples to write down their spiritual heritage that *we know of*, there is no accounting of extinct texts from prior cultures but this does not mean that they did not exist.

Case in point, the Dispilio Tablet also known as the Dispilio Scripture or Disc was carbon dated as being 7300 years old having been discovered in 1993 near Lake Kastoria Greece.

The tablet is older than Stonehenge and most pyramids by a few millennia! The Professor of Prehistoric Archaeology at the Aristotle University of Thessaloniki, George Hourmouziadis, stated that the tablet would overturn what we know about early writing in Europe as having originated in the Middle East via the Phoenicians and having been transmitted to the Greeks.

In other words, Europe had its own civilisation of the serpent-dragon long before the spread of eastern ideals reached the islands of Greece and the mountains and great plains of Europe. The Dispilio Tablet appears to be an actual script very similar to the way we write today versus the pictograms of Egypt. 4.

Should we consider this evidence against any ties between Atlantean Egypt and Europe? Is it too soon to make such a leap that Britain, Europe and Egypt could *not* have shared the same mother civilisation?

Let us use Furlong's example of the roughhewn standing stones of Britain versus the high art of the Egyptians' as our guide.

Is it possible that Atlantean writing did come to Europe but did not flower in the Middle East due to loss of life or perhaps fell out of fashion early on?

British Atlanteans

Is it possible that Atlantis had not only a script but also hieroglyphs; one transmitted to Egypt and the other to Europe?

Today the English language is a detailed and often contrary script to write let alone speak. But for ease of instant understanding we have an abundance of Ideograms to give us instant recognition in our world - from which is the appropriate room for our gender to powder our nose - to who has the right of way on the road.

The internet is replete with instantly recognisable imagery that helps us navigate a site. Even our homes are full of icons or glyphs such as the recycle logo on our empty containers. The list is endless and yet we have a complex and ancient form of language and writing.

"The currently-accepted historic theory taught around the world suggests that the ancient Greeks learned to write around 800 BC from the Phoenicians. However, a question emerges among scholars: how is it possible for the Greek language to have 800,000 word entries, ranking first among all known languages in the world, while the second next has only 250,000 word entries? How is it possible for the Homeric Poems to have been produced at about 800 BC, which is just when the ancient Greeks learned to write? It would be impossible for the ancient Greeks to write these poetic works without having had a history of writing of at least 10,000 years back, according to a US linguistic research." George Hourmouziadis 5.

The pyramids in China raise further uncomfortable questions as well as the recently discovered earthen pyramid in Ukraine.

There are many who contest the age of the Sphinx as being many millennia older than the pyramids and from an earlier culture. The Sphinx apparently suffers from erosion only possible from heavy rainfall which was only present prior to climate change during Hancock's time period for the Atlantean first collapse.

The Sphinx is oriented toward the constellation Leo which had its ascendancy 11,000 years ago and there are indications that its current face may have been re-carved by a much later pharaoh. Could it have once born the visage of a lion?

It may be argued that oral traditions often have greater strength over the written word through the long lens of history.

"According to Caesar up to twenty years of oral instruction was considered necessary before those who attended the schools of the Celtic Druids were ready for their final initiation into the mysteries. Chartres was the site of the great Druid university of Gaul, but from all over Europe the sons of important men went over to Britain, the mystic island of the North, to spend some years in a Druid college. The memory of the former universal tradition was preserved intact in Britain well into historical times, long after it had elsewhere waned." John Michell 6.

John Michell's comment on the survival of the Atlantean priesthood through oral tradition is quite striking.

In our modern world so dependent on the written word, it is easy to dismiss an oral culture such as the Druids. But their discipline was so high as to be military in its precision with the demand for perfection as absolute.

The Secret Dossier of a
Knight Templar of the Sangreal

Just as the aboriginal culture of Australia, the Druids did not forget their heritage and *did* pass it down. Even British historian Bethany Hughes argues in favour of a post Roman Druidic society stating that the Druids were not totally wiped out by the Romans but melted into the underground. Similarly the Templars survived through their own oral tradition. Modern Freemasonic culture relies on the same disciplined form of memorisation right down to the intonation and cadence of their spoken word and physical movements within a lodge.

Author Richard Heath makes this observation about the continuation of Atlantean culture:

"A culture or civilization is defined by what is in and what is out. The simple version of out is whatever is beyond the geographical or cultural borders of the empire. Some cultural components, while out, may from time to time be reviewed and then tolerated or have to be removed. The pre-classical corpus we have called "Atlantis" still existed around the time of Christ through many forms of belief and the different ethnic groups that held them. Thus, a tapestry of culture lay beneath, for example, the Roman Empire, whose main interest was the taxation of its great empire." Richard Heath 7.

I believe that the reason Atlantis was mentioned in the meeting with John Temple is that the longitude of the island itself is remembered in the continued building program of the Knights Templar across Europe as well as being a major energy centre on the Matrix Map:

"Sufficient evidence exists that a large input of sacred geometry and hence Atlantean number lore entered the Gothic civilization of the Middle Ages." Richard Heath 8.

The building program begun by the earlier British and European Atlanteans mirrored the celestial heavens on Earth, also following her sacred magnetic lines which have caused the earth itself to respond in physical geometric patterns. In other words a co-creative partnership. As Above So Below. We are the Earth and She - Us.

The Mysterious Number 325 and the New Atlantis

During the meeting with Comte de Medici I was told that the number 325 was all important in 'decoding' the map, but he did not disclose the entirety.

I have to admit that I am neither a mathematician and my sense of direction is atrocious at the best of times. As someone who has dealt with dyslexia from an early age I am used to my entire world flipping round the wrong way with my left literally becoming my right.

Although this can be amusing at times I don't exactly make the best navigator or dancer. I was rather chagrined that a meeting with a genuine modern Templar representative should include a map which needed 'de-coding', but I should not have been surprised as the Templars were known for their engineering and navigational skills and it seems they still are.

Certainly my area of expertise was more closely suited to history, comparative religion and symbolism. I've had a sharp learning curve and am still coming to grips with this information and can see the scope for further volumes as my own comprehension grows.

If my narrative attempts with maps and geometry appear to be that of an uncomfortable second language, other than my native tongue, then you would be correct! Therefore I'll make a brief foray into history before wrestling with the map.

Constantine

In an effort to be thorough, I cannot overlook the historical synchronicity of the year 325 AD in regards to the Matrix Map. It is the famous date for the Council of Nicaea, when Europe was turned towards Christianity through Constantine. His vision was of a unified people under one god, one empire and one emperor.

According to legend his head had been turned on the eve of the battle for the Milvian Bridge (October 312 AD) in a dream. He was instructed to emblazon the heavenly sign of God on the shields of his soldiers. He saw an 'X' with its 'head' turned in on itself and so the Chi Rho or Greek for Christos became part of the symbolic language of early Christianity.

His entire army apparently also had a vision of the cross overlaid on the sun. This mass vision could be explained by an optical illusion called a Sun Dog, a luminous ring which occurs by light interacting with ice crystals.

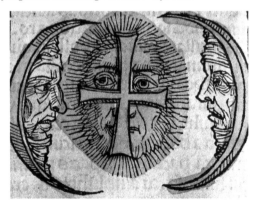

Sun Dog Illustration from the Nuremberg Chronicle by Michael Wolgemut and Wilheilm Peydenwurff, 1493 AD

There is a great deal of debate in academic circles regarding the political expediency of his decision. He himself may only have converted on his death bed or perhaps posthumously. However authors T. D. Barnes and Charles Matson Odah assert he was a committed Christian from early childhood. That he had felt ambiguous is possible, but he may also have hesitated initially due to a concern that it would be too controversial to be a known Christian amongst ambitious Roman pagans. He may not have wanted to endanger his throne should the timing for inclusion of the new religion be too precarious.

However things changed fast. Christianity was a new, growing and a strange cult of peace - quite boggling to the Roman mindset. The new consciousness of Christianity was flowing into the broken Roman world. The lure of a loving Sun/Son God of peace, who was deeply interested in the average person and kindly, had an instantaneous magnetic appeal. If not genuine, Constantine may have seen the future and seized on its popularity.

His mother, Empress or Saint Helena, may be the clue to the theory of early conversion. She was the first recorded archaeologist in the west for having made a successful expedition (327 AD) to the Holy Land to find the true cross.

One of the discovered nails was inserted (during the 7th century) into the Lombard royal lance, thus creating a bridge and Christianising the older tradition. The intriguing and ancient lance is on display at the Hofburg Palace, Vienna, Austria and was coveted by Hitler as the Spear of Destiny. He believed that as long as it was in his possession he would rule the world. He lost the spear and the war.

To say that Constantine is positively disliked in many Neo Pagan and New Age circles is an understatement. Author Laurence Gardner gives him a vitriolic review in Bloodline of the Holy Grail for the suppression of the Arians who held that Jesus was an intermediary, a god-man imbued with divine qualities and not actually *the* God. Simplified - the Council of Nicaea determined that Jesus *was* the ultimate God.

Through my own lens, I can actually see both points of view as humanity is a microcosm of the universe and therefore we are God.

Jonathan Black portrays what it must have been like for a hardened and macho Rome to meet a Christian 'lit up' on the inside whose external ambitions were of peace:

"So the Christian exaltation of meekness and humility turned everything upside down and inside out. The Christians clearly knew of new joys and satisfactions, new ways of being in the world." And "There were whole new worlds behind those eyes." 9.

Constantine freed slaves who converted and promised gold to the free. He became utterly dogmatic and ruthless. When his son inherited he tried to stem the tide and recover the initiatic impetus of Christ. Julian proclaimed religious tolerance but was murdered by hardliners who restored Constantine's macho form of religion. According to Black, the mystery school of Christ was driven underground.

Regardless of the cruelty of the messenger and the violent time period in which he lived, Europe embraced the Son of Man. The result of this would eventually lead to the end of slavery and greater freedom for women. Constantine's move to recognize a higher authority and accountability by choosing Christianity over the old system removed the threat of a despotic individual from being worshiped as an infallible god with absolute power in Europe ever again. Reform, though slow, was now possible. Divine revelation is just that – Divine. The flawed receiver is who he is – human.

British Atlanteans

Latitude, Longitude and the Sacred Ancient Measure

"Only by invoking the foot can we glimpse this entry into the world of ancient measurement and hence ancient thought." Robin Heath 10.

The Imperial Measurement provides a unique and sympathetic lens into ancient Egypt's past through the foot. If there is any doubt that the ancients knew the circumference of the globe, let us discus their measurement of the earth and its relation to time itself.

Otto Muck places Atlantis between the latitudes of 32 degrees and 40 degrees. Similarly, David Furlong also agrees.

For those of us who are geographically challenged, latitude is the horizontal measurement of the earth which is 'easily' established at any fixed point by the arc of the sun overhead and finding high noon.

The high seas have been travelled for millennia using this method. Longitude is the vertical measurement of the earth and a fairly new re-discovery.

Using the Imperial foot as his guide, David Furlong explains with aplomb the *latitude* and the location of Atlantis:

"The Earth is not a perfect sphere. Because of its rotation, the Earth bulges slightly at the equator and is flattened at the poles. This means that the length of each degree of latitude increases as one travels away from the equator. For example, there are 110,573 metres (362,679 feet) in one degree latitude at the equator. At the pole, this increases to 111,697 metres (366,366 feet). The latitude where the number of metres shifts from the 110,000 range to 111,000 is just under 39°. However, there are a group of ancient measures which make this shift between latitudes 32 ° and 33°. This group includes the Brasse and Remen, two measures derived from ancient Egypt. The Egyptians counted a minute of arc as being a 1000 Brasse, while the Remen was related to the cubit. The Brasse, for example, moves from 59,999 Brasse per degree on 32° latitude to 60,008 at 33° latitude, while the Remen shifts from 299,995 to 300,041 in the same way. Both the Brasse and the Remen are products of a system based on an 11.55 metre (38 feet) measurement. There are precisely 9600 of these units between 32° and 33° latitude. With factors of 8 and 12 (12X8=96), this number could have been chosen deliberately because it embodied important numeric symbolism. This suggests that, if Atlantis was the motherland of ancient measures, then its most likely position would be between latitudes 32° and 33°. David Furlong 11.

In relation to the above comment on 'factors' by Furlong, the number 8 has long been associated with the Templars as we have seen and is also a symbol of infinity.

The number 12 has many connotations from the 12 disciples to the 12 astrological signs and the 12 months of the year.

The Vernal Equinox, meaning 'equal' and 'night' in Latin, happens twice a year around March 20th and September 22nd, when due to the tilt of the earth's axis, the equator of the earth is 'equal' to the sun and there appears to be 12 hours of daylight and 12 hours of night, denoting yin and yang in perfect equal balance.

So, we have a direct correlation between the measure of the earth and spiritual meaning in relationship to the human being and how we've chosen to understand our environment.

The imperial measurement was founded in 1824 but it is interesting that the foot with its 12 inches relates to both our own mystical numeric culture and that of ancient Egypt the Brasse and Remen, especially where the earth herself is concerned.

Prior to unravelling the more practical aspects of the Matrix Map, I consoled myself with what I did know regarding the many layered meanings behind the number 325 which lends greater 'weight' to the actual usefulness of the number and other numbers on the map that I was also told had importance.

325

To illustrate, I separated out the number 32 from 5 as they relate to the tradition, history and the spiritual nature of the human being.

The number five has always represented humanity in the form of a pentagram which is also the symbol for Venus – love. In a prior chapter I mentioned that the orbit of Venus from the vantage of Earth, appears to make a five pointed star in the sky over an eight year period of time.

Returning to our sacred number 325 - If five is the number of mankind -five *plus* five is equated to God. 325 may be broken down as such:

$$3 + 2 = 5 \text{ (Mankind) and } 5 + 5 = 10 \text{ (God/Divine Creator)}$$

Ten is a representation of the Alpha and Omega. The digit one equals Alpha with its column appearance - and the digit zero equals Omega as the eternal Ouroboros.

It is not hard to see the male and female aspect of the Great Divine within the number 10 with its sword and grail depiction. In the occult world it is also represented as the chalice and blade.

Let us follow the number ten to ancient Judea. It is the equivalent of the first letter of the tetragrammaton of YHWH (Yodh He Waw He) or also pronounced – Yahweh – the first letter for the name of God in Hebrew and is written as Yod or Yodh.

Judaism also gave us Kabbalistic studies, its adherents hope to reunite with God by following its teachings literally upward through the Tree of Life and back to the source of creation, indeed the Tree of Life is a conceptual mapping of creation and the human being. The human nervous system could be said to resemble a tree with its many pathways.

Yod (the first letter of Yahweh) has been denoted as meaning 'the hand' and is the 20th pathway leading from Chesed the 4th sphere and to Tiphareth the 6th sphere. There are five fingers on a hand and the two spheres numerically add up to the number ten.

In relation to the Tarot Cards the above is explained in the personage of the enigmatic Hermit holding aloft his light. The figure of the hermit across the world has long held the mystique of being closer to the divine whether it is the Buddhist monk or the monk guiding those to Santiago de Compostela the Way of St. James with his bright lamp.

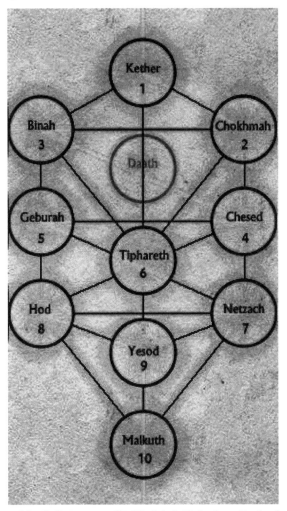

Kabbalah Tree of Life highlighting Da'ath

Any student of the Kabbalah will appreciate that there are 10 sephiroth or spheres which may also be seen as champagne glasses and 22 pathways intersecting together to form the Tree of Life.

Of course this adds up to the number 32 but there is a little known 11th sephiroth which is considered to be invisible Gnostic wisdom, hence adding up to the number 33; both these numbers (32 and the invisible 33rd) are therefore highlighted in an alchemical way.

The 11th hidden sephiroth, called Da'ath, is the key here literally and by its very nature, is shrouded in mystery as its very existence is beyond time and space.

The ancient Judaic system of the Kabbalah (simply put) believes that divine energy from above flows down through each sphere, filling it and as it over flows like a chalice and falls like a waterfall down to the next sphere it becomes more material in substance until finally reaching Malkhuth or the Earth plane.

It is a lovely way of visualising other dimensions as spilling down towards our own from the ethereal with each downward step becoming more substantial, having been infused with the goodwill of higher beings.

The number 33 is incredibly important to the human being as we have 33 vertebrae of the spine. The Caduceus and Kabbalah are an allegory for the spine and the dragon/serpent energy currents which lead upward to self-awareness. The dove in Christianity descending from above is the same metaphor of enlightenment and divine consciousness though less obvious pictorially.

Caduceus – Staff of Enlightenment

The human being is the embodiment of sacred number which is then extended outward to our world as a way of interpreting and sharing higher truths. As above so below may also be stated, as within as without. Mankind as the microcosm and macrocosm.

However the earth is the matrix from whence the physical form of the human being sprang. The Greek God Prometheus created man from the clay of the earth. The Goddess Athena breathed life or soul into mankind, thus sharing a similar creation myth with the Bible where man is created from the dust of the earth.

We see the allegory of the human spine and its 33 separate vertebra played out very well within Freemasonry. Progressing up the spiral stair gradually until reaching the

33rd degree where the higher truths unfold upon the 34th degree.

Our number 32 leads to 33, which in Freemasonry may only be conferred from above in recognition of service to community and to masonry as a whole.

It cannot be obtained by any other means. A reminder that gifts flow to us from above by serving others and a purposeful life well lived. Gaining recognition by those we respect and of our peers is a gratifying experience necessary to the human being for growth regardless of the path one may walk.

Speaking of the great number 33, one cannot but help thinking of the life of Jesus who was 33 years old at the end of his ministry, which is interesting in light of our subject.

"There are no coincidences."   *Comte de Mattinata de Medici*

Are there other connections between the Matrix Map and this legendary lost continent other than these seemingly insignificant lines drawn on a modern map?

The Albion Conspiracy

"I am standing on the prime meridian of the world, zero degrees longitude, the center of time and space, literally the place where East meets West. It's paved right into the courtyard of the Old Royal Observatory at Greenwich. At night, buried lights shine through the glass-covered meridian line, so it glows like a man-made midocean rift, splitting the globe in two equal halves with all the authority of the Equator. For a little added fanfare after dark, a green laser projects the meridian's visibility ten miles across the valley to Essex." Dava Sobel 12.

Travelling on land was quite dangerous, arduous and time consuming before the modern era of police, cars, trains and flights. Even so we still require great cargo vessels to traverse the seas to feed our massive consumer civilisation.

Is it any wonder that quicker sea routes were established as well as river navigation since time immemorial? Haulage of heavy goods was made easier by travelling by water and it was by and large easier to protect oneself.

The River Thames and its cousins around the world were the highways. Manmade and natural canals in Europe would rival the Thames in size and importance.

However travelling by sea was not without risk and those that did go forth on her waters would face many dangers if lost. There was nothing one might do if caught in a serious storm and one may find that the seabed would become a dark lost tomb along with any cargo on board.

Latitude has been used for hundreds of years and was no secret but finding a universal longitude (north-south measurement) sparked a tug of war lasting until the late 19th century.

Establishing a central universal meridian would help ensure the safety of lives and cargo at sea alongside better methods of measurement at sea. Not only was an accurate device needed for measurement but also a fixed location. Not even Isaac

Newton was able to answer the problem of longitude.

The race to establish the zero meridian from which all nations would determine their measurement of time and distance in relation to each other, would last decades.

Sailors instead would use the meridian nearest as established by a given country, using it as their place of departure and perhaps even their destination to guide them across dangerous seas.

One individual would use almost modern methods of mass media through the power of publication to shift all possible 'meridians' to Greenwich in London; in fact he himself moved the observatory from the centre of London to its current location.

Nevil Maskelyne was the fifth astronomer royal who chose to live on the Observatory site from 1765 until his death in 1811 and published a total of forty-nine Nautical Almanacs.

He listed the lunar-solar and lunar-stellar distances in the almanac based from his dearly-loved Greenwich Meridian. As a member of the Royal Society he was sent to the island of St. Helena in 1761 to observe the Transit of Venus.

His work would help establish the distance of the earth to the sun and therefore the size of the solar system. He would become known affectionately as the sailor's astronomer, so trusted were his techniques and easily available almanac. 13.

The Washington DC Meridian (a city built on hermetic sacred geometry) was to be a casualty of the Greenwich Meridian along with the famous Rose Line of Paris, but not without a meagre fight.

Greenwich won the accolade in 1884 during the International Meridian Conference which was actually held in Washington D.C.. Twenty six nations agreed that Greenwich would be the zero rose from which all longitude lines and time zones would be measured.

"Only the French refused to give up their claim and continued to recognize their own Paris Observatory meridian and the Rose Line as 0° until 1911. Even then, they could not bring themselves to refer to "Greenwich Mean Time," which was clearly a plot of perfidious Albion. Until 1978, the French referred to Greenwich Mean Time as "Paris Mean Time retarded by nine minutes twenty one seconds." Christopher Hodapp 14.

Though surely Washington D.C. was built as a New Jerusalem and was just as viable a choice; France also felt that their ancient meridian was of great value and did not want to lose the memory of it.

Dan Brown brought it to the wider population through The Da Vinci Code. Many monuments in France, according to Henry Lincoln, are aligned with the Paris Meridian. One of the legends behind The Rose Line of France is that one may find the Holy Grail beneath it.

In order to secure the memory of their rose, the French have created an unusual monument to The Rose Line which most people will never see when visiting Paris as they will walk right over it, literally.

Interestingly enough 135 small round bronze plaques were laid in 1994 on the Paris

Meridian, one of which bears the name of Arago. Apparently only 122 are referenced on maps which leave 13 'unaccounted' for.

One bronze rests over the Louvre inverted pyramid where Dan Brown romantically places the burial of the Magdalene.

The discs measure almost 5" across and are spread out north to south, spanning 5.7 miles which as we will see in a future chapter is significant as a distance marker.

The Arago Monument, as it is called, replaced an earlier monument to the 25th Prime Minister François Arago, which was melted down during the occupation of WWII.

Arago is well worth remembering as he led the way to abolish slavery in French colonies in 1848 and was a scientific polymath and a leading politician.

He was also the Director for the Paris Observatory until he retired to his home in the Pyrenees in 1853. He is now celebrated directly with the Paris Rose Line as long as the 'monument' is maintained. 15.

The shift of the zero meridian to Greenwich deliberately places the ancient mother culture of Atlantis on the Azores Plateau at 39°29'37.85"N and 32°59'29.67"W - which is to the east of Santa Das Flores. Its secret past and identity is hidden amidst the number lore of enlightenment.

It is interesting to note that Ignatius Donnelly published his book on Atlantis in 1882, two years prior to the International Meridian Conference of 1884. His book was very well received at the time and made him an instant star. Is it possible that the American Congressman had an influence on the decision of the Zero Meridian to be placed at Greenwhich in remembrance of Atlantis?

Today we think nothing of the accuracy of where we are going due to the wonders of GPS, but even this is not without fault. In fact 2011 saw the improvement of global positioning systems which increased their accuracy by a further 100 feet. Anyone who uses a sat nav knows that they are sometimes not 'spot on' but can often manage to get you near your target using a bit of common sense.

In the past and out at sea the problem of navigation is horrendous with no visible landmarks that allow for triangulation. One has only the Sun or Celestial/Lunar Navigation to sail by.

Mapping has come by leaps and bounds over the centuries and is still improving today. It is not easy to take a sphere which bulges in the middle due to gravity and create an accurate flat representation.

By its very nature it cannot be accurate. The farther one goes out from a central point the more one must compensate for inaccuracy. But we can come close to our chosen port of call.

If one takes the modern map of the world that I was given with its massive magnetic lines, one can clearly see that the Azores has a major energy centre over it at 32°/33° longitude, however using free Google Earth software those two sacred degree points are actually to the east of the last island by approximately ninety four miles.

The more refined software programs and localized detailed flat maps actually pull our sacred coordinates out slightly as they have the ability to hold more information.

The modern map I was given should be viewed as a symbolic representation of the earth and not meant as a nautical chart to sail from Britain to the Azores. Obviously one would need more information and navigation equipment to make such a journey.

But for now we must suggest that in the late 19th century, through the importance of number symbolism, the location for Atlantis was chosen.

Britain is specially marked by the new Rose Line as the Zero Meridian and thus it is drawn into the Atlantean legend. Due to the connection between the two sacred locations this means that Britain *is* the New Atlantis.

Stonehenge by © Gretchen Cornwall

1. Furlong, David. *The Keys to the Temple: Unravel the Mysteries of the Ancient World.* London: Piatkus, 1997. p. 41

2. Ibid p. 131

3. Ibid p. 134

4. Tsolakidou, Stella. "Prehistorc Tablet Calls into Question History of Writing." The Archaeology News Network:. July 16, 2012. http://archaeologynewsnetwork.blogspot.co.uk/2012/07/prehistorc-tablet-calls-into-question.html#.UHKbcK7F2kA.
Professor of Prehistoric Archaeology at the Aristotle University of Thessaloniki, George Hourmouziadis

5. Ibid

6. Michell, John. *The View over Atlantis.* London: Abacus, 1973. p. 171

7. Heath, Richard. *Sacred Number and the Origins of Civilization: The Unfolding of History through the Mystery of Number.* Rochester, VT: Inner Traditions, 2007.p. 156

8. Ibid p. 203

9. Black, Jonathan. *The Secret History of the World.* London: Quercus, 2010. p. 232

10. Heath, Robin. *Sun, Moon & Stonehenge: High Culture in Ancient Britain.* Cardigan, Wales: Bluestone Press, 1998. p. 166

11. Furlong p 133

12. Sobel, Dava, and William J.H. Andrews. *The Illustrated Longitude: The True Story of a Lone Genius Who Solved the Greatest Scientific Problem of His Time.* London: Fourth Estate, 1998. p. 197

13. Ibid p 197

14. Hodapp, Christopher. *Solomon's Builders: Freemasons, Founding Fathers and the Secrets of Washington, D.C.* Berkeley, CA: Ulysses, 2006. p. 174

15. Murdin, Paul. *Full Meridian of Glory: Perilous Adventures in the Competition to Measure the Earth.* New York: Copernicus Books/Springer, 2009. p. 125

Twenty Three

The Technology of the King

Religious Symbol or Ancient Technology?

Has there ever been a time in history when navigation, surveying and engineering was not only accurate but also considered a sacred art and as such was highly protected by its priestly caste? Yes and the evidence is around us the world over.

In my estimation, one singular recent historical discovery, which has been brilliantly decoded and reconstructed by author Crichton E. M. Miller - through sheer audacity and inspiration - has overturned modern understanding of the Templars and the ancient world. He has unraveled the true purpose behind what we have blindly called the Celtic Cross for hundreds of years throwing into vivid question our conceptions of religion and history.

"I will show beyond reasonable doubt that ancient man was capable of a form of understanding of such depth and subtlety that we only glimpse it today, occasionally and with untrained eyes. Furthermore that this ancient knowledge could be as old as 30,000 years or more and may reveal information about our changing, dynamic world that could affect our descendants and those of us who are still living in the next few decades." Crichton E. M. Miller 1.

According to Miller the Celtic Cross is not an edification of a religious belief but a scientific instrument to measure time, space and distance as well as being accompanied by a sublime ethos. Nothing says this more profoundly than this heart-wrenching statement by Miller in regards to the King of Kings:

"To be a carpenter was not a poor man's work as has been considered to be the case. Builders were held in same esteem as those who built Solomon's Temple and later the Mediaeval Cathedrals. These skills were based on religious principles, as considerable building work in those times was on religious construction and repair. They carried the respect of the church leaders as holy workers who practised their craft on religious buildings. Jesus and Joseph, his father, would have been members of a Guild, which would uphold considerable secrecy and furthermore, these members require the knowledge of geometry, mathematics and construction.

Christ was reputed to have spent considerable time in Egypt in Alexandria and Heliopolis. Both places were the centres of learning for the Greeks after the conquest by Alexander the Great, several hundred years earlier. I will show you that the crucifixion was an insult far greater than that currently believed. The cross was an instrument for measuring and finding levels, for surveying, map making, astronomy, astrology and mathematics. Jesus Christ, the last Pharaoh of the House of the Ram, was brutally murdered upon the instrument of his own knowledge of science and spirituality." Crichton E. M. Miller 2.

He equates the working cross with the staff of magicians, having crossed many borders from the Egyptians, Druids and Phoenicians the sea faring peoples of the bible.

Miller wanted to know how the Egyptians could have built the Giza pyramids with such accuracy using the primitive surveying equipment they are suspected of having.

He himself has a background as an engineer and architect. The simplistic tools did not 'do the job' of helping an ancient engineer create a masterpiece of precision.

He started building his own device with a plumb line and in a eureka moment Miller realised that he had built a Celtic Cross, which was comprised of working moveable parts that along with a plumb line would help with the difficult task of surveying, building and navigation.

What we see below is often viewed as a flat image but to Miller it sprang to life solving many problems of history in one fell swoop of inspiration and understanding. To my knowledge he is the only crypto historian to speak at a major university, Cambridge, in 2006 and 2007 by invitation and has been granted a patent for his discovery!

With kind permission - Photo of Miller's working Celtic Cross 3.
"Celtic Cross." Crichton EM Miller. http://www.crichtonmiller.com/

"The 'Celtic Cross' is the archetype of the sextant and the theodolite. It is also the archetype of the quadrant and the astro-labe. It is the physical manifestation of all construction, surveying, mathematics, astrology and astronomy" Crichton E. M. Miller 4.

Miller believes it is probable that the Templars found a working cross or plans to build one within Temple Mount which gave them unprecedented ability to travel the sea with accuracy not available to anyone for several hundred years to come. He also agrees that the Templars were able to sail to North America and also to South America with their advanced knowledge and echoes my own thoughts that they were the Feathered Serpents.

The Technology of the King

Since I have traced the sea-faring adventures of the Templars to the earlier Vikings and beyond it is difficult to say when they had a working cross since the stone Celtic Cross itself is of Dark Age origin.

It is highly probable that they had the Celtic Cross prior to Temple Mount. The Templars were excavating Temple Mount hundreds of years after many Celtic Crosses were erected. It is an interesting question. As I've already stated, the immortality of stone is the best way to ensure technology and the ethics behind it will remain for the future.

When did the purpose of the Celtic Cross become lost to time or did it secretly morph into other devices through the centuries such as a working magnetic compass?

Today the military often have technology first before it is allowed to flow to the civilian population. Could the Celtic Cross have experienced such a journey during the Templar period?

What does seem to be certain is that some Templar Navigators had an advantage over other rivals. Based on my conversation with John Temple it seems assured that historic Templar's had intuitive faculties able to link into the energy patterns of the earth and also had access to ancient technology such as the Celtic Cross both of which ensured a safe journey.

The Saint of the Compass

Catherine of Alexandria was a saint identified with the Templars and noted as being a 4th century scholar. According to legend she was to be tortured to death on a wheel spiked with knives, however when she prayed over the device it shattered to the amazement of onlookers.

Those bent on her death finally beheaded her with a sword. Her manner of passing is directly connected to St John the Baptist the main Templar patron.

Her three emblems are the quill, the wheel and sword. Joan of Arc claimed that the saint helped her to locate the hero Charles Martel's sword which in her hands became a rallying point for the French.

I'd always pondered why Saint Catherine was important to the Templars as the connection seemed quite vague. Nowhere in any book I've read over the years had I encountered any explanation for their interest in her.

In light of Miller's discovery of the Celtic Cross, I think it is easy to understand their fascination in her as a pictorial way of passing on the practice of sacred navigation.

Is it possible that the quill represents imparting of knowledge while the wheel serves as a *dual* device which is evident in the points of a working compass for navigation and also a tool for surveying, with the sword as a metaphor of the staff needed to support the Celtic Cross for surveying?

Caravaggio St Catherine 1598

I would like the reader to observe Caravaggio's painting above of Saint Catherine and remember her right hand which is delicately held over the blade. The wheel is the Templar compass of navigation.

The Technology of the King

The Compass

"Mariners at sea, when through cloudy weather in the day which hides the sun, or through the darkness of the night, they lose the knowledge of the quarter of the world to where they are sailing, touch a needle with a magnet, which will turn round till, on its motion ceasing, its point will be directed towards the north." Alexander of Neckam Between 1187-1202 5.

The compass is not such a recent invention as one might expect; indeed there is evidence that it reaches back millennia. The official date of its European invention is 1302 with its eight winds and central rose which has changed little over time.

During my search for a historic Templar link to the compass I came across documented references to the working compass prior and during the historic Templar period.

Of course any working compass must have a magnet which the Celtic Cross is not dependent upon. The early magnetic compasses only pointed to the north.

One still had to work out a passage through the position of the sun, moon or stars which is where the use of the Celtic Cross would be helpful. However during cloudy weather having an actual magnetic compass has an obvious advantage; therefore both may be a benefit when sailing and certainly the Celtic Cross as a surveying tool is preferred for obvious reasons.

Polar magnetic ore (naturally magnetized ore of iron) was worth its weight in silver due to its scarcity in Europe and only available in Scandinavia and in the Urals, which isn't a coincidence since the Vikings economically conquered Europe from Ireland to Constantinople! 6.

Floating magnets were in use and documented in Europe even though their actual function was not widely understood. The Faroe Islands which are north of the Shetlands were colonized by the Danish-Vikings. Sagas written down in approximately 1230 by these settlers speak of using a magnetic loadstone floating in a container to help them identify north while sailing.

By the time many sagas were actually written down they had been oral tradition for many decades, if not hundreds of years. The magnetic loadstone was known to be functioning as an early compass at the beginning of the 12th century in the Mediterranean and Baltic Seas. For this to be so widespread we are certainly looking at earlier and secretive usage prior to having been recorded. 7.

The earliest European mention of the compass in writing was by Aristotelian and theologian scholar Alexander of Neckam (1157 – 1217). He discussed the use of the compass for the English Channel in his treatise 'De utensilibus and De naturis rerum' written between 1187 and 1202. 8.

He taught in Paris but eventually returned to England to become the Augustinian Abbot of Cirencester in 1213 which was also the location of a Knights Templar preceptory. It would be inconceivable that the two monastic parties would not have crossed paths. 9.

Some five decades after the death of Alexander of Neckam the stunningly brilliant

The Secret Dossier of a
Knight Templar of the Sangreal

Pierre de Maricourt, a mysterious and by all accounts media shy French scholar, wrote the most significant breakthrough work of the Middle Ages on geomagnetism which was centuries ahead of its time and circulated until the 16th century. He had solved one of the great mysteries of generations in one inspirational flash. 10.

The "Epistola Petri Peregrini de Maricourt ad Sygerum de Foucaucourt, militem, de magnete"or in English, "Letter on the Magnet of Peter Peregrinus of Maricourt to Sygerus of Foucaucourt, Soldier" (1269) has been essentially described as a letter of 3500 words written to a possible 'friend' and 'neighbour' describing the magnetic nature and function of the loadstone as a magnet for use in a compass. 11.

"In his experiments with the loadstone, Petrus Peregrinus was the first to assign a definite position to the poles of a loadstone, and to give directions for determining which is north and which south. He proved that unlike poles attract and similar ones repel. He established by experiment that every fragment of a loadstone is a complete magnet. He was the first to pivot a magnetized needle and surround it with a graduated circle. He determined the positions of objects by their magnetic bearings as is done today in compass surveying. In his perpetual motion machine was the germ of an engine driven by a magnet!" Lloyd A. Brown 12.

The inventor of the European compass wrote in his letter to his so called neighbour, *"you will be able to direct your steps to cities and islands and to any place whatever in the world."* A very exciting prospect indeed for those interested in travelling the world such as the Templars. Included in the letter are technical drawings of a working compass and a perpetual motion machine! In a separate work he also lays out a detailed engraving of an astrolabe.

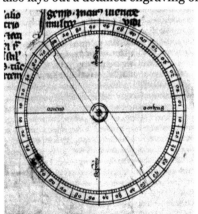

According to his student and fellow Aristotelian, Roger Bacon, Pierre de Maricourt was the only man of his day who understood perspective and considered him the 'perfect mathematician'. Bacon repeated de Maricourts' observations on magnetism in his own work "Opus Majus".

Epistola de magnete (1269)
http://en.wikipedia.org/wiki/File:Epistola-de-magnete.jpg

Though many credit Bacon with this breakthrough, it is clear by the evidence in the letter and reverence of Bacon towards his teacher that the knowledge came from

Peregrinus and was repeated by Bacon.

Bacon implied that his mentor had no restrictions of either state or clergy when it came to his observations on nature. Where he could have cultivated such a free mind set under the social restrictions of the day is not known and underscores an independent nature perhaps developed by a secret school of wisdom.

De Maricourt wrote of the importance of physical work which is interpreted today as gathering empirical and measurable evidence so important in scientific research and he is considered a rare example of a medieval experimentalist. 13.

De Maricourt was also known as Peter the Pilgrim (English for Peregrinus), he had been a crusader to the Holy Land hence the term 'pilgrim' as it was a common moniker of the day and associated with a perilous journey to the Middle East.

It is known that he served as a physician as well as a military engineer in the employ of Charles de Anjou in 1269. His duties included fortification of the camp, building offensive weapons such as catapults and setting mines. He was certainly a man of diverse talents along the same vein as Da Vinci.

Inspiration flooded into him during a siege, "...Peregrinus conceived a beautiful solution to a perpetual motion machine which operated on the principle of magnetic attraction. With success and immortality in sight, he sat down and wrote to a friend at home named Picard, telling him not only the story of his marvellous machine, but all about the properties of the loadstone – most of which he, himself, had discovered." Lloyd A. Brown 14.

Peter de Maricourt took his name from Maricourt-Picardy in France which is in the Somme department. Although this is not spectacular in itself, I find it interesting indeed that he lived only about 25 miles from the Notre Dame Cathedral of Aimes and more importantly the Cistercian Abby Notre-Dame du Gard which was 36 miles from the home of de Maricourt.

Both were centres of learning with Aimes being connected by a Roman road to Paris. It is thought he was of a noble family which could afford to educate him. Could he have been a younger son of nobility and joined the Templars? Could he have been Cistercian? In light of having been on crusade is it likely he may have been serving as an engineer lay brother of either order? Keeping in mind that Templars are Cistercians with swords. The proximity of his home of Maricourt to significant Cistercian sites leads me to believe he may have been educated by them prior to going on to Paris, the higher centre of learning.

Most educators of this time period were from wealthy families trained as clergy, therefore it is possible that de Maricourt was Cistercian having started his career closer to his home village near Aimes and or the Cistercian Abbey of du Gard. If he had been educated by them but had not officially joined, there is nothing to discount his civilian status as a secret Cistercian working on their behalf. It is an interesting question as to which order he might have belonged to.

Franciscan Friar and Englishman Roger Bacon was educated in Paris which may be where he met Peter de Maricourt who was his tutor and the only mentor he ever respected. The following quotations are from Bacon's *Opus Tertium*.

The Secret Dossier of a
Knight Templar of the Sangreal

"One man I know, and one only, who can be praised for his achievements in this science. Of discourses and battles of words he takes no heed: he follows the works of wisdom, and in these finds rest. What others strive to see dimly and blindly, like bats in twilight, he gazes at in the full light of day, because he is a master of experiment. Through experiment he gains knowledge of natural things, medical, chemical, indeed of everything in the heavens or earth." Roger Bacon 1214-1294, Opus Tertium 15.

Certainly this individual is being lauded as a Renaissance man by Bacon.

"Therefore he has looked closely into the doings of those who work in metals and minerals of all kinds; he knows everything relating to the art of war, the making of weapons, and the chase; he has looked closely into agriculture, mensuration, and farming work..." Roger Bacon 1214-1294, Opus Tertium 16.

Heralded as knowing "everything relating to the art of war..." could be an indication Peregrinus was Templar as the chivalric order was the gold standard of the day and they would have highly prized one such as Peregrinus. Bacon continues saying that with his mentors practical approach he was able to expose the fraud of conjurers and also notes that he had little time for the praise of high society or the limelight.

"As for reward, he neither receives nor seeks it. If he frequented kings and princes, he would easily find those who would bestow on him honours and wealth. Or, if in Paris he would display the results of his researches, the whole world would follow him." Roger Bacon 1214-1294, Opus Tertium 17.

I also find the address of the letter to his friend Picard-Sygerus to be of interest. (Picard) Sygerus de Fontancourt is identified as being a soldier and the following quote already mentioned above could be construed as a discussion of plans to travel afar, "*you will be able to direct your steps to cities and islands and to any place whatever in the world.*" 18. Could his 'soldier' friend have been a Templar with dreams of high adventure?

Perhaps we should address the issue of proximity to lend weight to a possible connection to the Templar/Cistercians? There are at least three Templar preceptories near Maricourt within a 37 mile radius or a two day ride; Vaux-Marquenneville, Becquigny and Villeroy.

Sygerus 'the soldier' was from Fontancourt which is across the river Somme from Maricourt, and nearer Aimes. His other name of Picard is directly linked to the region which is known as Picardy as we have seen and had its own dialect and was at one point independent of France until it was conquered.

He had access to the Cistercian and Templar locations as well as the centres of learning at Aimes. Where did the two meet? They were not actual neighbours as they were from differing locations. I would say with some confidence that the Cistercian and Templar preceptories were their common link.

The man had to have been likewise educated, otherwise a letter of such technicality would not have been sent to Sygerus as he would not have been able to read it or interpret the diagrams.

The letter's content alone suggests that there had been prior conversations on the topic of travel and the magnetic compass and other exotic machines with this particular man.

It also implies a great deal of trust for such original breakthroughs to be transmitted to a simple illiterate next door neighbour. Why did he not write letters to colleagues in Paris universities?

No, Sygerus had to have been a person of some ability and import during his day to have received such a letter. So is it possible that the term 'soldier' may have meant Soldier of Christ and that his friend Sygerus *was* a full blown Templar Knight discussing safe navigation on the high seas and new ways of powering a ship other than the sail?

The manner and date of Peter the Pilgrims death is not known. I enjoy the thought that he may have sailed off to the New World and to an unknown fate with Sir Sygerus on a secret Templar mission!

Peregrinus knew he had made the biggest scientific breakthrough of his age, he would not have entrusted it to an illiterate 'neighbour' as a gossip session over the garden wall and a cup of tea! It would only be entrusted to someone on a need to know basis who may have been capable of taking action on the information given to him, who may have even been a working colleague or employer.

Roger Bacon wrote of the desire for a fantastical world of the future which helped propel Western technology forward:

"Machines may be made by which the largest ships, with only one man steering them, will be moved faster than if they were filled with rowers; wagons may be built which will move with incredible speed and without the aid of beasts; flying machines can be constructed in which a man...may beat the air with wings like a bird...machines will make it possible to go to the bottom of the seas and rivers" Roger Bacon 1260 De secretis operibus 19.

Certainly we may extrapolate from Roger Bacon's futuristic insight a strong indication that this circle of companions were discussing, experimenting and possibly even implementing the technologies of the future during their own age for secret purposes such as travelling and surviving in the New World. It is a compelling image of Templar Knights in a Steampunk world.

The Secret Dossier of a
Knight Templar of the Sangreal

The Chaucer Astrolabe

"The astrolabe is intended to be used for both observation and computation. For observation, it is fitted with a ring so the instrument can be hung vertically while the position of the sun or a star is measured using moveable sights and a scale on the back of the instrument." James E. Morrison 20.

I find the above quote interesting that during this incarnation of the Celtic Cross it was required to hang the astrolabe since it no longer had its supporting staff.

According to author James E. Morrison only bronze astrolabes have survived down the centuries and that many of paper or wood have been lost. It is intriguing to know that there were certainly earlier representations of the astrolabe in different mediums such as paper and wood.

Geoffrey Chaucer (1343 – 1400), author of the Canterbury Tales, also started writing a treatise for a ten year old boy named Lewis, possibly his son, on the astrolabe, but it was never finished. Sadly the boy may have died thus ending Chaucer's motivation to finish the treatise.

It is considered the earliest technical manual in England. Included were notes on how the instrument functioned, tables of longitude, latitude and declinations. A theory of the motion of celestial bodies including the moon and also astrology were included.

His description of the object was so precise that he may have had the earliest known European astrolabe in his hands, thus it was named the Chaucer Astrolabe, which has been firmly dated at 1326, just nineteen short years after the Templar arrests of 1307.

It is an incredibly complex piece for its day indicating that the technology had been in existence for some time, but this piece is certainly a pinnacle having five separate plates and a great deal of written information in such a small space of approximately six inches across. Its composition may be a combination of brass and copper.

See photograph opposite:

"All five PLATES bear markings for the circles of the tropics and the equator. One of the plates is otherwise left empty. Plates 1a, 1b, 2a, 2b, 3a, 3b and 4a and 4b have markings for the almucantars every 5° (every 3° on 3a and b), markings for the unequal hours numbered 1 to 12, and the very unusual marking for the prime vertical (except on 4b), without markings for the astrological houses. They are laid out and labelled for the following latitudes ('Latitudo'): 1a) 32° 0' 'Jerlm' (Jerusalem); 1b) 35° 30', 'Babilonie'; 2a) 41° 50', 'Rome'; 2b) 44° 40', 'Motis pessulani' [Montpellier]; 3a) 48° 32', 'parisius'; 3b) 51°50', 'Oxonie' [Oxford]; 4a) 66° 0', 'Tab{u}la sub polo zodiaci'; 4b) 'Tabula sub Equinoctiali'." As qouted from http://www.britishmuseum.org

Note the dragon just inside the circumference which could be taken for an Ouroboros. Its head is in the upper right corner and its tale on the left. There are faces of two men, one smaller Morphic fish-man on the right and the other larger looks to have a bird as his hair and beard, both acting as celestial pointers.

The English creator of the device uses Latin, modern numerals and indicates 33 stars, one being Sirius or the Dog Star. The 'star pointer' on the astrolabe is actually a dogs head. Other star pointers are in the shape of birds.

According to the British Museum website the back also includes the equinoxes of March 13 and September 16 and no less than 46 saints. This is of interest as the date for Easter had not yet been fixed. The feast days of saints Dunstan, Augustine and Botulph are of particular interest for England.

The Chaucer Astrolabe may very well merit further investigation. The choice of the eight latitude locations is interesting. Montpellier of course is the capitol of the Languedoc-Magdalene country. The architect of the astrolabe has also chosen to indicate a latitude of not only Jerusalem as 32° 0' but also 'Babilonie' now modern day Syria.

The Secret Dossier of a
Knight Templar of the Sangreal

The Staff of Magicians

The Staff of Magicians associated with Miller's Celtic Cross instrument may find its reincarnation in Jacob's Staff.

The simple device had between one to four cross sections or transoms and was used for measuring angles, either in navigation or thrust into the ground for surveying and then further equipped with a compass.

I do think this is an echo of the Celtic Cross technology. It had morphed secretly down the centuries until its historical roots had been forgotten though the technology survived. It is interesting that the Celtic Cross seemed to have been taken apart, finding itself reinvented separately as the astrolabe and Jacob's Staff.

Eventually Jacob's Staff would be overtaken by the Sextant. Miller was right to ask how old was the Celtic Cross? The concept of the magicians staff left me with an image of Moses leading his people out of Egypt.

His staff also had the uncanny ability to turn into a serpent to the amazement of the Egyptian priests when he outclassed them in a duel of power.

As Moses was trained by the Egyptian priesthood and fused their religion into Judaic belief, one has to ask, who actually trained him as the Egyptian priests of the Pharaoh were unable to best Moses?

This suggests an ancient mystery school alongside that of the established one of the Pharaoh similar to that of the Underground Stream in Europe today.

As the Israelites wandered the desert was Moses using sacred navigational skills learned from an underground mystery school of Egyptian-Atlantean origin?

His staff might indeed be worth considering as ancient evidence. I would also like to state that I highly doubt Moses was actually lost, but took his people on a circular route in order to develop within them a new form of Judaism inspired by his unknown Egyptian teachers.

During my research on the compass I came across an enigmatic single piece of evidence regarding the Olmecs, who as you recall were building pyramid cities at the time of Christ dedicated to the Feathered Serpent. It appears that they too had a working compass!

Etching of the Jacob Staff, 1672, Practical Navigation by John Seller

"Considering the unique morphology (purposefully shaped polished bar with a groove) and composition (magnetic mineral with magnetic moment vector in the floating plane) of M-160, and acknowledging that the Olmec were a sophisticated people who possessed advanced knowledge and skill in working iron ore minerals, I would suggest for consideration that the Early Formative artefact M-160 was probably manufactured and used as what I have called a zeroth-order compass, if not a first-order compass. The data I have presented in this article support this hypothesis, although they are not sufficient to prove it. That M-160 could be used today as a geomagnetically directed pointer is undeniable. The original whole bar may indeed have pointed close to magnetic north-south. The groove functions well as a sighting mark, and the slight angle it makes with the axis of the bar appears to be the result of calibration rather than accident. A negative supporting argument is that M-160 looks utilitarian rather than decorative, and no function for the object other than that of a compass pointer has been suggested by anyone who has examined it critically." John Pike 21.

The royal capitol city of Atlantis was described by Plato as having a straight canal leading into a harbour. The canal system continued in a series of what may have been defensive circles with the city in the middle giving an overview appearance of what looks astonishingly like a Celtic Cross! Otto Muck's diagram captures this brilliantly.

Based on Otto Muck's drawing

I would like to remind the reader of the sacred number 325 and its relationship to the Alpha and Omega as discussed in the prior chapter:
"Returning to our sacred number 325 - If five is the number of mankind -five *plus* five is equated to God. 325 may be broken down as such:
3 + 2 = 5 (Mankind) and 5 + 5 = 10 (God/Divine Creator)"

Pictorially we have an interesting confluence of evidence between the Celtic Cross and the number 10 in relation to the Alpha and Omega. The number one as the Magician's Staff and the zero as the ancient compass or combined we have the Celtic Cross.

The Light of Navigation
Dutch sailing handbook, 1608, showing compass, hourglass, sea astrolabe, terrestrial and celestial globes, divider, Jacob's staff and astrolabe.

1. Miller, Crichton E. M. *The Golden Thread of Time: A Quest for the Truth and Hidden Knowledge of the Ancients*. Rugby: Pendulum Pub., 2001. p. 5
2. Ibid p 22.
3. Miller, Crichton E.M. "Celtic Cross." The , Crichton EM Miller. http://www.crichtonmiller.com/.
4. Miller, p. 42
5. Brown, Lloyd A. *The Story of Maps*. New York: Dover Publications, 1979. p. 127
6. Ibid, p. 128
7. Ibid, p. 128
8. Schmidl, Petra G. (1996–1997). "Two Early Arabic Sources On The Magnetic Compass". *Journal of Arabic and Islamic Studies* 1: 81–132 http://www.uib.no/jais/v001ht/01-081-132schmidl1.htm#_ftn4
9. APA citation. Kirsch, J.P. (1911). Alexander of Neckam (Necham). In The Catholic Encyclopedia. New York: Robert Appleton Company. Retrieved September 18, 2012 from New Advent: http://www.newadvent.org/cathen/10734a.htm
10. Grant, Edward. *Physical Science in Middle Ages*. Cambridge, MA: Cambridge University Press, 1978.p. 106
11. APA citation. Duhem, P. (1911). Pierre de Maricourt. In The Catholic Encyclopedia. New York: Robert Appleton Company. Retrieved September 18, 2012 from New Advent: http://www.newadvent.org/cathen/12079e.htm
12. Brown, Lloyd A. *The Story of Maps*. New York: Dover Publications, 1979. p. 128
13. Zilsel, Edgar, and Diederick Raven. *The Social Origins of Modern Science*. Dordrecht: Kluwer Academic Publishers, 2000. p. 93
14. Brown, p. 128
15. Bacon, Roger, and A. G. Little. *Part of the Opus Tertium of Roger Bacon, including a Fragment Now Printed for the First Time*. Aberdeen: University Press, 1912.
16. Ibid
17. "Petrus Peregrinus De Maricourt." Wikipedia. https://en.wikipedia.org/wiki/Petrus_Peregrinus_de_Maricourt.
18. Ibid
19. Roger Bacon 1260 De secretis operibus, As quoted in https://en.wikipedia.org/wiki/Petrus_Peregrinus_de_Maricourt.
20. Morrison, James E. *The Astrolabe*. Rehoboth Beach, DE: Janus, 2007. doi: p. 2.
21. "Military 1200 to 100 BC." Global Security. Accessed August 07, 2015. http://www.globalsecurity.org/military/world/mexico/history-1-olmec.htm.
Site maintained by John Pike

Twenty Four

The Keystone

"Caldbeck is the Keystone to the map" – John Temple

Caldbeck, meaning cold stream, is a tiny remote village in the north west of England in the county of Cumbria, known for its pastoral beauty.

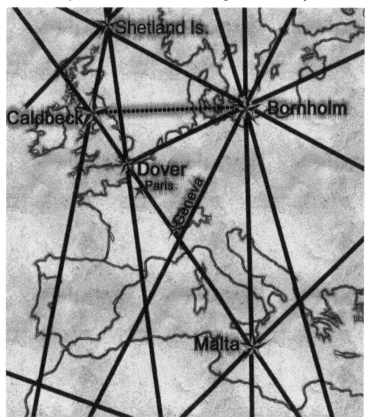

Map by © Gretchen Cornwall & based on the original map given by the Comte -
It may be viewed online at:
http://thesecretdossier.co.uk/maps-stars/

Caldbeck is the Keystone of the Matrix Map and sits at the apex of the kite in northwestern England and in a direct line to the Island of Bornholm famous for its Templar round churches.

The Keystone

I've spent a great deal of time pondering what the nature of a keystone actually is and how could this be relative to the Matrix Map I was given? According to the online Free Dictionary, the definition of 'keystone' is the following:

1. *Architecture* The central wedge-shaped stone of an arch that locks its parts together. Also called *headstone.*
2. The central supporting element of a whole.

The term 'keystone' rang many bells for me as I knew that this was also highly important to Freemasons. According to their allegorical tradition and biblical references, the architect Hiram Abiff was contracted through the King of Tyre by King Solomon to build the Temple in Jerusalem.

Hiram Abiff was an exceptional architect who is credited through legend to have discovered the supportive qualities of a keystone. The keystone sits at the apex of an arch and without it, the archway would collapse.

The architect is remembered in the 3rd degree Freemasonic allegorical tale where he is murdered by three jealous assailants who seek to find out the master builders' trade secrets. The three murderers were summarily executed for their crime. King Solomon respected and mourned the loss of the architect and wanted his memory to be enshrined.

I find the prior themes on the nature of a keystone quite interesting as they have withstood the test of time through their spiritual importance to masons and obviously to beautify and solidify a structure.

But since the nature of the map is magnetic and not of stone where else can I find substantial information that may shed light on this intriguing comment that a location can be a 'keystone' for an energetic grid?

He was also insistent that a person may interact with the grid suggesting a subtle energetic link between the earth and human beings. The use of the term 'subtle' may be a bit deceptive as John Temple believed that the energy in the lines are quite powerful.

'Subtle' may be a good way of describing the sensitivity required by the operative to engage with the Matrix Map and that at this stage we do not have a mechanical device to measure these energies. I'm not certain I want to ascribe the term 'art' to subtle energy interaction but since we are all unique individuals it is necessary for each one of us to discover the 'feel' of such a task with the guidance of intellectual instruction.

We do not have the ability to measure with a limited clockwork device the nature of the soul. But scientific experiments and personal experience of thousands of average and credible people bear out that we are energetic beings first, having a physical experience second.

That we are not a byproduct of chemicals, biology and mechanism – we are a byproduct of an energetic form of being called a soul. Does the earth herself have a soul that an aware human being might communicate with? Many indigenous cultures believe she does.

Perhaps this may be quite farfetched and beyond even pseudo-science but do bear with me here as I do have some rather interesting scientists to consult on what appears to be simply unverifiable mystic matters. Since architecture could not answer my questions regarding the nature of Caldbeck the Keystone, my search has taken me into the nature of Gaia, ley-lines, geology and Quantum Mechanics.

Gaia & Her Morphic Fields

"The morphic fields of mental activity are not confined to the insides of our heads. They extend far beyond our brain through intention and attention. We are already familiar with the idea of fields extending beyond the material objects in which they are rooted: for example magnetic fields extend beyond the surfaces of magnets; the earth's gravitational field extends far beyond the surface of the earth, keeping the moon in its orbit; and the fields of a cell phone stretch out far beyond the phone itself. Likewise the fields of our minds extend far beyond our brains." Rupert Sheldrake 1.

James Lovelock, independent scientist and environmentalist, developed the theory of the Gaia principle in the early 1970s. He saw in a flash that the earth was actually a self-organising and self-regulating biosphere. His ideas were pilloried by the scientific community but over the decades this trend has reversed. His theories have been taken forward by individuals such as Dr. Rupert Sheldrake, former fellow of the Royal Society and biochemist turned author who is challenging the scientific community further.

"I believe that not only in relation to controversial frontier areas of research, but also in more conventional areas, science needs democratizing. It has always been elitist and undemocratic, whether in monarchies, communist states, or liberal democracies. But is currently becoming more hierarchical, not less so, and this trend needs remedying." Rupert Sheldrake 2.

In his book Morphic Resonance, Rupert Sheldrake has explored mysteries of biology such as the cutting of a worm into multiple pieces. The worm does not die but becomes several living worms.

Sheldrake's research has developed the theory that our bodies, indeed all living beings including the plant vegetation of the earth, are governed by Morphogenic fields which 'know' how to align cells to correctly create the living being in question.

We share much of the same DNA as other creatures yet theirs and ours become what was intended through our antecedent, which is possible through the concept of Morphogenic fields which are passed down through a given species. Is it possible that a beneficial change in a species happens first in the energetic collective field prior to an evolutionary physical shift?

185

The Keystone

Mechanistic or clockwork theories for an organism cannot possibly answer all the questions raised by life. If one breaks a clock for example it cannot self-heal or replicate itself into an entire new being such as the worm. It cannot heal itself of a wound allowing life to continue, as many life forms are capable of depending on the gravity of the wound.

Mystics around the world have been studying the energetic nature of the human being for thousands of years; science is only just now coming to grips with the concept that we each have a pre-life existing energetic field or Morphic field as described by the brave Dr. Sheldrake.

"The mechanistic theory postulates that all the phenomena of life, including human behaviour, can in principle be explained in terms of physics. It is a form of materialism or physicalism, the theory that only material or physical things exist; they are the only reality. Materialism is opposed to the more commonsense view that minds affect bodies, and are capable of interacting with them." Rupert Sheldrake 3.

The lines on the Matrix Map take another leap forward from mere pen and ink to having greater substance. If Dr. Sheldrake is right about Morphogenic fields it may indeed give credence to John Temple's comment that the lines on the Matrix Map may have guided the great continent of Pangaea, through continental drift, to become the globe we know today. Sheldrake's research reinvigorates the study of what has come to be known as Ley-Lines or more correctly Ley-Energy.

The Old Straight Track

"We have seen how, with the decay of the old straight track, its mounds and mark stones became in many cases sites of castles and churches. No student of the ley, seeing how on the map ancient homesteads with ancient names seem drawn to the line like iron filings to a line of magnetic influence, can doubt that these also were planted on mark-points of the disused track. Sometimes it was a stone, sometimes at a sighting pond, as at Ingestone, where a cobbled causeway, successor to the old straight track, goes straight for the pond, the ley continuing through the house." Alfred Watkins 4.

Alfred Watkins was a keen antiquarian who made a startling discovery from the vantage point of his saddle. He was gazing across the countryside in the early 1920s when his whole world came into sharp focus. He realised he was gazing at an ancient scene that had been marked over millennia and preserved by successive cultures in the British landscape.

Ancient mounds with a single oak, leading away on a straight track to a pond and then across to an early church and finally in the distance, to a standing stone.

Straight tracks that were heroically dug into rocky landscapes not because of their ease of use but because they were (for example) in line with the rising sun on May Day.

Indeed the difficulty of digging some of these old tracks which connected significant landmarks suggests that they were chosen for their alignment and not due to use as sheepherding or travel.

Watkins organised a club, the Old Straight Track, to help him discover further precise alignments with stars, the sun and pre-Roman earthworks, stones and mounds.

They found webs of intersecting lines woven over the face of the earth radiating outward from each other. The term ley-line was developed as if to describe a moving directional current of energy across Britain that had been marked in antiquity.

Dowsers and other sensitives claim to be able to work with ley-energy. Indeed these serpentine energy lines enjoy the attention and respond with greater strength. These invisible lines snake between and connect with ancient places and old roads. Dowers believe that ley-energy is a form of subtle but powerful earth currents. Almost as if the current were the electrical veins of earth, carrying energetic vitality from one place to another.

Author and speaker Hamish Miller read engineering at St. Andrews and Edinburgh before teaching the art of dowsing. In his book The Sun and the Serpent, he and his co-author Paul Broadhurst set out to mark the entire length of the famous St. Michael and St. Mary ley-lines from Norfolk to Cornwall. They followed the 'currents of terrestrial force' or 'Spiritus Mundi' through ancient sites, localised tales of dragon fighting saints and Marion legends.

"Dowsing the actual energy involved brings a new dimension into play where the abstract concept assumes a reality that can be measured, or at least felt by most people. This in turn creates a fresh scenario where those who feel drawn into the mystery can personally interact with the elemental forces involved. What may appear at first to be an unsubstantiated theory crystallizes into a vivid experience that communicates itself to others. This in turn may have consequences that we can only guess at from our current level of understanding." Hamish Miller & Paul Broadhurst 5.

Working with earth energy as if She were a sentient being is not isolated to Europe. The art of Feng Shui practised in China for millennia believes that positive energy can be collected and guided through homes and even large city planning.

Areas of negative energy are avoided and those that are beneficial are cultivated as the Chi energy of the earth is focused to create positive balance for inhabitants. In China the dragon has long since been a symbol of energy either in the earth or the human being and may be either beneficial or negative. We find a similar correspondence in Europe with the ancient symbol of the dragon coursing through the landscape and through the Gaian-Participant. We are far more squeamish of these ideas than the Chinese and Japanese where the dragon is commonplace. It is a real detriment and in some cases a sad and myopic view held by many in the West of a quantifiable gift which we all share.

The Keystone

The Mysteries of Light: A Sacred Science

"If you want to find the secrets of the universe, think in terms of energy, frequency and vibration." Nikola Tesla, Inventor, 1856-1943

I would like to explore quantum theories as a possibility which could allow for the ley-energetic veins of Gaia and our Keystone in Caldbeck as the peak of the Matrix Map.

As I am not a scientist I cannot give a detailed theory, proven with mathematical equations, as to what might comprise a telluric line of earth energy or its relationship to the earth's protective magnetic shield and gravity.

Nor am I able to answer all of the questions laid out but to propose ideas in order to discuss possible explanations for these phenomena. To my knowledge, and pardon my ignorance if I am mistaken, I've not read in print anywhere a detailed discussion of the links between quantum theory and ley lines. However we may discuss in layman's terms the brilliant minds that have explored quantum theories and surmise their relevance to sacred energetic lines of Gaia.

Roughly speaking, classical physics cannot explain the odd behaviour of light, atoms and particles as its remit functions at the larger level of viewable objects. Though our daily world is seemingly predictable and stable, at the particle level we find a wild undiscovered country where the physical laws flummox our linear views of gravitational pull and time. But it is this small, wild world that determines our own and yet it disobeys the so-called laws of time and space which we use to govern our way of life.

The sub-atomic level is completely flexible backwards and forwards in time and where the very act of observing can shift an experiment. We must ask how much of our conception of linear time and physical reality is accurate as we are surrounded by phenomena in our world that should not exist with the Classical Mechanical world view.

Quantum Mechanics was developed in 1925 by physicist Max Planck which won him a Nobel Prize. His theories have been lauded by many scientists, built upon and proven time and again as measurable fact.

Free energy proponents and mystics have turned to Quantum theory as the principles allow and explain the relationship between humanity, our environment and ability to interact with each other and the earth with limitless potential and harmless sustainability.

Equations show that it is not possible to have a true void or emptiness at the sub-atomic level and that there is a quantifiable energy within the void; indeed fluctuations of electro-magnetic field energy at very high frequencies interact with all matter.

Zero Point Field has become the term for this binding energy which seemingly fills the vast space between the nucleus of an atom and the orbital electrons. It interacts with all elementary particles and becomes an actual energy source in itself. 6.

The Secret Dossier of a
Knight Templar of the Sangreal

The so-called void has been described as extremely dense, fierce and active with energy flying about in all directions at once. Its raw condensed mass comprises more material in one cubic centimetre than what is viewable with the most powerful of telescopes.

Remind yourself of this next time you step outside on a warm summer night to view the vastness of stars and consider a small centimetre in the palm of your hand holding more than the eye can see! 7.

Quantum theory is filled with paradoxes. Under its auspices energy, light and matter are one and the same, where one's actual location becomes flexible if not infinite through a concept known as the Multi-verse. Particles may behave as waves, by-locate instantly and appear simply due to the presence of an onlooker.

"If a quantum calculation predicts that a particle might be here, or it might be there, then in one universe it is here, and in another it is there. And in each such universe, there's a copy of you witnessing one or the other outcome, thinking – incorrectly – that your reality is the only reality. When you realize that quantum mechanics underlies all physical processes, from the fusing of atoms in the sun to the neural firings that constitutes the stuff of thought, the far-reaching implications of the proposal become apparent. It says that there's no such thing as a road untraveled. Yet each such road – each reality – is hidden from all others." Brian Greene 8.

Physicist and philosopher Niels Bohr (1885 – 1962) not only helped to establish quantum mechanics but also played a part in CERN – (European Organization for Nuclear Research) which is the largest particle physics laboratory in the world. His experiments on the nature of light helped turn Classical Mechanics on end.

Heated gas within a tube forms defined lines of light when viewed through a prism versus the diffuse rainbow effect that was expected. Bohr explained that the electrons which surround the nucleus of an atom leave a definite colour line depending on the speed that the heat forces them to travel.

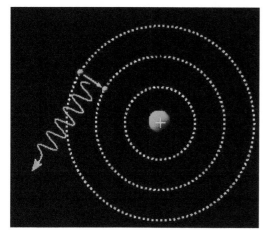

Bohr Model of the atom with an electron making a Quantum Leap. Free source Wiki

View the atom as a solar system where electrons have defined orbits such as planets. The oddity was that Bohr's Model decreed electrons could jump from one fixed orbit to another orbit without appearing to have actually travelled when heated/excited.

Each jump to another orbit has a specific colour of light which is emitted depending on the decreasing/increasing speed of the electron. Bohr's experiments gave us the term Quantum Leap as we are unable to follow the path of the leap. It just simply happens. What if we were to eventually understand this concept and apply it to travel? Instantaneous travel would change our lives and also allow for interstellar travel. 9.

Oddly, further experiments showed that electrons and photons (elementary particles which comprise light) behaved as water when forced through slits in a barrier and not as predictable direct sharp lines as was the expectation. How can a particle move like a wave which is an entirely different pattern of energy?

Is there a correlation between particle waves and ley-lines? How does it seemingly maintain the structure of a 'line' over vast miles, such as indicated on the maps I had been given?

Dowsers describe their experience with ley-lines as an energy wave which maintains its prescribed path over hundreds of miles such as a serpent tightly zigzagging its way over the surface of the earth. Are ley-lines or light-energy somehow connected to concentrations of electron particles/photons acting as waves?

Quantum Mechanics has led to lasers, computers and the entire field of modern microscopic electronics. Even though this technology has given us a new interconnected world, scientists still argue about its nature and the basic questions of reality such as the act of observation and measurement.

Niels Borh believed that the nature of reality is actually fuzzy. The act of measuring and observing a particle forces it to become viewable, therefore the observer is necessary to the experiment!

The observer is the participant in the experiment. Therefore there is no such thing as impartiality even in the human mind, though we do our best to behave as an observer in order to maintain the integrity of any project either in science or historical research, yet true separation is impossible as we are comprised of and part of the nature we are attempting to observe. The grand illusion is that we are separate and outside of the experiment of life and each other. Indeed that is why the experiment of the material exists in order to help us develop free will.

"...the universe begins to look more like a great thought than like a great machine'"
astrophysicist Sir James Jeans (1877 – 1946)

Studying the system from 'within' as in the field of Quantum Mechanics, whereby the act of observation alone dictates the outcome, leads to such questions as, 'how does G.O.D. observe the self?' we can never be outside of the system of energy that comprises the All.

The Secret Dossier of a
Knight Templar of the Sangreal

There are those that think human beings are mirrors reflecting the Divine back to the Source in order that the Source may behold itself allowing for sheer experience, love, compassion, empathy and growth.

Entanglement

Particles can become 'entangled' if their properties become linked. But if one sends these particles away from each other over thousands of miles and then perform an operation on one the other will respond! How is instantaneous communication between the two possible?

Einstein called this response 'spooky' and unsettling. Dr. Rupert Sheldrake implies that this very spontaneous particle behaviour allows for metaphysical activities between recipients whether plant, animal or human!

The secret of 'entanglement' seems to be the instantaneous nature of the energy between particles which would allow for faster than light travel, teleportation and perhaps speed of thought. This energy seems to flow both forwards and backwards in time – dare I call time travel a real possibility? The scientific community is divided on time travel.

Much has been made of the Tachyon particle which has never actually been seen and talk of it seems to be diminishing since the first decade of the mid 2000s. However that does not mean it does not exist. If a Tachyon particle is not responsible for 'entanglement' – the instantaneous stealth particle will eventually be found. We don't know how a Quantum Leap occurs, it just simply happens. Tachyon particles could be the bridge.

So far, physicists can only account for 4 percent of what the universe is made of, said Thomas Koffas, a physicist at Carleton University in Canada. "The remaining 96 percent," Koffas said, "we have no idea." 10.

In lieu of the Tachyon particle, currently all the attention is focused on the Higgs Boson which is said to give mass to physical matter, but true to the conundrum of Q.T. it is also the supporting matrix of the matter which it seemingly has helped to create.

To the chagrin of scientists it has been dubbed the 'god particle' by the press, however in sympathy with the press, it is easy to see the correlation with the divine.

Indications that the Higgs Boson is real were announced both in July of 2012 and in March of 2013 after successful tests at CERN with great excitement by the scientists involved. 11.

The Higgs Boson (AKA the scalar field and scalar boson) is very important as it will prove the theory of the Higgs Field and explain the Unified Field Theory or Zero Point Energy Theory. The Higgs Field can be described as water in which all matter flows through and is comprised of the same energy. 12.

The Keystone

It is hard not to compare this theory (which has had billions invested such is its importance) to George Lucas's the Force:

"The Force is what gives a Jedi his power. It's an energy field created by all living things. It surrounds us and penetrates us; it binds the galaxy together." *Obi-Wan Kenobi, Star Wars, Episode IV A New Hope 13.*

Teleportation

During the meeting an idea suddenly hit me and I boldly asked John Temple if the energy crossings on the map had anything to do with teleportation?

I was quite pleased that he stopped dead in his tracks and said spontaneously, *'yes, but you need three crossing lines and a special tool.'* He of course did not describe this 'tool' and at this stage all I can do is speculate on the nature of this mysterious device.

My first instincts were to consider the Ark of the Covenant and or the Breastplate of Aaron which is comprised of twelve stones. But of course I have nothing else to go on at this stage nor am I likely to have any further input on this issue. The question did leave me pondering the nature of time travel as well, since teleportation was confirmed; why not travel to a time and place?

Physics and philosophy collide on the subject of teleportation. At the present time we can only teleport photons and atoms. In the future the expectation is that we will be able to teleport molecules such as water, however teleporting DNA raises ethical questions.

At our current level of understanding the object to be teleported must be scanned and its information is transported while the original is destroyed. Who would then be arriving at the distant location? 14. What happens to the energy body or soul of the person?

As you know by now I do think that humans are immortal energy beings. Could teleportation in the future be akin to a Near Death Experience since the body dies before it is reconstructed at the other end?

Or would it be as if one fell asleep and woke up shortly after having been teleported? Those that think we are merely biological machines believe that the body being scanned will have died and that the teleported person having been reconstituted will be a new individual with hopefully the faculties and memories of the original still intact.

Will the teleported person be the same or different? Have the Templars that I met dealt with this issue and what conclusions did they draw upon? Again, I may only ask the question as an answer is not forthcoming. Perhaps I'll have further contact with them in the future on this issue?

Even though there are large questions to be asked and answered, it is becoming clearer through quantum mechanics that our experience is created out of energy first and the physical as an emanation of the divine second. Does a clear metaphysical understanding of how the universe functions negate the need for mechanistic devices or tools? Can an adept walk on water, walk through walls, teleport, heal and feed the masses? According to the scientific study of Quantum Theory the answer would be *yes* and it seems that as human beings we all have this innate capacity – the capacity to save ourselves and each other.

Is a Qubit a Cubit and Other Golden Questions

It may be many decades before teleportation of a human being is possible in the public domain. However other uses are more readily within reach. At M.I.T. Seth Lloyd is experimenting with a Quantum computer made of gold and brass – both metals are highly conductive of electromagnetism.

The computer is able to acknowledge or simulate quantum numbers which are 'entangled' such as a zero 0 and a one 1 – now imagine energy flowing between the two and either digit being able to act as the other.

Please see the article:
http://www.popsci.com/science/article/2011-10/seth-lloyd-particle-man
The director of the Center for Extreme Quantum Information Theory at MIT answers our biggest questions
By Flora LichtmanPosted 11.04.2011 at 2:52 pm

The potential for computing power will explode the speed of computers beyond our expectations creating a new world of possibilities. Ironically these numbers are called 'qubits' which has an Old Testament ring to them and is pronounced the same way as the biblical term cubit. The term is referring to a binary code of zeros and ones called bits. A conventional bit can either be a zero or a one but a quantum bit can be both! Or a qubit. 15.

This biblical term cubit caught my attention and I suddenly noticed that the quantum computer was made of gold with brass. The Ark of the Covenant was heavily overlaid with gold plate and there are those who think that part of the secret to the Ark is its ability to conduct electricity.

Is it possible that the Ark contained a free energy device similar to a portable Tesla coil? The Breastplate of Aaron also had gold as a key component surrounding the gems. Are we rediscovering lost secrets?

Is there an energetic spiritual connection between the metal gold, human beings and the Unified Field? I've spoken with psychics who claim that gold objects infused with their energy can augment intention in order to bring about a change in their situation.

The use of a gold signet ring with or without a gemstone in meditation practices or the occult is well documented through the centuries and eventually became a status symbol for the wealthy of the medieval era as hereditary treasures and to seal letters or documents.

Alchemists from Egypt to Medieval Europe have discussed the transmutation of base metal into gold both of the physical nature and also the inner nature.

Many who have had NDEs have reported seeing their surroundings infused with golden light. If the material world is an emanation or reflection of the Unified Field then gold and also the light of the sun must be a physical representation of higher thought.

There is no process on earth that actually creates gold – it is formed through the high impact of a super nova during the creation of earth, which seems fitting as we are speaking about the metal of the sun.

There is so much gold in the earth that if it were above ground we would all be knee deep in the metal of the sun!

The silica mineral Feldspar covers over 60% of the earth and is used in glassmaking and other items as a way to keep temperatures down while firing. Feldspar is the umbrella term for a variety of minerals. 16.

Feldspar can also be found in quartz and includes moonstone, sunstone, labradorite, amazonite and has been linked to the astrological sign of Aquarius. Quartz is the second most abundant crystal found in the earth after the Feldspar group. 17.

Healing with crystals is a very popular subject; indeed the usage of crystals within the New Age community comprises an actual industry. Those that work with crystals view them as sentient friends who assist the practitioner along their 'intentional' way.

I've even spoken with those who have given their crystals names. Sensitives claim to be able to feel energy coursing through their hands and the stones augmenting their own inner energies.

Since there is such an abundance of gold (which is a conductor of electromagnetism) and quartz (conductor of subtle energies) on the earth, are they in anyway attached to the mystery of ley-lines?

One would expect automatically that in areas dense with gold or feldspar-quartz, that there would be a higher amount of ley-lines. However this is not always directly the case. Or at least with our current knowledge of Feldspar as there is so much of it – performing a geological survey of the earth for its highest concentrations is considered a waste of time since it is in such abundance.

We also know that water is a conductor of electricity and dowsers have the ability to find water for wells. Water often follows ley-energy or magnetic lines and may be indicated with an ancient holy well.

China and Japan have acknowledged the elements of earth, air, fire, water, wood and metals for millennia in their sacred belief systems. In the western world we acknowledge only the first four but place a great deal of significance on 'tree-lore' or the green man of the wood and in pre-Christianity the smelting of metals was attributed to god-like powers.

The Secret Dossier of a
Knight Templar of the Sangreal

Pine Cones and Pigeons and Flight Oh My!

I would like to propose that there is a physical correspondence in the human being which might prove to be a link to gold, quartz, water and therefore telluric earth energy.

The Pineal Gland in the human brain has an odd pine cone shape and has been depicted in symbolist art going back millennia. It has been thought to be the seat of the third eye, middle pillar of the Kabbalah and the keystone of the human energetic system.

Mysteriously there are tiny calcite crystals on the Pineal Gland. Is the human body built to perceive and engage with earthly emanations such as gold, crystals and water along with telluric energy lines through the crystalline structure of the Pineal Gland?

John Temple also commented that I should consider the flight of pigeons and their ability to perceive magnetism, thus helping them to navigate over thousands of miles.

Researchers have now discovered that birds have infinitesimal iron clumps inside their inner ear which helps them engage with the earth's magnetic field and navigate! 18.

Humans do not have the iron sensitive compasses of the inner ear that all birds have, but we do have the crystalline Pineal Gland which could be our own interface with the energy systems of the earth.

Strings? Or Leys? Or Both?

String Theory within Quantum Mechanics may answer the question of the difference between telluric currents and the magnetic field of the earth.

Not having a scientific background I cannot answer how the magnetic lines on the Matrix Map can remain stationary yet magnetic north is moving at 40 miles annually and will find its new home over Russia in years to come. 19. Or how magnetic ley-lines seem to be independent of the magnetic field around earth. I can at this point only liken them to veins of energy.

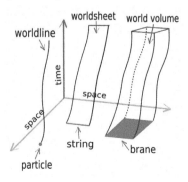

Diagram of String Theory and Branes: Wikipedia free of use by Stevertigo at en.wikipedia, 25 April 2005

Are ley-lines related to Strings or are they an 'emanation' of Strings such as gold, quartz and other higher physical vibrational forms of energy?

"String Theory which has evolved as part of Quantum Mechanics suggests that the universe is composed of vibrating filaments of energy, expressed in precise mathematical language. These strings of energy represent the most fundamental aspect of nature. The theory also predicts other fundamental objects, called branes. All of the matter in our universe consists of the vibrations of these strings (and branes). One important result of string theory is that gravity is a natural consequence of the theory, which is why scientists believe that string theory may hold the answer to possibly uniting gravity with the other forces that affect matter." Andrew Zimmerman Jones & Daniel Robbins 20.

Gravity is highly important to the earth's survival and must also affect ley-lines. These other forces that string theory may help unite are not only gravity but electromagnetic force, weak nuclear force and strong nuclear force. It is thought that after the Big Bang the energy produced was once unified but over time diverged into these four forces which govern our world today.

The earth's magnetic field is lopsided due to what might be the crystallizing and cooling of the inner core on the western side, whereas on the eastern it is actually melting, revitalising itself. The earth's iron core may be hotter than that of the sun and is forcing molten metals into vortices which stretch and twist magnetic field lines and also help create the protective field around earth. The process of the cooling inner core on one side and the melting on the other may be what is driving magnetic north towards Russia from Canada - instead of remaining stationary at true north. 21.

How this affects the stationary ley-lines I cannot say and if it were not for the plethora of sensitives who can 'read' a ley-line, I would say that ley-lines border on pseudo-science, but there is a phenomena happening here which can be supported through Quantum theory and real experience/experiment through handy dowsing rods.

Could the secret of ley-energy sit with the Higgs Boson Field/Unified Field? Where string theory (also called M-Theory – I've used string theory here as it is better suited to visually explain the concept to the lay person over M-Theory) suggests that energy flows in lines? But that it can also act as a wave? Therefore we have two symbiotic systems on earth, the stationary ley-energy lines and the ever-moving and evolving magnetic shield. 22. As we progress and understand quantum energies could we begin to understand ley-energies that sensitives claim to be able to detect? Can the theory of 'entanglement' explain how a dowser can find a missing object, detect water or gold and even hidden archaeological remains? Does 'entanglement' cast new appreciation on Remote Viewing of other places, people or even events in the past or future?

The Secret Dossier of a
Knight Templar of the Sangreal

"...at the core basis of the universe the foundation of the universe is a single universal field of intelligence, a field which unites gravity with electro magnetism, light with radio activity – with the nuclear force – so that all the forces of nature. ...are now understood to be one... they are all just different ripples on a single ocean of existence that is called the unified field..." John Hagelin, Ph.D. 23.

Quantum Mechanics may be our best path to understanding the human soul and the energies of earth in terms of brass tacks science. Until then we have the freedom to experiment as individuals or groups thus making up our own mind and empowering our own lives. The result of such experimentation is the discovery of the Matrix Map.

1. Sheldrake, Rupert. "Morphic Resonance." Articles and Papers -. September 09, 2009. http://www.sheldrake.org/Articles&Papers/papers/morphic/morphic_intro.html.
2. Sheldrake, Rupert, and Rupert Sheldrake. *Morphic Resonance: The Nature of Formative Causation*. Rochester, VT: Park Street Press, 2009. Introduction p. XXVII
3. Ibid p. 15
4. Watkins, Alfred. *The Old Straight Track: Its Mounds, Beacons, Moats, Sites and Mark Stones*. London: Abacus, 1974. p. 212
5. Miller, Hamish, and Paul Broadhurst. *The Sun and the Serpent*. Launceston, Cornwall: Pendragon Press, 1990. p. 27
6. Free Energy: The Race to Zero Point: Actors: Tom Valone, Tom Bearden, Troy Reed, John Hutchison, Dennis Lee Directors: Christopher Toussaint, Director, Harry DeLigter, Producer LightworksAV.com DVD Release Date: January 8, 2008 ASIN: B00136MBNO
7. Ibid
8. Greene, Brian. *The Hidden Reality: Parallel Universes and the Deep Laws of the Cosmos*. Penguin, 2012. p. 6
9. *Nova Fabric of the Universe*. Performed by Brian Greene. DVD. ASIN: B0056031LE Studio: PBS (Direct) DVD Release Date: 22 Nov 2011
10. Rosenblum, Bruce, and Fred Kuttner. *Quantum Enigma: Physics Encounters Consciousness*. 2nd ed. Oxford: Oxford University Press, 2011. p. 53
11. Koffas, Thomas. "A Second Higgs Boson? Physicists Debate New Particle." Fox News. April 15, 2013. http://www.foxnews.com/science/2013/04/15/second-higgs-boson-physicists-debate/#ixzz2VoAi8lmj.
12. "CERN Accelerating Science." New Results Indicate That New Particle Is a Higgs Boson. March 14, 2013. http://home.web.cern.ch/about/updates/2013/03/new-results-indicate-new-particle-higgs-boson.
13. Lucas, George, Director, 20th Century Fox, Star Wars, Episode IV A New Hope 1977
14. Michio Kaku: The Metaphysics of Teleportation http://www.youtube.com/watch?v=KcivmBojzVk http://bigthink.com
15. *Nova Fabric of the Universe*. Performed by Brian Greene. DVD. ASIN: B0056031LE Studio: PBS (Direct) DVD Release Date: 22 Nov 2011
16. Hamilton, Calvin, and Rosanna Hamilton. "Feldspar." Feldspar. http://

Two Templar Knights playing chess - c. 1283 AD

www.scienceviews.com/geology/feldspar.html.
Information adapted from "Minerals in Your World", a cooperative effort between the U.S. Geological Survey and the Mineral Information Institute.
17. Haxworth, Carly. "Healing Properties of Feldspar from Charms Of Light - Healing." Charms of Light. http://www.charmsoflight.com/feldspar-healing-properties.html.
18. Gray, Richard. "Iron Spheres in Ears May Help Birds Navigate." The Telegraph. April 26, 2013. http://www.telegraph.co.uk/science/science-news/10021789/Iron-spheres-in-ears-may-help-birds-navigate.html.
19. Adams, Guy. "Adjust Your Compass Now: The North Pole Is Migrating to Russia." The Independent. March 06, 2011. http://www.independent.co.uk/news/science/adjust-your-compass-now-the-north-pole-is-migrating-to-russia-2233610.html.
Movement of the magnetic north is causing problems for aviation, navigation and wildlife
20. Jones, Andrew Zimmerman., and Daniel Robbins. *String Theory for Dummies*. 1 Original Edition. Hoboken, NJ: Wiley Publishing, 2009. p. 9
21. Oskin, Becky. "Why Earth's Magnetic Field Is Lopsided." MNN. July 18, 2012. http://www.mnn.com/green-tech/research-innovations/stories/why-earths-magnetic-field-is-lopsided.
22. Don Lincoln of Fermilab, Educational video What is a Higgs Boson 7 July 2011 http://www.youtube.com/watch?v=Rig1Vh7uPyw
23. *What the Bleep: Down the Rabbit Hole*. Performed by John Hagelin Ph.D. Revolver Entertainment. DVD.Extended Interviews DVD 31 July 2006,ASIN: B000GPPPYA

Twenty Five

Heronian Tetrahedron

The Keystone of the Matrix Map, Caldbeck England, is at the apex of a Heronian Tetrahedron which the Comte de Medici stressed, during our meeting, as being of high significance.

I've taken the liberty of upending the map (see below) in order to understand its shape as being a 'kite' with Caldbeck in the north. He was quite insistent that it was a sacred geometric shape and had energetic significance of its own accord.

Before embarking on writing I did show this map to others with an interest in sacred geometry, they said it is highly unusual to have a sacred geometric shape that is not of a prime number or of an 'equal' form.

However for those who would argue that this is not a genuine form I would like to point out that many stone circles are of an elliptical unequal nature which align with stars on a particular day of the year.

Knowledge of elliptical orbits is quite sophisticated for any culture to have attained. It is quite natural to acknowledge the 'wobbly' countenance of our world in sacred monuments and also to 'notice' the same in Gaia's energetic veins.

As the map has led to many significant historical, important locations and also people, I do not have cause to doubt his assertion that this map is genuine. It is certainly the next step in our understanding of sacred geometry and the nature of ley-lines.

Of course the first noticeable feature is that of the cross within the kite formation itself. It is not equilateral as the Templar Cross Pâté but warped as if one were looking at the constellation of Cygnus expressed as an energetic cross over the earth.

We are looking at a flat representation of the curved surface of the earth just to complicate matters. The cross extends from Caldbeck through Saint John's Chapel (Bishop Auckland) in the Pennines to Bornholm Island and from the Shetland Islands to Dover. All known Templar locations.

The Heronian Tetrahedron was named after Hero of Alexandria (10 – 70 AD), a Greek mathematician and engineer. He is famous for his drawings of a steam engine, cuckoo clock, vending machine and the first attempt to harness the power of the wind through his wind-wheel. Much of his work is lost due to the burning of the Library of Alexandria by Christians in the 4th or 5th century. He is associated with Heron's Formula, for finding the area of a triangle from its side lengths. 1.

The Heronian Tetrahedron is not a flat two dimensional shape, but rises above the landscape and is comprised of four planes.

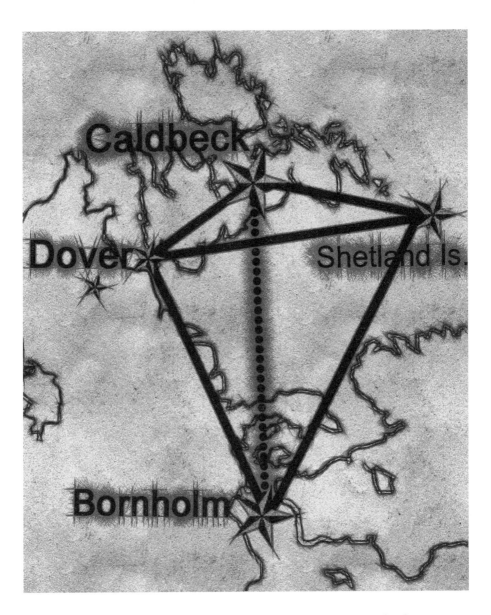

Map by © Gretchen Cornwall & based on the original map given by the Comte -
It may be viewed online at:
http://thesecretdossier.co.uk/maps-stars/

The Secret Dossier of a
Knight Templar of the Sangreal

"A Heronian tetrahedron, also called a perfect tetrahedron, is a (not necessarily regular) tetrahedron whose sides, face areas, and volume are all rational numbers. It therefore is a tetrahedron all of whose faces are Heronian triangles and additionally that has rational volume."

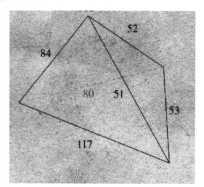

The following table gives the smallest pair of primitive integer Heronian tetrahedra with the same surface area.

area	volume	edges
64584	170016	595, 429, **208, 116**, 276, **325**
64584	200928	595, 507, **116, 208**, 276, **325**

Both above images are based on mathematician
Eric Weisstein of Wolfram Research 2.
http://mathworld.wolfram.com/HeronianTetrahedron.html

The table (page 269) is highly important as it contains the Hyper Perfect number 325 which has been explored at great length in prior chapters.

There is a second layer to the code of the Matrix Map which I will discuss shortly, where the Hyper Perfect number 325 plays a considerable role.

John Temple spoke of the Hyper Perfect number as a sacred key to the map along with the Natural Numbers 116 and 208. A k-hyperperfect number may be found under the umbrella of Natural Numbers.

Simply put, Natural Numbers help us with daily activities such as counting - for instance, we have 3 potatoes for dinner, 1, 2, 3 and we could use a 4th for another guest – or for placing objects in an order, so as to differentiate between them, such as there are 6 chairs and 1 table.

Heronian Tetrahedron

Natural Numbers may be used either with a zero or without and many ancient cultures developed the use of the zero from ancient Egypt, Babylonians, Olmec and Maya. Often a simple blank space was used to denote 'nothing' but also symbols had been developed in these ancient cultures as well. Dionysius Exiguus (c. 470 – c. 544) originated the Anno Domini era (AD) and the use of the Latin term 'nihil' meaning 'nothing' to act as zero. Though 'nihil' was helpful it was still very cumbersome compared to the breath of fresh air from the east. The use of an actual zero was noted in India approximately 600 AD. 3.

Heronian Triangle

"Given a Heronian triangle, one can split it into two right-angled triangles, whose sidelengths form Pythagorean triples..."

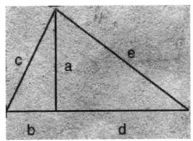

A triangle (page 270) with sidelengths c, e and $b + d$, and height a.
Text and table based on mathematician Eric Weisstein of Wolfram Research http://mathworld.wolfram.com/HeronianTetrahedron.html

Pythagorean Triples (under Euclidean geometry) forming a Heronian Tetrahedron, may have been developed by Greek mathematician and philosopher Pythagoras 6th century BC who was also the leader of his own metaphysical community.

A Regular Tetrahedron is one of the five Platonic Solids:

The Platonic Solids viewed as elemental energy and the shape of the Universe by Johannes Kepler Mysterium Cosmographicum 1600

The Secret Dossier of a
Knight Templar of the Sangreal

The five Platonic Solids have sides of Cube=Four, Tetrahedron=Four, Octahedron=Eight, Dodecahedron= Twelve and the Icosahedron = Twenty. Plato postulated that matter was formed out of the Solids at the level of what would be termed as the atom. Though proven incorrect in modernity his genius is undisputed for such a concept as to what might comprise physical matter prior to the advent of the microscope and the discovery of the atom.

It would be reductionist thinking to now simply brush aside Plato's reverence for the five geometrical progressions for together they also represent an entire philosophy. The Platonic Solids resolve themselves in the Vitruvian Man and the Pentagram.

Though the Solids are credited to Plato the 4th century philosopher and mathematician, there may be an earlier tradition of the concept.
Hundreds of carved stone balls have been found across Scotland and northern England of the Neolithic period 10200 BC – 2000 BC.

See Hart's site for copyright photos:
http://www.georgehart.com/virtual-polyhedra/neolithic.html 4.

Their purpose has been ascribed to art as their original function is simply not known. However they appear to be experiments in geometry, perhaps even a memory or relic of Atlantean Britain?

Crichton E.M. Miller, author of the Golden Thread of Time, suggests that some of them could have been used as plumb bobs by megalithic builders by tying a cord around the notches as their size of about 3" in circumference would be perfect. 5.

The stones do bear an uncanny resemblance to Platonic Solids which is the assertion of professor and architect Keith Critchlow. He has received a great deal of criticism regarding his theory, but over the course of an in-depth and mathematically driven chapter in his book, Time Stands Still, develops a strong argument that their creators had a deep knowledge of geometry. 6.

Though the Heronian Tetrahedron is not symmetrical with all sides being equal, it is still worth discussing the polyhedron or Regular Tetrahedron and its interesting historical background as noted by Plato, Kepler and its possible earlier British roots.

All of the Platonic Solids are found in the astonishing world of fractals.

Humanity, the Golden Mean and the World of Fractals

"Once our eyes have been opened to the fact that fractal objects possess a distinctive character and structure, and are not just irregular or random, it becomes obvious that the universe is full of fractals. Indeed, it may even be one." Arthur C. Clarke 7.

One cannot discuss the Holy Grail genre without its indelible links to the realm of sacred geometry which is a physical manifestation of the divine and our direct connection to the stars.

The practice of sacred geometry in art, sculpture, landscaping, architecture and city planning is akin to an act of creation or magical-prayer work often mirroring the heavens, planetary alignments and solstices. In fact the human being *is* walking sacred geometry and a fractal in motion.

As I said before, in China and Japan, the above statement would not cause them a moment of consternation as they embrace these concepts as a matter of course. It is part of their ancient heritage.

Western hermetical arts and city planning concepts raise eyebrows in religious circles, denial in academic circles and fear of the sinister in some of the conspiracy theory circles. What is an alchemist to do but remain silent and anonymous due to repercussions of a social nature or perhaps even physical violence?

The Golden Ratio or Phi Φ, was the measure used to build what is considered to be one of the most perfect of structures, the Parthenon of Athens and dedicated to Athena the goddess of war and wisdom.

In numerical terms this magical of all symbols by which so much has been built through the millennia including the pyramids, may be spelled out numerically as - 1.618 and is directly related to the ratio of the idealised body.

The medieval mathematician Leonardo Fibonacci (1170-1250) discovered that if one added the following digit to its prior correspondent, a sequence is born. Hence the Fibonacci Sequence:

0, 1, 1, 2, 3, 5, 8, 13, 21, 34, 55, 89, 144... and so on

Oddly, when one divides the larger Fibonacci numbers by the number preceding it you obtain values very close to, or exactly, of the golden number or phi: 89 / 55 = 1.618

This golden ratio may be found in floor plans, art and nature such as the famous sea-shell spiral.

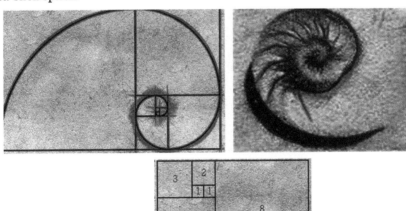

The Secret Dossier of a
Knight Templar of the Sangreal

Cut an apple open and the seeds will form a pentagram or a five pointed star, a shape whose triangles are based on the Golden Mean.

According to the developer of Phimatrix software, Gary Meisner, the body is based on patterns of fives:

- *5 appendages to the torso, in the arms, leg and head.*
- *5 appendages on each of these, in the fingers and toes*
  - *5 openings on the face.*
1. *5 senses in sight, sound, touch, taste and smell.*

The golden section in turn, is also based on 5, as the number phi, or 1.6180339
http://www.goldennumber.net/human-body/ 8.

We see the Golden Mean ratio reflected in the body. Using the finger as an example. The first two bones in your index finger will be equal in length to that of the third bone in your finger. Those three bones of your index finger will equal the length from the base of the finger to the wrist bone and so on.... Of course this is an approximation and will not bear out for each person exactly, but it is often the measure considered to be most pleasing to the eye and is therefore used by artists and architects.

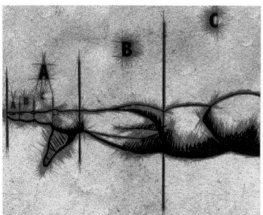 

Leonardo's Vitruvian Man using the Golden Mean of 1.618

"The Fibonacci numbers and the golden mean are not merely numerological curiosities. Rather, this scaling pattern appears to be built into a number of biological structures, or perhaps more appropriately, such structures appear to be constructed in part from a Fibonacci blueprint...." Bruce J. West & Ary L. Goldberger 9.

West and Goldberger found that the lungs were formed in the same manner as the Fibonacci Sequence. The trachea as 'one' branches off into 'two' lungs and then from there into the bronchial tubes in an asymmetric pattern. They termed this phenomena the "fractal/Fibonacci Lung Tree". Fractal anatomy is not isolated to the lung but may be seen in the heart, brain and vascular system.

West and Goldberger noted that Fibonacci scaling was also seen in plants and also the ratio of the total height of the human being from head to toe based on the measurement of naval to toe, as one unit and is approximately 1.62 very close to 1.618.

"What makes them [fractals] so useful in today's scientific research is that they have opened up entirely new ways to model nature. They give scientists a powerful tool with which to understand processes and structures hitherto described merely as 'irregular', 'intermittent', 'rough', or 'complicated'." Arthur C. Clarke 10.

Fractals are a very complex pattern of geometry that may be regular or irregular. Aside from the medical world's use of fractal geometry of scaling, which could not be done without the aid of computers, it has also given us dazzling entertainment and the ability to compress large image files and send them flying across the world.

The richness of our experience through mediums such as the internet has added colour where there was black and white – has added three dimensional space where there had been a simple stick figure. Computer animators depend on fractals to generate realistic landscapes from characters, mountains, clouds, trees and the minutia of leaves.

We could not conceive of a computer prior to their existence. Fractal geometry is the basis of new technology and science – it will be the primary tool of descriptive physical science and engineering for hundreds of years to come. We owe much to the scientific and creative genius of one man.

The Measure of Chaos

Mathematician, Benoit Mandelbrot (1924 – 2010) created the term 'fractal' (meaning broken glass) as well as developing the theory that anything 'rough' can be measured through fractal geometry. Such was the impact of his discovery that the series of intricate and infinite geometric patterns he developed were given his name. 11.

When I first learned of the Mandelbrot Set I felt as if I were looking at a divine pen sketching itself across the universe of its own free will.

Mandelbrot discovered that there was a certain order to what appeared to be chaos, such as clouds, galaxies and blood vessels. Repeatable patterns could be seen in ferns as well as in humble broccoli.

The Secret Dossier of a
Knight Templar of the Sangreal

No matter how large or how small the M. Set is always the same in configuration, truly a microcosm and macrocosm of ultimate geometry.

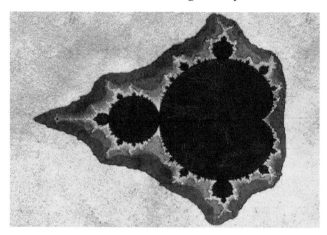

The M. Set appears to be a very strange looking bug or any multitude of organic shapes. I highly recommend Arthur C. Clarkes film and book, The Colours of Infinity, which dramatically explains the significance of the Mandelbrot Set.

No matter how far 'down' or 'up' the scale the pattern is repeated. Further along on the strange creature, it appears that it may have what could be described as hairs where the pattern splits into two without end and has the uncanny appearance of bronchial or tree limbs.

Everywhere in nature one looks you will see fractal patterns. The M Set is a wild but simple formula that can replicate itself through a mathematical two-way street and describe the roughness and irregularity of life around us. In essence there is nothing that could not now be measured or mapped!

Dr. Ian Stewart, professor of mathematics, believes that we should be able to predict the future. *"It's not whether god plays dice but how god plays dice."* 12.

The M. Set allows for order and chaos, classical Newtonian Physics and Quantum Physics to co-exist, Dr Michael Barnsley describes our experience superlatively *"...This is how god created a system which gave us free will. The most brilliant manoeuvre in the universe, to create something in which everything is free".* 13.

We are made up of dynamic responsive energy freely available to all, which cannot be metered, charged for or controlled. It is our holistic birth right and our future.

"...perhaps there is some structure, if one can use that term, deep in the human mind that resonates to the patterns in the M-set." Ian Stewart 14.

Many who have ingested hallucinogens can actually see the M. Set and other psychedelic patterns similar to Hildegard Von Bingen's mandala style artwork.

We see this complex geometric artwork across multiple cultures from Hindi, Buddhism, Native American and Islam. Does the mind have a way of processing fractal geometry? If we and all around us are related to Quantum Fractals such as the M. Set, it stands to reason that we would be able to intuitively perceive our world as we are the very hardware with ethereally installed software allowing us to

207

communicate with creative energy.

"Carl Jung would have been surprised – and delighted – to know that thirty years after his death, the computer revolution whose beginnings he just lived to see would give new impetus to his theory of archetypes, and his belief in the existence of a 'collective unconscious'. Arthur C. Clarke 15.

Is the mind sensitised to perceive the quantum mechanics of the universe? How does it affect our consciousness? This is an interesting question considering the engravings on the back of this 1st century Celtic mirror and the Julia Set fractal below to it.

Photo by Fuzzypeg, all rights released
The Desborough Mirror Celtic (England) 50 BC-50 AD The British Museum, showing the spiral and trumpet decorative theme of the late "Insular" La Tène style
http://en.wikipedia.org/wiki/Celtic_art

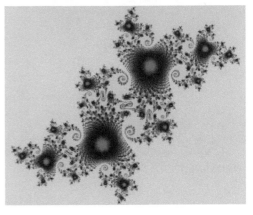

A Julia set, a fractal related to the Mandelbrot set
http://en.wikipedia.org/wiki/Fractals
Created by Wiki User Eequor
http://en.wikipedia.org/wiki/
File:Julia_set_(indigo).png

"The Mandelbrot Set is, as I have tried to explain is essentially a map. We've all read those stories about maps that reveal the location of hidden treasure. Well, in this case the map IS the treasure!" Arthur C. Clarke

The Secret Dossier of a
Knight Templar of the Sangreal

The Comte said exactly the same thing about the Matrix Map being the treasure itself when it was given to me at our first meeting.

I can't escape the similarity of the kite shape of the Mandelbrot Set as compared to the Heronian Tetrahedron. The two seem to overlay comfortably with one another and help explain the irregularity of the Heronian Tetrahedron.

The further I studied the Heronian Tetrahedron the more astonished I became as we have a physical link to this oddly shaped kite. Dr. Tidjani Negadi of the Physics Department, Faculty of Science at the University of Oran in Algeria has discovered a direct mathematical and physical link between amino acids, our DNA and the Heronian Tetrahedron. Amino acids are the building blocks of life and may have been seeded by radioactive dust from space creating the soup out of which life began.

He may very well have found the key as to why molecules form stable structures allowing for growth.

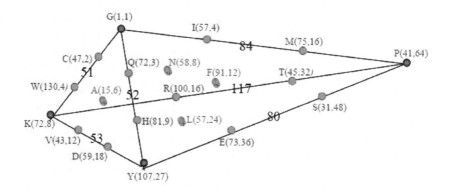

Figure 2: The heronian tetrahedron "117" hosting the 20 amino acids

Negadi, Tidjani. "The Irregular (integer) Tetrahedron as a Warehouse of Biological Information

Now, I'm not a scientist but I offer this selection of his paper to you for consideration:

"Abstract: A "variable geometry" classification model of the 20 L-amino acids and the 20 D-amino acids, based on twenty, physically and mathematically, labeled positions on tetrahedrons, and extending Filatov's recent model, is presented. We also establish several physical and mathematical identities (or constraints), very useful in applications.

The passage from a tetrahedron with (possibly) maximum symmetry to a tetrahedron with no symmetry at all, here a distinguished integer heronian tetrahedron, which could "describe" some kind of symmetry breaking process, reveals a lot of meaningful biological numerical information.

Before symmetry breaking, and as a first supporting result, we discover that the L- and D-tetrahedrons together encode the nucleoncontent in the 61 amino acids of the genetic code table and the atomcontent in the 64 DNA-codons.

After a (geometric) symmetry breaking, and also an accompanying (physical) "quantitative symmetry" restoration concerning atom numbers, more results appear, as for example the atom-content in this time 64 RNA-codons (61 amino acids and three stops), the remarkable Downes-Richardson-shCherbak nucleon-number balance and, most importantly, the structure of the famous protonated serine octamer Ser8+H+ (L- and D- versions), thought by many people to be a "key player" in the origin of homochirality in living organisms because of its unique property to form exceptionally stable clusters and also its strong preference for homochirality." Negadi, Tidjani 16.

The Heronian Tetrahedron –
The Shape of Things to Come

The Heronian Tetrahedron mathematically promotes a Torus which is a geometric shape best thought of as a donut and one which many physicists' think may indeed be the shape of the universe. Interestingly enough CERN's Large Hadron Collider in Switzerland is constructed in the shape of a large Torus. 17.

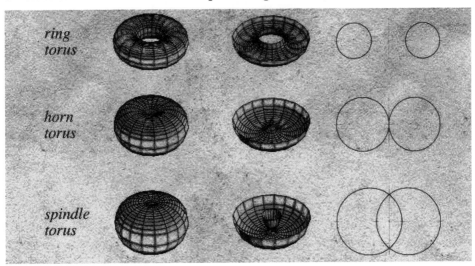

ring torus

horn torus

spindle torus

Torus drawing is based off of a drawing from Mathworld

Profoundly the pattern of the atmospheric circulation around earth may be idealised as a Torus. According to Nassim Haramein of the Resonance Project Foundation, the same flow of our atmosphere can be understood as the movement of the universe. Earth is not stationary but hurtling through space at a vast rate with other galaxies moving to the breath of the universal Torus just as the atmosphere flows around earth.

Magnetic Shield of Earth in the shape of a Torus

At every scale of existence the flow of energy and the Torus may be found such as in the red blood cell or the shape of an apple.

The Torus has a representational mathematical skeletal structure which is called the Vector Equilibrium (cuboctahedron) and was termed by architect, futurist and inventor R. Buckminster Fuller (1895 – 1983).

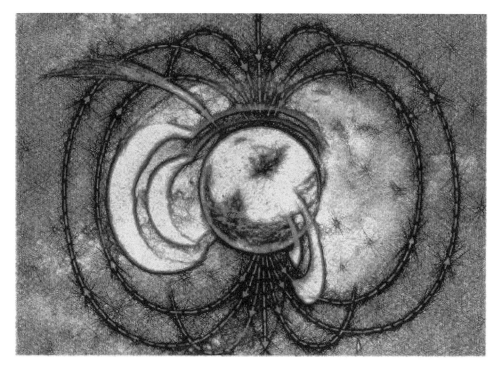

"Emptiness at the Center: All four planes of all eight tetrahedra, i.e., 32 planes in all, are congruent in the four visible planes passing through their common vector equilibrium center. Yet you see only four planes. Both the positive and the negative phase of the tetrahedra are in congruence in the center. They are able to do this because they are synchronously discontinuous. Their common center provides the locale of an absolutely empty event." R. Buckminster Fuller 18.

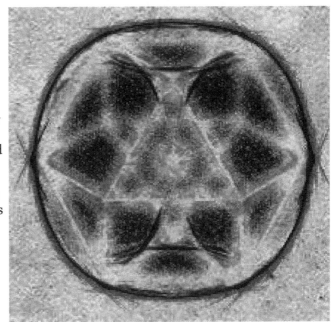

The centre of the Vector Equilibrium may be viewed as a three dimensional twelve wind compass and is a very stable equal structure. The energy which flows around this 3-D compass is the Torus.

Life for us however becomes even more interesting with the Torus as it is the basis for the 64 point pyramid. If each pyramid is then viewed as a sphere the Flower of Life pattern is born. The Flower of Life is a symbol that can be seen in ancient cultures around the globe.

There are modern mystics who claim that our 64 point DNA reflects these sacred geometric themes.

The Secret Dossier of a
Knight Templar of the Sangreal

The Vector Equilibrium may be mathematically expressed to include an overlay of the Kabbalistic tree of life.

"Equilibrium between positive and negative is zero. The vector equilibrium is the true zero reference of energetic mathematics. Zero pulsation in the vector equilibrium is the nearest approach we will ever know to eternity and God: the zero phase of conceptual integrity inherent in the positive and negative asymmetries that propagate the differentials of consciousness." R.Buckminster Fuller, Synergetics 19.

The Torus has been said to be the source of free energy devices and capable of tapping into the Zero Point Energy Field of Quantum Mechanics, such as the Tesla coil and is the answer to a sustainable, clean and free future.
Our ability to perceive the energetic beingness of the world and each other has been studied by Dr. Gary E. Schwartz, one of the most brilliant minds of our time. He has waded into this muddy, highly emotive discussion putting his distinguished career in peril.

In his book, The Afterlife Experiments Dr. Gary E. Schwartz asks the question:

"If it could be proved beyond a doubt and in an entirely convincing way, if it could be proved scientifically that life and love are eternal-
> would your love be enhanced,
> would your fears vanish,
> would your purpose in life be magnified?" 20.

He conducted powerful, academically-accepted experiments on life after death or the study of the post physical reality, concluding that we are immortal energy beings that continue to learn and love.
According to Dr. Schwartz the soul continues after the body dies and his findings leave the door wide open on the subject of reincarnation.

He challenges us by asking:

"How would life be different for you if you knew that just as patterns of dynamic light from distant stars continue to expand into the universe, our light, our dynamic information and energy, our soul and spirit not only continue to expand into the universe but live and grow just as we do on the earth? That the living soul can be likened to a dynamic living rainbow, a vibrating spectrum of visible and invisible energies that shimmer and shine forever?" 21.

If we are immortal beings then surely we cannot be alone as the same creative Source behind our existence must conduct and flow through the rest of creation? Hence our ability to navigate through ley-lines.

Heronian Tetrahedron

Dr. Schwartz states:

"...in the case of evolution, just because growth and increases in complexity appear to occur naturally does not mean that evolution is non-intelligent. Evolution-and what scientists term natural evolution-may require invisible external fields modulated by intelligence, that is, intelligent evolution." 22.

He suggests that we must listen to these invisible fields, which is exactly what our ancient ancestors did in deep caves and the mystery schools of today practice. But because we are human beings this path is open to us all as it is hardwired in our DNA.

We evolved to experience God, reflecting the Divine back to the Source through acts of empathy and appreciation, thus being part of the continued growth of the Divine.

In his book The G.O.D Experiments, Dr. Schwartz offers an anagram of a universe that is a Guiding-Organizing-Designing process, asking us to merge faith with science based observation of the natural world and spiritual world outside of dogma. As our own souls are androgynous, so is the ultimate nature of God with the complete freedom to express through the male or female element.

Dr. Schwartz indicates the sun as the major factor in our evolving consciousness. Since time immemorial we have looked to the sun for life on earth and indeed even worshiped it as a god in some cultures, such as the great kingdom of Egypt who acknowledged both the sun and Cygnus the Swan as vital to all life. In our current age of Pisces, Jesus takes over the role of sun god from Apollo breathing new messages of life into our collective unconscious.

The good doctor states that:

"The sun is a complex dynamical system that emits a wide spectrum of energies and information – from micro and radio waves, through infrared waves, light waves in the visible spectrum, and ultraviolet waves, to X rays and gamma rays." He continues, "We are all highly interconnected with the sun's bands of energy and information." 23.

If the Heronian Tetrahedron creates a Torus which also is an energetic production form – if the human being is attuned to the earth and in symbiotic relationship to the ley-energies – what could an aware person achieve through the Matrix Map?

The Secret Dossier of a
Knight Templar of the Sangreal

1. Alexandria, Hero Of. The Pneumatics of Hero of Alexandria. Lexington, KY: CreateSpace Independent Publishing Platform, 2009.
2. Weisstein, Eric. "Heronian Tetrahedron." -- from Wolfram MathWorld. http://mathworld.wolfram.com/HeronianTetrahedron.html.
3. http://en.wikipedia.org/wiki/Dionysius_Exiguus
4. Hart, George W. "Neolithic Carved Stone Polyhedra." Neolithic Carved Stone Polyhedra. 1998. http://www.georgehart.com/virtual-polyhedra/neolithic.html.
5. Miller, Crichton E. M. The Golden Thread of Time: A Quest for the Truth and Hidden Knowledge of the Ancients. Rugby: Pendulum Pub., 2001. p. 262
6. Critchlow, Keith, and Rod Bull. Time Stands Still: New Light on Megalithic Science. London: Gordon Fraser Gallery, 1979. p. 132
7. Stewart, Ian, and Arthur C. Clarke. The Colours of Infinity: The Beauty and Power of Fractals. Clear Books, 2004.
8. Meisner, Gary. "The Human Body and the Golden Ratio - Phi 1.618: The Golden Ratio." Phi 1618 The Golden Ratio. May 31, 2012. http://www.goldennumber.net/human-body/.
9. West, Burce J., and Ary L. Goldberger. "Physiology in Fractal Dimensions,." American Scientist, The Scientific Research Society. http%3A%2F%2Fwww.jstor.org%2Fstable%2Fi27854710. p 356, , Vol. 75, No. 4, July-August 1987 Sigma Xi,
10. Stewart, Ian, and Arthur C. Clarke. The Colours of Infinity: The Beauty and Power of Fractals. Clear Books,
    2004. P. 12
11. Wolfram, Stephen. "The Father of Fractals." WSJ. November 22, 2012. http://www.wsj.com/articles/ SB10001424127887324439804578107271772910506. Re: Mandelbrot
12. DVD Interview: The Colours of Infinity: The Beauty and power of Fractals, contributors Ian Stewart, Sir Arthur C. Clarke, Benoit Mandelbrot, Michael and Louisa Barnsley, Will Rood, Gary Flake and David Pennock, Robert R. PrechterJr. And Nigel Lesmoir-Gordon, ISBN 1 904555 05 5, Clearpress UK
13. Ibid
14. Stewart, Ian, and Arthur C. Clarke. The Colours of Infinity: The Beauty and Power of Fractals. Clear Books, 2004. P 41.
15. Ibid p. 34.
16. Negadi, Tidjani. "The Irregular (integer) Tetrahedron as a Warehouse of Biological Information." MArXiv. 2012. http://marxiv-org.lieblich.us/?query=id%3A1207.3454#?query=id%253A1207.3454&page=0&type=search&_suid=143896245400106304131115 6425. Abstract: This paper is devoted to a new classification of the twenty amino acids based on the heronian (integer) tetrahedron.
17. Marshall, Michael. "Five Snacks That Are Shaped Like the Universe." Newscientist.com. August 03, 2009. http%3A%2F%2Fwww.newscientist.com%2Farticle%2Fdn17535-five-snacks-that-are-shaped-like-the-universe.html.

18. Fuller, R. Buckminster, and E. J. Applewhite. Synergetics: Explorations in the Geometry of Thinking. New York: Macmillan, 1982.
19. Ibid
20. Schwartz, Gary E., and William L. Simon. The Afterlife Experiments: Breakthrough Scientific Evidence of Life after Death. New York: Pocket Books, 2002. p. 15
21. Ibid p. 24
22. Schwartz, Gary E., and William L. Simon. The G.O.D. Experiments: How Science Is Discovering God in Everything, including Us. New York: Atria Books, 2006. p. 119
23. Ibid p. 122

The floriated cross on the tombstone of Sir Thomas de Bray, a known Templar Knight. Note the cross added to the lower right side. The tombstone is now affixed to the wall of Saint Kentigerns, Caldbeck Cumbria. © Gretchen Cornwall 2009
Further discussion on the cross and location in the next chapter -

The tombstone of Sir Thomas de Bray, a known Templar Knight
It is now affixed to the wall of Saint Kentigerns, Caldbeck Cumbria.
© Gretchen Cornwall 2009

Twenty Six

Vesica Piscis - the Alchemical Marriage in Caldbeck Cumbria

Imagine two beings surrounded by their own flowing energy of the Torus – these two seemingly independent beings now step towards one another, within each other's space; what is then apparent is the overlay of their individual energy Torus creating a third form of a combined energy called the Vesica Piscis.

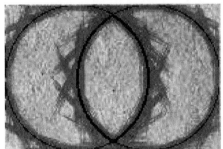

Vesica Piscis

This ancient symbol of the Alchemical Marriage and resultant Trinity is abundant with meaning. It is the birth canal of new life, the gift of clear sight or All Seeing Eye and the beginnings of the Christian fish symbol whose original meaning is the ability to traverse the inner planes of self-knowledge. Each of us as individuals are imbued with the capacity of the Alchemical Marriage as it is our birth right as human beings.

In early sacred western art the original way to depict a saint was by a Vesica Piscis which surrounded the entire body, later medieval and Renaissance art shifted this whole body glow, giving way from the eye of the Vesica Piscis and reducing it to a simple halo surrounding the head.

"What many people don't know is that every line in the Tree of Life, whether it has 10 or 12 circles, measures out to either the length or width of a vesica piscis in the Flower of Life. And they all have Golden Mean proportions. If you look carefully at the super-imposed Tree of Life, you'll see that every line corresponds exactly to either the length or width of a vesica piscis. This is the first relationship that became visible as we came out of the Great Void." Drunvalo Mechizedek 1.

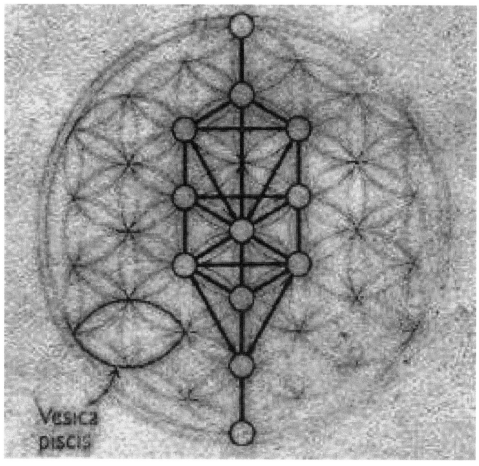

Caldbeck and the Vesica Piscis

Relationship is the perfect term for the Vesica Piscis which has been documented in the landscape across Europe from standing stones to Cistercian-Templar locations. I found this relationship played out to dizzying array, spanning out from Saint Kentigern's church in Caldbeck Cumbria, the Keystone of the Matrix Map.

Caldbeck the Holy Centre

An early medieval mystery has been noticed within the last thirty years. Radiating out from a significant central hub are standing stones, churches, wells, cairns, burial mounds, straight tracks and castles, forming a circle where each spoke on the geographical wheel is approximately six miles long or usually and rather more

Vesica Piscis - the Alchemical
Marriage in Caldbeck Cumbria

precisely 5.96 miles.

After pondering the Heronian Tetrahedron I wondered if Saint Kentigern's might be one such location? In all my years of research I have never come across such a proliferation of sites laid out in the pattern of a compass in the landscape, radiating out from Saint Kentigern's Church in Caldbeck. My initial mild interest was eclipsed by exhilaration by the literal net of connected sites laid over this rural part of Cumbria.

Usually the spokes of the wheel are modest, comprising of only three to six locations while being remarked upon as significant. I'm still dazzled when I look at the map around the area of St. Kentigerns. I am certainly willing to accept that I may have been a bit over enthusiastic, however with that said and an error margin of maybe five locations, I am still left with an abundance and to be honest, many more that I did not even include as it would have been very challenging to create a readable diagram for a book over flowing with all but the most significant sites.

I consider these spokes in the wheel to be a memory infused into the land and associated with the Celtic Cross technology and a further method of mapping ley-lines within a circle formation.

Saint Kentigerns' Caldbeck (AKA St. Mungo)
25 Churches, Holy Wells & Monuments
Within a 5.96 Mile Radius
Inner circle = 4.96 Miles

There were significant numbers of locations that led me to consider an additional inner circle of 4.96 miles from the Caldbeck Centre. This is a unique feature and not one I've come across in other compass maps of this nature. Indeed this inner ring feature might easily be continued at one mile increments towards the centre, such are the numerous monuments surrounding Caldbeck.

As one can see, not all locations are exact but it is understood that it is not always possible to build on the exact spot due to bogs, hillsides, water, rocky conditions or property lines and human error can enter into the equation as well, as triangulating a location over six miles is difficult even with clear line of sight. Given these caveats the following illustration is quite amazing.

I chose to start my diagram and those following, from the bottom, moving from left to right as one might read a book and flowing in a counter clockwise direction.

Explorer Map, Ordnance Survey, OL 5 1:25 000 scale - was used for the Caldbeck investigation, shown on the opposite page. The circle (and following circle) for the diagram is six inches in diameter and meant as a representation only though all effort has been made as to accuracy. All locations may be seen using the online software program 'Get A Map by Ordnance Survey' and also' Google Earth'.

Vesica Piscis - the Alchemical Marriage in Caldbeck Cumbria

The stream from the top of the steps down to St. Kentigern's Well
© Gretchen Cornwall 2009

Opposite - Saint Kentigern's Church, Caldbeck,
looking up from the well & stream
© Gretchen Cornwall 2009

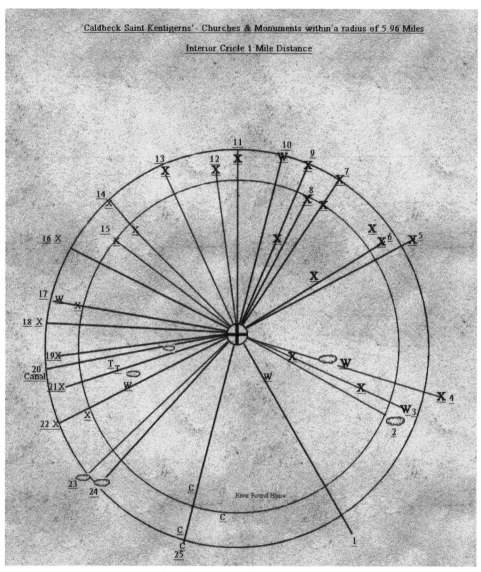

Map by © Gretchen Cornwall

Key to the Compass Map
X = Church or Monument
W= Holy Well
⬭ = Earth works – Stone Circle – Moat – Settlements
C = Cairn
T = Tumulus

223

Vesica Piscis - the Alchemical
Marriage in Caldbeck Cumbria

1. White Well - St. Mungo's
2. Earthworks Enclosure
3. Hesket Newmarket (Sundial House) – St Kentigerns' - Thanet Well
4. Castle Howe – Holy Well – Chapel Lamonby
5. Christ Church
6. St Mary's – Castle Gate & High Head Castle –
7. All Saints – St Judes (ruined)
8. Rose Castle (Bishops of Carlisle Residence)
9. St James - Hawks Dale Hall
10. Fountain Head
11. St James
12. Holy Trinity
13. Jenkin Cross
14. St Hilda's to Roman Fort
15. Isel Kirk Hall
16. Bolton All Saints
17. Carlisle Gate – Well Head
18. All Saints
19. St James Ireby
20. Church Strand Canal
21. St James
22. Elfa Well – St James – Ruthwaite Tower
23. Moat – Dry Medieval Earthworks
24. Castle Howe

The Ancient Cross Circle of Holme Coltrume Abbey

I was to find much more than I expected yet again through a secondary circle after much experimentation with other possible surrounding sites. Though there are many other possible secondary circles the one portrayed below was the most abundant with ancient and medieval sacred places easily connecting with the Caldbeck circle to form a Vesica Piscis.

The centre of the Ancient Cross Circle lays near a very old market cross (converted to a war memorial) in Blennerhasset. The area is steeped in the legends of Viking invaders who later converted to Christianity and erected Celtic knot stone crosses in many villages.

The Secret Dossier of a
Knight Templar of the Sangreal

Directly north of the ancient market cross the line moves through Saint Mungo's which is Saint Kentigerns alternative name in the area, straight up to the Cistercian Abbey of Saint Mary's which as you will see has played a secret part in the survival of the Templar Knight Order. Due south lays the Elva Stone Circle.

The true centre of this circle appears to be void of a monument; this does not mean that it has always been so as a standing stone could have been moved by a farmer at one point. I've also seen other circles of this nature devoid of anything in the centre yet still have astounding landmarks forming a circle within the 5.96 mile radius rule.

As you can see in the diagram Stone How and the Carling Stone are in a direct line with each other within the circle. As in the Caldbeck circle there is an inner ring at 4.96 miles distance from the centre another truly remarkable feature and overlaying exactly with the Caldbeck points for an unprecedented creation centre of the Vesica Piscis. What this inner circle may mean I cannot say at this point but with so many locations as evidence it should not be ignored as a possibility.

Key to the Ancient Cross Circle
X = Church or Monument
W= Holy Well
⬭ = Stone Circle

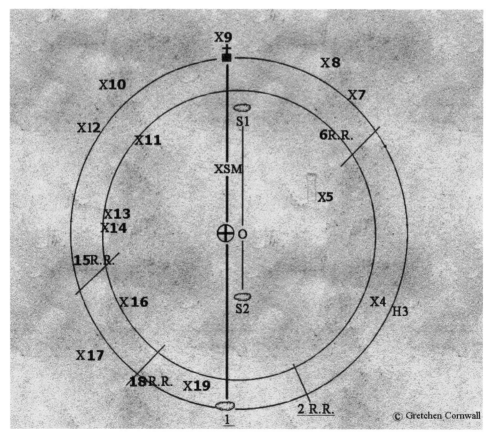

© Gretchen Cornwall

Vesica Piscis - the Alchemical Marriage in Caldbeck Cumbria

Map opposite by © Gretchen Cornwall
Explorer Map, Ordnance Survey, OL 4 1:25 000 scale -
was used for this investigation.

1. Elva Plain – Stone Circle
2. Roman Road (Ley-Line-Intersection at Bassenthwaite CA12 4RG)
3. Armathwaite Head – Hill
4. Chapel Farm & Resevoir (Denoting extinct church)
5. Roslin Castle
6. Roman Road (Ley-Line-Intersection at Red Dial CA7 UK)
7. Saint Marys – Wigton
8. Lesson Hall (Corruption of Lascelles, ruined, 1st recorded in 1578)
9. Saint Marys & Remains of Cistercian Abbey – Abbey Town
10. Holme Saint Cuthbert (need postal code or near place name)
11. Chapel Moss & Hill – Possible location of ruined church of
    St. Roche 1327 *
12. Saint James – Edderside
13. Hayton Castle – Hayton
14. Saint James – Hayton
15. Roman Road – Allerby
16. Saint Mary's Sundial – Gilcrux
17. Saint Bridgets – Bridekirk
18. Roman Road - (Ley-Line-Intersection Redmain CA13 UK)
19. Isel Hall (Peel Tower – Lawson Arms)

Inner Circle Locations of Note

XSM – Saint Mungos' of Bloomfield & Moat

⊕ Ancient Cross of Blennerhasset, Cumbria

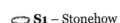 **S1** – Stonehow

S2 – Carling Stone

X5 - Castle Roslin (similarity of name to Rosslyn Chapel in Scotland is interesting. Also Rose Castle is just north east of Caldbeck)

The Secret Dossier of a
Knight Templar of the Sangreal

The Caldbeck Vesica Piscis

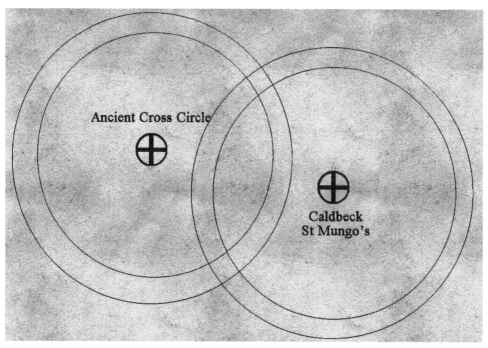

Ancient Cross Circle

Caldbeck
St Mungo's

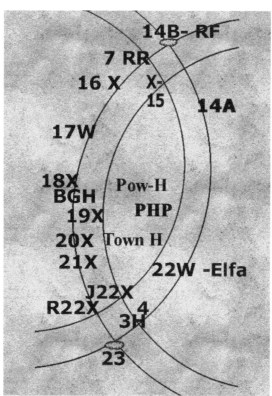

Vesica Piscis - the Alchemical Marriage in Caldbeck Cumbria

Maps opposite by © Gretchen Cornwall

Larger View of the Centre of the V.P.

X = Church or Monument

W = Holy Well

⬭ = Moat or Roman Fort

H = Place name use of the word 'head'

Starting from the bottom – counter clockwise (left to right)

23 = Moat – Dry Medieval Earthworks
3 H = Armathwaite Head – Hill
4 = Chapel Farm & Resevoir (Denoting extinct church)
J22X = Saint James, Uldale
22W – Elfa Well
14 A = St Hilda's to Roman Fort
14B = Roman Fort to St Hilda's
15 X = Isel Kirk Hall
7 RR = Roman Road (Ley-Line-Intersection at Red Dial CA7 UK)
16 X = Bolton All Saints
17 W = Carlisle Gate to Well Head
18 X = All Saints
BGH = Bolton Gate Head
19 X = St James Ireby
20 X = Church Strand Canal
R22 X = Ruthwaite Tower

Inner Vesica Piscis

Pow Heads
PHP = Pow Head Plantation
Town Head

Pow is an old family name whose origins are of Brittany in France having come over with William the Conqueror in 1066 AD. In medieval French slang it means peacock, eventually finding its way into Elizabethan slang with various spellings. Another possibility is that it means pool. The Cumbrian dialect would often drop the final sound of the 'L' in the word 'pool' leaving one with 'po' or 'pow' with variations in spellings over time.

The definition of 'head' has become a geographical term for a hill ending in a cliff or steep drop or the beginnings of a river. I find it interesting and rather synchronistic that the word 'head' is used across the area as if there were no imagination or other options; especially within the Caldbeck circle where I counted well over forty place names containing the word head. There were far too many locations to create a readable drawing in this work.

I have scoured other locations of note pertaining to the Templars, other random locations and only found a few if any place names containing the word. Only a few places containing the word 'head' may be considered properly connected to the landscape due to their physical features.

Saint John the Baptist was the patron saint of the Knights Templar and famously met his end by decapitation. As I was to find out during the meeting with Comte de Medici, they proliferated in the area after escaping from France. Is it possible that their patron saint is remembered in the landscape through a seemingly innocuous place name?

Much has been made of the Vesica Piscis and its sacred and geometric meaning. I decided to research what esoteric Freemasonry had to say about this shape and came across a very good article by Brother William Steve Burkle.

Burkle discovered varying explanations regarding the sacred circle which is the basis of the V.P. However the most profound explanation was that of the circle with two straight lines on either side with a dot in the centre. The straight lines astronomically depict the two saint John's separated by six months – the dot being the sun and the circle representing earth's orbit between the summer and winter solstice. 2.

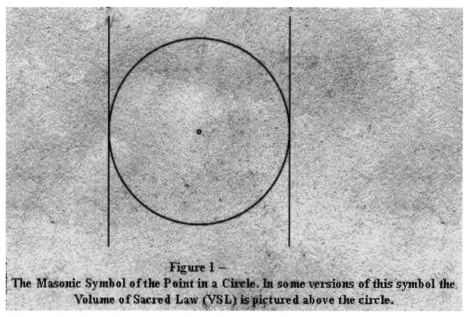

Figure 1 –
The Masonic Symbol of the Point in a Circle. In some versions of this symbol the Volume of Sacred Law (VSL) is pictured above the circle.

He also found a reference to an Egyptian connection:

"Early Egyptian monuments are carved with the Alpha and the Omega or symbol of God in the center of a circle embordered by two upright parallel perpendicular serpents, representing the power and wisdom of the Creator. The symbol apparently came into Masonry from an operative practice, known to but a few Master workmen on Cathedrals and great buildings."

Vesica Piscis - the Alchemical
Marriage in Caldbeck Cumbria

Brother Burkle's article contains many geometric experiments with the symbolic circle, dot and its two straight lines.

The symbol is a guarded ancient glyph encapsulating the knowledge for the building of monuments, city planning and astronomy; it seems as if it is also one to be internalized as a metaphor of self-knowledge.

1. Melchizedek, Drunvalo. The Ancient Secret of the Flower of Life: An Edited Transcript of the Flower of Life Workshop Presented Live to Mother Earth from 1985 to 1994. Vol. 1. Flagstaff, AZ: Light Technology Pub., 1998. p. 41
2. Burkle, William Steve, Bro. "The Point Within A Circle." PS Review of Freemasonry. http://www.freemasonsfreemasonry.com/point_within_circle.html.

Twenty Seven

The Mystery of the H.T. & the
British Ordnance Survey National Grid

The British Ordnance Survey National Grid was born out the Jacobite rebellion when Highland hopes sought to place Bonnie Prince Charlie on the throne. Charles Edward Stuart's ambitions were dashed with the loss of 1500 lives during the battle of Culloden in 1745. Forced to quit his claim he fled to Italy living out his life in exile.

English forces on the run up to the final battle were constantly one step behind the Highland Scots as they simply did not have knowledge of the difficult terrain. Often maps would be devoid of important points such as a river, correct location of a mountain and rest locations such as a local inn or farm. The population understandably confounded matters by using local place names or slang, instead of given names recognized on many existing but inaccurate maps.

The history of the 'Office of Ordnance' finds its roots in the latter 14th century when gunpowder and advancements in weaponry demanded professional guidance and was given space in the Tower of London.

It became an independent military body which saw many changes between 1414 and 1855 (officially beginning in 1544), whose primary interest was originally artillery and supplying the navy, but grew and became more complex over hundreds of years. Eventually it became known as the Board of Ordnance and also included a scientific corps encompassing artillery and engineering. It was only natural that cartography would become a necessary art and science to support artillery and engineering needs.

The Edinburgh-born, Lieutenant Colonel David Watson, recognized the need for better intelligence to stave off further rebellion in the north of Scotland and the ever present and real concern of invasion from the continent.

King George II gave Watson the charge of creating a military survey of the Highlands which would later be rolled out over the decades to the Isle of Man, Ireland and England. It was a large scale endeavour and considered time well spent during the Napoleonic Wars.

Though born out of conflict, today it is freely available for the public to help plan walks across the pristine beauty of the British Isles and to mark historical places of interest such as ancient churches, wells and stone circles which are often not on a regular road map. The Ordnance Survey Grid or OS is now a self-funding civilian organisation worth millions of pounds per year and has easily shifted into the computer age. 1.

As time progressed so too did the accuracy of the Ordnance Survey maps. Between 1783 and 1853 the Principal Triangulation of Great Britain took place using the Ramsden Theodolite, the most sophisticated method of line of sight measuring at that time.

The Theodolite was used to 'triangulate' in order to find an accurate distance between three locations the third location helping to diminish errors. Measuring

The Mystery of the H.T. & the
British Ordnance Survey National Grid

distances via triangles is an ancient practice. In the Europe of 1533 the process was introduced to the science of map making. Gemma Frisius published his article on using triangulation which was widely disseminated and eventually came to Britain by the end of the century. Its techniques were used to develop the first OS maps.

The symbol below is called a 'benchmark' and is sometimes confused with medieval priest's sundials, but was created to mark a building which was used in triangulation mapping. Many churches carry this mark due to the fact that they are often on high ground. It is an interesting symbol to ponder in light of philosophy.

The Re-triangulation of Great Britain commenced in 1935, yet again updating OS maps to an even greater level and replacing prior efforts. Concrete pillars were built across Britain on hill tops in order to create a permanent station for measurements. One may still see at least opposite pillars in the distance on a clear day.

The OS Grid is different from finding a location via latitude and longitude. The math to convert one to the other are very complex and the two systems are considered separate requiring software to make the conversion between the two.
The USA has its own grid of a similar nature again born out of a military purpose, such as being able to traverse the immediate area with accuracy.

The OS Grid is a flat representation of Britain. There are 100 squares each measuring 100 kilometres and each square is identified with two letters. The lettered square is then divided into 10 kilometre squares numbering from 0 to 9 and is always read from the left (Eastings) to right (heading in an Easterly direction) and then upwards to the North or (Northings).

Due to copyright laws I am unable to reproduce the diagrams here. Please visit the O.S. site for more information http://www.ordnancesurvey.co.uk/

The Heronian Tetrahedron's three points in Britain are overlaid with the OS Grid exactly.

The OS Grid is specific to Britain and therefore does not cover Bornholm or any other country where the energetic lines travel. The difficulty inherent in rolling this system out to other parts of Europe is that the further one moves out from Britain as the central point the more one must compensate for exponential errors and of course there are political borders and agreements to cross.

The fact that the OS map overlays the Matrix Map is quite challenging to comprehend. It is impressive that the contemporary intuitive Templar, well versed in 21st century math and cartography, noticed correlations between Templar sites, ley-lines and quantum mechanics.

The Secret Dossier of a
Knight Templar of the Sangreal

As I'd already noted earlier, John Temple had said that the Order found it necessary to give the map system to a member of the public as they were surprised no one had discovered it yet.

He went on to say that the duty of each Grand Master was to visit the important Templar locations on the map at least once. He did not qualify this with any timeframe such as the Templar historic period or during the OS Grid's public creation and outing. Since the order is alive and well today he may very well have meant this in a modern context.

The three locations in Britain on the Matrix Map which align with the Ordnance Survey Map

Dover TR 325 400

Caldbeck NY 325 400

Shetlands HU 325 800

One can't escape the notice of the first three digits used for the Eastings in all three locations – 325 – our magic number. The second set of numbers refers to the Northings.

John Temple explained that either a Templar official or guest may be given coordinates to a location such as Caldbeck NY325 400 and that when their identity was confirmed the individual would be taken to a secret location within a three to six mile radius of the coordinates.

Does this distance have anything to do with our Vesica Piscis radius of up to six miles? Each '325' designation was considered a holy place in itself but that there may be a hidden temple within the three/six mile radius as well and or a meeting house. More investigation on this front seems warranted.

I will cover the historic significance of Caldbeck (NY 325 400) and Dover (TR 325 400) in later chapters with a brief nod to HU 325 800.

HU 325 800 Near Swinister Mainland Shetland Islands

Researching HU 325 800 in the Shetlands has been more problematic regarding Templar Knight occupation. The location near Swinister on the mainland island appears to be quite rural with disused mines and an ancient burial mound. Indeed it could be that the mining activity was the main interest of this location?

The Shetlands along with the Orkney Islands were colonized by Norway in the 8th century. The Orkney Islands in particular were the province of Earl Sinclair of Rosslyn.

If there is a secret temple in HU 325 800 I have yet to find it, indeed its significance may be long past as the sea-faring and mystic traditions of the Vikings melded with the later Templar Historic period.

I decided to investigate other '325' locations not associated with the energy lines on the Matrix Map - and was rewarded with an astonishing discovery. I had uncovered five sites with historic and modern Templar links.

Temple Scotland NT 325 600

Royston Cave TL 325 400

Templar Newsum or Temple Newsam SE 400 325

Irvine, North Ayrshire NS 325 400

Westgate-On-Sea TR 325 700

Edward I Monument NY 325 610

(I have chosen to include the Edward I Monument as it was mentioned several times during the meeting – though it is technically outside the parameters)

Temple Scotland NT 325 600

The location of NT 325 600 is currently the site of an 18th century palatial mansion called Arniston House, which is just up river from Temple Scotland and within an easy ramble.

The political dynasty of the Dundas family, which includes many notable freemasons, has owned the land since Henry VIII's time when it was purchased from under the Hospitallers.

Balantrodoch (now Temple) had been the seat of power in the north prior to the order's dissolution and whose property comprised a large farm which today would have encompassed Arniston House.

Rosslyn Chapel, Balantrodoch's famous cousin, is just 6.5 miles north along the B7003. I found this very intriguing and certainly seems to fit within the parameters of the mapping system I was given.

Rosslyn Chapel lays directly on the Heronian Tetrahedron line from Caldbeck up to the Shetlands using *Ordnance Survey Great Britain OS Travel Map Route 2008 1:625 000* that I was given.

Henry Herbert Phillip Dundas of Arniston, Third Baronet (1866 – 1930) has a memorial marker within the ruined church of Temple along with his wife who survived him by another ten years. Carved into the grave slab are their names opposite one another and between is the tall stemmed compass rose.

Interestingly enough, it was the ancestor of the Third Baronet, Robert Dundas 1685–1753, that became the surrogate father and mentor of David Watkins. The Dundas family has Freemasonic connections, a direct link to the poetically ruined church of Temple Scotland and also the birth of the first Ordnance Survey mapping system.

The Secret Dossier of a
Knight Templar of the Sangreal

Royston Cave TL 325 400

The Royston Cave was discovered in 1745 beneath an ancient crossroad. Carved from soft chalk, the bell-shaped vault is covered with an array of medieval religious artwork that had once been painted.

Saint Catherine with her wheel, the holy family, hearts and a mystery as to its usage continue to intrigue us. Author Sylvia P Beamon believes there is enough evidence to suggest it had been a secret place of Templar worship. Nearby is the Church of Saint John the Baptist which is the only surviving remnant of the Augustinian Priory of the 12th century.

Templar Newsum AKA Temple Newsam, SE 400 325

Due West of West-Garforth Leeds was a large preceptory engaged in farming. Notice I have switched the number sequence around but it is interesting that such a major Templar site is encompassed by these coordinates.

Irvine, North Ayrshire, Scotland NS 325 400

The presence of the Knights Templar are remembered in local listed buildings and place names. Irvine was a major capitol and port during Robert the Bruce's time also within five miles of Kilwinning, considered to be the home of the Mother Lodge of Scotland's Freemasons and also where the ruins of a Benedictine Abbey still stand.

Westgate-On-Sea, Kent TR 325 700

The town of Westgate was once farming land under the auspices of Dent de Lion Castle of which only the tower gate remains. The Isle of Thanet has a very old subterranean initiation culture which is evident in the nearby Margate Shell Grotto, the secret temple correlating with the Westgate-On-Sea code reference. The exact O.S. point however, should you choose to visit it, correlates with this office building.

I was curious to understand to a greater degree why Caldbeck had been chosen as the Keystone. Sitting down with the map it became clear. The three locations of Dover, Caldbeck and Swinister simply make the most sense in order to achieve a triangle with Caldbeck at the apex. The direct line from Caldbeck to Bornholm is a dead giveaway in regards to Templar lore.

Dover was chosen over Westgate-On-Sea as Dover leads us through Geneva to

Malta, likewise two significant Templar locations. The other five Templar locations listed above would not provide us with the needed triangulation points that form the basis for the Keystone of the Matrix Map and the math behind its all-important Heronian Tetrahedron.

Upon further thought, I decided to see what the 325 locations would look like joined up on Google Earth. The 325 energy centres form a large serpentine pattern over the entire length of Britain the backbone of the isle. The labyrinth of Chartres Cathedral has been miniaturized by some Tantric practitioners for the desk top or as an actual item of meditation which they use to 'walk the labyrinth' with their finger or a stylus. I think that just such a meditation can be achieved with the above locations, joined with one's own lower energy centre and walking up the spine of the Isle as well as one's own body. A marriage of the individual to the land takes place outside of time and space.

Synchronicity

Intriguingly these adepts have either, unconsciously or with some guided intuitive purpose, over hundreds of years, tapped into a universal sacred geometry stream and encoded it within the OS Grid.

As discussed earlier, human beings who have this awareness tend to intuitively gravitate to the fractal micro-macrocosm embedded within our personal Unified Fields and relate it easily to the Morphic Fields of Gaia.

Had there been some prior mapping code where the number 32 + 5 were enshrined within this society in a practical manner that might have allowed those with the knowledge to find their way across land and sea, eventually being laid down within the OS Grid by David Watson and those geniuses that followed him? It is an interesting question.

If there had been a practical application for 325 prior to Watson, perhaps it was remembered in Freemasonry's 32nd and 33rd degrees? Author David Ovason of Shakespeare's Secret Booke believes he has found a code enshrined in the Notre Dame Cathedral of Paris stained glass window of the Madonna and child. Her halo is comprised of 33 round and lozenge shaped glass. The use of the number 33 was encoded in a variety of forms within the written word from at least Dante's Divine Comedy through the most notable of alchemists, poets and scientists. Ovason has traced the number 33 through Nostradamus, John Dee, Robert Fludd, Frances Bacon and others. 2.

It cannot be considered coincidence that the locations of some of the most important Templar sites in Britain fall directly on the Matrix Map points, nor can it be simply dumb luck that the medieval Templars built their preceptories on or near OS Grid reference points of '325' – a better term for this so-called coincidence is 'synchronicity' developed by Carl Jung who continued to expound upon the concept over his lifetime. As a result of his own work and time spent with physicists he came up with this interesting diagram regarding the relationship between energetic forces.

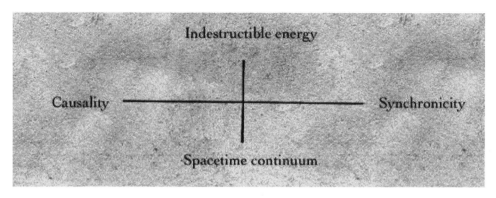

"Synchronicity is an ever present reality for those who have eyes to see." Carl Jung (1875 - 1961) 3.

This is a complex subject for whom Jung excelled at analysing from all angles but here I've chosen to express in as succinct way possible and callously disregarding his fine ability with nuance.

Jung had spent a great deal of time with physicists of both the Classical and also the growing world of Quantum Mechanics. He considered that humanity as Archetypes may interact with the Unus Mundas or One World via Synchronicity as an expression of a waking dream from which we had much to learn.

I am writing this in the New Year of 2014 and have had a follow up meeting with the Templars. I'll leave you with a quote given to me by Comte de Medici in regards to having raised the issue of synchronicity:

"Once the world has rid itself from coincidence, and embraced the concept of intuitive Synchronicity, all obscurity will be illuminated."

1. Hewitt, Rachel. Map of a Nation: A Biography of the Ordnance Survey. London: Granta, 2010.

2. Ovason, David. Shakespeare's Secret Booke: Deciphering Magical and Rosicrucian Codes. Forest Row, East Sussex: Clairview, 2010.

3. Crowley, Vivianne. Thorson's Principles of Jungian Spirituality. London: Thorsons, 1998.

Twenty Eight

Escape to the North

The 14th century fleet slipped away from La Rochelle, the nerves of those on board the vessels taught as the rigging, silence being all important.

Ships laden with legendary silver and gold, treasures, documents and brethren – all battle hardened and grim men. They knew that their lives and that of the Order had changed completely. Almost 200 years of Gnostic chivalry driven underground on 13 October 1307.

According to an eyewitness account, 18 Templar ships disappeared in the dead of night, leaving the Paris Temple empty except for their leader and a skeleton crew of loyal followers. Hoping to clear their name by legal means and through the loyalty of the king of the church, the only political figure they were bound to obey, Clement V - their only hope. Mysterious, poignant and sought after over the last 700 years, from which ports did the Templar ships make their escape?

Sitting across the table from a modern day Knight, I was given a hidden history of the small rural village of Caldbeck and the county of Cumbria by a man who could trace his family back hundreds of years.

His manner was quick and decisive in order to divulge all he could in the time the meeting allowed. I was hard pressed to keep up with pen and ink as he had barred any recording.

My contact relayed that three ships had split off from those leaving La Rochelle and headed north to the Cistercian Abbey of Holme Cultram on the Northwest Coast of Cumbria. It was a fascinating claim and very precise.

There were some 500 men on board the ships. He stated quite clearly that they had dismantled the vessels and slept in shifts amongst their Cistercian hosts to hide their numbers.

Most were encouraged to join the local community by marriage, business or farming. Their beards were shaved and their skills were merged with local guilds.

John Temple said that by 1320 integration was complete. Other ships took important relics to Nova Scotia where they would be out of reach of plunder and their sanctity retained.

The border of Cumbria was fluid in the 14th century and during this period the abbey was within the English side. Intriguingly Comte de Medici said that Edward I & II knew there were Templars gathered near Holme Cultram's surrounds and that they wanted their help or resources in battle against Robert the Bruce.

Holme Cultram was founded in 1150 by Prince Henry of Scotland with monks from Melrose Abbey which had been seeded by French Cistercians.

It is built from the famous Cumbrian red sandstone found across the area. It became one of the British Isles' richest abbeys through the wool trade and was apparently larger than Carlisle Cathedral.

Carlisle Cathedral has been the seat of religious power in the north for hundreds of years and has 8 bays which match Le Madeleine, Vezelay in France as mentioned.

The Secret Dossier of a
Knight Templar of the Sangreal

Holme Cultram originally had a much larger footprint with nine bays but is now reduced to six. It would be interesting to visit the Cistercian abbey on the summer solstice through to St. John's day and perhaps witness the same event down the central nave watching the light shining from the upper windows or clerestory.

Though Holme Cultram had a wealthy royal benefactor it was not necessary to be rich as far as the Cistercians were concerned. In fact one of the reasons why the order was so popular was that they made it affordable for patrons with less money and rank to start their own monastery.

It was a far less expensive franchise to buy into than the other religious houses and more democratic, thus paving a new way forward and reducing the exclusivity of extreme upper echelons. 1.

Robert the Bruce sacked Holme Cultram leaving it financially crippled on 17 June 1322 even though his father the Earl of Carrick was laid to rest within its sanctum in 1304. 2.

The abbey never regained its footing, such was the damage, and was plagued by a further two centuries of border reivers. At times it was used as a fortress for the local population as shelter.

I have often wondered if the Bruce had been looking for Templar treasure. Had he dreamt of obtaining the Ark and other legendary relics? He had Templars amongst his own military operating as the original Order in Scotland.

Were some of them privy to the inventory and personnel aboard the vessels from La Rochelle? Had they been to Holme Cultram before going north? It leads to a rather challenging question.

If the Bruce was looking for (legendary or ordinary) riches was this an indication that the Templars who found themselves on either side of a national border, having committed themselves to family life and the need to protect their homes, perhaps facing the untenable position of conflict with brothers across any given border and in this case with Scotland? It seems a likely scenario and perhaps not out of choice either.

Edward I was cruelly determined to have Scotland, fulfilling his Arthurian dream of a united crown. Neither the King of Scotland nor of England were about to surrender their political positions regarding their neighbour across the fence. Such a rigid stance drags all peoples of both nations into conflict.

The Cistercian delegates on either side visited with one another until war broke out and also during the truce between wars when the delegates continued to meet their contemporaries.

So it seems that politics was the wedge driving hostilities between the Templar-Cistercians and their northern brethren which were then laid aside during truce periods.

Another point to muse over – Templars dispersed to many European countries for political protection but also to prevent another major catastrophe – with brothers on either side of the border - hopefully some if not all would succeed as an organisation even if the politics of war reared their ugly head.

An interesting record from Edward II's Close Rolls reveals the sad state of the besieged Abbey of Holme Cultram. He petitions other houses to take in their brethren until such a time that it is safe enough for them to return.

The date is just one year off from John Temple's narrative that the integration of

Templars was complete by 1320. It is not certain if the abbey had been abandoned entirely but obviously only a few brave monks could have sustained themselves.

"1319, Aug. 18. King Edward II requests the abbey of Tintern to admit to the Collegium William de Bromfeld, a monk of Holcoltram, whom the king is sending them that they may minister to his necessities as one of their own brothers until he shall cause ordinance to be made concerning his estate, or until the house of Holcoltram, which is of the same Order as they are, be released from its oppressions, as the king wishes for assistance for the monks of that house or other houses of the same order, because the possessions and goods of the abbey have been so wasted by the invasions of the Scotch rebels that they are now insufficient for the maintenance of the abbot and convent." 3.

By 1324 the situation seems to have improved for the monks as a demand of wine and grain is made by Edward II which means that the area had to have been stable enough to farm and trade:

"1324 May 10. To the bailiff of Holmcoltram. Order to cause all the ships of that port, capable of carrying 40 tuns and upwards of wine and grain, to be prepared and found without delay, so that they shall be ready to set out on the king's service at three days' summons, and not to permit such ships to go to parts beyond the seas." 4.

Protection from one's king often came with a price, such as demands for hospitality, food and wine which also caused a financial burden to religious houses unlucky enough to be founded too near a disputed border or on the way to battle.

Nor was Holme Cultram the only victim of the Bruce's incursions against England's religious houses. In 1316 he ventured down the coast and attacked the abbey of Calder completely laying it to waste amongst other smaller houses.

His next port of call was the peninsula of Barrow-in-Furness. He carried off plunder and captives for ransom from the powerful Abbey of Furness. Though it had its own wooden defences and harbour on the island of Piel across from the abbey on the mainland, it proved no use against the Bruce's men.

He raided them again in 1322 but the abbot went out to meet him with a charm offensive that probably cost his house a great financial sum and invited him to dinner thus saving the abbey from a further physical hit. 5.

As safety issues continued Edward III finally gave Furness abbey permission to build a crenulated mote and bailey castle for defense on Piel Island in 1327. 6.

I found it interesting to explore Furness abbey in regards to John Temple's assertion that at least three ships had landed 70 miles north at Holme Cultram. I wondered why some had not made landfall with Furness as it was the more important of the two abbeys, though both were powerful with harbours, trading with the Isle of Man and Ireland. Is it possible that Furness had taken in refugees and treasures as well? Could this have been part of the motivation of Robert Bruce or was it strictly financial and to keep them from being useful as a strategic source for the English?

Is it possible that Furness was too powerful and thus visible to have had extra priests and lay-brothers suddenly appear? Both harbours would have been able to absorb Templars disguised as Cistercian priests.

My contact made no mention of any other landing site for Northwest England except to confirm that ships had gone to Nova Scotia, but it is nonetheless interesting to explore.

The abbey of Holme Cultram was in a very strategic position which Edward I exploited on his three main campaigns of 1300, 1303 and 1306 - having used the harbour at Skinburness for the new fleet from the five powerful Cinque Ports of south east England. 7.

The abbey had trading vessels in the harbour of Skinburness on the coast of the Solway Firth and during the wars with Scotland their ships had to be escorted to Ireland and the Isle of Man by the ships of the English King.

The date is not known but the harbour and town were destroyed by a massive storm. Between the years of 1301 August through 1304 April the landscape was completely altered, making it unusable. Many must have perished, buried alive as the land was washed out to sea. It was so devastating that Edward I gave permission to move all and sundry to Newton Arlosh meaning, New Town on the Marsh.

He gave the Abbey permission to build a new parish church dedicated to Saint John the Baptist. Though they had permission it seems that the new church was not built as we see it today until the reign of Edward III.

There may have been an initial structure with the fortified Peel tower added in the 1360s. This may be an indication of the conflict and lack of funds that the abbey was experiencing during the wars. The permissions to run a market, fair and upgrades to the harbour of Skinburness granted to the community by the king were then transferred over to Newton Arlosh under the Abbey's auspices.

I've not been able to determine the exact location of a new harbour but that it was in proximity to Newton Arlosh is assured. Certainly there was one as Edward I brought ships up from Dover with men, horses and heavy goods.

It was simply common knowledge that the monks had built a new harbour. They had to have landed somewhere with ease of use and the ability to shift supplies to Holme Cultram which Edward I used as storage for a time with soldiers garrisoned at Carlisle.

I was told that the Templars would have used the same harbour and then dismantled the ships. Upon the death of Edward I in July 1307 the campaign halted and the bulk of his fleet would have dispersed leaving it possible for the Templars in October to have landed without too much difficulty of being seen.

Another indication as to the importance of Holme Cultram were the demands on its abbots as ambassadors not only to report back to the mother house in France but also to the English King. Records remain of passage being granted to the Abbot of Holm Cultram via Dover Cinque Port to the mother house of Citeaux Abbey, France.

The Abbots had also been asked to sit at Parliament on the order of Edward I as he valued their observations and knowledge of law. Edward I was famous for his regard of intellect, law and had created Parliament, a step towards democracy, if unintended as such. Many historians credit him with the beginnings of English democracy and the advancement of law. 8.

Holm Cultram was chosen as the meeting place where the Scottish king's major supporter, the brave Bishop of Glasgow, Robert Wishart, swore allegiance to Edward I for the fourth time in October of 1300, witnessed before English lords,

French and the ambassadors of religious houses. He must have been a cool customer to have stared the feared Edward I in the face with Scottish Independence held in the forefront of his heart. 9.

The wrongs of history die slowly in the heart of humanity. During my visit to Cumbria I asked a few people about the Peel towers. To my surprise they were still angry at the aggressive border reivers and their business of kidnapping for profit - before, during and after the victory of Robert the Bruce, as if it were yesterday.

Fortified churches with defensive Peel towers were built across the region during the reign of Edward III in response to the continued problem. During the discussion, praise for Edward I quickly followed. It was a highly interesting moment and was a psychological mirror for events played out the world over whenever an injustice is perpetrated. The high cost of an eye for an eye policy when neither side is willing to see themselves as anything but the victim and not an aggressor.

Physical evidence of the English King's long standing admirers can be seen today. The Edward I Monument was erected in 1685 at Burgh by Sands Cumbria NY 325 610. It is popularly held that it is the exact location where he died at the age of 68 on 7 July 1307, on his way to invade Scotland but fell ill of dysentery. He may have been staying at Holme Cultram and died enroute whilst going north on campaign. His epitaph at Westminster Abbey reads, 'Here is Edward I, Hammer of the Scots, 1308. Keep Faith.'

The Scottish Wizard

Holme Cultram hosted heads of state, prelates, scholars and of course Templars. She is also known for the final resting place of Michael Scot the Wizard (1175 – 1232), who may have been to the abbey more than once and spent his final years living as a monk.

He may have been born in Cumbria which of course at varying times was part of Scotland, hence the name Michael Scotus. He was a polymath of great scope with a deep understanding of mathematics and medicine. "Michael Mathematicus" may have been the tutor of Leonardo Fibonacci. He practiced alchemy and was Frederick II's court astrologer and possible lover. Frederick II was akin to Charles II in his fascination with science, arts and intellectual pursuits.

Michael Scot studied in Oxford, Paris, had no compunctions consulting Rabbis for knowledge, 'as a means of penetrating through the older world of material research.' 10.

The occult arts were part of science well into the early 18th century and were part of university life. According to a mysterious chapter written by 'a friend' in the book, Some Records of a Cistercian Abbey, Michael Scot was trained across the full spectrum possible in arcane lore.

'At the ancient universities of Salamanca and Toledo, he would be initiated into the mysteries of the black arts, astrology and alchemy, chiromancy and physiognomy.' 11.

The Secret Dossier of a
Knight Templar of the Sangreal

He was also feared by some even though he was courted by two Popes and invited to become the Archbishop of Cashel, Ireland and Canterbury, England.

> "A wizard of such dreaded fame,
> That when in Salamanca's cave
> Him listed his magic wand to wave
> The bells would ring in Notre Dame." 12.

Dante gives him short shrift in his Divine Comedy for daring to make predictions on the future, even though he appeared to be accurate according to historical accounts.

It is my assertion that if the 'wizard' had become an Archbishop, Dante's prejudices would have lifted. However he was exonerated by the positive attentions of Edward I as an intellectual and had been knighted by Alexander III which is quite a dualist feat!

He was well travelled across Europe and translated from Arabic into Latin Aristotle's works and authored books that were widely circulated for centuries.

Holme Cultram, Melrose Abbey and Glenluce in Scotland, all Cistercian Abbeys, claim the privilege of final resting place for the scholar and diplomat which suggest he may have visited them all. Was he a lay-brother Cistercian? Entwined with legends of Cistercian burials are that he was interred with his books of arcane wisdom, which according to legend no man may read due to their dangerous content. His tomb has never been found. 13.

Holme Cultram's Decline

The abbey was unable to maintain its structures upon the dissolution by Henry VIII in the 16th century though it was not destroyed like so many of its sisters. Its footprint shrank due to lack of funding, the stones of the cloisters and outbuildings having vanished into the growing nearby town.

It was renovated in the 18th and 19th centuries as it had long been in use as a parish church. Unfortunately I took a very blurry photo of its one remaining green man - whose face had been traumatized by time - the vine growing from either side of his mouth still very evident. There are also many decorative Freemasonic graves in the old graveyard with compass, square and images of the sun.

Having fought for its existence by constant aggressors and the needs of poverty, the great masterpiece of Cistercian architecture, though still imposing, was to suffer a modern blow, one dealt in ignorance and total lack of empathy for the lives of the community that it served.

It had been the victim of a mindless attack in June 9 2006 by a teenage arsonist who stole £5.00 from the donations box and left a community stunned. Thankfully only one stained glass window was lost but the ancient beamed roof had to be totally replaced. Now at the time of this writing of late 2013, they are still in need of funds to complete the renovation so that it may be brought back into service.

I visited the abbey in 2009 and had the privilege of being shown the archaeological digs which revealed the cloisters and further foundations by the Reverend David Tembey. The scope of the ancient foundations was impressive and I found myself wishing that it still stood in its former glory. I had gone to the abbey in the hope that perhaps I might just find a clue to the Templars having lived here for a time. It was a long shot and I knew it, however the more recent Masonic graves gave me hope.

Later I came across this wonderful illustration of mason marks within the church:

Having ducked under a low door lintel, I made the steep climb up a narrow turnpike stair to the inner bell-cot with the Reverend. The view was a once in a lifetime opportunity above the high altar to look down the long dark nave towards the large Romanesque entrance - and out through the 16th century porch.

Conservationists were at work below under lamplight - the windows having been boarded up - as the stained glass had yet to be returned from their safe storage and the dust of work was everywhere.

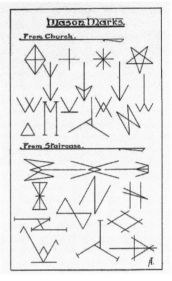

Masonic Marks Illustration –
Some Records of a Cistercian Abbey: Holme Cultram

I had a bird's eye view through the high arched windows of the old inner bell tower and though sad that the grand old place had suffered, I looked forward to its rescue and felt privileged I was standing with Reverend Temby amongst the high graceful stone which had been raised nine centuries earlier that whispered of so many secrets.

The nave remains the only original medieval Cistercian structure serving in England today. Now called the Church of Saint Mary, she is a rare and one off gem deserving of funding and resurrection.

Please contact the Church of Saint Mary's if you'd like to assist with a donation:
http://www.holmecultramabbey.org.uk/

The Secret Dossier of a
Knight Templar of the Sangreal

A newly cut corbel (one of 30 planned) of red sandstone with an open hand, crescent moon and two bees. A fitting symbol of Holme Cultram's future.

Photo by © Gretchen Cornwall 2009

1. Stöber, Karen. Late Medieval Monasteries and Their Patrons: England and Wales, C. 1300-1540. Woodbridge: Boydell Press, 2007. p. 12

2. Grainger, Francis, and W. G. Collingwood. The Register and Records of Holme Cultram. Kendal: T. Wilson & Son, 1929. p. 136-148

3. Cal. Close Rolls, 13 Ed. II, Amble.

4. Cal. Close Rolls, 17 Ed. II, Westminster.

5. Farrer, William, and J. Brownbill. "Houses of Cistercian Monks: The Abbey of Furness." Houses of Cistercian Monks: The Abbey of Furness. http://www.british-history.ac.uk/report.aspx?compid=38348&%3Bstrquery=++Date+accessed%3A+03+October+2013. Volume 2 (1908), pp. 114-131

6. Gilbanks, G. E. Some Records of a Cistercian Abbey: Holme Cultram, Cumberland. London: W. Scott, 1899. p. 75

7. Grainger, Francis, and W. G. Collingwood. "Records : The Abbey in the Thirteenth Century." Records : The Abbey in the Thirteenth Century. http://www.british-history.ac.uk/report.aspx?compid=49537&strquery=. pp. 126-136

8. Grainger, Francis, and W. G. Collingwood. "Records : The Abbey in the Thirteenth Century." Records : The Abbey in the Thirteenth Century. http://www.british-history.ac.uk/report.aspx?compid=49537&strquery=. pp. 126-136

9. Wilson, J. "Houses of Cistercian Monks: The Abbey of Holmcultram." Houses of Cistercian Monks: The Abbey of Holmcultram. http://www.british-history.ac.uk/report.aspx?compid=39957&strquery=.

10. Gilbanks, G. E. Some Records of a Cistercian Abbey: Holme Cultram, Cumberland. London: W. Scott, 1899. P. 59

11. Ibid p. 60

12. Ibid

13. Brown, J. Wood. An Enquiry into the Life and Legend of Michael Scot. Edinburgh: D. Douglas, 1897

Twenty Nine

Saint Kentigern & the Grail Connection

There are ten churches in Cumbria dedicated to the Celtic bishop, Saint Kentigern meaning head-chief, (527 – 612) and whose alternative 'pet name' is St. Mungo, meaning 'dearest friend'. He was also known to the Welsh as Cynderyrn. Kentigern's hagiographic (symbolic) birth and life history, some of which was drawn from older sources by the Cistercian monk Jocelyn of Furness in the 12th century, reads like the Greek myth of Perseus.

His mother the Brythonic Princess Tenaw became co-patron saint and founder of the city of Glasgow. Her father was King Lot and her brother was the Arthurian knight Gawain.

According to 12th century monastic writer Jocelyn of Furness, she had been raped by the hero, Owain ab Urien, Prince of Rheged who then deserted her, but I think this is a false account.

Jocelyn claimed he was using older documents from Ireland which no longer exist. Tenaw was of course from Scotland yet he was drawing on her story from an Irish source. It is my opinion that the story became garbled over time and place and perhaps confused with another individual or purposefully embellished for some unknown effect through Greek myth. By the time Jocelyn came by the account centuries later it had become degraded. However the odd colourful story can be decoded through the name of the princess herself.

The dreadful tale continues stating that her father, King Lothus of Laudonia (Lothian), found out she was pregnant and had her thrown off a cliff in a chariot. 1. Tenaw survived the fall and managed to escape in a coracle across the wide girth of the Firth of Forth and found safe haven with Saint Servanus in Fife who protected her and her son, later tutoring him.

The story is off beam as Servanus was not born for another 100 years and the harsh conditions of Kentigerns birth, having survived a pre-natal cliff fall onto stony ground, is straight out of a Greek myth and is overly dramatic if not impossible. 2.

Prince Urien is noted to have been married to a princess named Laudine, whom he was loyal to all his life. He was a great knight and hero eclipsing King Arthur himself. Why would he rape a woman when he himself was known to be a man of honour? I don't believe he did. The name Laudine is derived from the name of her father's kingdom, Laudonia. Tenaw is Laudine and had actually married Prince Urien. They were one and the same person. The name Tenaw became separated from her place name (Laudine) in error or purpose to create two different women. Perhaps it was a shotgun wedding and her father King Lot may very well have been furious by the young lovers but I highly doubt he threw his pregnant daughter over a cliff. After many Arthurian adventures Urien returned to his wife, winning her love.

There may be another explanation for Jocelyn having augmented Kentigerns story with the introduction of Greek myth and overtones of virgin birth. Zeus had been amorous with the mother of Perseus and when the pregnancy was discovered by her human husband, he had her thrown over a cliff in a casket. Perseus survived to become a hero and was secretly assisted by his hidden father and the gods through his life.

The inheritance of Jesus' descendants through the Merovingians was imported from France and could be the reason for this Greek myth to have been transposed over the historical St. Kentigern. Somewhere in Tenaw's past looms a Merovingian, perhaps her mother. Trade between the powerful Merovingians of Paris to England is a known quantity and there were royal marriages and treaties.

There is no record of Jocelyn prior to his time in Furness aside from a stint in Ireland, but his name may hail from Brittany. That he may have actually been a Breton is highly probable.

Chrétien de Troyes Arthurian tales were avidly followed by the Troubadours and Templars having spread out from France. Elements of this can be traced through Jocelyn's narrative. As a French Cistercian of Breton heritage, it is likely he was fully versed in de Troyes having had immediate exposure to it and either wove it into Saint Kentigerns life story or recounted a more accurate past. 3.

Also to recap chapter one, the events of King Arthur were native to Cumbria, so it is only natural that Jocelyn would have absorbed knowledge of the Pendragon heritage from Cumbria, France and Ireland.

The mystery deepens as Kentigern's fourth miracle of the salmon and the ring come to us straight out of the Cistercian Abbey of Orval in Belgium.

Jocelyn tells us that the Queen of Strathclyde was accused of adultery by her husband. The King ordered her to give up her wedding ring which he claimed she had given to a lover, when in reality he had thrown it into the river. Kentigern directs one of his disciples to go to the river and fish for a salmon. Having done so the priest returns with the fish from which Kentigern then pulls out the missing ring saving the lady's honour and life.

As a Cistercian having visited Orval, Jocelyn would have become familiar with the original story of the abbey's foundation by the Countess Matilde di Canossa (1046 – 1115) whose grandfather was the Duke of Lorraine.

The Countess 'just happened' to be visiting when she dropped her wedding ring in a stream. In her dismay she prayed for its return. A fish jumped out of the water with the gold ring in its mouth. Matilde, greatly relieved, proclaimed that the valley was indeed 'gold' hence the name of the location gold valley (or-val). She then gifted the monks with the funds to build the abbey.

It would be naïve not to explore this story further and dismiss it as a quaint medieval legend. Upon closer examination a great deal may be extracted.

"...this band of monks was led by an individual called 'Ursus' – a name which the 'Prieure documents' consistently associate with the Merovingian bloodline. On their arrival in the Ardennes, the Calabrian monks obtained the patronage of Mathilde de Toscane, Duchess of Lorraine – who was Godfroi de Bouillon's aunt and, in effect, foster-mother. From Mathilde the monks received a tract of land at Orval, not far from Stenay, where Dagobert II had been assassinated some five hundred years earlier." Baigent, Leigh, Lincoln 4.

Dagobert II was supposedly the last of the Merovingians when the line was cut off by the Carolingians in collusion with the church, but it is thought that his son had been safely taken to the British Isles, had children and the line continued secretly. The implication being that the Prince Ursus, now a monk, was descended from Dagobert II.

As a reminder, Godfroi de Bouillon was the first ruler of Jerusalem and intimately involved with the Templars. Ursus was not only an original founding monk from Orval but was Godfroi's tutor and co-instigator of the first crusade. Orval had been a place of initiation where Nostradamus was shown an arcane book which inspired him to write many of his quatrains. 5.

In the area surrounding Orval, Merovingian tombs were discovered and there are indications that a prior Merovingian church may be encompassed within the Cistercian abbey.

Matilde comes down through history to us as a successful warrior queen; protecting her lands by riding out in front of an army against the Emperor Henry V who she routed in various battles.

He was left with no choice but to crown her 'Imperial Vicar Vice-Queen of Italy', a ceremony which is memorialized as part of a May festival in the Italian region of Emilia. 6.

Is there a deeper meaning behind the legend of the returned ring from the waters by a fish which had been charmed through prayer? A fish is a being capable of traversing the etheric dimensions symbolized by water initiates of European legend have power over the forces of nature, it is a dual metaphor. The priest is the fish and the fish is nature, himself, which he has mastered.

Is there a memory of this western European tradition of a hidden circle of colleagues and a hidden priestess, memorialized by the Knights of the Garter? A tradition of a mystical round table, hidden goddess and Mary Magdalene - brought from Orval and embedded into the life of St. Kentigern?

The ring is a direct link to inner practices of the alchemical marriage, the secrets of astronomy and building as explored in chapter twenty six. Jocelyn casts Kentigern in the role of the Grail Knight whose priestly abilities to affect the physical saves the life of his queen.

Kentigern's four miracles, including the ring, are composed within the crest of the city of Glasgow.

Here is the bird that never flew – *Power over death, man & beast*

Here is the tree that never grew – *enflamed branch providing life-saving heat*

Here is the bell that never rang – *Kentigern brings a church bell from Rome*

Here is the fish that never swam – *the Merovingian Orval legend*

Aside from the messianic ability to raise the dead, Kentigern is also on the same footing as Moses. Jocelyn recounts the saint parting the waters of the Forth in order to flee persecution by jealous students. 7.

Saint Kentigern was invited by the King of Strathclyde to live in his court and

The Secret Dossier of a
Knight Templar of the Sangreal

helped him gain the post of Bishop of Glasgow. The cathedral according to legend was built on the place of his final hours and his tomb still draws pilgrims today.

He met and befriended Saint Columba of Iona and also St. Cuthbert famous for the Lindisfarne Gospels which is the earliest illuminated manuscript of England. His life of course is strewn with miracles from raising a dead bird to life and also that of a man while still a child himself. 8.

At the hand of Jocelyn, Saint Kentigern became a Cistercian prototype and knightly hero whose symbolic life is not dissimilar to that of Saint Bernard.

The Keystone Church

Caldbeck was initially founded by Augustinian monks with permission and support from Holme Cultram as a hospital and place of respite for travelers. It does sound familiar to the Templars' public role in the Middle East, to protect the roads for pilgrims. They continued the practice of baptism from the tiny well by the side of the stream that runs through Caldbeck. The name itself translates as cold-stream. The Augustinians believed Saint Kentigern had utilized this well during his time when walking the hills of Cumbria.

A Templar Knight Buried at Caldbeck

One of the names I was given was Sir Thomas de Bray whose grave slab of the mid thirteenth century is carved in the fashion of a compass rose and to a highly skilled level. The sandstone grave slab was brought into the small church and affixed to the wall to ostensibly protect it from the elements but I was to learn it is a ceremonial protection symbol which guards the door and creates a 'cross in the landscape'.

It appears to my own untrained eye that the sword, carved to the left of the original floriated cross, was done at a later time to indicate he was indeed a knight, likewise a small equidistance cross was carved into the stone just under the right side of the rose.

The compass rose itself is raised above the main stone but the carved sword is not which lead me to think that it may have been done as a posthumous courtesy.

My contact said that Sir Thomas was a Templar and his grave slab certainly is carved in the traditional manner of the Order for this time period. His name had been carved onto the stone as well which is unusual for a Templar as most grave slabs, though carved with a device, did not include an actual name.

"Mediaeval Slab by Vestry door: raised floriated Cross (Sword
to dexter) Inscription on edge nearly chiselled away.
R.............De BR........."
[Thoms de Broy] 9.
(As quoted from Monumental Inscriptions in the Church and Churchyard of
Caldbeck, Cumberland. See pages 213 & 214 for photos)

249

Gargoyles from the arched entryway to Caldbeck's Church
by © Gretchen Cornwall 2009

Through my own research I was to find that the name de Bray is old French and part of a group of families known as the Ouseley Group that supported William the Conqueror and were rewarded for their help after the invasion through land gifts spreading out over England, Wales and Ireland.

Over time many branches of the family dropped the 'de' in order to appear English and not French as difficulties rose between the two countries. 10.

What I find interesting is that Caldbeck is not too far from Scotland. Scotland and France were known as the Auld Alliance, it would not necessarily be a negative in the northern England/Scotland border region to have continued using the 'de' Bray French connection with Scotland as a neighbour and possible ally.

Sir Thomas was actually from Kirkby Thore, a combination of names colliding under different two different cultures and religions. Kirk means literally church and Thor is the Norse god of thunder, an indication of the areas Viking heritage.

Kirkby Thore is a stone's throw from Temple Sowerby, both of which are 24 miles S.E. of Caldbeck. Due to his proximity to the old preceptory of Sowerby, still active at the time of the death of Sir Thomas in 1247 AD, it is very likely he was a Templar as my contact has stated. There appears to have been no children but the family line carried on through its cousins. But many Templars had been known to marry and then trade their secular life for monastic duties.

What I do find interesting is that he was buried at Caldbeck 24 miles to the north. I was hard pressed to find any information about him and so must speculate on his connection with and also why he was interred in Saint Kentigerns rather than Temple Sowerby, Holme Cultram Abbey, or his place of birth. It may simply be he or his brethren wanted him placed at their spiritually significant Keystone. Had they known that the church was sitting on a power vortex? How could they not have?

His parents, Amabilis Waldeve de Barford and Sir Robert de Broy, were supporters of the Cistercian Abbey of Holme Cultram, having gifted the Abbey 16 acres of their own land near Temple Sowerby. Other members of the Waldeve family were also engaging in the donation of fields and lands to the abbey across Cumbria. These activities are a strong indication of a northern family tie to both the Temple and the Cistercians, supplying lands, resources and men. 11.

The Comte de Medici is not related to Sir Thomas de Bray but the medieval knight was part of the broader Templar family. The Comte is however related to the famous huntsman of Cumberland, John Peel, also buried in the cemetery of St Kentigerns.

Having stayed in this beautiful area a few times, I had learned by speaking with the locals that many had proudly made a claim of kinship to John Peel. He is popular indeed as a local historical celebrity!

The Huntsman, John Peel,
Gravestone,
Photo by
© Gretchen Cornwall 2009

The stone is beautifully carved out of white marble rather than the rose coloured sandstone freely available in Cumbria, with graceful immortal acanthus leaves, roses, oak leaves and a subtle All Seeing Eye above the Peel hound.

Close view of John Peel's grave stone with his famous fox hound
and the All Seeing Eye. © Gretchen Cornwall 2009

Long term friend John W. Graves wrote three songs dedicated to Peel one of which is so popular it is sung today. Graves predicted with accuracy that the song, D'Ye Ken John Peel, would be repeated for years to come, *'By Jove, Peel, you'll be sung when we're both run to earth."* 12.

The song is a march for two British regiments and one Canadian regiment. Legend holds that three pubs were named after his favourite dogs and also a large province of Australia, Peel Region. 13.

Controversially, Peel died with debts and enjoyed a pint. But many imbibed too much during the this time. During his funeral three thousand people attended as he was well liked. Even by present day standards this is quite the huge turn out! Those present paid his debts such was their affection for him.

The Secret Dossier of a
Knight Templar of the Sangreal

John Peel
by John W. Graves 1795-1886

D'YE ken John Peel with his coat so gray
D'ye ken John Peel at the break of the day?
D'ye ken John Peel when he's far, far away,
With his hounds and his horn in the morning?

'Twas the sound of his horn call'd me from my bed,
And the cry of his hounds has me oft-times led ;
For Peel's view holloa would 'waken the dead,
Or a fox from his lair in the morning.

D'ye ken that bitch whose tongue is death 1
D'ye ken her sons of peerless faith 1
D'ye ken that a fox with his last breath
Curs'd them all as he died in the morning ?
'Twas the sound of his horn, &c.

Yes, I ken John Peel and auld Ruby, too,
Ranter and Royal and Bellman as true ;*
From the drag to the chase, from the chase to the view,
From the view to the death in the morning.
'Twas the sound of his horn, &c.

And I've follow'd John Peel both often and far,
O'er the rasper-fence and the gate and the bar,
From Low Denton-holme up to Scratchmere Scar,
When we vied for the brush in the morning.
'Twas the sound of his horn, &c.

Then, here's to John Peel with my heart and soul,
Come fill fill to him another strong bowl :
And we'll follow John Peel thro' fair and thro' foul
While we're wak'd by his horn in the morning.
'Twas the sound of his horn, &c.

"These were the real names of the hounds which Peel in his old age said were the
very best he ever had or saw." J. W. G. 14.

Saint Kentigern & the Grail Connection

The Cross in the Landscape

Along the iron fence of the church perimeter in the front of the grounds is the Roughton Stone Monument. It is an important memorial but also a marker for a cross in the landscape in the south.

Text from accompanying plaque:

"The Roughton Stone – In the 19th century, this stone was used in its original circular form to process minerals in the mining area of Roughton Gill, Caldbeck. It is placed here in tribute to the mining men and their families who lived and worked in the Gill for four hundred years and who now lie at rest in this churchyard."

The Roughton Stone © Gretchen Cornwall 2009

My Templar contact alluded to a 'Cross in the Landscape' using the Hyper Perfect numbers (116, 208, 325) which were discussed in the Chapter on the Heronian Tetrahedron. After multiple experiments, I did locate the cross but also a series of triangles within the church yard.

254

Produced With Google Earth Software

The Roughton Stone is indicated with a yellow tack at the front of the church yard closest to the street at the bottom of the photo. Following a diagonal line northwest, it connects to the John Peel monument. The other main crossing line follows the path from the front gate to the front door of the church.

The apex of the church where the high altar is located, is actually the point where it is cited on the Ordnance Survey map as being NY 325 400. The stream, Caldbeck can be seen to the north of the church.

The red tacks on the left near the church wall to the west, indicate the first triangle of 116°. The John Peel stone is simply marked in the photo as J.P. – the Francis Mattinson stone guards the west gate and completes the first triangle.

I was told that Francis Mattinson (Died 20 Sept 1823) was a descendant of John Peel and a Templar and therefore his family memorial stone was of importance.

255

The white 'kite' or cross is the 325° triangle from the Francis Mattinson stone to the church pathway for the door. Produced With Google Earth Software.

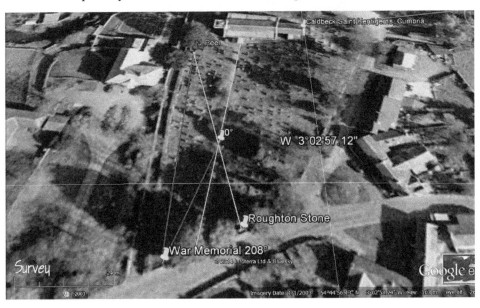

The War Memorial triangle of 208° sits next to another Mattinson family monument in the south. Produced With Google Earth Software.

Melancholia I

Melancholia I by Albrecht Dürer 1514 Engraving

Melancholia I is one of the most contemplated occult images to come out of Europe. It is full of mystical symbolism, much speculated upon by numerous writers down the centuries. The tools are of a practical nature indicating that there is a work aspect to heightened awareness. The angelic figure is that of the artist's soul, strongly androgynous, appearing to suffer from malaise or depression.

He has all the tools and knowledge one could want surrounding him, having through steep labour achieved his goal. He has passed through the 34 steps of the magic square. The Angelic Knight, now a Metatron, knows that there are two further steep mountains to climb and his work must commence yet again.

The graves and monuments of St. Kentigerns church yard are replete with symbols which match the above engraving. The compass may be found in multiple. John Peel's monument shares pride of place between the fox hound and the all Seeing Eye. The rising sun near the Melancholia I banner and sleeping hound is a match for the eye and hound on the Peel stone.

Please notice the cherub busy writing in the engraving, an indication that future work is commencing if not still young. He sits on a stone grinding wheel in echo of the Roughton Stone Monument.

The geometric stone to the left in the engraving which is being worked on or dressed is a code in itself. The actual shape of the stone is debatable and the basis for what is now called the Dürer's Solid. Essentially it is a polyhedron with a faint human skull. It has also been called a Chamfered tetrahedron.

'In the mathematical field of graph theory, the Dürer graph is an undirected graph with 12 vertices and 18 edges. It is named after Albrecht Dürer, whose 1514 engraving *Melencolia I* includes a depiction of Dürer's solid, a convex polyhedron having the Dürer graph as its skeleton. Dürer's solid is one of only four well-covered simple convex polyhedra.' 15.

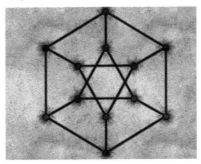

Author of graphic, Koko90, http://en.wikipedia.org/wiki/File:D%C3%BCrer_graph.svg

I find this an intriguing graphic based on Dürer's Solid which I have taken the liberty of rotating 90° to illustrate Solomon's Seal or Star of David.

Melancholia I is worth the attention of a book so I will give it only a passing nod here in order to highlight the symbolic language that the polymath Dürer was so well versed and its incarnation in the church yard of Caldbeck.

The figure in Melancholia I has been called an 'angel' since day one, and I'm not disputing this, but another way to explain the image of the feathered wings is that of a Knight of the Swan. In fact the winged being is both.

Caldbeck, home of the Knights of the Swan

When I embarked on this project I considered Cygnus the Swan and its impact on the ancient world and the Christian. I omitted this as I had thought the content of my work was already overflowing the cup. However during the early months of 2014 - I had an email from John Temple suggesting I should look into Cygnus and that it had always been important to the Templars. The Knights of the Temple were also the Knights of the Swan! I could not ignore the connections between the swan and the knights any longer.

Godfrey de Bouillon claimed descent from Helyas who was simply and mysteriously a Knight of the Swan. It is possible that the etymology of Helyas is also that of the solar god Helios and his chariot.

The name is also synonymous with the prophet Elijah in Greek and later Latin. Elijah raised the dead, performed miracles and may have been reincarnated as John the Baptist as references in the Bible seem to attest. Though this may sound strange, it is not unheard of in the early Celtic, Buddhist and Hindu belief structures for such an event to take place. The prophet Elijah takes on the rays of the sun through Mount Horeb and ascends, undying, in a chariot of fire.

In the Judaic tradition, Enoch, Noah's ancestor, was a priest-king. He ascends on a horse – having bypassed the chariot – to heaven at the age of 365 years and is transformed into an angelic Metatron. He does not die but is taken up at the end of a cycle whose years match the exact days of our modern calendar. The other patriarchs in his line live to many hundreds of years. The difference is significant and ties Enoch to the wisdom of astronomy and to an ancient tradition of soul journeying.

The Chevalier of the Cygne, Helios, becomes Lohengrin under the pen of German poet and knight, Wolfram von Eschenbach (1170 – c. 1220). Lohengrin enters Arthurian lore as the son of the perfect knight, Percival.

Lohengrin comes to the aid of a damsel but under the mysterious condition she not ask his name. When I encountered this it hit me that his request for silence is a distinct reference to a secret Order of Knights. Lohengrin was able to help the maiden as she promised not to reveal his identity which could have endangered his circle.

The swan in British lore goes back hundreds of years. The Mute Swan has been traditionally 'owned' by the British Crown since the 12th century. Every third week in July since the 15th century, the census/ceremony of Swan Upping takes place on the River Thames. The birds are no longer a food source but are caught, assessed and released. 16.

In 1304 Edward I was invested as a knight and swore an oath to god on two swans decorated with golden nets. 17.

I wondered if the constellation Cygnus might have inspired the search for the Heronian Tetrahedron by the present day Knights of the Swan? Had they found a sympathetic layout in the church yard? Below are my experiments with the constellation overlaid on top of St. Kentigern's and also across western Europe.

Cygnus Experiment One Opposite

During Cygnus Experiment One, I aligned Cygnus with the War Memorial line which intersects nicely with the John Peel stone, the wings enfold the church and the star named 'V' to the left of Deneb at the top of the cross sits nicely near St. Kentigern's Well. The black dots and green lines of Cygnus are an acurate portrayal of the constellation.

Saint Kentigern & the Grail Connection

Cygnus Across the Caldbeck Church Yard

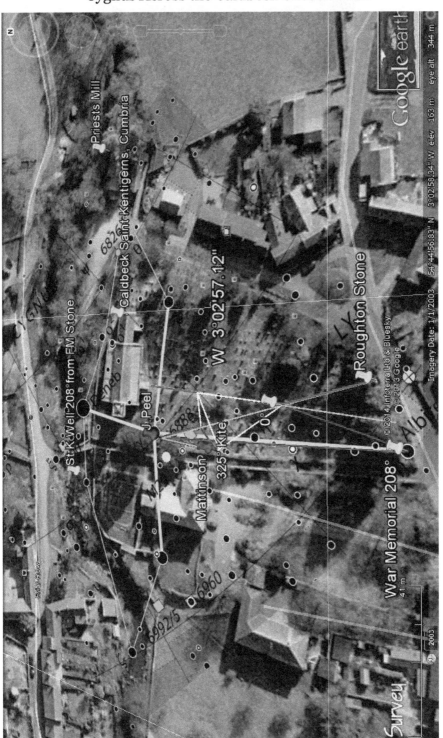

Cygnus Experiment One Produced With Google Earth Software

The Secret Dossier of a
Knight Templar of the Sangreal

Saint Kentigern & the Grail Connection

The Secret Dossier of a
Knight Templar of the Sangreal

The Cygnus Two experiment on the left opposite page, may make more sense with the alignment of the church path. The left cross bar intersects perfectly with the apex of the 116° J.P. & F. Mattinson memorials.

Cygnus Experiment Three
Prior Page - Produced With Google Earth Software

In this European experiment with Deneb at Caldbeck the line follows the H.T. to Dover. It is not a perfect match to the Matrix Map as Cygnus diverges from Geneva to the east of Italy instead of a straight line to Malta. Nonetheless I find the correlation interesting as Geneva was an important Templar retreat after 1307.

Author Andrew Collins of the Cygnus Mystery sites evidence through millennia for the impact of the constellation including the Egyptian priesthood. 'Everywhere Cygnus became associated with the cosmic source of life and death, and the transmigration of the soul.' 17. It was revered as a celestial temple by early European Shamans whose interpretive cave art depicted the position of Cygnus in the night sky. Collins made a stunning discovery upon reviewing the work of NASA's Mike McCollough.

Cygnus X-3, which is not visible to the naked eye, emits radioactive forces through a powerful galactic garden hose. Its jet stream is pointed right at earth. '...relativist jets originating from a microblazar were responsible for a rapid acceleration in human evolution at the height of the last Ice Age.' 18.

Collins noted that in the 1980s deep underground facilities in the USA and Europe which had been heavily shielded from exterior interference, were looking for proof of nucleon decay. The experiments were unable to detect their objective which would have proven the Grand Unified Theory. As of 2012 the theory remains only a possibility.

I will sidestep an explanation of this as I am not a physicist and it bears little influence on this section except the unexpected outcome of the experiment. Repeated tests found something altogether different. Cygnets! Poetically named from the parent source. These shielded and sterile labs deep within the earth detected gamma radiation coming right from the central cross of the constellation Cygnus! 19.

Had the Shamans of the Magdalenian Age in S. France commune through astral means with the Northern Cross? Had they detected its powerful stream of light through intuitive means and followed it back to its source and we are only just now scientifically discovering its impact on humanity?

There is only one explanation for humans to go deep into a dark mountain when it is not necessary for survival. Indeed anthropological evidence shows that it was not for the purpose of living, but to journey through the inner planes to the home of the Swan kingdom.

The impact of radiation both for healing and destruction on human DNA is well documented. It seems that Cygnus has been rearing cygnets on earth since the beginning.

Why had the Templars chosen the large and graceful white bird which is the swan as an emblem? Had they come across the same stream of radiation out of the constellation Cygnus through soul travel as had earlier European Shamans? Had they gained their respect of the swan from their own experiments in caves? The cave is very important to early Christian legends such as the Magdalene levitating in a seated position, living out her life in a cave.

Knights, embodying the serene qualities of a swan, are beautifully imagined by the Arthurian tales and Melancholia I by Albrecht Dürer.

Caldbeck's Sun Dial

Mass dials or sun dials were carved onto the south facing wall of a church near the priest door or main entrance. Initially very simple in nature and enabled the priest to determine morning, noon and evening calls to prayer. The bell would then be rung to alert the faithful to come to the church and were Europe's earliest forms of a clock.

Sun dials have led some to believe their function related to greater mysteries as many have been found where the sun does not reach them – such as under the cover of a porch or actually to be found inside a church. Such ideas are quite exciting but their adherents have not factored in that churches of such great age were remodeled several times over in their history.

Porches were added in Elizabethan or Victorian periods cutting out the sunlight and rendering the sun dial useless. Entire walls were moved with the stonework used in other areas with little care as to the original markings orientation. Originally the mass dial was exactly just that – a means of telling the time of day.

The Caldbeck sun dial enjoys the rare benefice of its original position on the upper right side of the priest door on the south wall of the ancient church. It is approximately 7" in diameter and to a high standard with a deep cut circle and the base of the gnomon still in place.

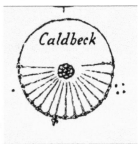

by Rev. William Slater Calverley

At some point nails and lead were driven into the central hole, possibly to support the gnomon or its replacement. Time has obscured its clarity but one can see the drilled holes on the circumference and the corresponding seventeen rays. A small cross marks high noon at the lowest point and projects slightly out of the circle. It is thought that the four drilled holes on the outside of the circle to the right represent four pm.

"The number of rays and holes is seventeen, but one ray is evidently marked beyond the diameter, making the number of divisions in the half circle sixteen, and thus bringing us again into contact with the octaval system of time division common among the Angles, in which daynight is divided into eight equal parts, sub-divided into sixteen, and again sub-divided into thirty-two." 20.

The priest door, centre and between the two windows, has been walled in at some point. The sun dial is still in place to the upper right of the doorway. Many thanks to John Price, President of the Caldbeck and Local History Society for the above photo.

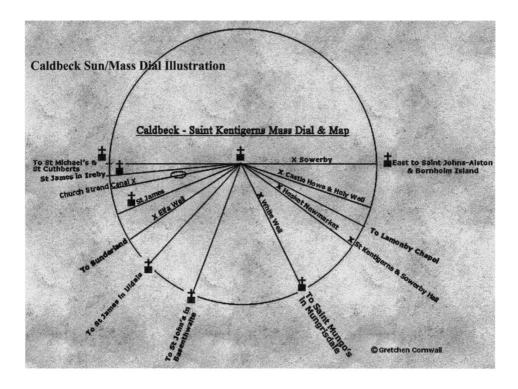

Saint Kentigern & the Grail Connection

As a point of interest, following the Southwest ray of the Caldbeck sun dial we are led to the church of Saint Bega in Bassenthwaite. A 13th century crucifix with skull and crossbones at the foot was discovered during a recent restoration of the church. It had been hidden to protect it from either Cromwell or overzealous reformers and is now at the treasury of Carlisle.

The opposite diagram is simply an exploration into the possibilities that there may be more to the Caldbeck dial than meets the eye. It is representational only and in an effort to leave no stone unturned.

As I mentioned earlier much has been ascribed to these mysterious little carvings but this sun dial is in its original position and if compared to an ordnance survey map, its rays do lead to other significant locations.

It may be circumstantial only - as the number of rays fit with the above quote on the 'octaval system' of the early medieval period. If the church is a hub, according the Templars, then perhaps as the Keystone of the Matrix Map, could it be the compass rose of multiple mapping systems over centuries of use?

It is thought that sun dials were in use from the 11th century up to the 16th century when actual clock technology developed. However the Reverend William Slater Calverley has made a very good argument that they date to a much earlier time period of several hundred years. He makes the point that the Bewcastle Cross sun dial has not been added or altered in any way and is therefore original.

The illustration (right) is that of the Celtic Cross of Bewcastle Cumbria, which dates to the 7th century. It is covered with runic inscriptions, John the Baptist, Christ and possibly a figure of St James with an eagle, flora and fauna are amongst the Celtic knot work.

It is a beautiful fusion of Viking art encompassing both the old religious style and the acceptance of an incoming new impetus. One can clearly see the sun dial which appears to have twelve to thirteen hours on the south side of the cross. It is clearly a sophisticated work undertaken by experienced stonemasons.

Drawing by Rev. William Slater Calverley

I would like to suggest that post Norman (1066) stone churches replaced their wooden counterparts and therefore earlier sun dials. Based upon the 7th century sun dial on the Bewcastle Cross it seems likely that they were in wider use. Had they also been the basis for solar town planning? The sun is a powerful navigation tool and would have been very useful to mark not only the time but also locations. Had the Dark Age warriors actually planned their villages based on the rays of the sun and marked it on their Celtic Crosses and early churches based upon a division of hours on the sun dial? Is the Caldbeck sun dial and its corresponding rays a map to local

The Secret Dossier of a
Knight Templar of the Sangreal

places of importance planned by marking the rays of the sun in the landscape?

"Caldbeck and Caldbeck Fells are worth all England else"
Queen Elisabeth I

During the meeting with John Temple he quoted the above and also said mysteriously that the Templars of the time were very angry with her for having stated publically that there was a secret of great wealth in Caldbeck Cumbria.

How he could have known this I do not know. What we do know is that during Queen Elisabeth's reign she signed the charter of the Mines Royal in 1564 giving Daniel Hechstetter of Augsberg Germany the leadership over mining for copper in nearby Keswick Cumbria. He brought over some 200 German miners as their expertise was far more robust than the English miners. Their ability to tunnel, retrieve ore and smelt copper was superb. Had they been of Templar extract?

It was highly necessary for Elisabeth to be independent of Europe as a source for copper as the danger of being cut off in the channel was very real. Spain had its eye on England and it was known that they were preparing to invade. Elisabeth needed fine copper for making cannons to defend the nation.

A Visit to Caldbeck Fells

"Slept at Mr. Younghusband's public-house, Hesket Newmarket. In the evening walked to Caldbeck Falls, a delicious spot in which to breathe out a summer's day-- limestone rocks, hanging trees, pools, and waterbreaks--caves and caldrons which have been honoured with fairy names, and no doubt continue in the fancy of the neighbourhood to resound with fairy revels." Dorothy Wordsworth 21.

During a research visit I stayed at Rose Castle Farm B&B run by the very hospitable Hetherington family. The nearby Rose Castle itself has been the traditional home of the Bishops of Carlisle since the 13th century. I was fortunate to be given a private tour of the lovely ancient place as it is closed to the public. Initially a mote and bailey, a Pele tower was built in the 14th century and the castle has been extended using the local stone which is a beautiful pink tone, perhaps having influenced the name.

On another occasion I stayed at the old Oddfellows inn and pub in the centre of Caldbeck itself, both trips were memorable, beautiful and interesting experiences.

Caldbeck and the surrounding countryside suffered badly during the Foot and Mouth Epidemic of 2001 and 2002, causing farmers to lose their stock and tourism all but ceased.

It was a very emotional time as many family businesses, generations old, had folded leaving little income generation in parts of Cumbria which was hardest hit by the disease. As a result Prince Charles became a patron and frequent visitor to Caldbeck where he inaugurated one of three charities, known as 'Rural Revival

Projects' or the Northern Fells Rural Project (NFRP) in Caldbeck. 22.

In the years since the catastrophe Caldbeck has rebounded to become a favourite tourist location with breathtaking fell walks, heritage centres and has seen the doubling of property prices.

Hesket Newmarket is a lovely village 1.5 miles from Caldbeck with its own cooperative microbrewery, the Old Crown. The locally sourced meals and fantastic beer are well worth the journey and don't forget to try a pint of Doris' 90th Birthday Ale!

"Hesket Hall is a square house with a large central chimney, built around 1630 for Sir Wilfrid Lawson of Isel Hall, twice MP for Cockermouth. The shape of the house is all angles and annexes – the story goes that it was built this way so that shadows from the twelve corners of the building act as a sundial." Contributors of Visit Cumbria 23.

Hesket Hall is very interesting with its direct relationship to the sun. One can see this played out in Isel Hall, just a few miles from Brassenthwaite where the image of the sun is repeated throughout the old country house.

In the years since the catastrophe Caldbeck has rebounded to become a favourite tourist location with breathtaking fell walks, heritage centres and has seen the doubling of property prices.

Hesket Newmarket is a lovely village 1.5 miles from Caldbeck with its own cooperative microbrewery, the Old Crown. The locally sourced meals and fantastic beer are well worth the journey and don't forget to try a pint of Doris' 90th Birthday Ale!

"Hesket Hall is a square house with a large central chimney, built around 1630 for Sir Wilfrid Lawson of Isel Hall, twice MP for Cockermouth. The shape of the house is all angles and annexes – the story goes that it was built this way so that shadows from the twelve corners of the building act as a sundial." Contributors of Visit Cumbria 23.

The Lawson Arms – Statuary at Isel Hall ©
Gretchen Cornwall 2009

The Secret Dossier of a
Knight Templar of the Sangreal

Projects' or the Northern Fells Rural Project (NFRP) in Caldbeck. 22.

Hesket Hall is very interesting with its direct relationship to the sun. One can see this played out in Isel Hall, just a few miles from Brassenthwaite where the image of the sun is repeated throughout the old country house.

Temple Sowerby

I would be remiss if I did not at least in brief mention the preceptory of Temple Sowerby. I had started a geometric investigation of the surrounding area and it had nowhere near the monuments that Caldbeck enjoyed.

I decided not to pursue the Vesica Piscis as the comparison was underwhelming. It may very well be that I have missed an important point that bears further geometrical research, but in the effort to focus on the Matrix Map, Caldbeck and historical background, I decided to be circumspect. Many of the places of interest surrounding Sowerby are simply too close to the old preceptory, nullifying the pattern of the 5.96 mile radius needed.

Only the name of the nearby village indicates that there had been a preceptory here at all. The small village sits on an old Roman road in the Eden Valley and retains its old Maypole on the green. According to Victorian writers there had been a legend of two Celtic crosses on the green as well but no trace now exists of them. 24.

The Knights Hospitaller, like most Templar properties, took control of Sowerby. Upon the reformation the Dalston family was given the property which has since passed into the National Trust.

The stately 18th century home had incorporated prior buildings but it is thought that the actual Templar footprint is gone. In fact I have not come across references to the preceptory in other historical books as if it had never existed. I found the same to be true of Holme Cultram. Both locations had been forgotten by historians.

The Acorn Bank Garden & Watermill (Templar preceptory) is known for its orchids, 250 medicinal and culinary herbs. It is surrounded by rural beauty and old woodland which the Templars would have been well used to treading. Today one may take a stroll through the woods in their footsteps. It is a lovely day out and well worth a visit. If there are still secrets here the trees hold them now.

1. Shirt, David De. *Kentigern in Cumbria: His Presence and His Cult*. Maryport: De Shird, 2006.

2. APA citation. Hunter-Blair, O. (1910). St. Kentigern. In The Catholic Encyclopedia. New York: Robert Appleton Company. Retrieved October 16, 2013 from New Advent:

3. Medieval Sourcebook: Cynthia Whidden Green: Saint Kentigern, Apostle to Strathclyde:

A critical analysis of a northern saint. A Masters Thesis Presented to The Faculty of the Department of English University of Houston In Partial Fulfillment of the Requirements for the Degree Master of Arts © Cynthia Whiddon Green December, 1998

4. Baigent, Leigh, Lincoln p. 83

5. Baigent, Leigh, Lincoln p. 139

6. Fraser, Antonia. *The Warrior Queens*. Anchor Books, 1990.

7. Whidden Green

8. "Historical Preface: 1508-1546." Historical Preface: 1508-1546. http://www.british-history.ac.uk/report.aspx?compid=47903&strquery=saint+Kentigern.
Charters and Documents relating to the City of Glasgow 1175-1649: Part 1 (1897), pp. XLVIII-LXX.

9. Editorial Committee: Ursula Banister, Michael Curwen, John Price © Caldbeck & District Local History Society 1996 Reprinted 1997 Revised 2000 Copies of this publication may be obtained at Greenleaves Bookshop, Priests Mill, Caldbeck, Wigton, Cumbria CA7 8PR (016974 78369). ISBN 0 9526009 1 9 As quoted from Monumental Inscriptions in the Church and Churchyard of Caldbeck, Cumberland. Edited by James Wilson. Dalston W R Beck 1897.

10. http://rootcellar.us/bray.htm

11. 158. (C. p. 128; D. art. 81).—Adam f. Waldeve de Kyrkebythore confirms [no. 157]. Witnesses [from H. 2]—W. de Stotevill, etc. [The witness was sheriff of Cumberland 1198 and of Westmorland 1200–1202 and died in 1203 (C. & W. Trans., N.S. xiii, 38). Date c. 1200.]

12. Gilpin, Sidney. *The Songs and Ballads of Cumberland: To Which Are Added the Best Poems in the Dialect ; with Biographical Sketches, Notes, & Glossary*. Carlisle: G. Coward, 1865. p. 414

13. http://en.wikipedia.org/wiki/John_Peel_(huntsman)

14. Gilpin, p. 417

15. "Dürer Graph." Wikipedia. http://en.wikipedia.org/wiki/D%C3%BCrer_graph.

16. "Swan Upping." Wikipedia. http://en.wikipedia.org/wiki/Swan_Upping.

17. Collins, Andrew. *The Cygnus Mystery: Unlocking the Ancient Secret of Life's Origins in the Cosmos*. London: Watkins Pub., 2007.

18. Ibid p. 250,

19. Ibid p. 263, p. 274

20. Calverley, William Slater, and W. G. Collingwood. *Notes on the Early Sculptured Crosses, Shrines and Monuments in the Present Diocese of Carlisle*. Kendal: T. Wilson, 1899. p. 92

21. Wordsworth, Dorothy, and John Campbell Shairp. *Recollections of a Tour Made in Scotland, A.D. 1803*. Edinburgh: Edmonston and Douglas, 1874.

22. http://www.northernfellsgroup.org.uk/cms/about-us/

23. http://www.visitcumbria.com/car/hesket-newmarket/

24. Calverley, p. 54

Thirty

The Erasmus Obelisk and the New World

"The importance of 444 and 555 or 54 degrees, not 52 degrees"
Comte de Mattinata de Medici

As an island nation, England marshalled the sea for its defense against the Continent and to increase trade. Indeed England's power over the sea is legendary and needed proper administration to function.

The Cinque Port confederation, meaning five, had been charged with monitoring the S.E. Coast since the mid-12th century if not informally before as an extension of the ancient Saxon Shore Forts. In exchange for military action on behalf of the king, the Cinque Ports were granted tax exemptions and almost literal self-governance. 1.

The five main ports were Dover, Hastings, Hythe, New Romney and Sandwich. Dover was under a great deal of Templar control and oddly Margate became a 'Limb' of the Port of Dover in 1229 AD despite the small issue that it did not have a harbour allowing for heavy goods until 1320 AD. 2. Margate was at this time a small fishing village on the Isle of Thanet at the extreme S.E. tip of England just east and north of Dover. There are three main towns on the Isle, Margate, Ramsgate and Broadstairs with smaller hamlets nearby.

This is not to suppose that landing in Margate by sea was impossible as fishing, sheep and corn exports are historically noted. But certainly an intimate reason was applicable between the Templars of Dover and their interest in Margate which is adjacent to Westgate-on-Sea TR 325 700. The secret of Margate will be shared in a later volume.

Since the Templar fleet was the backbone of movement between Nova Scotia, the Middle East and Europe why would they not have been keenly interested in absorbing the Cinque Ports? As secular naval ports under their control or direction, is it not possible some Templar ships were accepted into the Cinque Port fleet?

It is an interesting question as I do not think that all ships headed towards Scotland. I believe they split up to increase their chances of survival. They had a great deal to offer their new host whoever that might be. Is it possible that their commercial vessels just continued under the auspices of the Cinque Ports where fleeing just was not necessary?

Ramsgate belonged to the much closer Cinque Port of Sandwich south of Thanet which is nearer than the deep water port of Dover. I find this intriguing that Margate would be associated with Dover rather than neighbouring Sandwich.

As far as I'm concerned this puts Margate on the map with the Templars as distinguished and separate from other neighbouring towns of Thanet. Dover became the most important of the confederation with Margate under its wing.

Many early records of the Port of Dover were lost during a move from the Market Place in 1836 - some of the loss is attributed to water damage. The British Library has the medieval records that remain.

The Erasmus Obelisk and the New World

The main bulk of records start from the early 19th century. But it is on record that the Cinque Port of Dover appointed a deputy Mayor to Margate - or St. John's as it was also known at the time - and the head justices of Dover would travel to Margate to adjudicate local disputes. Taxes from Margate were actually paid to Dover as a result and separate from church taxation to the See of Canterbury which seems rather extraordinary. The See of Canterbury owned half the Isle of Thanet and the Minster Abbey owned the other side. The Isle was therefore entirely under the auspices of the church, but one of its small insignificant villages was paying taxes and being monitored by the Templars of Dover.

What exactly could have caused their interest in Margate to be peaked is currently unknown to the broader public but hopefully with the insight of my Templar contact some of these questions may be answered. I am working on a book focusing on the Isle of Thanet and its initiatory and alchemical past.

Image section from Thomas Elmham's Mappa Thanet Insule –1413-1414 AD – Historia Monasterii S Augustini Cantuariensis

This segment from Thomas Elmham's map of the early 15th century of the Isle of Thanet shows four figures, two of which are certainly churchmen.

The figure with the staff seems to evoke St Christopher as he wades into the water with a smaller figure on his back. The man being taken to the ferry carries the cross pattée, a known Templar emblem.

The passenger in the small ferry looks like an emissary sent out to greet the newcomer; he also has a cross on the front of his clothing though it is very simple in nature.

Elmham, an intellectual of St Augustine's Abbey in Canterbury, chose to make a distinction between the two priests through the differences in their clothing but more noticeably the crosses they are wearing. Is the visiting figure on the left a Templar?

Edward Wedlake Brayley wrote in 1817 that Margate's name was derived from Mere-gate Old English for Sea-Gate. "Margate, anciently called St John's, from the Saint to whom the Church is dedicated, is a market town...." 3.

Today Margate is known as a seaside resort rather than part of a naval defence administration.

The Secret Dossier of a
Knight Templar of the Sangreal

Famous Visitors & Residents

My main interest in the Isle of Thanet is its hidden past and how it relates to the Templars. However a quick walk through time seems mandatory in order to create a flavourful repast.

Many notables visited, lived or were born on Thanet during the Victorian era on up to present day.

Queen Victoria loved Ramsgate as a girl, other remarkable visitors included Vincent Van Gogh, and queen of the occult world, Madam Blavatsky in 1824. The landscape artist Turner made it a point to stay in Margate where he said that the light was the best in the world. Charles Dickens wrote David Copperfield in Broadstairs within the shadow of a Gothic castellated house said to have inspired Bleak House. The poet and Pre-Raphaelite painter Dante Gabriel Rossetti fell ill with Bright's disease and came in hopes of a recovery. Sadly he died at a friend's home on Easter Sunday in 1882 and was buried at the Birchington cemetery.

Renowned architect, Augustus Pugin, died at the early age of 40 in 1852 and had developed the Gothic Revival style. He was the main designer behind the Palace of Westminster and its famous clock, Big Ben. We owe him a debt of gratitude for the many romantic architectural gems created in his life. Two of which, his home, The Grange and the neighbouring church of St Augustine's in Ramsgate. Very sadly due to his conversion to Catholicism he never achieved the status he deserved in Anglican England until recent years.

Artist Tracy Emin grew up in Margate and remains an avid supporter with frequent high profile visits. This is but a brief list of the interesting people that have lived or passed through Thanet's shores drawn here by its beauty, history and rare sandy beaches.

Courage was a requirement in order to live on the Isle in centuries past due to its proximity to the continent and the ever present danger of invasion on up to Napoleon and Hitler.

In May of 1940 every fishing boat or leisure craft capable of crossing the channel from Thanet did so in order to rescue the trapped British Expeditionary Force and allied French soldiers in Dunkirk. Dubbed the Little Ships of Dunkirk – some 700 vessels left Ramsgate Harbour, making repeated crossings in order to rescue 338,000 men.

Author and Assistant Provincial Grand Master, E.D.Y. Grasby wrote that during WWII the population of Broadstairs alone had gone from 13,500 to a mere 2000 due to the threat of bombings from the air. 4.

Grasby further states:

"Ramsgate, with its harbour and naval base, possessed deep shelters and its three Lodges carried on in spite of 3,700 air raid and 86 shelling warnings, although their Masonic Temple was one of many damaged." 5.

These shelters he writes of are now reopened in 2014 for the general public. The Ramsgate Tunnels were built to protect the public during WWII.

273

The Erasmus Obelisk and the New World

The Royal Air Force of Manston held back the aggressions of the Kaiser during WWI and Nazi Germany of WWII. The Manston Spitfire Museum is a testament to the brave men who repelled enemy attacks in both world wars.

The Spitfire was equipped with the swift Merlin engine which revolutionized flight and gave the much needed edge to the British. It is not uncommon to hear folks remark that the spirit of the Arthurian age had returned as promised to save Britain in her darkest hour, such was the importance of the Merlin engine.

The King's Obelisk

Thanet's sandy beaches and proximity to London saw it become the favoured resort of the middle classes and Royal patronage in the 18th, 19th and 20th centuries.

The Hoy boats from the 1730s onward allowed for inexpensive, quick and fairly safe travel from London down the coast. The sea air, kind microclimate and beautiful vistas were considered a healing and restful break from smog-ridden, fast-paced London.

Ramsgate boasts the only royal harbour in Britain. King George IV bestowed the accolade upon the town in 1821 for the warm hospitality he received. He had chosen the harbour as his embarkation point on numerous occasions to Hanover where he was also King.

A 52.5 foot or 16 metre high obelisk was erected to mark the harbours royal status in 1822 for the return visit of King George. The foundation stone was laid by Lord Liverpool, Lord Warden of the Cinque Ports and weighs 100 tons and is cut from solid Dublin granite. 6.

Inscribed in English and Latin-

To George the Fourth
King of Great Britain and Ireland
The Inhabitants and Visitors of Ramsgate
and the Directors and Trustees of the Harbour
have erected this Obelisk as a grateful record
of his Majesty's gracious condescension
in selecting this Port for
his Embarkation on the 25th September
in Progress to his Kingdom of Hanover
and his happy Return on the 8th November 1821

The Ramsgate obelisk was inspired by the riches out of Egypt which would influence architecture, fashion and treasure hunters (lately known as archaeologists) for decades to come.

Napoleon's army was defeated in Egypt by the British in 1801 and thus all the monuments, antiquities, including the Rosetta Stone, now in the British Museum, fell into the hands of the British.

Napoleon was also interested in Masonic links to Egypt but had lost his valuable hoard.

To say that interest in the ancient culture was high is an understatement as it was actually a fever that gripped Europe and now the British were in command of the flow of antiquities.

As thanks to the British, the Egyptian government gave a massive obelisk to the nation to commemorate the victories of 1801 which had repelled the French from Egypt. The gift was made years later in 1819.

"In 1798 Napoleon Buonaparte, with forty thousand French troops, landed on the coast of Egypt, and soon conquered the country. Admiral Nelson destroyed the French fleet in Aboukir Bay; and at a decisive battle fought within sight of Cleopatra's Needle in 1801, Sir Ralph Abercrombie completely defeated the French army, and rescued Egypt from their dominion." 7.

Un-deciphered at the time, the obelisk was apparently named Cleopatra's Needle by local people though pre-dating the famous queen by 1000 years - the name has stuck.

One of a pair which is now in New York, the red granite monument carved from a single stone, stands 21m/69ft high and weighs 224 tons. Its weight is more than double of the Ramsgate obelisk. The cost to move the single cut stone from Egypt was prohibitive, dangerous and thought impossible.

Sir William Curtis, resident of Ramsgate, was a friend of King George IV whose home he stayed during the night of his departure for Hanover. Curtis and co. would have known of the exciting gift to Britain which had been well received, but also disappointingly, the will and skill to move the behemoth was sorely absent.

The Ramsgate Obelisks spirit cousin lay in the desert sands until 1877 when William James Erasmus Wilson (1809 – 1884) resurrected it from its prone position where it had been laying for nearly 2000 years at Heliopolis.

The great philanthropist, Doctor Wilson, was a preeminent surgeon and known as the father of dermatology. He was also Vice President of the Society of Biblical Archaeology and as such was keenly interested in Egyptology. 8. Wilson's deep interest also flowered from his position as a 33° Mason and a Templar Knight Commander.

Erasmus Wilson was knighted for his efforts to bring the needle to London where it sits on the Victoria Embankment. He funded the operation to the tune of £10,000.00 (approximately £210,000.00 today) a princely sum at the time and engineered the means by which it could make the hazardous journey.

An Oxford Professor, among other notable positions, Sir Erasmus Wilson was a great believer in cleanliness to improve various health aliments from skin to respiratory diseases, and as such was an advocate of steam baths which became a great Victorian pastime. From an aesthetic point of view we can be grateful to him for suggesting a daily bath or shower.

He lived his remaining years in Westgate on Sea in Thanet, having contributed £30,000.00 to the Royal Sea Bathing Hospital, expanding it greatly. As a Director his influence on the cutting edge hospital, which opened in 1791, was broad.

As a committed Christian he was deeply concerned for the health of the poor, especially many children with T.B. from London who were brought to the hospital.

It was thought that the sea air in Thanet was of such exceptional quality that just breathing it could heal maladies. He had the Gothic Chapel built next to the hospital where the front of the nave was vacant of pews in order to allow for wheel-chairs. As always he was ahead of his time by providing for disabled access long before the term was even coined.

In the driveway of the hospital is a bronze statue of Sir Erasmus Wilson, (son of a Scottish naval surgeon) a tribute to his humanity and ingenuity. He was a physically courageous man, industrious and likeable with a Dickensian sense of humour. 9.

His statue within the circular drive is to be considered a metaphorical column or more specifically an obelisk. The Erasmus monument points directly to the New World. I would not have known of his statue's relevance if John Temple had not shared it with me, asking for its inclusion in this book.

Sir Erasmus Wilson © Gretchen Cornwall 2014

The statue of Sir Erasmus had at one point looked out to sea before he had been moved to his current situation. He now faces the chapel.

The Obelisk

The nature of the obelisk is that of a ray of sunlight frozen in time through the medium of stone. The long shaft of the classical monument is capped with an actual pyramid expressing the lofty state of the mega-structure.

The base of the pyramid is of course the perfect square represented by the number four and is the most stable of structures. The apex is the central column or inner obelisk which rushes up to the top point culminating in the eye of god and is indicative of the number five.

The obelisk is a holy monument representing the completed soul and an invocation of the Heavenly-Solar Light on a particular site on earth. Joined together with obelisks across the miles, energetic lines are created or acknowledged.

The Erasmus monument forms the central base for the inner column which leads to the apex of a trans-Atlantic energy obelisk connecting to the Washington

Monument. For ease of future discussion I'll call this energetic light structure the Erasmus Obelisk.

The Erasmus Obelisk investigation below relies on the importance of 0 degrees, 45 degrees and 54 degrees. Obviously both five and four are the numbers of our pyramidal-obelisk from which an exciting synchronistic structure of light is developed. The distance of the Erasmus Obelisk to the Washington Monument, DC = 54° Degrees

To appreciate the connection between the Erasmus Obelisk and Washington D.C. requires a brief explanation of the sacred geometric plan for the city.

The Washington Monument

The Washington Monument was at one time the tallest man-made structure on earth, standing at 555 feet in honour of George Washington the first President of the USA and Commander in Chief of the Continental Army.

It was eclipsed by the Eiffel Tower when it was built in 1889, itself also effectively an obelisk. The Wa. Monument of course looks nothing like the former President which was controversial at the time but when considering his Masonic links and the 'real intention' of sacred city planning, the meaning is clear.

Many studies have been done regarding the hermetic-geometric layout of Washington D.C. Amongst the multitude a few stand out. The brilliant tomes written by Ovason, Tompkins, Hancock and Bauval are sane, measured and without paranoia.

They've explored in great depth the relationships of intersecting boulevards to each other, celestial bodies, solstices and monuments which form sacred patterns. I would also like to add to this short list the brilliant philosopher, Jim Edgar, though his work is not to be found on a bookshelf but online and without cost at:

http://dcsymbols.com/ 10.

His work is of a singular nature, correcting discrepancies and omissions of other authors. He is a master of this subject.

His site is very graphic intensive but I will do my best to condense a few major points as it relates to the Erasmus Obelisk.

Jim Edgar has made an *exhaustive* study of the earliest maps and histories of those involved in the original city planning of 1791 which continued over the decades. The layout of the city is that of three major templates from which other Kabbalistic and Masonic symbols rotate. He discovered a dissection of the Great Pyramid, Metatron Cube and Tree of life which overlay each other.

In his video called The Great Pyramid and the Washington DC Map - available on YouTube – Edgar reminds us that Enoch who lived 365 years was taken up to heaven and transformed into Metatron the Archangel. This story is found within the Royal Arch degree in Masonry and therefore its inclusion in the city planning is made clear.

According to Edgar, New Hampshire Ave is formed by 54 degrees which is larger than the base angle of the Great Pyramid of 52 degrees discovered in 1836. However the city planning maps were done in 1791-1792 without accurate measurements but not outside of the knowledge of ancient Egyptian cosmic measurements.

With amazing insight he found that Potomac Avenue was the Descending Passage and Pennsylvania Avenue was the Ascending Passage of the Great Pyramid! The angle of the two streets where they meet is 26.5 degrees exactly that of the Great Pyramid.

Bonaparte Before the Sphinx, (ca.1868) by Jean-Léon Gérôme, Hearst Castle

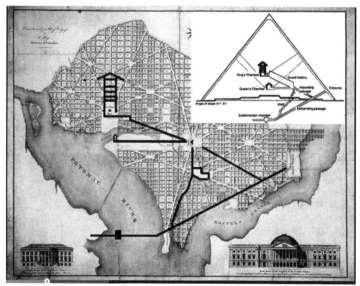

© Jim Edgar's presentation 11.
on http://www.youtube.com/watch?v=-hqVwDT2iWU

The White House represents the Kings Chamber and the Washington Monument represents the Queen's Chamber, which is exactly under the apex of the Great

279

The Erasmus Obelisk and the New World

Pyramid. Interesting that the Queens Chamber should be central to the apex and that the King's is offset? The Erasmus Obelisk shown to me by my contact culminates on the Wa. Monument and is inside the Queen's Chamber of the Great Pyramid of the capitol city.

The pentagram in the street layout as shown below is left unfinished in order to 'trap the devil' (read Faust) preventing harm from coming to the city and its population; quite the opposite intention of the claims of ill-informed anti-Masonic hysterics. Unfortunately, fear, gossip and sex sells – few want to hear good news.

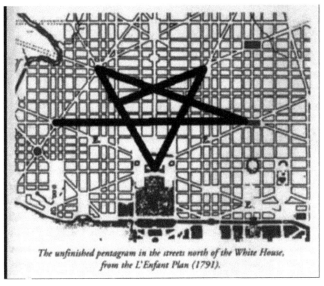

The unfinished pentagram in the streets north of the White House, from the L'Enfant Plan (1791).

© Jim Edgar - http://www.youtube.com/watch?v=-hqVwDT2iWU 12.

To 'complete' the pentagram in order to tell another story which will become the Metatron Cube and Tree of Life – Edgar drew the following lines on the L'Enfant Plan of 1791.

© Jim Edgar - http://www.youtube.com/watch?v=-hqVwDT2iWU 13.

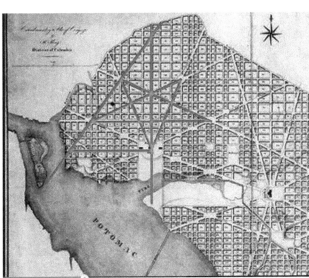

The Secret Dossier of a
Knight Templar of the Sangreal

The pentagram becomes the grid for the street plan. Measuring the base angles of the isosceles triangle which forms the pentagram gives us 54 degrees with an apex of 72 degrees. According to Edgar's colleague Jim Alison, the measurement seemed to echo the creation triangle used by the Egyptians known as the MR triangle of 36-54-90. The measurements of the pentagram display the city planner's knowledge of ancient Egyptian faith and also their expression of the building blocks of the cosmos.

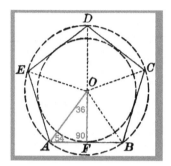 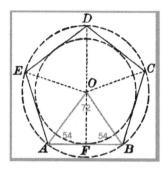

© Jim Edgar - http://www.youtube.com/watch?v=-hqVwDT2iWU 14.

The dimension of the base line casing stones of the Great Pyramid were not known until after 1836. How did the city planners of 1791-1792 come within 2 degrees let alone know the exact interior measurements of the Great Pyramid or that there was a subterranean chamber? Had there been a secret expedition? Edgar asks the pertinent question 'what else' can we learn about the Great Pyramid from the avenues of Washington D.C.? Egyptologists today have speculated that there must be further hidden chambers within.

The marriage of heaven and earth is to be found at the Capitol Building facing due west, with its symmetrical cross-quarter day markers of Maryland Ave and Pennsylvania Ave.

Sunset in Nov & Feb   Sunset in May & Aug

The Capitol Building 1850 Maryland Ave on Left - Wa. Mo. in the centre distance – Penn Ave on Right.

Cross-Quarter (meaning four) days are halfway between the solstices and the equinoxes giving us twelve spokes to the calendar year.

One Cross-Quarter day marks the statistical cold height of winter in early February whilst the opposite warm spike is that of early August. Edgar puts these weather peaks down to the 6th of each corresponding month, sometimes this event is expressed on the 7th to the 8th. The other two cross-quarter dates fall in May and November.

The sun sets in November and February on the aligned Maryland Ave and on Pennsylvania Ave in May and Aug. Washington D.C. is aligned to four sunsets not just one - and to two avenues not just a singular avenue! What can this mean?

According to astrology the months of May, Aug, Nov and Feb all relate to the houses of the fixed signs Taurus, Leo, Scorpio and Aquarius. The corresponding icons represent the bull, lion, man and an eagle of the four gospels of Matthew, Mark, Luke and John.

So, by implication the above study is an invocation of the four gospels for the blessing of the city and therefore the new country and based on the New Testament. I must ask as I have in prior chapters regarding the time wasting subject of heresy, when is a Christian – not a Christian? And is that up to other 'rival' Christian denominations or outside antagonists to decide? No, it is not.

I highly recommend reading Jim Edgar's dissertation and watching his videos as they are truly stunning and brimming with positive implications and real scholarship.

http://www.youtube.com/watch?v=-hqVwDT2iWU 15.

I have taken a screen shot of the pertinent monuments in Google Earth to better illustrate the points of the Cross-Quarter days culminating in the four major sunsets in the west.

A broad corridor which is the National Mall, creates line of sight kinship with the Lincoln Memorial to the Washington Monument and the Capitol Building at the eastern most point. If we stand at the Washington Monument and face east we will catch the rising sun.

One can see in the east at early nightfall in July - the 'Summer Triangle' formed by Deneb of the constellation Cygnus, Altair and Vega the brightest star of the three. Aside from Venus and Jupiter, Sirius is the brightest object in the night sky. The Egyptians marked their New Year with the heliacal rising of Sirius.

"The ancient Egyptians devised a method of telling the time at night based on the heliacal risings of 36 stars called decan stars (one for each 10° segment of the 360° circle of the zodiac/calendar)." 16.

The Secret Dossier of a
Knight Templar of the Sangreal

Sirius is the undisputed star of ancient Egypt. It was and is important to gnostic Christianity and also esoteric masonry.

However I do think that the city planner's main intention was that of the sun in relation to the Washington Monument. In Masonry, noon is of the greatest import due to the sun's brightest moment during the day. *'Let there be Light, and there was'*.

I've read varying accounts of the time from exactly 12 noon to Ovason who states that it was 1:30 PM for the laying of the cornerstone on July 4th 1848, of the Washington Monument.

Google Earth Software image of the Capitol Building & Washington Monument. The National Mall with the Cross-Quarter avenues marked in yellow with the Erasmus Obelisk in white touching the Washington Monument.

The number four is played out with the sunset avenue markers. The rising of the sun on the Wa. Monument gives us the total number of five celestial events including the sun.

Was there another ancient inspiration for the plan of the famous city layout? The National Mall with the Washington Monument bears a striking resemblance as an enlarged version of Constantine's 4th century Hippodrome. 'Hippo' meaning horse in Greek, could seat as many as 100,000 people for chariot races and other public events for his new shinning Christian city. He had imported from Egypt the Obelisk of Thutmose III and also the four headed Serpent Column from the Delphi temple in Greece. The Walled Obelisk was built much later to commemorate Constantine VII.

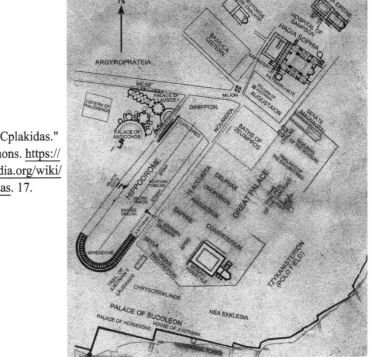

Cplakidas. "User:Cplakidas." Wikimedia Commons. https://commons.wikimedia.org/wiki/User:Cplakidas. 17.

The angle of the Hippodrome's obelisks denoting the centre of the arena is, however, closer to 51° due east to the rising sun which is a striking synchronicity tying Washington DC, Constantinople and the Erasmus Obelisk together.

According to the Encyclopaedia Britannica, the sides of the Great Pyramid rise at an angle of 51°52' – such an exact measurement was only recently possible. An invisible hand outside of time and space seems to be at play here bringing the ancient Egyptian culture together with Constantinople and the new Washington D.C.

The Washington Monument was originally meant to be an equine statue but this was changed in 1836 to a costly and elaborate Greek column surrounded by a colonnade, a chariot with the hero George Washington and 30 statues of his compatriots around him. A winged Egyptian Sun Disc was also included in the design which suggests to me that the National Mall and the Washington Monument had solar inspiration. Due to cost the entire effort was reduced to the tallest man-made structure in the world at that time - an elegantly simplified Egyptian ray of light known as an obelisk.

It is clear to see by the broad width of the National Mall by comparison to the sunset avenue markers, that the Wa. Monument high noon is of great importance. The 'spire' of the Erasmus Obelisk touches the Washington Monument and is marked in white above.

The Secret Dossier of a
Knight Templar of the Sangreal

The Erasmus Obelisk

The Prime Meridian is the zero base of the Erasmus Obelisk reaching from Britain and France, intersecting with the Heronian Tetrahedron, across Nova Scotia to the Washington Monument.

Listed below are the coordinates for the illustration above provided by John Temple.

North Sea (North base of Obelisk)

54°54'54.54"N

0° 0'0.00"E

Intersects the Heronian Tetrahedron & Extends to -

North Atlantic – Labrador Sea

54°54'54.54"N

54°54'54.54"W

Saint-Cybardeaux, France (South base of Obelisk)

45°45'45.45"N

0° 0'0.00"E

Extends to -

Atlantic Ocean – (Nova Scotia)

45°45'45.45"N

45°45'45.45"W

Kolbec (Nova Scotia)

45°45'45.45"N

63°48'48.63"W = Starting Point Kolbec/Apex

Newport Tower, Rhode Island, USA distance to the Cathedral in Newport Wales = 46.4° Degrees

Newport Tower, Rhode Island, USA:

41°29'09"N 71°18'36"W

41.4858°N 71.3099°W

Cathedral Newport Wales:

51°34'59"N

2°59'55"W

Westford Knight

42°35'15.48"N

71°26'4.65"W

Westford Knight to Newport Tower = 1.10 ° Degrees

Ross Castle

44°44'23.18"N

64°27'26.33"W

The Erasmus Obelisk and the New World

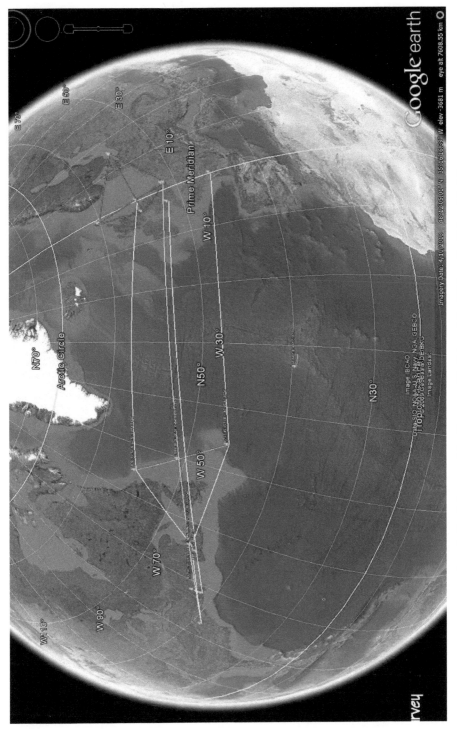

Google Earth image of the Erasmus Obelisk and the H.T. on the Prime Meridian

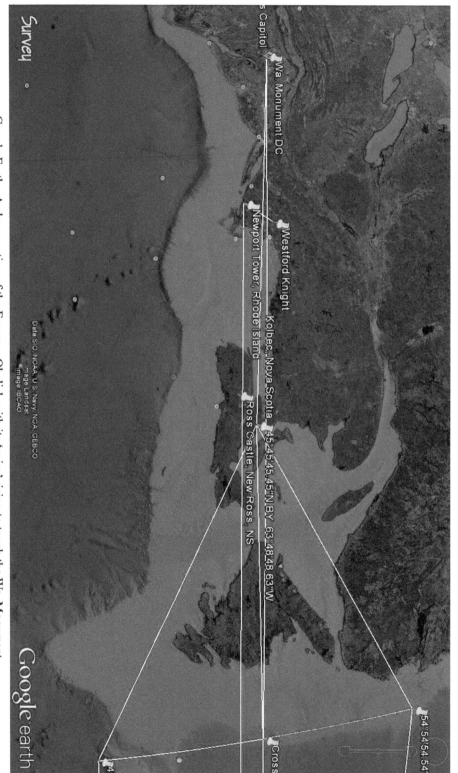

Google Earth - A close section of the Erasmus Obelisk with its 'spire' rising to touch the Wa. Monument.

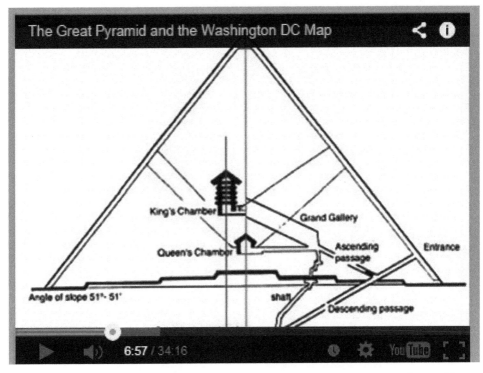

Jim Edgar's screen shot of the Kings and Queens chamber at mark 6:57 minutes. 18.

I have surmised that the spire of the Erasmus Obelisk represents the risen sun at high noon. The Queen's Chamber within the Great Pyramid also represents an obelisk and the apex of the pyramid is the spire of the risen sun.

The situation takes another very interesting synchronistic turn. Please consider the following image on the next page with coordinates in the east using the number four and five in repeated patterns:

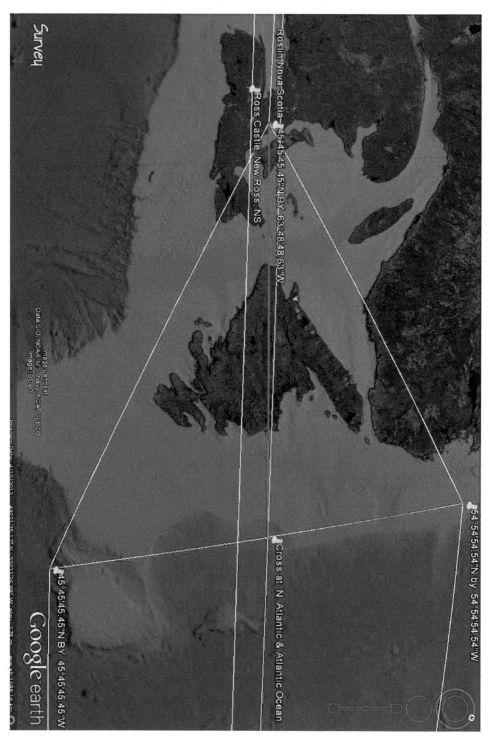

The Erasmus Obelisk and the New World

The line marked in red above marks the actual apex of the light monument located at Kolbec, Nova Scotia 45°45'45.45"N - 63°48'48.63"W and intersects the Erasmus Obelisk line in yellow. The spelling for Kolbec in the UK is actually Caldbeck which was discussed at length in earlier chapters. Within 1.46 miles of Kolbec is Roslin Nova Scotia!

The centre line, yellow, created from the Erasmus monument at the Royal Sea-bathing hospital, Westbrook in Margate travels to the Washington Monument just missing the actual apex of the pyramidal triangle.

If the red centre line of the Erasmus Obelisk is the Queens Chamber, can it be possible that the secondary horizontal line in white which begins at the Newport Cathedral in Newport Wales, 51°34'59"N - 2°59'55"W represents the 'Kings Chamber'? It intersects with Ross Castle in New Ross, Nova Scotia and finds its apex at the Newport Tower, Rhode Island!

As for the small towns of Kolbec and Roslin, Nova Scotia, what undiscovered Templar archaeological treasures lay waiting to be discovered?

The Rosslyn Matrix

The phrase 'Rosslyn Matrix' was coined by author Ashley Cowie for his book of the same name. He pondered the mysterious carving in the crypt of Rosslyn Chapel which is on the south wall. Cowie wondered if the odd carving which resembles an electrical pylon, at first glance, could not have actually been a representation of an actual surveying tool. Curators of Rosslyn Chapel assert it is a representation of one of the many load bearing pinnacles; however Cowie rightly states that it in no way shape or form comes close to any of the pinnacles adorning the mid-15th century chapel.

Cowie discovered that the lattice work bore strong similarities to Ptolemy's system for mapping the northern hemisphere of the known world. The base of the matrix represented the equator.

"The number of times the map projected round to complete the circle was twenty-four which of course equals the number of hours in a day. Thus, by simply dividing 360 by 24, one twenty-fourth section of arc, it corresponded to 15 degrees. The carving represented precisely 15 degrees of longitudinal arc. Therefore it also defines a specific time. This 15 degree section, this one twenty-fourth of a global arc, is also the equivalent of one earth hour, the time it takes for earth to rotate 15 degrees on its axis." 19.

Based on Ashley Cowie's photo from the Rosslyn Matrix 20.

The chapel's neighbour, Roslin Castle, held a scriptorium during the 15th century. Now in the National Library of Scotland, the Rosslyn-Hay manuscript described Ptolemy's geographical treatise which had been treasured by the earls and signed by William Sinclair builder of the chapel! 21.

The Secret Dossier of a
Knight Templar of the Sangreal

Just when the carving was laid down is difficult to know since the crypt predates the chapel by 250 years. However its neighbouring carving on the opposite wall is that of an arch in the chapel above. Plus we have the evidence of Ptolemy's geographia in the Sinclair library. The Rosslyn Matrix appears to be a device inspired by Ptolemy but what genius could have reinterpreted prior surveying tools into this masterpiece? St. Catherine's wheel or compass is also one of the carvings in the crypt.

As well as being an actual portable standing device - is the Rosslyn Matrix a Mural sextant? The first such was constructed in the 10th century in Iran. With a radius of twenty meters the mural sextant measured sixty degrees arc on a wall aligned along a meridian arc with the ability to calculate seconds. 22. The link between Islamic scholarship and trade with the west is well established. Could the knowledge of Mural sextants from the Far East have reached the earls of Roslin? Could it have flowed in the opposite direction and earlier European models are either misunderstood or lost?

The concept for the enigmatic carving as both land and celestial surveyor's tool was brought to my attention by Comte de Medici. In a prior chapter I highlighted the work of Crichton E. M. Miller who had back-engineered the Celtic Cross technology. I had further outlined the possible progression of this into St Catherine's compass and Pierre de Maricourt's 12th century letter outlining the magnetic properties of the loadstone. He had also made strides concerning the astrolabe. Later generations developed Jacob's Staff with its transoms. All seem to echo their later cousin, the Rosslyn Matrix, which can be no misfit to the underground technology of the Templars.

The illustration opposite was created in Adobe Photoshop with a screen capture from Google Earth of the Erasmus Obelisk which is shown in white. The Rosslyn Matrix image in red was developed from Cowie's original photo.

The Heronian Tetrahedron is visible in the upper right corner intersected by the Prime Meridian or zero degrees.

The Erasmus Obelisk and the New World

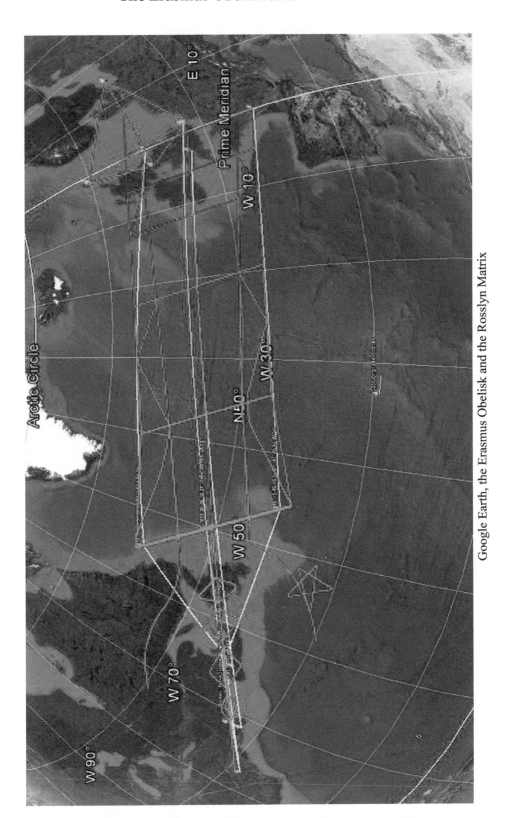

The Secret Dossier of a
Knight Templar of the Sangreal

Cowie made a separate study of the lozenge shapes, determining they were directional, tied to the solstices and surprisingly were actual locations in Scotland. The Comte decided to take the carving off the wall and apply it to a map of the world and then sent the coordinates to myself for implementation. Using the Rosslyn Matrix as a synchronistic location marker proved to be stunning. Please see the results listed in number sequence below.

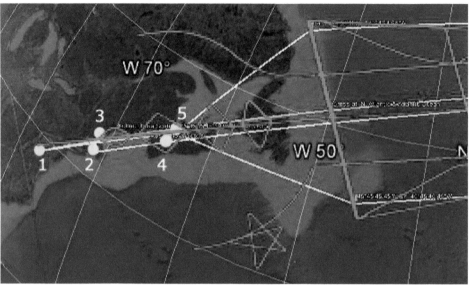

Google Earth, the Rosslyn Matrix Chalice and the five Templar monuments

1. Washington Monument D.C.
2. Newport Tower, Rhode Island
3. Westford Knight
4. Ross Castle
5. Kolbeck & Roslin, Nova Scotia

I'd like to point out the symmetrical ideal of the numbers four and five in the four lozenges and the pentagram in relation to the concept of 444 – 555 and 54 degrees.

The chalice also takes in Newfoundland. Its provincial capital is St John's in the S.E. – Cape Spear is just further on from the capitol. It was the first North American proto-colony having first been visited by Henry VII's contract captain, John Cabot in 1497.

Stella Maris

The cup of the R.M. is a bit wobbly to such an extent that it looks careless. How could precision-driven stonemasons have built Rosslyn chapel and yet carved such a lazy structure on its crypt wall? Cowie deduced that the grail may outline the path of Stella Maris AKA Venus as viewed on the horizon. The morning and evening star dips below our line of sight and returns to become the Horns of Venus.

The pentagram appears to be sliding down the left side of the cup, indicating celestial movement. The five pointed star is also the path of Venus over an eight year period in the night sky. Moses the leader of the Jewish peoples and Egyptian priest is often shown with horns. Could this be a remembrance of astronomical knowledge which he would have been trained to use?

Applied as a landmark relational tool the chalice of the R.M. holds Nova Scotia within its dimensions highlighting enigmas associated with the Knights Templar adventures in the New World. It appears that the Roslin Templars built land markers along the directional lines of the Rosslyn Matrix in the New World. The carving of the device on the chapel itself held keys to their secret locations and method of navigation.

Is there anything else that may be deduced from the pentagram of Venus in relation to the New Jerusalem? Author Robert Lomas states that the number five represents the divine nature of humanity if we will only reach for it. The five steps up to the second degree of Masonry leaves the world of human suffering and negative animal expression behind and flowers into the kingdom of the Initiates. 23. Humanity can embrace the fifth kingdom, their inner five pointed star and connection to the unknowable climbs. We are at the beginning of our next phase of evolution and not the culmination. We are so much more than we imagine and with so much more to look forward to!

"For those who learn to perceive it, this Morning Star will break forth in full splendour, its rising bringing peace and salvation to those who faithfully and obediently pursue it." Robert Lomas 24.

Ezekiel, Chapter's 1 and 2, use the number five in three instances to describe a fiery vision of god:

1 Now it came to pass in the thirtieth year, in the fourth month, in the fifth day of the month, as I was among the captives by the river of Chebar, that the heavens were opened, and I saw visions of God.

2 In the fifth day of the month, which was the fifth year of king Jehoiachin's captivity, The Bible, King James Version

Ezekiel continues the infusion of number play using 'four' no less than thirteen times. He describes four beings with qualities in multiples of four. Their features comprised of an ox, eagle, man and lion with four wings, hands and wheels which moved in accord with each other. As the conglomerate Being approached Ezekiel a blue sapphire throne appeared and the figure of a man spoke to the priest from above the four winged creatures.

The image reminded me sharply of the Light Beings that Dannion Brinkley reported in his book Saved by the Light wherein he describes a Near Death Experience. Dannion found himself transported to a Light Cathedral, seated, and facing the high altar where thirteen Light Beings stood. Twelve of the individuals represented the astrological houses and bore the visages of their associated icons. The central figure embodied the twelve around 'him' and appeared to have all their qualities, as if they were a group mind with the brightest individual as their leader. 25.

The Secret Dossier of a
Knight Templar of the Sangreal

Did the Templars have visions of the same Light Beings that Dannion Brinkley spoke of when he had been pronounced clinically dead for 20 minutes? Were the Templars introducing Biblical number symmetry into navigation (or from it?) and developing temples on synchronistic locations to embody the values of higher dimensional beings and that of their ancestor Jesus? Based upon the assembled evidence in preceding chapters I would have to say for myself I am certain this is the case.

The practice and recognition of sacred geometry in the landscape is an allegory for the inner citadel and higher dimensional planes of existence. The use of the obelisk is an invocation to the heavenly solar Christ to bless, by infusing His Light, on a particular location and at the centre of those invoking Him.

The Four Crowned Martyrs

The importance of the numbers four and five are revisited in an historical memory of relevance today. The simple phrase, 'the Four Crowned Martyrs' is ultimately a statement of political freedom, religious reform and representative of the rise of working class guilds and their craft secrets.

The legend bears a direct tie to the Isle of Thanet through St Sebastian and St Augustine. St Sebastian's chapel has all but disappeared but according to old maps and legends was just off of Poor Hole Lane on Chapel Hill also called Sacketts Hill. The names are testament in themselves that there had been a chapel there in centuries past.

According to the 13th century Golden Legend written by Jacopo da Voragine, Sebastian assisted in the burial of four Christian martyrs of the 4th century AD.

The men were specialists in their field as soldiers and clerics of the Roman Empire. As Cornicularii, they were in charge of record keeping for their regiment which was incredibly important since most were illiterate. These men are considered to be part of what is called the 'First Group' under the umbrella of the Four Crowned Martyrs. The 'Second Group' comprised of five sculptors also died at the hand of Diocletian.

Group One is honoured on August 8th and Group Two is honoured on November 8th which again occurs near the Cross Quarter days of high summer and the beginning of fall. Both Groups became the patrons of medieval masons for their joint abilities of record keeping and stonemasonry.

Bede noted that there had been a church dedicated to the nine men in Canterbury. Saint Augustine had spent time in a monastery near the basilica of Santi Quattro Coronati where the nine saints' relics had been located. It seems an easy reach that he had brought their memory to England although it is also possible that their legend was already being commemorated by the Romano Britains. Is it possible that the lost chapel of St. Sebastian's on Thanet had a connection to the extinct chapel in Canterbury through the Four Crowns? It is the only place name on the Isle which is not Brythonic, Romano-Britain or of Norse decent and is therefore unique.

The nine men jointly are called the Sancti Quatuor Coronati which inspired an academic journal & lodge in London called the Quatuor Coronati which began in 1884 and whose emblem is a lozenge with four crowns and swords. Their founding members also were nine in total.

The Erasmus Obelisk and the New World

"Nothing could throw more light on the connection between the Roman Collegia and the medieval Gilds, so far as England is concerned, than the discovery of some earlier history of the Church of the Four Crowned Martyrs at Canterbury, and the mention by Bede of its existence in A. D. 619, at the time of the great fire which nearly destroyed the city and only stopped when this church was reached." 26.

The church of the Four Crowns in Canterbury must have been built in stone and therefore survived the fire. The original Anglo-Saxon wood structures would have burnt but a stone structure built by a Christianized Roman Collegia of stonemasons would have remained. Could St. Sebastian in Margate been its twin? Half of Thanet prior to the Reformation had been under the See of Canterbury. I would think that this connection is probable.

There are ancient, tantalizing hints across Europe, that an evolving Roman Collegia of stonemasons became the working class medieval guilds and in jointure with the Cistercians – evolved into the Knights Templar. That their predecessors were here in humble Thanet many centuries prior appears more than credible.

Within eighteen years of the nine saints' murder, Constantine, who had fought with his father in Britain, adopted the new faith. It was only natural that the hard working Christian artisans of Rome chose the Four Crowns as their patrons. It was indeed a choice which spoke of democratic values on behalf of the esoterica within the guilds to venerate the nine men.

The Shepherds of Arcadia

'Et In Arcadia Ego' by Nicolas Poussin, 1637 - 1638

The Secret Dossier of a
Knight Templar of the Sangreal

The large estate of Shugborough Hall in Staffordshire contains many Neoplatonic follies but one stands out amongst them and even the casual observer must admit it holds a secret in plain sight. Many including Charles Dickens have tried to crack the code of the Shepherd's Monument and failed.

The strange mid-18th century carving was adapted from the Nicolas Poussin painting of the prior century. The image is reversed from the painting called 'Et In Arcadia Ego' meaning 'Even in Arcadia, I Am'.

'Et In Arcadia Ego' is also an anagram for 'I Tego Arcana Dei' which translates to 'Begone! I conceal God's Secrets' - a suitable warning to those seeking to loot a tomb holding precious secrets.

Aside from the reversal of the painting a sarcophagus with a wreath and pyramid was included on top of the tomb along with an enigmatic code below it.

The Shepherd's Monument © Gretchen Cornwall 2011

The code of ten letters is oddly spaced just under the carving of the shepherds

O.U.S.V.A.V.V.
D.   M.

Author and historian, Dave Ramsden has come up with what I believe to be the best solution for the monument. In his work, Unveiling the Mystic Ciphers, Ramsden has decoded the famous ten letters to reveal the name Magdalene. The woman looking over the ponderings of the Shepherds has long been linked to the Magdalene.

Thomas Anson (1695 – 1773) the owner of the estate and the designer for the monument had been inspired by ancient Egypt. Amongst the books in his library was a copy of the Askew Codex.

"This codex contained the first known Coptic translation of the *Pistis Sophia*, a gnostic gospel in which Mary Magdalen played a significant role as a spiritual leader." 27.

Ramsden asks the pertinent question, how did Anson know of the relevance of Mary Magdalene as the Gnostic Gospels were not discovered until the 20th century. He postulates that Anson was part of an existing mystery tradition that valued the Magdalene's role as the Goddess of Christianity and the Queen of Heaven.

Amongst Poussin's pastoral scene are sacred geometry links to the landscape of Rennes le Chateau. The Seal of Solomon and the Pentagram formed by Templar and Cathar landmarks dotted the countryside. The over-all geometry of the Poussin painting is based on the pentagon.

Many have wondered if the tomb in southern France that Poussin used in the painting was that of the Magdalene. The Shugborough Monument has reversed the image which some have taken to mean that her relics are now in Nova Scotia. The tomb was destroyed by the owner of the property in France to prevent tourists with buckets and spades digging up his land. It is now against the law to attempt any exploratory digging in the region such has been the proliferation of treasure hunters.

I pondered my own photo of the Shugborough Monument along with Henry Lincoln's geometry patterns and felt inspired to measure the angle of the pyramid atop the sarcophagus which led me to consider the broader picture.

I was rewarded with a pentagon! It is highly significant as the pentagon is the focal point of the geometry for the Poussin painting from which the geometrical patterns Lincoln found to back engineer the Templar landmarks in France.

I borrowed Jim Edgar's encircled pentagon from his work on the Washington D.C. city plan on the following page. The photo of the carving is tilted and therefore not to scale. I am not able to present it 'square on' but the measurements are real. The top of the pyramid is 108° and the entire pentagon is sympathetic to both Lincoln's experiment of the Poussin painting and Jim Edgar's Masonic plan of Washington D.C.

I believe that Thomas Anson who designed the Shugborough Monument had conducted the same geometry experiment as Henry Lincoln with the same results on the Poussin painting. He discovered that Poussin had designed the painting around the Pentagon which forms the five pointed star. Did he actually discover its relation to the landscape as Henry Lincoln had? It is possible.

Anson became a Fellow of the Royal Society, studied law and architecture with a focus on Greece. His estate is strewn with references to Greek and Egyptian mythology which includes paintings and statues of goddesses.

He formed the Dillettanti Society with the Earl of Sandwich and was acquainted

The Secret Dossier of a
Knight Templar of the Sangreal

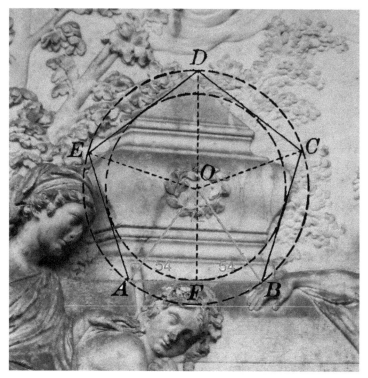

Photo by © Gretchen Cornwall –
Pentagon overlay based on Jim Edgar's graphic

with Lord Dashwood of the infamous Hell Fire Club. He supported the Egyptian Society and made many trips to Europe.

Anson encoded the key to his findings in the sarcophagus topped with a capstone upon the original tomb in the Poussin painting. He wanted to let the onlooker know he had reverse-engineered the painting and its secrets and found Her.

Anson had a portrait of himself done wearing 'oriental' costume; was he telling us that he held a Gnostic Christian view of the world which sprang out of Egypt and was reincarnated into Mary Magdalene as the new Eve and her husband, Jesus? The Magdalene was the first to see the risen Christ. The tradition of her as the redeemed new Eve began in the 3rd century according to Ramsden.

In wonderful synchronistic harmony perhaps Anson also knew that 54° degrees was the key to the resting place of an important Saint and or other highly sensitive objects known to have been taken to Nova Scotia. His brother was, after all, Admiral George Anson, who paid for the Shugborough Monument. It appears that the Shepherds of Arcadia are still watching over the legacy of the Magdalene in the French countryside, England and in Nova Scotia.

1. Hillier, Caroline. *The Bulwark Shore: Thanet and the Cinque Ports*. London: E. Methuen, 1980.

2. Cawthorne, Bob. *The Isle of Thanet Compendium*. Broadstairs: Scribble and Doodle Books, 2007. p. 44

3. Brayley, Edward Wedlake. *Delineations Historical and Topographical of the Isle of Thanet and the Cinque Ports,*. Vol. Volume 1. 1817. p. 19

4. *The Province Of Kent 1770-1970*. Canterbury: J. A. Jennings, 1970. p. 82

5. Ibid p. 82

6. "Ramsgate Obelisk." Obelisk. http://www.ramsgatetown.org/history/landmarks-monuments/obelisk.aspx.

7. King, Reverend James, Rev. *Cleopatra's Needle: A History of the London Obelisk, with an Exposition of the Hieroglyphics*. London: Religious Tract Society, 1886. p. 40

8. Strange, F. G. St. Clair. *The History of the Royal Sea Bathing Hospital, Margate, 1791-1991*. Rainham, Kent: Meresborough Books, 1991. p. 75

9. Ibid p. 75

10. Edgar, Jim. "From Pentagram to Pyramids:." Masonic and Kabbalistic Symbols In the Washington D.C. Map. http://dcsymbols.com/.

11. Edgar, Jim. "The Great Pyramid and the Washington DC Map." YouTube. http://www.youtube.com/watch?v=-hqVwDT2iWU.

12. Ibid

13. Ibid

14. Ibid

15. Ibid

16. "Heliacal Rising." Wikipedia. http://en.wikipedia.org/wiki/Heliacal_rising.

17. Cplakidas. "User:Cplakidas." Wikimedia Commons. https://commons.wikimedia.org/wiki/User:Cplakidas.

18. Edgar, Jim. "The Great Pyramid and the Washington DC Map." YouTube. http://www.youtube.com/watch?v=-hqVwDT2iWU.

19. Cowie, Ashley. *The Rosslyn Matrix*. East Kilbride: Wicker World, 2006.

20. Ibid. p. 70

21. Ibid 68

22. "Sextant." Wikipedia. http://en.wikipedia.org/wiki/Sextant_(astronomical).

23. Lomas, Robert. *The Secret Science of Masonic Initiation*. London: Lewis Masonic, 2008. p. 25

24. Ibid 37

25. Brinkley, Dannion, and Paul Perry. *Saved by the Light: The True Story of a Man Who Died Twice and the Profound Revelations He Received*. New York: Villard Books, 1994. p. 50

26. Clarke, C. Purdon, Bro., and Stephen Dafoe. "Masonic History." The Four Patron Saints Of Masons. http://www.masonicdictionary.com/fourcrown2.html.
Quatuor Coronati Lodge in 1919

27. Ramsden, Dave. *Unveiling the Mystic Ciphers*. New York: CreateSpace, 2014. p. 88

Thirty One

The Stars of the Magdalene

The Neoplatonic School, which infused itself into western Kabbalistic practices, used the five-pointed star as a symbol of recognition. According to later Gnostic Christians it represents not only Jesus and the five wounds of the crucifixion, but also the Magdalene. In Freemasonry it exemplifies the five senses and the five points of brotherhood and in the inverted form, the Daughters of Job. Thanks to Brother Gerald Gardner, the pentacle is the sign of recognition for Neo-Pagans.

The pentagram appears as the heraldic devise of Sir Gawain in the 14th Century poem Sir Gawain and the Green Knight. The poem states that the five-pointed star originated with King Solomon and is the key to the 'work'.

Many truths in one simple line drawing from which spring deeper sacred geometrical images of antiquity and – like the layers of an onion – further stories which lead one ever on through the garden.

The five-pointed star had become the emblem of Western Enlightenment worth a book - in a single and elegant image.

Esoteric Freemason, Brother William Steve Burkle Kt, 32° of http://www.freemasons-freemasonry.com, describes in his article with beautiful detail, how the Rosicrucians absorbed ancient knowledge from the Platonic mystery school and Kabbalistic thought into the human form calling upon the Christ to dwell within.

Figure 3 - The Pentagram Labeled to indicate the significance of each apex (After Regardie)

Based on Brother William Steve Burkle Kt, 32°, The Tetragrammaton, the Pentagrammaton, and the Adam Kadmon: A Fusion of Christian and Hebrew Mysticism. http://www.freemasons-freemasonry.com/Adam_Kadmon.html 1.

The points of the pentacle absorbed within the body represent the five elements on the tree of life. It is the evolved name of the Tetragrammaton from Yod Heh Vav Heh or Jehovah into the Pentagrammaton Yod, Heh SHIN, Vav Heh pronounced as Yeheshuah the name of Jesus.

http://www.freemasons-freemasonry.com/
Adam_Kadmon.html 2.

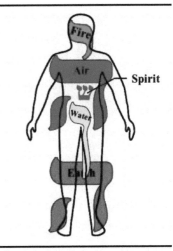

The illustration to the right is no less than a standing meditation, and if pressed for space 'drawing' the pentagram in the air in front of oneself may also be done or silently done. It is a prayer asking for the Divine One to manifest within from above.

How does Mary Magdalene fit into this explanation? Obviously Judaic mysticism predates her and the above outlines a male presence but Jesus brought in a new impetus and she came with him. As always with Templarism we must look deeper. According to Judaic beliefs Shin is the feminine spirit of god and means to dwell.

Figure 6 – The Adam Kadmon formed from the Pentagrammaton, and representing Jesus.

Shin is the first letter of the Shekinah who was sent by god to dwell among humanity as protection and blessing. She is the wife of God whose predecessor is Isis.

When the Shekinah is acknowledged in the Temple all those present cover their eyes and do not look upon her countenance as she is potent and will cause them irreparable damage or death. The warning is very similar to the dangers of not being prepared or authorized to touch the Ark of the Covenant otherwise death or serious injury will follow.

Her presence protects those voluntarily blindfolded within the Temple. The hands of the Rabbi raised over the congregation mimic the letter Shin and is the hand sign used by the wonderful Leonard Nimoy as Spock in Star Trek. 3. https://www.youtube.com/watch?v=DyiWkWcR86I

From the Synagoge of Enschede Mozaiek by Kleuske

The Secret Dossier of a
Knight Templar of the Sangreal

'If two sit together and the words between them are of the Torah, then the Shekinah is in their midst' Rabbi Hananiah ben Teradion (ca,135 CE) 4. The ancient Judaic saying is hauntingly familiar and echoed in Matthew 18:20, 'For when two or three are gathered together in my name, there am I in the midst of them'. KJV.

The act of including the Divine Feminine in the five pointed star symbol is healing and equalizing for those who follow any of the three major religions.

Gnostic Christians who knew of the marriage between Jesus and the Magdalene adopted the pentacle as a way to perpetuate the practical information and the ideal of priestly marriage. The pentacle has been found in French cathedrals which spread out across Europe through the Templars.

Author Alan Butler ascribes the pentacle to the goddess in Christianity and outlines in his book - The Virgin and the Pentacle - how Freemasons kept alive the memory of Isis through the Virgin Mary and the Goddess of Reason.

In December of 1793 the "Goddess of Reason" was enthroned in the Notre Dame Cathedral of Paris. It was an act by the Revolutionaries that placed science in the forefront and was meant to dispel blind acceptance of religion without vetting the provenance behind it.

The actress Mlle Maillard was dressed in the robes of the goddess and lit a candle on the high altar. 5. Her candle would become the Torch of Truth in the hand of Beauty, the Statue of Liberty which dispels ignorance thus protecting humanity.

Through Roman hands in England, this same goddess was Britannia with her trident, which is an allusion to the Spear of Destiny. The light held aloft by the Statue of Liberty is also doubly the Spear of Destiny.

Athena-Minerva was the only female virgin birth in religious myth by her father the king of the gods, Zeus. The smith-god Vulcan was called to Zeus to help relieve a tremendous headache which had plagued him.

Vulcan split the monarchs head open and out sprang a fully grown daughter dressed in armour with innate wisdom and gifts for humanity. She carried the spear and wore the helmet of invisibility with an owl as her totem. Her visage has been traced from Isis to the Greeks and Romans and finally to the Statue of Liberty.

Minerva Expelling the Vices from the Garden of Virtue by Andrea Mantegna (1502)

303

The Stars of the Magdalene

The Thirteen Lady Liberties of France

The French gifted the great New York icon of welcome to their revolutionary brethren of North America. The French rather than erecting their own massive statue of Lady Liberty chose to build the scaled down versions listed below:

*Île aux Cygnes - or in English - Swan Island in the River Seine

Pont de Grenelle

*Luxembourg Gardens Musée d'Orsay

*Musée des Arts et Métiers

Flame of Liberty, Life size copy of the torch

(Pont de l'Alma tunnel near the Champs-Élysées)

*Barentin near Rouen

*Saint-Cyr-sur-Mer- Frédéric Bartholdi

*Poitiers

*Lunel

*The Musée des beaux-arts de Lyon in terracotta

*Châteauneuf-la-Forêt, near Limoges in the region of Haute-Vienne, Limousin

*An "original" Bartholdi replica at Roybon (near Grenoble)

*Colmar France of the Alsace Loraine region in 2004 –

*Bordeaux

*Saint Martin des Champ, Paris France

I have endeavoured to be thorough in the list and hope I've not missed another French Lady Liberty. There are many more statues around the world and one may even be found in England in Leicester and dates from 1925.

Lady Liberty is an allusion to Lady Philosophia or the Wisdom of Sophia and her Seven Rays of Knowledge or Gnosis. The New York monument wears a seven rayed crown and stands atop a tower which looks hauntingly like the Tower of the Tarot.

Author Laurence Gardner put forth an interesting theory that the Tower card actually sprang from the Magdalene's name as a pictorial pun. The tower is attacked by lightning sent by the Roman Church out of their fear of the Bloodline of Christ. 6. In generalized readings it is meant as utter catastrophic change.

(Below: A maiden has the power to tame the unicorn, fresco, by Domenico Zampieri, 1602)

The Secret Dossier of a
Knight Templar of the Sangreal

An early medieval incarnation of these themes comes from Magdeburg, Germany.

The image is the ancient coat of arms for the city of Magdeburg, which was founded by Merovingian descendant, Charlemagne, in 805 AD. She carries a sword of truth & protection with the triumph of the palm branch, the symbol of Jesus as the physical King of Israel.

The Architectural Language of Lady Liberty

1880 by the artist Everett

Lady Liberty is all about number play and symbolism. I've only scratched the surface of her story here but wish to hit upon the highlights.

She stands on a plinth which is actually a tower. There are three exaggerated vertical 'windows' on each face of the tower supported by four columns which of course is a trinity but also echoes the number seven. Below this configuration are ten roundels on each face which speaks of the spheres of the Tree of Life.

The Tower sits in the centre of a three tiered pyramid. Its base is an eleven pointed star which is an odd configuration, especially in architecture. The base is actually the remains of a disused fort. However the 'coincidental' clue can be found in the Tree of Life.

Da'ath is the eleventh sphere of invisible and unknowable power, hardly written about and considered to be of the deepest of mysteries by Kabbalistic practitioners. Most renditions of the Tree of Life will exclude this centre; it has only been in recent years remarked upon more freely in books on the subject and online.

© software image curtesy of Google Earth

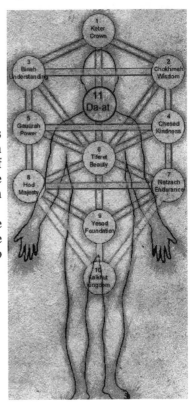

When overlaid onto the human form, Da'ath is the centre of the throat and mouth which indicates sound vibration or the 'Word' of creation. It is associated with Knowledge encapsulating the 13th path which is the High Priestess of the Tarot deck.

The architect of Lady Liberty, Frédéric Auguste Bartholdi 1834-1904, was known to have Free Masonic and esoteric connections and also supported the Suffragette movement.

306

The Secret Dossier of a
Knight Templar of the Sangreal

The 'M' Hand Sign of the Magdalene.

In the recent documentary for America Unearthed, Scott Wolter follows the trail of the Magdalene and discovered with new eyes that the Statue of Liberty held secrets.

Her left hand holds a notched Keystone which is a direct link to masonry and the fingers of her hand are moulded to form an 'M'. Wolter believes this is meant to signify Mary Magdalene; I think he is right. 7.

Although it could be argued that the 'M' stood for Masonry but why could it not be both?

In the documentary Scott Wolter was then directed by a Sinclair descendant to visit the ancient abbey of Saint Martin des Champ, Paris. In front of the church is a replica of the Statue of Liberty with her hand of course forming the letter 'M'.

Meskens, Ad. "Statue of Liberty." October 30, 2009. 8. The Keystone and the 'M' hand sign for the Magdalene.

The church visited by Wolter was founded by the Merovingians. There are many sarcophagi of the family dating from the 6th to 7th centuries.

What are the odds that Lady Liberty should be directly in front of this particular church when it might be said there were innumerable other locations where it could be visited and seen more readily by the public?

Wolter also discovered that the painter of a Christopher Columbus portrait used this hand gesture. The left hand is across his body in the very same gesture as Lady Liberty. Columbus himself started using a 'hooked X' in his own signature - the topic was covered in chapter sixteen.

I was astonished while watching the America Unearthed programme as several months back I had used the Caravaggio portrait of St. Catherine (chapter 19, the Technology of the King) to illustrate the Templar compass with the Saints educational quill. I was rewarded when examining the painting after the documentary – she had the same hand sign!

Posthumous portrait of Christopher Columbus (1451 – 1506)

by Sebastiano del Piombo, 1519

I was delighted to find the same sign in nine further paintings by Caravaggio! Saint Matthew and the Angel, Entombment, Madonna of Loreto, The Calling of Saints Peter and Andrew, Christ on the Mount of Olives, Madonna of the Rosary (Madonna del Rosario) , Crowning with Thorns, Portrait of a Courtesan, and the Fortune Teller. I felt prompted to look at other works by the master painter.

St Catherine of Alexandria by Caravaggio 1598, Thyssen-Bornemisza Museum

Martha and Mary Magdalene, Caravaggio

Though neither figure in the above painting by Caravaggio uses the 'M' gesture. I'd like to point out that Mary Magdalene is holding a white five petal flower. Her abdomen seems distended as if she is pregnant. A comb and cosmetic pot are on the table in front of her, symbols of self-observation and of course that of vessel-hood.

Her left hand rests on a convex and darkened mirror which is reflecting a lozenge, the symbol of feminine fertility, energy and pregnancy. The mirror does not reflect the image of Martha opposite the mirror or anything for that matter. Why is this? It is meant to highlight Mary as a Black Madonna. The lace of reflection of anything else but the lozenge tell of impenetrable secrets.

The fingers of both her hands are very awkward. Try sitting yourself and imitating these positions. Very difficult. These postures are deliberate. The five fingers of her hand whisper the number nine with the four pointed lozenge. She is the very image of the Four Crowns as discussed in the prior chapter and speaks of the inclusion of the feminine in this Gnostic form of Christianity.

The ring finger of each hand seems to be highlighted by this difficult pose. In various parts of Europe it is the right hand which the ring rests denoting marriage and in western tradition it is the left hand. Here Caravaggio makes a point to highlight the left hand ring finger and right.

While Martha is supposedly trying to persuade Mary Magdalene to convert to Christianity and give up vanity she is lower in the frame, in shadow and as a result is the secondary image which the eye falls upon. This painting is sheer misdirection. We're supposed to be looking at the bride of Christ who is wearing the green of fertility and red. Martha, whose image is diminished, is wearing the same colours though not with the same amount of impact. Martha is actually following and imitating Mary the Magdalene.

The Magdalene was the first Christian. She was the first to speak to Jesus upon his resurrection and alerted the disciples to follow. Martha did not need to 'convert' the Magdalene as she was a main supporter of Jesus from the start. Of course she was – they were married!

The 'M' gesture is repeated in a further painting of Saint Catherine by student painter, Bernardino, a protégé of Leonardo and Caravaggio.

Is there an argument against the 'M' as referring to the Magdalene? Could it not refer to the Virgin – I would have to say that a dual meaning as in the Statue of Liberty must be entertained as there must be an 'exoteric' public explanation to avoid difficulties – plausible deniability is a must within the underground stream.

Adoration of the Magi, detached fresco, 1520-25

Bernardino Luini - State Art Museum of Azerbaijan

The painting on the left was also created by Bernardino Luini and is bold in its imagery.

Please note the prominent vessel at the foot of the Virgin and the other two of varying sizes.

She, like her handsome husband, has auburn hair and they are of a compatible age. Joseph does not have the infirmity of age usually shown in religious paintings of the pair.

The Secret Dossier of a
Knight Templar of the Sangreal

I believe we are looking at the next generation, Jesus, Mary M. and their child.
Joseph is the one holding his hand as an 'M'.

The painter Bernardino Luini has continued the tradition of Leonardo and Caravaggio in his own work. The hand gesture continues into the future but also stretches into the past. I found near to 200 paintings spanning the centuries from the 15th to of course the Statue of Liberty.

How can the letter Shin and the 'M' hand sign be reconciled as having the same intention when the finger positions are different?

I believe that Lady Liberty - with her hand poised over the Keystone of Illumination - is a coded form of the Hebrew letter Shin. Rather than use what is known to be a Jewish hand gesture in xenophobic medieval Europe, the proponents of the Bloodline reversed the finger positions from Shin to form an 'M' *however* it is interchangeable with a 'W' and for a very good reason.

Julius Schiller (1580-1627), a lawyer and cartographer from Augsburg Germany, published the star chart titled Coelum Stellatum Christianum in the last year of his life with colleague Johann Bayer and artist Lucas Killian. He replaced all of the constellations with Biblical scenes and persons as if the night sky was a vast stained glass window of a cathedral.

I visited Germany and was surprised by the many references to Mary Magdalene in medieval architecture over and above other countries I've visited. Schiller's inspiration for his new cosmology came out of the underground culture around him.

I took these three photos of the gate into Castle Lorenstein which is just south of Dresden. The figures left to right adorn an archway into a paved courtyard. Shown

311

opposite.

The picture on the left is clearly Mary Magdalene and the other two reminded me of the bared right knee in masonry. Oddly the centre figure is feminine with her left knee exposed and seems to echo the heraldic image of the city of Magdeburg whereas the priest is more easily recognizable as a male Freemason. All three images share the shell of Venus or St. James and this motif is repeated in the castle.

Sculptures date from apparently the 17th century
© Gretchen Cornwall 2011

The new constellations were never popular and soon forgotten but the tome is a beautiful work of art. Schiller and his associates are considered top cartographers by today's standard and ahead of their time.

Saint Catherine appears with her compass and a cherub floats above her with the Spear of Destiny. Eve appears with the apple but also the Tau Cross hanging above her head.

The Virgin Mary is minimized totally in his chart but her parents are large and highly visible. Is this a commentary on the controversial virgin birth of the Virgin Mary that was instituted in the 15th century? It would seem so as her parents are large figures in the night sky but their daughter is absent. It seems that Schiller chimed with St. Bernard's view that the virgin birth of the Virgin was not possible with her two distinctly named parents so evident.

Schiller has other motives behind his artistry and makes a definite separation point between the mother of Christ and his wife.

Curiously he changed Cassiopeia's throne with Mary Magdalene, a very prominent constellation in the northern hemisphere which revolves around Polaris and one which tells a story of depth both in Classical Greek and in Gnostic Christianity.

The Magdalene sits with a Mona Lisa smile next to the empty sepulchre of the risen Christ which was previously Andromeda. She holds her emblem of her children in her lap and a sceptre of streaming stars in her left hand.

The Secret Dossier of a
Knight Templar of the Sangreal

The copyright image of the Constellation of Mary Magdalene as Cassiopeia is available on my website:
http://thesecretdossier.co.uk/maps-stars/

Cassiopeia has always been known as the throne; placing the Magdalene on this throne puts her in the position as the new Queen of Heaven. As the throne revolves in the night sky it forms the letter 'M' and respectively the letter 'W' both are interchangeable and meant to form the double initials 'MM' of the bride of Christ which are remembered in the secret hand sign of the Statue of Liberty and hundreds of paintings.

In Greek mythology Cassiopeia was the queen of Ethiopia which became one of the first Christian nations. The queen made the mistake of publicly stating her daughter Andromeda was more beautiful than the nymph-daughters of a sea-god named Nereus. Poseidon became angry with her comment and sent the monster Cetus to destroy the kingdom. The hero Perseus, assisted by Athena, saved the day and married Andromeda.

Oddly it is the only constellation group from Classical mythology to be immortalized in the stars as a reminder of an entire story. The group is formed of five individuals, the king of Ethiopia – Cepheus, Cassiopeia his wife, Andromeda, Perseus and the monster Cetus – often called the Whale constellation. It is the story of a family which makes Schillers choice of interchanging Mary with the Queen of Ethiopia much more interesting and of course both have a connection to Christianity.

Andromeda's rescue by Perseus has evolved into a favourite motif by painters such as Frederic Leighton where the monster becomes a dragon and the hero wins the bride of Hieros Gamos; A visual story which is identical to Saint George and the Dragon out of Turkey.

The Greeks believed Cassiopeia to have been a real woman who may have also been the queen of king Phoenix of the Phoenicians known also as the great sea-peoples.

Cassiopeia has become known as a form of derision as her throne revolves around the North Star causing it to be viewed upside down as the night progresses. Some depictions of the queen of Ethiopia are of her holding on desperately as the night sky turns.

She has been accused of being vain as a result of her revolving throne, but oddly it is in a prime position in the sky and cannot be missed. However, all the constellations revolve in like manner. Viewed as the Magdalene constellation, she turns around the only fixed star of true north which I believe in Schiller's context is Christ.

She is often seen holding a palm branch. Some images of her are shown with her holding a mirror said to reflect her vanity. However one must remember the motto, 'know thyself'. This aphorism is Greek as discussed earlier and was one of the Delphi Oracle maxims.

Schiller was able to see the comparisons between Cassiopeia and Mary Magdalene. Both held mirrors, had been mothers to an important bloodline, held the secrets of sacred science and were misunderstood through history – possibly on purpose by their adherents and certainly by those who would have nothing to do with their necessary human counterpart – women.

The Holy Grail of the Tarot

The famous deck of cards published in 1910 was devised by the scholarly mystic-author A.E. Waite through the illustrator Pamela Colman Smith. Waite became a Freemason after having been Catholic and was also a member of many occult groups in London.

The Rider-Waite deck is based off of the Marseille cards which include the practices of alchemy and go back centuries. Waite spent a great deal of time in France and I believe he was privy to the secrets of Mary Magdalene.

ACE of CUPS.   The Ace of Cups from the famous Rider-Waite Tarot Deck

I've pondered the symbolism around this deck for some time and I found myself looking at the Ace of Cups with some bemusement.

Nowhere in his writings does he make comment on the odd sigil emboldened on the Ace of Cups which is held out by an inter-dimensional hand to the earth plane. His book titled The Pictorial Key to the Tarot ignores any explanation at all of the odd sigil which he designed.

It neither looks like an 'M' or a 'W'. It could be either one or another or both! Most commentaries on the subject site the sigil as an 'M' but is it? The art of it is almost careless and therefore contrary to the rest of the deck, but I believe it is deliberate as to mislead the onlooker.

Could this be an odd joke that he based his Tarot deck on the Marseille cards and his last name is Waite so the simple answer must be that this is a cross between the two initials? Why did he choose the Ace of Cups for this inside joke, because he had been Catholic? But he had left the church and became a Freemason. This initial as it is shown is nowhere else in the deck at all.

Had he spent time with Gnostic groups in France and had been told of the correlation between Mary Magdalene and Cassiopeia? Had he re-discovered it himself? Had he come across Schiller's work?

The imagery of this card is amazing. An equal lateral cross (or host) is being lowered into the cup by the dove and a divine hand is lowering the grail onto the earth plane. Five streams pour forth from the cup and on it are three bells which evoke the power of sound. The word made manifest - and or - could the bells be equivalent to three children?

In Waite's book titled laboriously and beautifully – The Hidden Church of the Holy Graal: Its Legends and Symbolism. Considered in their Affinity with Certain Mysteries of Initiation and other Traces of a Secret Tradition in Christian Times.– there are references to the Cathars and their murder at the hands of the Inquisition, noted with great sympathy by Waite.

He also discusses the Templars as having gifted a crystal vessel to Henry III containing the Sangreal or the Royal Blood on page 33 - this episode took place in the year 1247 AD. 9.

On page 555, Waite discusses the emergence of the Hallows within the Holy Graal legends that had flowed east to west through Germany and France through the Swan Knights of King Arthur. The Hallows and their respective keepers were originally hereditary. 10.

Waite states that the Templars replace the Swan Knights in Germany during the mid-13th century. But it is clear that the Chivalric Order of the Templars are the Swan Knights in their public guise, which is what I was told. Later in Waite's tome he states in his chapter heading that the 'Hallows of the Graal Mystery Re-Discovered in the Talismans of the Tarot'.

Waite's deck is not without the Divine Feminine; in fact she follows on directly from the Magician or what I would term the realised Christ figure.

Card number two is the High Priestess who represents the Shekinah and holds the Tora in her lap. She is seated between the pillars of Boaz and Jachin with an equal cross on her blue dress, a horned crown and behind her a tapestry protecting the hidden mysteries. She is the Moon following the Sun Magician.

The pomegranates on the tapestry behind her are a potent symbol of life and the palm leaves, yet again, echo Jerusalem's returned King. This card is controversial and has been named the Popess in other earlier versions, perhaps representing the legendary Pope Joan. As a result it was banned for centuries but Waite decides to re-introduce her perhaps as a tribute to Mary Magdalene?

Waite never mentions a strict location for the story of his tarot deck to unfold but I can't seem to get away from the architecture that repeats in various cards throughout.

His sympathy with the plight of the Cathars is interesting and it is known he visited the area. Could the castle of Carcassonne be immortalized in the cards? The building style bears a striking resemblance to the towers, walls and sunny aspect of southern France as envisioned in the deck.

The Cathars were expelled from Carcassonne in 1209 crushing the stronghold of the Occitan resistance. It is an intriguing question as to where Waite placed his Tarot card journey.

Cards where the medieval city-scape are played out include The Chariot, King of Pentacles, Six of Cups, Four of Pentacles and the Four of Wands, the latter of which is the most remarkable of all the cards as a match for Carcassonne. There is a small arched bridge in the middle right of the image. The actual bridge into Carcassonne is long and straight but this could not have been managed in a rectangular small card. The cards may be found online quite easily.

During a research trip to Cumbria in 2011 I came across a few anomalies which I filed away. As more information came to light about Mary Magdalene remembered as Cassiopeia, I kept coming back to a few photos I had taken.

Newbiggen is a tiny farming community adjacent to Temple Sowerby in Cumbria. Historically the rich family who owned the manor house were neighbours to the Templar preceptory and I've often pondered if they might have been sympathetic and helpful to the knights in their darkest hour?

The manor house is privately owned and the ancient church next door is still in use with many of its medieval ornamentation preserved.

Outside Saint Edmunds and detached from it stands, what appears to be, a bell tower or shrine for the statue of a saint of about 12 or so feet tall. I've actually never seen a detached tower of any size next to a church in Britain. If it is a shrine why was it so tall as to not be able to see the enclosed saint, or leave a votive offering? Why was it built?

The Newbiggen Cumbria tower &
Ceiling of Saint Edmunds Church © Gretchen Cornwall

The ceiling inside the church is painted with five pointed silver and gold stars which are the armorial device of the Crackenthorpe family who took over the manor house and patronage of the church in 1332. For some reason a square of stars was framed and singled out from the rest of the ceiling. This pattern of stars stayed in my mind and haunted me for some time...

Recently I was outside looking up at the night sky. The moon was bright and I decided to gaze upon MM/Cassiopeia when I realized I could only count four of her stars due to the brightness of the moon - rather than the five main stars which show up on a dark night! I immediately thought of the Newbiggen church! Is there a correlation between a full moon and this constellation? Had it been noted in centuries past by the Crackenthrope family?

Is the constellation of MM remembered in the church of St. Edmunds Cumbria? Is it 'just' coincidence? I decided to include the tower and the painting of stars for your own musings in this chapter.

The Secret Dossier of a
Knight Templar of the Sangreal

The Soul of the Rose 1908 - John William Waterhouse

1. Burkle, William, Bro. "The Tetragrammaton, the Pentagrammaton, and the Adam_Kadmon." The Tetragrammaton, the Pentagrammaton, and the Adam_Kadmon. February 28, 2012. http://www.freemasons-freemasonry.com/Adam_Kadmon.html.
2. http://www.freemasons-freemasonry.com/Adam_Kadmon.html
3. Whitney, Christa. "Live Long and Prosper: The Jewish Story Behind Spock, Leonard Nimoy's Star Trek Character." YouTube. https://www.youtube.com/watch?v=DyiWkWcR86I. Produced by Wexler Oral History Project at the Yiddish Book Center
4. "Shekhinah." Wikipedia. http://en.wikipedia.org/wiki/Shekhinah.
5. Butler, Alan. The Virgin and the Pentacle: The Freemasonic Plot to Destroy the Church. Winchester: O Books, 2005. p. 125
6. Gardner, Laurence p. 252
7. The Templars Deadliest Secret: Evidence Exposed and Part Two The Chase. Performed by Scott Wolter. The History Chanel, 2015. TV. America Unearthed Season 3
8. Meskens, Ad. "Statue of Liberty." October 30, 2009.
9. Waite, Arthur Edward. The Hidden Church of the Holy Graal: Its Legends and Symbolism. S.l.: Yogi Pub. Soc., U.S. p. 33
10. Ibid p. 555

Thirty Two

Philosophia - A Medieval Tracing Board

Herrad of Landsberg (1130 – July 25, 1195) was contemporary with Hildegard of Bingen and was the abbess of Mont Sainte-Odile in Alsace which was founded, of course, by a Merovingian princess. The abbey is only sixty eight miles or 110 kilometres from Magdeburg.

Herrad compiled an ambitious encyclopaedia of 12th century knowledge as a comprehensive guide for the education of her nuns. Hortus Deliciarum, or the Garden of Delights, was begun in 1176 and completed in 1185, containing over 300 illuminations. Multiple hands took part but Herrad wrote, edited and guided the manuscript. The majority of the poems and hymns are attributed to her. The beautiful illustrations were by other artists.

Sadly the great volume was lost in a fire when the Library of Strasbourg burnt in 1870 during the Franco-Prussian War. The illustrations and works that we have available to us today are as a result of the skilled copyist Christian Moritz Engelhardt in 1818 and publishers Straub and Keller who released the text during 1879 to 1899.

The most comprehensive academic study of the work was done in 1979 by a team of six under the leadership of Rosalie Green for the Warburg Institute of London and is a rather weighty tome of some expense.

Herrad of Hohenburg, as she is also known, drew on the works of theological writers from as far away as Byzantium, but also goes beyond the Bible by including Plato, Socrates, Aristotle and Cicero. It is thought she had access to the libraries of two other nearby priories. 1.

She included references from Bernard de Clairvaux. Mariology is quite apparent in the text and details the life of the Virgin. In one image King Solomon is in peaceful repose ensconced in bed which represents the Virgin as the womb of the church. 2.

Herrad was only 23 years old when St. Bernard passed away but she had entered the priory of Hohenburg at a very young age and therefore her knowledge of him was quite relevant.3. Had she met him? Difficult to say but he had toured Germany. Regardless she included his views having had access to copies of his works.

Amongst the illustrations in the volume is a sun driving a chariot which bears a striking resemblance to the chariot of the tarot cards as well as the wheel of fortune. The wheel is being turned by a woman on a throne which stands on a triple peaked mountain. Of course it would not be complete without a representation of the astrological signs.

I also came across a very odd trio of church leaders; the central figure is wearing what can only be described as a narrow pyramidal hat! It is worn by a man meant to represent the office of the Pope and he appears four more times in the tome.

The Secret Dossier of a
Knight Templar of the Sangreal

An Apostle, a Pope and a Bishop 4.

Landsberg, Herrade De, Rosalie B.. Green, Michael Evans, Christine Bischoff, Michael Curschmann, Thomas Julian Brown, and Kenneth Levy. *Hortus Deliciarum*. Vol. II. London: Warburg Institute, 1979. p. 520 - Tab VII PL 165 - Image origin online: http://artmediaeval.blogspot.co.uk/

One of the most fascinating plates from the Hortus Deliciarum is the *Philosophia et septem artes liberales* or Philosophy and the Seven Liberal Arts.

The Seven Liberal Arts were considered by Greeks to be a complete circle of geometry, astronomy-astrology, arithmetic, rhetoric, music, grammar and dialetica. All Seven Arts were necessary in the Classical world for the complete understanding of the art of war and to be a good citizen.

The outer circle reads in Latin and translated in English below:

Philosophi sapientes mundi et gentium clerici fuerunt. +Hec exercicia que mundi philosophia investigavit investigata notavit scripto firmavit et alumnis insinuavit. Septem per studia docet artes philosophia hec elementorum scrutatur et abdita rerum.

'The wise men of the nations, the philosophers of the world and the clergy that had gone before + These exercises noted that the search for philosophy through investigation and confirmed in writing are suggested for the students. Seven teaches skills through studies of philosophy and explores these elements and hidden things.'

What 'hidden things' could the Abbess Herrad be referring to? I hope that I have teased out one or two possibilities amongst my theories below.

Lady Philosophy is central in the painting and supported by the secular works of Socrates and Plato who sit beneath her. The inner circle, which surrounds her and the two poets of truth, reads in Latin as:

'Arte regens divina que sunt ego philosophia subjectas artes in septem divido partes' and translates into English as 'Arte guiding philosophy by which they will subject the arts into seven parts.'

The secondary outer circle portrays the muses of the Seven Liberal Arts, each within their own descriptive archway.
Outside the sanctity of the protective circle are four poets of magic each inspired by infernal realms as pictured by the four black birds whispering in their ears.

Philosophia et septem artes liberales from the Hortus Deliciarum 12th Century, compiled by Abbess Herrad of Hoenburg or Landsburg.
Original image from https://commons.wikimedia.org/wiki/
File:Hortus_Deliciarum,_Die_Philosophie_mit_den_sieben_freien_K%C3%BCnsten.JPG

The Secret Dossier of a
Knight Templar of the Sangreal

I chose not to dwell on all of the Muses but there are a few which caught my attention due to their curious nature and relevance to prior chapters.

I found the muse of Dialetica (pictured on the right of the Philosophia) to be interesting as she is holding the head of a hound as this was considered an aggressive skill required in Greek life in order to defend oneself in court.

St. Bernard was also noted during his life as having the ability to 'bark' with assertiveness during a debate to win his argument. Is there also a reference here to the God Star or Dog Star of Sirius? I wondered if the muse holding the head of the 'wise' dog might be in reference to St Bernard?

I found the trio of Arithmetic, Geometry and Astronomy to be of particular interest.

The muse of Arithmetic on the left is holding a string of counting beads which number twenty-two. Her left hand is obscuring one of the beads. Oddly there are three beads held between her hands and a total of nine on either side of her hands. What code is the Muse of Arithmetic hiding with her message of 9-3-9? See below for a larger image.

The main theme of the painting is the number seven. I immediately tumbled to the thought that perhaps the reason for the number of the beads might be that of the feast day of July 22nd for the feast day of Mary Magdalene?

Her archway bears a strange inscription: Arithmetica. – Ex numeris consto quorum discrimina monstro the number of words in Latin is seven. Or in English, 'The differences between the numbers of a monster' – is this a warning to adherents of the Bloodline to be forewarned of enemies and to count their numbers?

In the book of Revelation the number seven is played out nineteen times. There are instances of the number seven as being positive but in the instance of the seven headed dragon threatening the pregnant woman clothed in white, with a crown of twelve stars, on her head, it is quite threatening.

It is thought that the seven headed dragon in this instance may be referring to the Seven Hills of Rome and its determination to wipe out the Bloodline. Since there are positive representations in the book of Revelations is it also possible that the number seven in the context of the above could refer to the seventh month of July?

Gematria

Gematria is a stunning figure when broken down and gives credence to the muse of Arithmetica as being a warning signpost to the Sangrael.

The archway reads - Geometria; circulus. – Terre mensuras per multas dirigo curas.

Into English - I direct the measurement of the earth through many cares.

The translation into English reads as if the muse is practicing alchemy. She is not just measuring the earth, she is directing the material plane as an initiate with great care and perhaps 'through many' obstacles. In her left hand she holds a staff that meets the point of a compass held in her right hand.

Note the fold of her skirt from her right hip as it dissects the long staff and follow it down to the foot. The staff, compass and fold of Geometria's skirts form an 'M'.

Astronomia

Astronomia. – Ex astris nomen traho per que discitur omen.
'Is learned by means of which the name of an omen is pulled from the stars.'

What omen one must ask? The Abbess illustrates astrological signs in the encyclopaedia as well; the search for omens is an allusion to the use of astrology. Oddly Astronomia is holding a jar or vessel with a lid in her left hand which is of course the traditional symbol of the Magdalene.

Astronomia is counting the five stars above her head which brings to mind all the varied meanings behind the number five as visited in the prior chapter. Is she counting the stars of Cassiopeia? The configuration is not identical but I thought it important to consider the possibility that this could be a representation of

The Secret Dossier of a
Knight Templar of the Sangreal

Cassiopeia's throne introduced for the first time as the constellation of Mary Magdalene.

I've overlaid a transparent image of the constellation over the stars of the original painting. The transparent image is exact in its proportions for Cassiopeia but the problem of medieval inaccuracy in drawing is apparent here, if of course, my theory is correct in the first place.

The star closest to the muses head is not where it should be if this is meant to be the Celestial 'M'. It appears squished into the arch as if the artist had started on the lower right hand side and by the time he/she reached the upper left hand side, realized their error and had to place the fifth star in a misaligned manner.

The other possibility is that it is a coded and purposeful error in order to hide the configuration. Granted, it is a theory, however when examining the other images and the Merovingian establishment of the abbey the Magdalene aspect of these stars comes into sharper focus.

The above two muses are in opposition to each other as are their corresponding 'M' & 'W'. An exact representation of the turning throne in the night sky of Cassiopeia.

Please note the faces which can be seen at the top of the left hand column and its partner on the right hand side of Astronomia below. I believe that this marks Geometria and Astronomia out as a pair meant to be taken into consideration together. The two faces do not appear on any of the other columns.

In this experiment of the two muses, I placed the 'W' of the constellation in blue as just resting above the finger of Astronomia. The original placement of the stars is above.

Philosophia A Medieval Tracing Board

Lady Philosophia

The Queen of Heaven is centre with seven green streams of knowledge pouring out of her heart to the lower planes. She wears a crown of three presences and holds a very curious banner. The translation from Latin of the banner reads: All wisdom is from the Lord God, only those who desire the flame of love achieve wisdom.

I'd like to offer up the banner of Sophia as a representation of the Constellation of Mary Magdalene which may have inspired the cartographer Schiller in the 17th century. The banner has the sprawl of the Celestial 'M' and its five points echo the themes of Arithmetic, Geometry and Astronomy.

As always in Holy Grail matters there are multiple meanings. Are the three faces of Philosophia's crown the children of Mary Magdalene? Beyond this are the five stars of the constellation and the streams of the Seven Liberal Arts.

The number sets above play an important role in the Freemasonic Tracing Board as transmitted by the Templars.

The Secret Dossier of a
Knight Templar of the Sangreal

The Tracing Board

The Tracing Board (left) of the Second-Degree Fellowcraft and its curved stairway of higher awareness. The steps are separated into sections of the numbers Three, Five and Seven. 5.

The first three steps are the three working tools of this degree the Plumb, the Square, and the Level. All three instruments were used in medieval architecture by masons. In speculative masonry they represent the moral fortitude of honesty, virtue and that all are travelling upon the Level of Time. 6.

The five steps are asking us to use all our senses Hearing, Seeing, Feeling, Smelling and Taste. Our entire body must be engaged on the path of the next seven steps which are the Seven Liberal Arts.

Of the second tracing board representing the Fellowcraft Second-Degree, Lomas states that -

"Philosophy is the Porchway to Truth and its pursuit widens human understanding." Lomas 7.

I find the correlations between the 12th century work of Abbess Herrad and the Tracing Board of the Second-Degree to be fascinating.

As a successor to Saint Bernard and Hildegard of Bingen, Herrad created a work that would impart the 'hidden' knowledge of Philosophia, not just as a static encyclopaedia, but as a living document for the future whose vibrant images held the secrets of the Merovingian's.

Like the Masonic Tracing Board, Herrad's Philosophia contains practical instruments which may be used in an allegorical sense for the work of the inner domain and of course the necessary external application to create a flowering microcosm of civilization within the walls of her abbey.

The initiatic themes illustrated by Herrad transmitted down the centuries through Templarism and are of an individual nature, meant to develop the heart, mind, body and soul. A never ending road marked by shining gates.

The banner below was created from Philosophia's and represents the 'W' and 'M' of the constellation of Mary Magedalene.

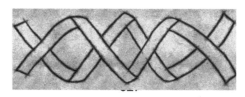

The Accolade 1901 by Edmund Blair Leighton

1. Lillich, Meredith P. The Gothic Stained Glass of Reims Cathedral. University Park, PA: Pennsylvania State University Press, 2011. p. 277

2. Griffiths, Fiona J. The Garden of Delights: Reform and Renaissance for Women in the Twelfth Century. Kindle ed. Philadelphia: University of Pennsylvania Press, 2011. p. 74

3. Ferzoco, George, and Carolyn Muessig. Medieval Monastic Education. Bloomsbury Publishing, 2001. p. 89

4. Landsberg, Herrade De, Rosalie B.. Green, Michael Evans, Christine Bischoff, Michael Curschmann, Thomas Julian Brown, and Kenneth Levy. Hortus Deliciarum. Vol. II. London: Warburg Institute, 1979. p. 520 - Tab VII PL 165 - Image origin online: http://artmediaeval.blogspot.co.uk/

5. Sickels, Daniel, 33. The General Ahiman Rezon and Freemason's Guide: Containing Monitorial Instructions in the Degrees of Entered Apprentice, Fellow-craft and Master Mason ... To Which Are Added a Ritual for a Lodge of Sorrow ... Also, an Appendix, with the Forms of Masonic Documents, Masonic Trials, Etc. New York: Masonic Pub. and Manufacturing, 1867.

6. Ibid p. 120

7. Lomas, Robert. The Secret Science of Masonic Initiation. London: Lewis Masonic, 2008.

Thirty Three

Final Comments

My goal for writing this book was multi-fold and certainly a highlight has been to discover new evidence for the existence of the Knights Templar into our modern age. Having entered the fray, I caught the attention of a royal priest of this gnostic order and am privileged to have been given the family history of the Comte de Mattinata de Medici and hither to undisclosed information such as the Templar Matrix Map of the world.

How is a journey such as this engaged? How do we recognize the still voice within? We all have the capacity for the imaginative, intuitive response which leads to greater powers of preception if exercised. Those who treat this faculty as an artful science gain the most from the human experience and are able to carry the torch with a backward glance at tomorrow.

Extraordinary faculties lay dormant in all humanity unless they are first acknowledged as 'real' and then pursued with great rigour against the resistance which life throws at us. It is not unlike having the determination, self reliance and personal responsibility to go to the gym on a daily basis.

Once this light within is acknowledged, we must then extrapolate that the Light of our soul was gifted to us by a Greater Architect than ourselves. The more we traverse this path a sense of awe grows at the beauty, complexity and inclusive, ever-self-sustaining Matrix from which we draw our immortal lives. Our Energetic-Being is the key to the material world and our place in it. Quantum Mechanics is beginning to catch up and prove what gnostic mystics and alchemists have been sharing with us for centuries.

Great spiritual athletes are able to sense and participate in the magnetic energy life of the Earth in symbiotic relationship and growth. The Templar Matrix Map of the World is the direct result of applied and organic skills. I am certain there is more to discover in regards to the map and now that the map is in the hands of the public its certain physical merit may be engaged with...

The Knights Templar as a genre is vast, covering millenia. It was my hope to write a book that explored the many facets involved with an eye towards it being a platform for future volumes.

The Templar Knights are real, modern and are the children of Mary Magdelene and King Jesus. Celtic Christianity which is inclusive of men and women as married priestly partners thrives in the wild and pastoral beauty of the Lake District.

Final Comments

The Secret Dossier is the result of a lifetime of study for my part and gifts of information direct from the Comte himself. More will be revealed in the future.

The Princes of Rheged in Cumbria thrive, carrying the banner of the Arthurian dragon tradition, strengthened with the Merovingian and Medici Renaissance achievements. The Comte is in the process of writing his own book, Pennies From Heaven, due out in the near future. Keep in touch via my own website for release date information:

http://thesecretdossier.co.uk/

Sincerely, Gretchen Leslie Cornwall
August 20th 2015

The author at Stonehenge

Epilogue

Mattinson Shield

When I sat down a year ago to write 'Final Thoughts' it had not occurred to me that this volume would have further loose ends to tie up. The printed book provided an opportunity to include recent discoveries in an epilogue.

Rather than trying to pick apart the chapters to insert the following information, expediency and also curtesy won out. Those who have already bought the ebook will certainly enjoy the new art work in the printed word but also appreciate that the following will be at their fingertips quickly.

It has been an exciting year and I feel a great sense of accomplishment at seeing the book develop into print. I am looking forward to the future and new developments with my Templar Knight contact, the Comte de Mattinata de Medici and his knightly colleagues.

The Shield

The Mattinson coat of arms includes many alchemical emblems. The Griffin is symbolic of strength, leadership and courage. It is an amalgamation of a lion and eagle, a ferocious mix indeed!

The beastie is ancient in origins, with its roots in Egypt, Persia and resurgence in popularity during the Renaissance. In fantasy, author J.K. Rowling uses the Griffin as the symbol of House Gryffindor in the Harry Potter series. The symbol is not dissimilar to the chimera which St. Bernard likened himself to...

"Griffin mythology reads a lot like dragon mythology in that griffins were thought to be very wise and wily characters who spent a good deal of time seeking out and guarding gold and treasures. Other legends have the griffin as a trickster, much like the Sphinx, who would challenge people with riddles in a contest of wits. The winners would get to keep their lives and treasures, and the losers... wouldn't. The Sphinx also has the body of a lion."

As quoted from: http://www.gods-and-monsters.com/mythology-griffin.html

Fresco of a Griffin in the throne room at Knossos, Crete, taken by Wiki user:

User:Paginazero

Apart from the dangers of meeting a Griffin, Christianity embraces the essence of the beast in the New Testament. The gospels Matthew, Mark, Luke and John are associated with four divine symbols: The Man or Angel, Ox, Lion and the Eagle of St. John the Devine.

Above the Griffin on the shield is a chevron, often given to knights as a distinction for military service during the middle-ages. The chevron is still used today by American military and law enforcement agencies but also continues as a heraldic device.

Contained within the chevron are two equally balanced Scales of Justice on a gold field. Above the scales are golden two bees, both sitting on a black background, the symbol of constancy and loyalty. The Griffin also sits on a black background.

The comparison of the Mattinson coat of arms with that of St Bernard de Clairvaux is easy to understand as he is the patron saint of bee-keepers.

Bernard de Clairvaux

Artist unknown

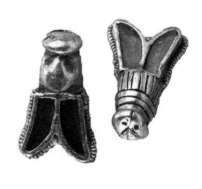

Merovingian bees from the tomb of
King Childeric I

Mattinata Italy

The Man in the Leather Mask was exiled to Mattinata Italy from the French Court
by his own mother Queen Marie de Medici as discussed in chapter one.

Mattinata Italy is within the Province of Foggia, a protected nature reserve and is
famous for its beaches and crystalline waters. Its roots go back into pre-history. The
remains of a Roman settlement may be visited and also those of the Benedictine
Abbey of Santissima Trinità.

The town was originally tied to its neighbour the ancient capital of Monte
Sant'Angelo. The Sanctuary of Sant'Angelo is dedicated to Saint Michael and was
rebuilt by Charles I of Anjou in the 13th century who ruled over the region. One of
its main features is an octagonal tower which stands guard over the front portal of
the church.

St. Bernard visited the Sanctuary in its earlier form, as well as British pilgrims on
their way to the Holy Land. St. Francis carved a tau cross on the entrance to the
grotto.

The town of Mattinata based its coat of arms on an Indo-European mother figure.
She survived down the millennia under varying guises and is directly related to the
area for its gorgeous sunrises as a source of eternal hope.

Mattinata had been called Matinum by the Romans after the goddess, Matuta of
the Morning Sunrise or Mother of the Morning Star. It's interesting that they chose
to relate the sun with a 'morning star'. Technically this is correct as the sun is a star
and Venus a planet, which is also known as the evening and morning star.

Epilogue

The Mattinata shield is under tight copyright protection –
I've re-created it here but not with accuracy. Please read the description for greater clarity. If you'd like a better view of the shield, visit the Mattinata Italy site for the origianl shield:
http://www.comune.mattinata.fg.it/

The upper left section of the shield is the Morning Star over the blue sea with sixteen rays of light. Eight compass points are straight the other half are curved. The shield is diagonally bisected with the town's motto, 'Lux Vera Illuminet' or 'the true light shines'.

Above the crest is a castellated crown in the form of a stone tower, of Our Lady of the Most Holy Mary of Light. It has nine arch doorways above three larger. The castellation's are also nine in number.

The crown is a nod to the abbey church Maria Della Luce which was built in the 12th century. Certainly, Prince Henri would have visited the church if not prayed there on a regular basis during his exile.

Below the motto is a green verdant field, blue sky and the successful olive tree which grows so happily in the sun.

The town was memorialized in the song 'Morning' - composed by Ruggero Leoncavallo in 1904 and recorded by Enrico Caruso of the same year for Gramophone Company.

> The dawn, dressed in white,
> has already opened the door to the sun,
> and caresses the flowers with its pink fingers.
> A mysterious trembling seems to disturb all nature.
> And yet you will not get up, and vainly
> I stand here sadly singing.
> Dress yourself also in white,
> and open the door to your surrender!
> Where you are not, there is no light;
> where you are, love is born.
> Where you are not, there is no light;
> where you are, love is born.

The Secret Dossier of a
Knight Templar of the Sangreal

The Morning Star, Fisherman and Scholar

Greek scholar Archytas and friend to Plato met his end on the beach of Mattinata during a storm which wrecked his ship. His body remained unburied on the shore until a fisherman scattered sand across him thus freeing him from the physical world and making it possible for Archytas to cross over the river Styx. Otherwise, according to Greek religion, he would have wandered for 100 years, trapped on the wrong side of the veil without friend or guide.

The fisherman was lead to the site of the body by the warm rays of the morning mother sun after the storm had passed.

Archytas has been dubbed the father of mathematical mechanics. Plato gave him the accolade of philosopher king in The Republic.

I found this episode to be very interesting and likened it to 'modern soul guides' sometimes called 'ghost hunters' whose province it is to speak to the dead who may not realize they'd passed. Confusion occurs with someone who has suffered a violent and frightening death and they are unable to leave this plane.

Could the fisherman have had the ability to sense Archytas? Was the philosopher lost between worlds? Perhaps the philosopher had not known he had perished and was freed by the actions of the fisher-man? For some reason this event was remembered over the millennia and is now bound up in the legends of Mattinata and that of the morning star.

The Black Dub Monument – Charles II

A lichen covered obelisk, called the Black Dub Monument, sits on Crosby Ravensworth fell. It is a windswept and rugged place but so were the men who rested in the valley below on August 8th 1651, the date on the obelisk. Their king, Charles II, newly crowned, was on his way from Scotland to London with the army when he stopped to drink the water at the source of the river Livennet.

On one side of the obelisk is the carved profile of the king, a crown, a lion and inscription.

Here at Black Dub
The Source of the Livennet
King Charles The II
Regaled His Army
And Drank of the Water
On His March From Scotland
August 8 1651

Epilogue

Black Dub translates as black water or black hole. Oddly the source of the river is about 1 kilometre away and not on a dreary hill memorialized by the self-taught sculptor John Bland.

He had built the obelisk in 1840 which in itself was a mystery; what prompted him to create it in the first place? He was considered eccentric but what were his reasons for placing the monument in what might conceivably be called the 'wrong place'?

There is a small stream flowing past the monument that is associated with the Livennet but it is not the source and seems to dry out in summer. However the landscape may have changed over the years, but by a kilometre in two hundred years?

Could there have been another reason for placing the obelisk where it sits? Perhaps a meeting that was considered private which John Bland discovered or was told of a few centuries later?

Lady Anne Clifford relates the event in her precious diary:

"On 8 August, 1651, His Most Gracious Majesty King Charles II with his army on his way from Scotland passed Appleby about 7 miles to the West."

Lady Anne was one of the wealthiest women in England and had survived Cromwell by sheer force of will to rebuild her castle and the whole of the north with churches, schools and hospitals, providing life reviving employment after the Civil War. She was an amazing woman indeed.

I believe that Lady Anne and certainly, Prince Henri Mattinata de Medici, met King Charles II, who was after all, the nephew of the Man in the Leather Mask; perhaps on the spot where the obelisk stands. Patterdale, the home of Prince Henri, was due west of Black Dub by 30 miles.

Charles II was of course the patron behind the Royal Society and also was deeply interested in hermetic and alchemical teachings. Since this is the case, meeting with his uncle, the priest-king of Cumbria, would have been a natural consideration, if not an initiatic one.

The Erasmus Obelisk Revisited

I recently had a dream which I believe to have been a spontaneous soul journey or astral travel. I was flying over the earth and looking down at the cities and landscape. I was over a modern glass skyscraper shaped like an obelisk, not too dissimilar to the 30 St. Mary Axe or 'Gherkin building' in London.

I could see down into the roof which melted away and though I knew it had floors which would have obstructed normal viewing, the centre of it was hollow and filled with light as if it were a physical rainbow. The coloration was mostly crystalline however but I knew it contained all possibilities.

On waking, I could not help but think of the scientist/occultist Isaac Newton and the experiments using a crystal for light refraction and optics.

The Secret Dossier of a
Knight Templar of the Sangreal

The dream implied that humans, by building, can interact with the energies of earth which are often tied to alignment with the stars. We are building obelisks today in the same way that the Egyptians had but perhaps without the religious undertones, however having effect on earth energies just the same. The further considerations of this are too many to indulge here...

"If I have seen further than others, it is by standing upon the shoulders of giants."
Quote by Isaac Newton

I was asked by the Comte to have another look at the Erasmus Obelisk which crosses the Atlantic and to include it in the Epilogue.

The diagonal lines, if measured with a giant compass creates an inner circle. He used the term, 'isometrics' which means 3-d drawing. The circle appears to draw the attention to a 'light mountain' or 'pyramid' in the middle of the Atlantic.

The tip of the obelisk is the Newport Tower in Rhode Island and leads through the 'circle of light' to Newport Wales and St. Woolos Abbey. There is a direct line from the abbey to Rosslyn, of course, which runs along the border of Wales up through Scotland.

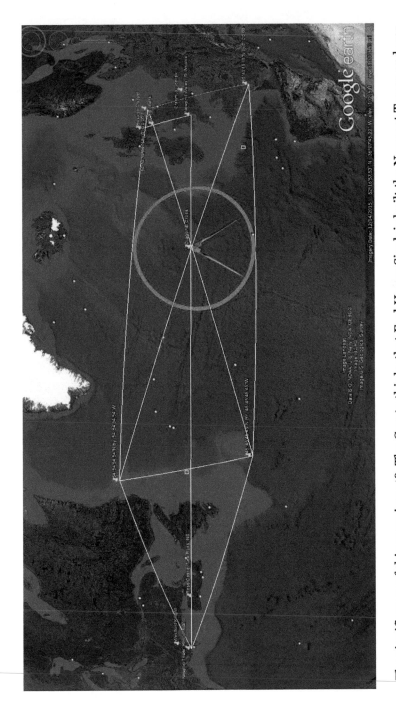

The significance of this experiment? The Comte thinks that Earl Henry Sinclair built the Newport Tower and was aware of the 'light obelisk' across the Atlantic and perhaps even thought of it as a 'light bridge'.

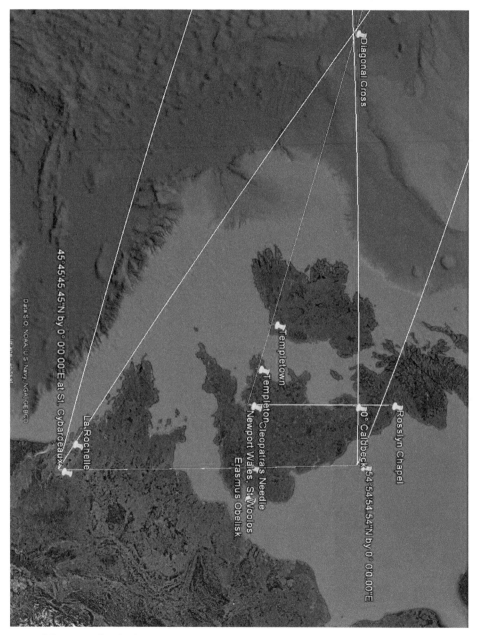

Oddly enough, the line from Newport Wales to the Newport Tower takes in two
Templar preceptories, Templeton in Wales and Templetown Ireland as shown in the
above map.

The Sinclair's trace their ancestry to the dreaded Vikings and may have had secret

Epilogue

instruments for navigating the oceans which is why they were successful. The Templars of course were part of their descendant stream.

If this seems preposterous, examining an English shipwreck from 1592 should prove interesting:

"An oblong crystal the size of a cigarette packet was next to a pair of dividers – suggesting it was part of the navigational equipment."
http://www.bbc.co.uk/news/world-europe-21693140

The legendary 'sunstone' mentioned in ancient Viking writings was thought to be a myth; a magical talisman that aided the captain at times when the sun was behind the clouds.

If it seems farfetched that the Vikings used this to find North America and even more preposterous that the Sinclair's did so; then what was one doing on a sunken wreck from the 16th century? It was a secret worth keeping, passing down and also is an indication of the Templars surviving in England, not just in Scotland.

Had Isaac Newton been aware of the Viking sunstone? As an educated man he may very well have known of the Norse Sagas and been inspired to experiment with its crystal matrix.

The Knights Templar took the light of the immortal soul very seriously as well as the light found in the physical counterparts of the Viking sunstone, light bridges, magnetic lines and monuments. Some of these monuments such as the Newport Tower drew down the light of specific stars onto earth, others such as the obelisk or Celtic crosses, creating new towers of light on earth or reinforcing ancient lines and vortexes. Light Bridges, Pyramids and Obelisks - Consious Emmanations from the Divine Mind- As Above So Below.

"I'm going to build my secrets into the geometry of these buildings because I know that books can burned but buildings not so easily."
Thomas Jefferson

Sincerely,

Gretchen Leslie Cornwall
October 13th 2016

For more information please visit -
http://thesecretdossier.co.uk/

Bibliography

* Adams, Guy. "Adjust Your Compass Now: The North Pole Is Migrating to Russia." The Independent. March 06, 2011. http://www.independent.co.uk/news/science/adjust-your-compass-now-the-north-pole-is-migrating-to-russia-2233610.html. Movement of the magnetic north is causing problems for aviation, navigation and wildlife

* Addison, C. G., and Robert Macoy. *The Knights Templars*. New York: Masonic Pub., 1842.

* Alexandria, Hero Of. *The Pneumatics of Hero of Alexandria*. Lexington, KY: CreateSpace Independent Publishing Platform, 2009.

* Asbridge, Thomas S. *The Crusades: The Authoritative History of the War for the Holy Land*. Reprint ed. New York: Ecco Press, 2011.

* Bacon, Roger, and A. G. Little. *Part of the Opus Tertium of Roger Bacon, including a Fragment Now Printed for the First Time*. Aberdeen: University Press, 1912.

* Baigent, Michael, and Richard Leigh. *The Temple and the Lodge*. New York: Arcade Pub., 1989.

* Baigent, Michael, Richard Leigh, and Henry Lincoln. *The Holy Blood and the Holy Grail*. London: Century, 2005. 158.

* Bailey, James. *God-Kings and the Titans: The New World Ascendancy in Ancient Times*. S.l.: Hodder and Stoughton, 1973.

* Begg, Ean C. M. *The Cult of the Black Virgin*. 2nd ed. London: Arkana, 1996.

* Bernard, Samuel John Eales, and Francis Aidan Gasquet. *Some Letters of Saint Bernard, Abbot of Clairvaux*. London: J. Hodges, 1904.

* Black, Jonathan. *The Sacred History: How Angels, Mystics and Higher Intelligence Made Our World*. Quercus, 2013.

* Black, Jonathan. *The Secret History of the World*. London: Quercus, 2010.

* Brayley, Edward Wedlake. *Delineations Historical and Topographical of the Isle of Thanet and the Cinque Ports,*. Vol. Volume 1. 1817.

* Bredero, Adriaan Hendrik. *Bernard of Clairvaux: Between Cult and History*. Grand Rapids, MI: W.B. Eerdmans, 1996.

* Brinkley, Dannion, and Paul Perry. *Saved by the Light: The True Story of a Man Who Died Twice and the Profound Revelations He Received*. New York: Villard Books, 1994.

* Brown, J. Wood. *An Enquiry into the Life and Legend of Michael Scot*. Edinburgh: D. Douglas, 1897.

* Brown, Lloyd A. *The Story of Maps*. New York: Dover Publications, 1979.

* Burkle, William, Bro. "The Tetragrammaton, the Pentagrammaton, and the Adam_Kadmon." The Tetragrammaton, the Pentagrammaton, and the Adam_Kadmon. February 28, 2012. http://www.freemasons-freemasonry.com/Adam_Kadmon.html.

* Burkle, William Steve, Bro. "The Point Within A Circle." PS Review of Freemasonry. Accessed August 07, 2015. http://www.freemasons-freemasonry.com/point_within_circle.html.

* Butler, Alan, and Stephen Dafoe. *The Warriors and the Bankers*. Hersham, Surrey: Lewis Masonic, 2006.

Bibliography

* Butler, Alan. *The Virgin and the Pentacle: The Freemasonic Plot to Destroy the Church.* Winchester: O Books, 2005.

* Butler, Cuthbert. *Western Mysticism: The Teaching of SS. Augustine, Gregory, and Bernard on Contemplation and the Contemplative Life.* London: Kegan Paul International, 2000.

* Calverley, William Slater, and W. G. Collingwood. *Notes on the Early Sculptured Crosses, Shrines and Monuments in the Present Diocese of Carlisle.* Kendal: T. Wilson, 1899.

* Cawthorne, Bob. *The Isle of Thanet Compendium.* Broadstairs: Scribble and Doodle Books, 2007.

* "CERN Accelerating Science." New Results Indicate That New Particle Is a Higgs Boson. March 14, 2013. http://home.web.cern.ch/about/updates/2013/03/new-results-indicate-new-particle-higgs-boson.

* Charpentier, Louis. *The Mysteries of Chartres Cathedral.* London: Research into Lost Knowledge Organisation; Distributed by Thorsons, 1972.

* Clarke, C. Purdon, Bro., and Stephen Dafoe. "Masonic History." The Four Patron Saints Of Masons. http://www.masonicdictionary.com/fourcrown2.html.

Quatuor Coronati Lodge in 1919

* Clayton, Mary, Mrs. "CCED: Persons Index." CCED: Persons Index. Accessed August 05, 2015. http://db.theclergydatabase.org.uk/jsp/persons/CreatePersonFrames.jsp?PersonID=15631

* Coelho, Paulo, and Alan R. Clarke. *The Pilgrimage: A Contemporary Quest for Ancient Wisdom.* London: Thorsons, 1997.

*Coffin, Robert A. London Burns & Oates, 1868.

* Collins, Andrew. *The Cygnus Mystery: Unlocking the Ancient Secret of Life's Origins in the Cosmos.* London: Watkins Pub., 2007.

* Corbin, Henry. *Temple and Contemplation.* London: KPI in Association with Islamic Publications, London, 1986.

* Cowie, Ashley. *The Rosslyn Matrix.* East Kilbride: Wicker World, 2006.

* Cplakidas. "User:Cplakidas." Wikimedia Commons. https://commons.wikimedia.org/wiki/User:Cplakidas.

* Critchlow, Keith, and Rod Bull. *Time Stands Still: New Light on Megalithic Science.* London: Gordon Fraser Gallery, 1979.

* Crowley, Vivianne. *Thorson's Principles of Jungian Spirituality.* London: Thorsons, 1998.

* Cruttenden, Walter. "An Ancient Message for the Future - Graham Hancock Official Website." An Ancient Message for the Future - Graham Hancock Official Website. August 26, 2012. http://grahamhancock.com/cruttendenw2/.

* "Database." Cumbria Archive Service Catalogue. http%3A%2F%2Fwww.archiveweb.cumbria.gov.uk%2FCalmView%2Fdefault.aspx.

Cumbria Archive Service Catalogue, Carlisle, DCC/2/27, General Memoranda Book of Sir John Lowther

* Donnelly, Ignatius. *Atlantis: The Antediluvian World.* New York: Dover Publications, 1976.

* Douce, Francis. *The Recreative Review, or Eccentricities of Literature and Life*. London: Wallis and, 1821.

* "Dürer Graph." Wikipedia. http://en.wikipedia.org/wiki/D%C3%BCrer_graph.

* Duignan, Brian, ed. *Medieval Philosophy: From 500 to 1500 CE*. 1st ed. New York, NY: Britannica Educational Pub. in Association with Rosen Educational Services, 2010.

* Edgar, Jim. "From Pentagram to Pyramids:." Masonic and Kabbalistic Symbols In the Washington D.C. Map. http://dcsymbols.com/.

* Edgar, Jim. "The Great Pyramid and the Washington DC Map." YouTube. http://www.youtube.com/watch?v=-hqVwDT2iWU.

* Farrer, William, and J. Brownbill. "Houses of Cistercian Monks: The Abbey of Furness." Houses of Cistercian Monks: The Abbey of Furness. http://www.british-history.ac.uk/report.aspx?compid=38348&%3Bstrquery=++Date+accessed%3A+03+October+2013. Volume 2 (1908), pp. 114-131

* Ferzoco, George, and Carolyn Muessig. *Medieval Monastic Education*. Bloomsbury Publishing, 2001.

* "Fliegel Jezerniczky Expeditions." Fliegel Jezerniczky Expeditions. http://www.fjexpeditions.com/frameset/uweinat_inscription.htm.

* Frale, Barbara. *The Templars and the Shroud of Christ*. New York: Skyhorse Pub., 2012.

* Fraser, Antonia. *The Warrior Queens*. Anchor Books, 1990.

* Fuller, R. Buckminster, and E. J. Applewhite. *Synergetics: Explorations in the Geometry of Thinking*. New York: Macmillan, 1982.

* Furlong, David. *The Keys to the Temple: Unravel the Mysteries of the Ancient World*. London: Piatkus, 1997.

* Gardner, Laurence. *Bloodline of the Holy Grail: The Hidden Lineage of Jesus Revealed*. Shaftesbury, Dorset: Element, 1996.

* Gaud, Henri, Jean-François Leroux-Dhuys, and John Crook. *Cistercian Abbeys: History and Architecture*. Köln: Könemann, 1998.

* Gilbanks, G. E. *Some Records of a Cistercian Abbey: Holm Cultram, Cumberland*. London: W. Scott, 1899.

* Gildas, M. *The Catholic Encyclopedia*. New York: Robert Appleton Company, 1907.

* Gilpin, Sidney. *The Songs and Ballads of Cumberland: To Which Are Added the Best Poems in the Dialect ; with Biographical Sketches, Notes, & Glossary*. Carlisle: G. Coward, 1865.

* Goldberg, B. Z. "The Sacred Fire: Book Three. In the House of the Lord: Chapter II. Romance in the Church." The Sacred Fire: Book Three. In the House of the Lord: Chapter II. Romance in the Church. Accessed August 05, 2015. http://www.sacred-texts.com/sex/tsf/tsf15.htm.

* "Graham Hancock on Plato and Atlantis." YouTube. http://www.youtube.com/watch?v=TdQ0P6k8inc.

* Grainger, Francis, and W. G. Collingwood. "Records : The Abbey in the Thirteenth Century."

Bibliography

Records : The Abbey in the Thirteenth Century.
http://www.britishhistory.ac.uk/report.aspx?compid=49537&strquery=

* Grainger, Francis, and W. G. Collingwood. *The Register and Records of Holm Cultram*. Kendal: T. Wilson & Son, 1929.

* Grant, Edward. *Physical Science in Middle Ages*. Cambridge, MA: Cambridge University Press, 1978.

* Gray, Richard. "Iron Spheres in Ears May Help Birds Navigate." The Telegraph. April 26, 2013. http://www.telegraph.co.uk/science/science-news/10021789/Iron-spheres-in-ears-may-help-birds-navigate.html.

* Grayson, Janet. "St. Bernard of Clairvaux." CATHOLIC ENCYCLOPEDIA:. 2012. Accessed August 05, 2015. http://www.newadvent.org/cathen/02498d.htm.

* Greene, Brian. *The Hidden Reality: Parallel Universes and the Deep Laws of the Cosmos*. Penguin, 2012.

* Greenia, Conrad. Number Nineteen ed. Vol. 7. Kalamazoo: Cistercian Publications, 1977.

* Griffith-Jones, Robin. *Mary Magdalene: The Woman Whom Jesus Loved*. Norwich:
        Canterbury Press, 2008. As quoted in the Preface

* Griffiths, Fiona J. *The Garden of Delights: Reform and Renaissance for Women in the Twelfth Century*. Kindle ed. Philadelphia: University of Pennsylvania Press, 2011.

* Hallam, Elizabeth M. *Chronicles of the Crusades: Eye-witness Accounts of the Wars between Christianity and Islam*. Godalming, Surrey: CLB, 1997.

* Hamilton, Calvin, and Rosanna Hamilton. "Feldspar." Feldspar. http://www.scienceviews.com/geology/feldspar.html.
Information adapted from "Minerals in Your World", a cooperative effort between the U.S. Geological Survey and the Mineral Information Institute.

* Hancock, Graham, and Santha Faiia. *Heaven's Mirror: Quest for the Lost Civilization*. London: Penguin, 1999.

* Hart, George W. "Neolithic Carved Stone Polyhedra." Neolithic Carved Stone Polyhedra. 1998. http://www.georgehart.com/virtual-polyhedra/neolithic.html.

* Haxworth, Carly. "Healing Properties of Feldspar from Charms Of Light - Healing." Charms of Light. http://www.charmsoflight.com/feldspar-healing-properties.html.

* Heath, Richard. *Sacred Number and the Origins of Civilization: The Unfolding of History through the Mystery of Number*. Rochester, VT: Inner Traditions, 2007.

* Heath, Robin. *Sun, Moon & Stonehenge: High Culture in Ancient Britain*. Cardigan, Wales: Bluestone Press, 1998.

* "Heliacal Rising." Wikipedia. http://en.wikipedia.org/wiki/Heliacal_rising.

*Henry, William. "Secrets of The Cathars - Why the Dark Age Church Was Out to Destroy Them." Secrets of The Cathars. http://www.bibliotecapleyades.net/esp_autor_whenry04.htm. Originally Published in Atlantis Rising Dec. 2002 http://www.atlantisrising.com/

* Hewitt, Rachel. *Map of a Nation: A Biography of the Ordnance Survey*. London: Granta, 2010.

* Hillier, Caroline. *The Bulwark Shore: Thanet and the Cinque Ports*. London: E. Methuen, 1980.

The Secret Dossier of a
Knight Templar of the Sangreal

* "Historical Preface: 1508-1546." Historical Preface: 1508-1546. http://www.british-history.ac.uk/report.aspx?compid=47903&strquery=saint+Kentigern. Charters and Documents relating to the City of Glasgow 1175-1649: Part 1 (1897), pp. XLVIII-LXX.

* Hodapp, Christopher. *Solomon's Builders: Freemasons, Founding Fathers and the Secrets of Washington, D.C.* Berkeley, CA: Ulysses, 2006.

* Hodgson, Natasha R. *Women, Crusading and the Holy Land in Historical Narrative.* Woodbridge, Suffolk, UK: Boydell Press, 2007.

* Hopkins, Marilyn, Graham Simmans, and Tim Wallace-Murphy. *Rex Deus: The True Mystery of Rennes-le-Château and the Dynasty of Jesus.* Shaftesbury: Element, 2000.

* Jones, Andrew Zimmerman., and Daniel Robbins. *String Theory for Dummies.* 1 Original Edition. Hoboken, NJ: Wiley Publishing, 2009.

* Kaleem, Jaweed. "'The Gospel Of Jesus' Wife,' New Early Christian Text, Indicates Jesus May Have Been Married." The Huffington Post. September 19, 2012. Accessed August 05, 2015. http://www.huffingtonpost.com/2012/09/18/the-gospel-of-jesus-wife-_n_1891325.html?utm_hp_ref=mostpopular.

* King, Reverend James, Rev. *Cleopatra's Needle: A History of the London Obelisk, with an Exposition of the Hieroglyphics.* London: Religious Tract Society, 1886.

* Koffas, Thomas. "A Second Higgs Boson? Physicists Debate New Particle." Fox News. April 15, 2013. http://www.foxnews.com/science/2013/04/15/second-higgs-boson-physicists-debate/#ixzz2VoAi8lmj.

* Krstovic, Jelena, and Gale Cengage. "Bernard of Clairvaux Essay - Critical Essays - ENotes.com." Enotes.com. February 01, 2010. Accessed August 05, 2015. http://www.enotes.com/topics/bernard-clairvaux#critical-essays-bernard-clairvaux. Vol. 71

* Landsberg, Herrade De, Rosalie B.. Green, Michael Evans, Christine Bischoff, Michael Curschmann, Thomas Julian Brown, and Kenneth Levy. *Hortus Deliciarum.* Vol. II. London: Warburg Institute, 1979. p. 520 - Tab VII PL 165 - Image origin online: http://artmediaeval.blogspot.co.uk/

* Leadbeater, C. W. *Freemasonry and Its Ancient Mystic Rites.* New York: Gramercy Books, 1998.

* "The Legacy of the Knights Templar." By Mystic Realms. http://www.lundyisleofavalon.co.uk/templars/tempic055.htm.

* Lillich, Meredith P. *The Gothic Stained Glass of Reims Cathedral.* University Park, PA: Pennsylvania State University Press, 2011.

* Lomas, Robert. *The Invisible College: The Royal Society, Freemasonry and the Birth of Modern Science.* London: Headline, 2002.

* Lomas, Robert. *The Secret Science of Masonic Initiation.* London: Lewis Masonic, 2008.

* Lomas, Robert. *Turning the Templar Key: Martyrs, Freemasons and the Secret of the True Cross of Christ.* Hersham: Lewis Masonic, 2007.

* Mackenzie, Agnes Mure. *Robert Bruce, King of Scots.* Edinburgh: Oliver & Boyd, 1934. Chapter XI

Bibliography

*Markale, Jean. *King of the Celts: Arthurian Legends and the Celtic Tradition.* Rochester, VT: Inner Traditions, 1994.

* Marshall, Michael. "Five Snacks That Are Shaped Like the Universe." Newscientist.com. August 03, 2009. http%3A%2F%2Fwww.newscientist.com%2Farticle%2Fdn17535-five-snacks-that-are-shaped-like-the-universe.html.

* Martin, Sean. *The Cathars: The Most Successful Heresy of the Middle Ages.* Edison, NJ: Chartwell Books, 2006.

* Marvin, Laurence Wade. *The Occitan War: A Military and Political History of the Albigensian Crusade, 1209-1218.* Cambridge, UK: Cambridge University Press, 2008.

* Matos, Carolina. "Archaeology: Prehistoric Rock Art Found in Caves on Terceira Island – Azores | Portuguese American Journal." Portuguese American Journal. August 27, 2012. http://portuguese-american-journal.com/archeology-prehistoric-rock-art-found-in-caves-on-terceira-island-azores/.

* Mayer, Hans Eberhard. *Studies in the History of Queen Melisende of Jerusalem.* Cambridge, MA: Harvard Univ. Pr., 1972.

* Meisner, Gary. "The Human Body and the Golden Ratio - Phi 1.618: The Golden Ratio." Phi 1618 The Golden Ratio. May 31, 2012. http://www.goldennumber.net/human-body/.

* Melchizedek, Drunvalo. *The Ancient Secret of the Flower of Life: An Edited Transcript of the Flower of Life Workshop Presented Live to Mother Earth from 1985 to 1994.* Vol. 1. Flagstaff, AZ: Light Technology Pub., 1998.

* Meskens, Ad. "Statue of Liberty." October 30, 2009.

* Michell, John. *The View over Atlantis.* London: Abacus, 1973.

* "Military 1200 to 100 BC." Global Security. Accessed August 07, 2015. http://www.globalsecurity.org/military/world/mexico/history-1-olmec.htm. Site maintained by John Pike

* Miller, Crichton E. M. *The Golden Thread of Time: A Quest for the Truth and Hidden Knowledge of the Ancients.* Rugby: Pendulum Pub., 2001.

* Miller, Crichton E.M. "Celtic Cross." The , Crichton EM Miller. http://www.crichtonmiller.com/.

* Miller, Hamish, and Paul Broadhurst. *The Sun and the Serpent.* Launceston, Cornwall: Pendragon Press, 1990.

* Morison, James Cotter. *The Life and times of Saint Bernard, Abbot of Clairvaux: A. D. 1091-1153.* London: Macmillan, 1868.

* Morris, W. P., Reverend. *The Records of Patterdale.* Kendal: T. Wilson, 1903. https://archive.org/details/recordsofpatterd00morr.

* Morrison, James E. *The Astrolabe.* Rehoboth Beach, DE: Janus, 2007. doi:p. 2.

* Muck, Otto Heinrich. *The Secret of Atlantis.* London: William Collins Sons & Co, 1978.

* Murdin, Paul. *Full Meridian of Glory: Perilous Adventures in the Competition to Measure the Earth.* New York: Copernicus Books/Springer, 2009.

The Secret Dossier of a
Knight Templar of the Sangreal

* Negadi, Tidjani. "The Irregular (integer) Tetrahedron as a Warehouse of Biological Information." MArXiv. 2012. http://marxiv-org.lieblich.us/?query=id%3A1207.3454#?query=id %253A1207.3454&page=0&type=search&_suid=143896245400106304131156425. Abstract: This paper is devoted to a new classification of the twenty amino acids based on the heronian (integer) tetrahedron.

* *Nova Fabric of the Universe*. Performed by Brian Greene. DVD. ASIN: B0056031LE Studio: PBS (Direct) DVD Release Date: 22 Nov 2011

* Oldenbourg, Zoé. *The Crusades*. London: Phoenix, 2001.

* Oskin, Becky. "Why Earth's Magnetic Field Is Lopsided." MNN. July 18, 2012. http://www.mnn.com/green-tech/research-innovations/stories/why-earths-magnetic-field-is-lopsided.

* Ovason, David. *Shakespeare's Secret Booke: Deciphering Magical and Rosicrucian Codes*. Forest Row, East Sussex: Clairview, 2010.

* Partner, Peter. *The Murdered Magicians: The Templars and Their Myth*. Oxford: Oxford University Press, 1982.

* "Petrus Peregrinus De Maricourt." Wikipedia. https://en.wikipedia.org/wiki/Petrus_Peregrinus_de_Maricourt.

* Philip, Jean-Yves Leloup, and Joseph Rowe. *The Gospel of Philip: Jesus, Mary Magdalene, and the Gnosis of Sacred Union*. Rochester, VT: Inner Traditions, 2004.

* Phillips, Graham. *The Templars and the Ark of the Covenant: The Discovery of the Treasure of Solomon*. Rochester, VT: Bear &, 2004.

* Picknett, Lynn, and Clive Prince. *The Templar Revelation: Secret Guardians of the True Identity of Christ*. New York, NY: Simon & Schuster, 1998.

* Porete, Marguerite, Edmund Colledge, Judith Grant, and J. C. Marler. *The Mirror of Simple Souls*. Notre Dame, IN: University of Notre Dame Press, 1999.

* *The Province Of Kent 1770-1970*. Canterbury: J. A. Jennings, 1970.

* Ralls, Karen. *Knights Templar Encyclopedia: The Essential Guide to the People, Places, Events, and Symbols of the Order of the Temple*. Franklin Lakes, NJ: New Page Books, 2007.

* Ramsden, Dave. *Unveiling the Mystic Ciphers*. New York: CreateSpace, 2014.

* "Ramsgate Obelisk." Obelisk. http://www.ramsgatetown.org/history/landmarks-monuments/obelisk.aspx.

* Rawnsley, H. D. *Literary Associations of the English Lakes*. Vol. 2. Glasgow: J. MacLehose and Sons, 1901.

* Rengers, Christopher. *The 33 Doctors of the Church*. Rockford, IL: TAN Books and Publishers, 2000.

* Robinson, John J. *Born in Blood: The Lost Secrets of Freemasonry*. New York: M. Evans &, 1989.

* Robinson, John J. *Dungeon, Fire, and Sword: The Knights Templar in the Crusades*. New York: M. Evans &, 1991.

* Rome, Malcolm Moore in. "Vatican Paper Set to Clear Knights Templar." The Telegraph. October 05, 2007. Accessed August 05, 2015. http://www.telegraph.co.uk/news/worldnews/

Bibliography

1565252/Vatican-paper-set-to-clear-Knights-Templar.html.

* Roover, Ryamond De. *The Three Balls of the Pawnbrokers*. Vol. XX. Business Historical Society. Business Historical Society, 1946.

* Rosenblum, Bruce, and Fred Kuttner. *Quantum Enigma: Physics Encounters Consciousness*. 2nd ed. Oxford: Oxford University Press, 2011.

* Rosselli, Francessco. *Aristotle's Physics*. Pope Clement VII. 1445 – before 1513

* Runciman, Steven. *A History of the Crusades*. Vol. II. London: Penguin, 1952.

* Russell, Duncan, Bro. "Lodge St. Andrew #518 Province of Aberdeenshire East Grand Lodge of Scotland." Lodge St. Andrew 518,freemason,masonic. April 25, 2004. Accessed August 05, 2015. http://www.standrew518.co.uk/.

* Schaff, Philip. *History of the Christian Church, Volume V: The Middle Ages. A.D. 1049-1294*. 1882.

* Schipperges, Heinrich. *The World of Hildegard of Bingen: Her Life, Times, and Visions*. Collegeville, MN: Liturgical Press, 1998.

* Setton, Kenneth Meyer. *A History of the Crusades*. Vol. I. Philadelphia: Univ. of Pennsylvania Pr., 1958.

* "Sextant." Wikipedia. http://en.wikipedia.org/wiki/Sextant_(astronomical).

* "Shekhinah." Wikipedia. http://en.wikipedia.org/wiki/Shekhinah.

* Sheldrake, Rupert. "Morphic Resonance." Articles and Papers -. September 09, 2009. http://www.sheldrake.org/Articles&Papers/papers/morphic/morphic_intro.html. Publisher: Park Street Press; 4 Rev Exp edition (9 Sep 2009) ISBN-10: 1594773173 ISBN-13: 978-1594773174

* Shirt, David De. *Kentigern in Cumbria: His Presence and His Cult*. Maryport: De Shird, 2006.

* Sickels, Daniel, 33. *The General Ahiman Rezon and Freemason's Guide: Containing Monitorial Instructions in the Degrees of Entered Apprentice, Fellow-craft and Master Mason ... To Which Are Added a Ritual for a Lodge of Sorrow ... Also, an Appendix, with the Forms of Masonic Documents, Masonic Trials, Etc*. New York: Masonic Pub. and Manufacturing, 1867.

* Silverberg, Robert. *The Realm of Prester John: With a New Afterword*. London: Phoenix Press, 2001.

* Sobel, Dava, and William J.H. Andrews. *The Illustrated Longitude: The True Story of a Lone Genius Who Solved the Greatest Scientific Problem of His Time*. London: Fourth Estate, 1998.

* Sri, Magilia. "Municipality of Mattinata." Mattinata.it/. http%3A%2F%2Fwww.mattinata.it%2Fnews%2F19260%2Fha-sessant-anni-e-li-dimostra-tanta-storia-tradizioni-e-cultura.

* Stein, Walter Johannes, Irene Groves, and John M. Wood. *The Ninth Century and the Holy Grail*. London: Temple Lodge, 1988.

* Stewart, Ian, and Arthur C. Clarke. *The Colours of Infinity: The Beauty and Power of Fractals*. Place of Publication Not Identified: Clear Books, 2004.

* Stöber, Karen. *Late Medieval Monasteries and Their Patrons: England and Wales, C. 1300-1540.* Woodbridge: Boydell Press, 2007.

* Strange, F. G. St. Clair. *The History of the Royal Sea Bathing Hospital, Margate, 1791-1991.* Rainham, Kent: Meresborough Books, 1991.

* "Swan Upping." Wikipedia. http://en.wikipedia.org/wiki/Swan_Upping.

* Sweeney, Emmet John. *Atlantis: The Evidence of Science.* New York: Algora Pub., 2010.

* Swidler, Leonard J. *Jesus Was a Feminist: What the Gospels Reveal about His Revolutionary Perspective.* Lanham, MD: Sheed & Ward, 2007.

* Tarassi, Massimo0. *The Buyer: The Medici Family from Its Origins to the Fifteenth Century.*
in G. Cherubini and G. Fanelli (curr.) op. cit, Pg 2.

* Taylor, Rupert. *The Political Prophecy in England.* New York: Columbia University Press, 1911.

* *The Templars Deadliest Secret: Evidence Exposed and Part Two The Chase.* Performed by Scott Wolter. The History Chanel, 2015. TV.
America Unearthed Season 3

* Thomas, Charles. *Christian Celts.* Stroud: Tempus, 2003.

* Tsolakidou, Stella. "Prehistorc Tablet Calls into Question History of Writing." The Archaeology News Network:. July 16, 2012. http://archaeologynewsnetwork.blogspot.co.uk/2012/07/prehistorc-tablet-calls-into-question.html#.UHKbcK7F2kA.
Professor of Prehistoric Archaeology at the Aristotle University of Thessaloniki, George Hourmouziadis

* "Ulpian." Wikipedia. https://en.wikipedia.org/wiki/Ulpian#cite_note-3.

* Underhill, Evelyn. "Mysticism: Part One: The Mystic Fact: VI. Mysticism and Symbolism." Mysticism: Part One: The Mystic Fact: VI. Mysticism and Symbolism. http://www.sacred-texts.com/myst/myst/myst09.htm.

* Vauchez, Andre, and Adrian Walford. *Encyclopedia of the Middle Ages.* Chicago: Fitzroy Dearborn Publishers, 2000.

* "The Villeneuve Du Temple of Paris." Templar Site : The 'Villeneuve Du Temple' of Paris. http://www.templiers.org/paris-eng.php.

* Waite, Arthur Edward. *The Hidden Church of the Holy Graal: Its Legends and Symbolism.* S.l.: Yogi Pub. Soc., U.S.

* Wallace, Douglas. "Native American Haplogroups: European Lineage." DNA Learning Centre. http%3A%2F%2Fwww.dnalc.org%2Fview%2F15188-Native-American-haplogroups-European-lineage-Douglas-Wallace.html.

* Wallace-Murphy, Tim, and Marilyn Hopkins. *Rosslyn: Guardian of the Secrets of the Holy Grail.* New York: Barnes & Noble Books, 2000.

* Warner, Marina. *Alone of All Her Sex: The Myth and the Cult of the Virgin Mary.* 2nd ed. OUP Oxford, 2013.

* Watkins, Alfred. *The Old Straight Track: Its Mounds, Beacons, Moats, Sites and Mark Stones.* London: Abacus, 1974.

Bibliography

* Weinzweig, Paul, and Pauline Zalitzki. "Humans Are Free." Atlantis Discovered in the Bermuda Triangle: The Sunken City Features Giant Pyramids and Sphinxes [Complete]. http://humansarefree.com/2014/02/atlantis-discovered-in-bermuda-triangle.html.

* Weisstein, Eric. "Heronian Tetrahedron." -- from Wolfram MathWorld. http://mathworld.wolfram.com/HeronianTetrahedron.html.

* West, Burce J., and Ary L. Goldberger. "Physiology in Fractal Dimensions,." American Scientist, The Scientific Research Society. http%3A%2F%2Fwww.jstor.org%2Fstable%2Fi27854710.

p 356, , Vol. 75, No. 4, July-August 1987 Sigma Xi,

* *What the Bleep: Down the Rabbit Hole*. Performed by John Hagelin Ph.D. Revolver Entertainment. DVD.

Extended Interviews DVD 31 July 2006,ASIN: B000GPPPYA

* Whitney, Christa. "Live Long and Prosper: The Jewish Story Behind Spock, Leonard Nimoy's Star Trek Character." YouTube. https://www.youtube.com/watch?v=DyiWkWcR86I.

Produced by Wexler Oral History Project at the Yiddish Book Center

* Wilson, J. "Houses of Cistercian Monks: The Abbey of Holmcultram." Houses of Cistercian Monks: The Abbey of Holmcultram. http://www.british-history.ac.uk/report.aspx?compid=39957&strquery=.

* Wolfram, Stephen. "The Father of Fractals." WSJ. November 22, 2012. http://www.wsj.com/articles/SB10001424127887324439804578107271772910506.

Re: Mandelbrot

* Wood, Michael. *In Search of the Dark Ages*. New York, NY: Facts on File, 1987.

* Wordsworth, Dorothy, and John Campbell Shairp. *Recollections of a Tour Made in Scotland, A.D. 1803*. Edinburgh: Edmonston and Douglas, 1874.

* Zilsel, Edgar, and Diederick Raven. *The Social Origins of Modern Science*. Dordrecht: Kluwer Academic Publishers, 2000.

CPSIA information can be obtained
at www.ICGtesting.com
Printed in the USA
LVHW071212211218
601354LV00018B/476/P